# URBAN POLITICS
## Third Edition

Third Edition

# URBAN POLITICS

Bernard H. Ross, The American University
Murray S. Stedman, Jr., Temple University

F.E. PEACOCK PUBLISHERS, INC. ITASCA, ILLINOIS 60143

To Nettie and the memory of Len
Both of whom taught me to love the city.
B. H. R.

# CONTENTS

# Preface to the Third Edition

Writing a book is truly a learning experience. Not only do the authors learn more about the substantive issues in their field, but they also learn the meaning of collegiality and professionalism. Few books are solely the product of the authors' own efforts and this book is no exception. A number of people contributed their talents and their time to improve the manuscript.

Myron A. Levine of Albion College (formerly of The American University) assisted us from the beginning in revising and updating this third edition. His review of the entire manuscript helped us to restructure the book as well as to think through a number of concepts and issues. His contributions were of great value in completing the work. Beverly Cigler, North Carolina State University, also read the entire manuscript and recommended numerous substantive and organizational changes.

David Walker of the Advisory Commission on Intergovernmental Relations read the chapters on intergovernmental relations and clarified some of our ideas and provided updates on some data. Charles H. Levine of The Brookings Institution read the chapter entitled "Financing Urban America" and directed us to relevant sources of information. Joel Miller and John Coleman of the U.S. Bureau of the Census were always available to answer questions, provide materials and correct our misinterpretation of census data.

Numerous friends and colleagues contributed to the work directly and indirectly through their conversations, encouragement, and knowledge. We have listened and gratefully borrowed from them. Several of these people need to be mentioned: Henry Cohen, New School for Social Research; A. Lee Fritschler, The Brookings Institution; Steve Diner, The University of the District of Columbia; Richard Zody of Virginia Polytechnic Institute and State University; Patricia S. Florestano, the University of Maryland; and Louise White, George Mason University.

Students in numerous urban courses at both American and Temple Universities were helpful in their questions, comments and opinions concerning issues and concepts which are discussed in this edition.

Several students were directly involved with the research. Judy Carra, David Perrin and Isabelle Schoenfeld at The American University spent many hours in the library gathering data and checking facts and citations. Barbara Schwemle did much of the research for the finance chapter. Parts of the manuscript were typed and retyped by Susan Gifford, Mary Kay Almy, Joan Boswell, Robin Adkisson, Celinda Hadden, Lucy Kent and Mindy Cebulski.

The support of Ted Peacock of F. E. Peacock Publishers is gratefully acknowledged as well as the very competent editorial assistance provided by Joyce Usher.

A special debt of gratitude goes to James J. Murray III, American Council on Education, who has been an inspiration and an encouragement to both authors. Jim was the editor on the first two editions of the book and has remained involved in the process of completing this third edition. His patience, wisdom and friendship are greatly appreciated.

Bernard Ross expresses a special note of recognition to Marlene and their three children, Jeffrey, Joanne and Carolyn, whose support and understanding made the writing of this book much easier.

B. H. R.
M. S. S.

# INTRODUCTION

Writing a textbook on any subject is an enlightening and educational experience for its authors. This is particularly true in the field of urban politics and administration, since the field has changed so much in the past generation. In the 1950s some sociologists were examining the patterns of influence in local governments, and political scientists were concerned with city structure and the formal institutions of government. But on the whole, few scholars turned their attention to the study of urban and metropolitan affairs.

During the 1960s, however, numerous changes began occurring in cities as well as in the study of urban politics. Social scientists examined the decision-making patterns in cities and helped us understand how power and influence were exercised in urban areas. Some of these studies have become classics in the field and are often used as introductions to the study of urban affairs.[1]

During the latter half of the 1960s much of the attention focused on urban areas concerned the urban riots and their causes. National and state commissions were created to examine the riot areas to ascertain what had precipitated the outbreaks of violence and to suggest how could it be controlled and possibly eliminated in the future.

Two different schools of thought emerged on how to reduce the potential for civil violence in the future. The federal government, beginning with the Johnson administration, developed numerous programs to aid lower-income urban residents. Job training, housing, community development, health care, and education were some of the areas where the federal government began spending billions of dollars to improve the quality of life primarily for the urban poor.

Many of the low-income residents of the inner city had a perspective on this problem different from that of the federal government. While the federal programs expended funds and created jobs, a number of community leaders felt that the strategy for changing their current living conditions required more than money. Some of these leaders organized community groups and began exerting pressure on local officials to devolve more power and decision-making authority to the community and its leaders. This perceived threat to governmental authority created many conflicts among elected officials, local bureaucrats, and community leaders. The resolution of these conflicts took many forms, and in almost all large American cities today there is evidence of power sharing arrangements that resulted from this conflict.

The growth and expansion of federal aid continued into the 1970s, with control over the expenditure of federal grant monies often the goal of contending community and government officials. With the growth of federal aid there came an increase in government regulations and guidelines on how programs were to be administered. The increase in regulations meant that more and more city programs were being directly affected by the federal government, which was having a greater impact on the way decisions were being made.

In the mid-1970s, as community leaders and city officials began finding ways to resolve their differences, a new problem began emerging. Escalating interest rates, high inflation, and local government mismanagement all combined to bring New York City to the edge of bankruptcy. Several other cities also experienced severe financial problems, and academics and practitioners began examining the issues of resource scarcity, cutback management, and contracting out.

During the late 1970s and early 1980s we have seen a continuation of fiscal stress in both cities and states. Skyrocketing federal budget deficits, accompanied by social program cutbacks, high unemployment, and high interest rates, have forced most local governments to adopt very stringent financial practices. Budgets have been tightened through any or all of such expedients as tax increases, job freezes, employee layoffs, increases in user fees, program cutbacks, small salary increases, and deferred maintenance.

In the past decade local government officials have gone from an era of high federal spending for state and local programs, and the problems inherent in obtaining and managing these grants, to an era of federal and state budget cuts in social programs and a demand for professional financial management in all areas of local government.

Several different themes might be used in a textbook on urban politics that seeks to examine the issues outlined above. Based upon our view that urban political and administrative life has been changing rapidly in the past generation, we have chosen to focus on power, how it is distributed and how it is exercised in the urban political arena. It is this theme, we believe, that will help students understand the fundamental issues and conflicts in urban America.

Power, however, often means different things to different people in different situations. Viewing the same set of circumstances, a government official and a community leader may render very different judgments on how power is distributed and exercised. This occurs because often we do not have agreed-upon definitions for terms, and a term such as *power* can be confused with *influence*.

For purposes of this book, influence is defined as the ability of party A to persuade or cajole others to act or think as A suggests or wants. If one imagines that influence runs along a continuum, with one end characterized by coercion (i.e., severe penalties imposed for noncompliance), this area of coercive influence is often called power. Power implies the threat or the use of sanctions—physical or otherwise—to achieve compliance.

One way to assess the distribution of power in urban areas is to examine the institutions of government and the amount of formal power delegated to each. Our intention is not only to do this, but to go beyond the formal power structure and determine if there are, in fact, individuals and organizations active in influencing decision-makers and in exercising power to alter political and administrative decisions. Some of the non-governmental organizations involved in influencing government decision-making are business groups, labor unions, churches, and civic associations.

In the past two decades we have witnessed the growth of additional non-governmental organizations that have become very active in local government decision-making. These non-formal or non-traditional organizations are community or neighborhood organizations or single issue, ad-hoc, city-wide groups determined to *prevent* highways, incinerators, etc., or pushing *for* better schools or mass transit. These non-traditional organizations have increased in importance in the past twenty years and represent a recent addition to the traditional techniques of distributing and exercising power in urban and metropolitan areas.

Our intention is to examine the major institutions, actors, and issues in urban politics and to analyze how power is exercised in different situations. In this way we hope to learn more about where we have been and where we are so we can better understand how to improve the quality of life in urban America in the future.

## NOTES

1. Robert A. Dahl, *Who Governs? Democracy and Power in an American City* (New Haven: Yale University Press, 1961); Edward C. Banfield, *Political Influence* (New York: Free Press, 1961); Wallace Sayre and Herbert Kaufman, *Governing New York City: Politics in the Metropolis* (New York: W. W. Norton, 1960); Peter Bachrach and Morton S. Baratz, "Decisions and Nondecisions: An Analytical Framework," *American Political Science Review* (September 1963): 632–642; Theodore J. Lowi, "Machine Politics—Old and New," *The Public Interest* 9 (Fall 1967): 83–92; Edward C. Banfield and James D. Wilson, *City Politics* (New York: Vintage Books, 1963); Nelson W. Polsby, *Community Power and Political Theory* (New Haven: Yale University Press, 1963); and Scott Greer, *Metropolis: A Study of Political Culture* (New York: John Wiley and Sons, 1963).

# 1. THE URBAN SITUATION

People have been living in cities for a very long time; probably, in fact, since 7000–6000 B.C. Although it was thought until recently that the earliest cities were founded about five millenia ago in the great valleys of the Tigris and Euphrates, new archaeological evidence indicates otherwise. In the summer of 1961, a British archaeologist, James Mellaart, discovered the remains of Catal Hüyük on the Anatolian plain of Turkey. The city spanned the period 7000–6000 B.C., and its populations must have run into the thousands.[1] One problem in reconstructing the histories of ancient cities, however, is the fact that they were prehistoric, i.e., predated the development of writing. By the time there is anything resembling a permanent record, the city has already developed into a mature form.[2] As a result, the earliest urban developments must be reconstructed from artifacts and from what seem to be a logical series of transitions.

On this basis, the usually accepted evolution is from hunting camp to agricultural village to the beginnings of a primitive urban settlement. However, not all experts agree on this sequence. Jane Jacobs, for instance, thinks that the jump from hunting camp to urban settlement was the more likely pattern of development. In her reconstructions of urban history, early agriculture took place within the city's walls, not as a prelude to urban settlement. Yet the dominant viewpoint, expressed by Lewis Mumford and others, is that the city at a very early date evolved from the village, which contained in primitive form many urban structures and symbols.[3] By 2500 B.C., Mumford declares, the essential features of the city had taken form.[4] Formerly, isolated groups came together and settled permanently in one place.

In telescopic form, the general history of cities in the West is well-known. The Golden Age of the ancient Greek cities, especially Athens, occurred during the period between 500 and 400 B.C. When the center of world power shifted to Rome, the emphasis is placed, quite properly, on the ability of the Romans to manage their own city and to create other cities wherever the Roman legions went.

With the collapse of the Roman Empire, the urban civilization Rome had created rapidly eroded. During the so-called Dark Ages, the urban arts were neglected, abandoned, and forgotten. Fortunately, urban culture even-tually revived, coming to a high level of achievement by the twelfth century in the West. During this remarkably creative medieval period, new towns and cities were established, the arts were reborn, and the self-governing city came into its own. At the end of a long evolutionary process, the remarkable civilizations of such city-states as Venice, Genoa, and Florence rose. In the politics of these Renaissance cities, one finds a good deal of the flavor, if not necessarily the same tactics, of a modern urban area. For instance, the Flor-entine attitude toward politics was that it was a highly important and intrigu-ing "game." For such reasons Machiavelli's *The Prince* continues to be a readable and instructive text in how to operate in a vigorous political world.

## CITIES IN AMERICA

The first permanent English settlement in America was Jamestown, Virginia, founded in 1607. Although more a beachhead in the wilderness than a city, Jamestown was followed by the establishment of towns up and down the Atlantic coast, the majority of which failed to develop into any-thing resembling urban centers. Among the exceptions were Boston, New-port, New York, Philadelphia, and Charleston, S.C.—all splendid ports—which rapidly outgrew their village status and became sites of significant commercial activity.

America was primarily an agricultural nation; at the time of the Ameri-can Revolution, some 95 percent of the American people were engaged in agriculture. But the westward expansion of the early years of the republic brought with it a notable increase in the number of nascent cities, such as those which now abound in the old Northwest Territory. Yet it was the Civil War that most profoundly influenced the development of American urban life. The cities of the South were decimated by the war, which, on the other hand, stimulated manufacturing and commerce in the cities of the North and West. The demographic expansion of these cities was often staggering; for example, the population of Brooklyn jumped from 202,000 in 1854 to about 302,000 in 1865. By 1900, Brooklyn had more than 1,000,000 people.

With this rapid urban growth came new problems of urban govern-ment. The age was the heyday of boss rule based on large blocs of immigrant voters. It was also the age of the sweatshop, child labor, and the "robber baron." Mark Twain referred to it scathingly as the Gilded Age. The un-planned, uncontrolled expansion of cities during the nineteenth century left a legacy of problems that still remain to be dealt with, not only in America but in the rest of the Western world as well.

## Urban Communities

Since most American cities are in a county, the question may arise as to why the county, as a subdivision of a state, cannot itself exercise the functions normally associated with a city. Why, in short, is it necessary to have municipal corporations? Or are they, in fact, superfluous? Why can't county governments do what city governments do?

The answers to these questions are deeply rooted in American history. To begin with, it must be noted that the county was originally conceived as a unit of rural government. As such, its powers were those that befitted the conditions of the time and the area. This is perfectly understandable when one recalls that only about three percent of the American people lived in cities at the time the Constitution was written in 1787. Residents of urban areas were obviously the exception rather than the rule in 1787.

But persons who did live in urban areas had special needs and requirements. For example, cities of the colonial era required, as they do now, special arrangements for public safety, economic regulation, and certain minimal public services. Since such services could be provided for neither by the existing county nor through an unincorporated (i.e., legally powerless) settled area, it was necessary to seek a special legal status for sizeable settlements. The device used was the municipal charter, given by the colonial legislature, which created a municipal corporation and allocated the necessary governmental authority to meet the felt needs of the area. There was nothing at all new about this practice, for English cities had been created for hundreds of years through royal charters and, later, through acts of Parliament.

In short, special conditions required a special governmental form—the municipal corporation—on both sides of the Atlantic. In the United States, the function of incorporation is no longer carried out by a special act of a state legislature. The common practice is to provide by statute that urban areas meeting certain specifications regarding population will automatically be incorporated.

## Why the Urban Situation Is Worthy of Study

One of the most compelling reasons for studying urban affairs is the deeply felt conviction that knowledge has, or at least ought to have, some potential relationship to power. To know something about a social situation is to create the potential for taking some reasoned action related to it. Knowledge as to how social processes operate brings with it the chance of controlling the end products of such processes. Even in the absence of positive controls over the outcome, knowledge results in an understanding that might otherwise be impossible to achieve.

Such beliefs underlie the modern study of urban affairs, a study that is multidisciplinary. It includes not only all of the social sciences, but history, architecture, engineering, law, and city planning as well. As its multidisciplinary nature would suggest, the study of urban affairs has a complex background. The concentration on urban matters as a specialized area dates from the relatively recent realization of the impact cities have upon human life in general. To put the matter differently, the growth of cities and the spread of their influence over whole national and international societies is now thought to be the major social transformation of modern times. And industrialization has been credited as the key factor in this vast and continuing change.

In studying urban history, modern historians consider the relative importance of such factors as population, technology, environment, and the sociopolitical organization.[5] Not surprisingly, social scientists, employing a somewhat different vocabulary, ferret out the same key factors. These may be defined as the demographic aspects (population size, composition, and distribution), ecological aspects (the spatial and temporal dimensions of community life), structural aspects (the organization of communities and their parts), and behavioral aspects (sociopsychological facts of the community, including group membership, attitudes, and values).[6]

To the political scientist concerned with urban affairs, the perspectives of historians and social scientists are of great value. Nonetheless, the emphasis of political scientists is somewhat different from that of their colleagues. For political scientists in general, and urban political scientists in particular, the focus is on power. They are interested in such questions as: Who holds power? By what means? What are the rewards for persons who go along with the in-power group? What are the sanctions to be used against those who defy the in-group? How are political wars fought? What are the relationships between principal political organizations and leading interest groups? What are the relationships among interest groups? How does the public perceive the political activity in the community? Additional questions of structure, finance, and administration also interest political scientists, but the above illustrations are probably sufficient to indicate the general orientation of urban political scientists.

## THE PRESENT URBAN SITUATION

Americans are much less confident about the future of their cities today than they were sixty or a hundred years ago. Despite the excesses, the vulgarities, and the injustices of Twain's Gilded Age, the feeling persisted that in the long run the country, and its urban areas, would improve. Indeed, the belief that progress was almost automatic was deeply embedded in American culture. Recent developments, such as race riots, deteriorating housing, and the lowering of educational achievement, have done much to undermine this optimism.

The situation was summarized by the then unofficial spokesman for America's big-city mayors, Mayor John V. Lindsay of New York City, in an address before an international audience delivered on May 27, 1971, at Indianapolis.[7] After reminding his listeners of the historic ambivalence of Americans toward urban life, Lindsay listed some of the problems facing modern U.S. cities. The two most important, he said, were race and poverty. "Together," he added, "they have brought frustration and despair, polarization and fear, and finally violence and disorder."

How had the central cities become the "repository" of these problems? This had occurred, the Mayor asserted, because of the vast population shifts that had taken place during the previous twenty years. For instance, in New York City, a million poor blacks and Puerto Ricans had migrated into the city, while a million whites had opted to live in the suburbs.

The Mayor saw no prospect at all that his city could meet its social problems without federal help. He ridiculed state aid as too little and too restricted. He suggested that machinery be established so that the twenty-five U.S. cities with a population of more than 500,000 be classified as "national cities" and deal directly with Washington. In short, he called for giving these cities about the same powers that the states now possess.

Not all of the delegates to the Indianapolis conference agreed with Lindsay's prescription, but there was general concurrence with his diagnosis. Many of the mayors were quick to point out, however, that the situations in their own cities were by no means so grim as that in New York. Even so, there was a general feeling that the urban condition had deteriorated in cities large and small and in all sections of the country. The optimistic mayors were those who thought that the decline had been arrested in their own cities.

Since the Indianapolis conference, much has happened to bear out some of those dire predictions about urban life. In the mid-1970s New York City went to the brink of bankruptcy, which necessitated intervention by state and federal actors to avoid a financial catastrophe. New York recovered, and even began experiencing a downtown boom, although some of its nationally known neighborhoods, such as the South Bronx and the Bedford-Stuyvesant section of Brooklyn, still remain as examples of extreme urban blight.

New York, of course, has not been the only city to experience severe financial hardships. Cleveland, Philadelphia, and Detroit all have been on the brink of major financial problems and bankruptcy. The cities of the Northeast and the Midwest have been particularly hard hit, while the cities of the South and Southwest (often referred to as sunbelt cities) continue to grow and prosper, although they are experiencing numerous problems associated with rapid growth.

The economic recession of the early 1980s also began taking its toll on the sunbelt. Unemployment in Alabama, Mississippi, Louisiana, and Kentucky skyrocketed, and states like Texas and Louisiana began borrowing from the federal government to pay unemployment insurance claims because their state funds were depleted. Most of these claims were filed in the large cities.

## Why Are the Urban Areas in Bad Shape?

In one way, it is strange that there is so much talk of "an urban crisis." A great deal of solid evidence points toward a continuing improvement in certain aspects of urban life. By any measurements, there is less poverty in the cities today than there was fifty years ago; housing is improved; more people go to school, and stay there longer; and the treatment of racial and ethnic groups is far superior to what it was in the 1920s, when discrimination against minorities was overt and was sanctioned by most Americans. Why then, on the part of the mayors and of nearly everyone else, is there so much unhappiness with the present situation?

The most immediate explanation is that the improvements have not kept up with rising expectations. As Edward C. Banfield has put it, "although things have been getting better absolutely, they have been getting worse relative to what we think they should be."[8] The result, of course, has been fairly massive discontent on the part of substantial segments of the urban population, especially slumdwelling black and Hispanics.

The debate over whether or not America's largest cities were in crisis escalated considerably in the late 1970s. Few commentators on the subject took time to carefully define what they meant by crisis. A crisis implies some degree of immediacy and magnitude. Using these characteristics, the litany of problems confronting urban areas did not convincingly establish the existence of a crisis.

Poor and unsanitary housing, costly and inefficient transportation systems, understaffed classrooms, high unemployment rates, and deteriorating tax bases are all serious problems facing America's cities. But do they constitute an urban crisis? Since each of these problems has plagued urban areas for numerous years and has not affected a majority of the urban population in any one city, it is difficult to label this condition a crisis. A more accurate conclusion would be that America's largest cities are facing a number of specific functional crises, which have been negatively affecting large numbers of urban dwellers for a long time. However, most of these problems have been recognized by public officials, who have developed policies, appropriated funds, and implemented programs to minimize the hardships felt by those unfortunate citizens. Thus a series of functional crises do not necessarily add up to a nationwide urban crisis.

The urban crisis debate begun by Banfield in the early 1970s became more volatile in 1978 with the publication of T. D. Allman's "The Urban Crisis Leaves Town and Moves to the Suburbs."[9] In his article, Allman argued that the northern cities had unemployment rates similar to those in the South and that capital investment was substantial and continuing in many of the downtown areas of the nation's largest cities. Allman, citing a Rand Corporation analysis, further argued that while suburban areas showed impressive growth rates in the 1960s, growth slowed markedly in the 1970s, allowing the central cities to narrow the gap.

One of Allman's major contentions was that many of the problems faced by urban areas were now spreading beyond the city limits. Using FBI crime reports, for example, Allman pointed out that crime was decreasing in larger cities and northeastern and midwestern cities, while it was increasing in southern and western cities.[10]

In short, Allman believed that the urban crisis argument was overemphasized and outdated. Poorly conceived and administered federal programs, coupled with a fiscal crisis, helped to create a mistaken image that America's cities were in crisis. A more careful reading of the data clearly showed that America's largest cities, particularly in the Northeast and the Midwest, were nowhere near the crisis levels articulated by some politicians, academics, and journalists.

Shortly after Allman's article appeared, the staff of the Office of Community Planning and Development of the Department of Housing and Urban Development (HUD) prepared a rebuttal in which they stated that Allman's article "presents a misleading, often inaccurate and inconsistent portrait of America's urban problems and the status of its larger distressed cities."[11]

In the HUD response, each of Allman's arguments was discussed and refuted to show that, in fact, America's cities were facing severe economic, social, and political problems that could not be minimized by using a few positive examples. The HUD response relied upon numerous documents produced by the U.S. Bureau of the Census, the Brookings Institution, the Urban Institute, congressional committees, and interested academics.

In each instance, the HUD paper was able to cite data that contradicted the Allman assertions or updated his figures, permitting a different interpretation. In some cases the HUD paper supplied "more accurate data" and accompanied it with a "more sophisticated analysis." In the areas of communities selected, employment data, private investment, property values, migration patterns, and revenue base, the HUD analysis found Allman's interpretation misleading and occasionally inaccurate. According to the HUD report, Allman had failed to recognize "that the Nation's distressed cities, especially central cities, are becoming the focus of social and economic distress in this country."[12]

But it is useful to go beyond this attitudinal explanation to one based on historic economic development. In this view, the cities have failed to create a humane environment because the city planning was left to the private sector, not to government officials. Sam H. Bass Warner, Jr., in his historical study of Philadelphia, puts it this way: "Cities have failed. Why? Under the American tradition, the first purpose of the citizen is the private search for wealth; the goal of a city is to be a community of private money makers."[13] Warner dates the basic problems of the cities from about the middle of the nineteenth century. Since that time, their successes and failures have depended upon the unplanned outcomes of the private sector. "What the private market could do well U.S. cities have done well; what the private market did badly, or neglected, our cities have been unable to overcome."[14]

This tradition of "privatism" found in Philadelphia, Warner believed, had been repeated in other cities, including Cincinnati, St. Louis, Chicago, Detroit, Los Angeles, and Houston. As a result, these cities lacked the desire, power, wealth, and talent necessary to create a "humane environment" for all of their citizens.

## Why Have the Problems Not Been Solved?

Several general explanations may account for the failure to solve urban problems. One is that constitutional and other restrictions tie the hands of the municipalities. A second is that private enterprise alone cannot create a decent environment for the totality of the citizenry. A third is that we continue to create new problems (and expectations) while solving the old ones, with the result that we are never satisfied. Yet overshadowing all of these explanations of urban problems is the general trend toward social change and its continuing impact on the political institutions of the country, including the urban political institutions.

Consider some of the key indices of social change in the U.S. during the last forty years. From 1940 to 1970, the population increased from 131 million to over 197 million, a growth of over 50 percent. Between 1970 and 1980 the population increased another 10 percent, to more than 220 million. The migration from rural to urban areas has resulted in a vast decrease in the number of people living on farms, from 30 percent of U.S. population in 1920 to 6 percent in 1966. It is not likely to increase in the near future.

The 1970 census revealed that a majority of the people now living in metropolitan areas lived outside the central cities. By 1980, the Census Bureau reported that 75 percent of the nation's population resided in Standard Metropolitan Statistical Areas (SMSAs). (For a full discussion of metropolitan areas and their political and administrative problems, see Chapter 8.) However, 30 percent of that population lived in the central cities, while 45 percent lived in the non-central city part of the SMSAs. This latter area, consisting primarily of the suburbs, doubled in percent of U.S. population and tripled in numbers of people between 1950 and 1980.[15]

TABLE 1.1
Metropolitan and Nonmetropolitan
Population: 1950 to 1980
*(Reflects areas as defined at each census)*

| Area | 1950[1] | 1960 | 1970[2] | 1980 |
|---|---|---|---|---|
| Population (Millions) | | | | |
| United States | 151.3 | 179.3 | 203.2 | 226.5 |
| Inside SMSA's | 84.9 | 112.9 | 139.4 | 169.4 |
| Central cities | 49.7 | 58.0 | 63.8 | 67.9 |
| Outside central cities | 35.2 | 54.9 | 75.6 | 101.5 |
| Outside SMSA's | 66.5 | 66.4 | 63.8 | 57.1 |
| Percent of U.S. | | | | |
| United States | 100.0 | 100.0 | 100.0 | 100.0 |
| Inside SMSA's | 56.1 | 63.0 | 68.6 | 74.8 |
| Central cities | 32.8 | 32.3 | 31.4 | 30.0 |
| Outside central cities | 23.3 | 30.6 | 37.2 | 44.8 |
| Outside SMSA's | 43.9 | 37.0 | 31.4 | 25.2 |

[1]Including Alaska and Hawaii.
[2]1970 tabulated population excluding subsequent corrections.
Source: *Standard Metropolitan Statistical Areas and Standard Consolidated Statistical Areas: 1980* (Washington, D.C.: Bureau of the Census, October, 1981).

Indices of gross national product, public debt, and taxation showed sustained growth throughout this period. For most of the 1970s similar increases were reported in many manufacturing industries, particularly in computers, mass communications, and other high technology fields. Service industries such as computer software, research and consulting firms, data collections and information companies, and state and local government also revealed remarkable growth rates. These indices of rapid social change in the United States have generated demands that have subjected the existing social and political institutions to tremendous stress. These demands range from specific ones, such as better police protection, to general objectives, such as equality of opportunity and an improved physical environment. Under the circumstances, it is understandable, if not entirely forgivable, that America's urban political institutions have found it difficult to cope with new problems and situations. In later chapters, this situation will be examined in more detail, but for the moment, it may be helpful to explain the process of urbanization more thoroughly.

## Urbanization

Urban politics takes place within an environment of its own, one that is distinct, but not isolated from the national or international political setting. Even though the cities have their own political environment, this environment does not insulate them from national trends and tides. The "urban crisis" of our time is in large measure part of the larger crisis that has been affecting American life. For example, while the cities have become, to repeat former Mayor Lindsay's remark, the repositories of the problems of race and poverty, it is not the cities that created the problems in the first place. These problems may be attributed largely to the failure of the national government to develop and sustain consistent and humane policies in the economic and social spheres. Nor are the cities even remotely capable of solving such problems by themselves.

Yet the cities do have problems and conditions that are unique and with which they must deal as best they can. By any standards, there has been an urban explosion, and this has, in fact, brought about a genuine social revolution in big and small cities and their suburbs. Though a good deal of evidence could be cited to illustrate urban growth, the most spectacular figures relate to population. A few statistics suggest the magnitude of the transformation. The population of the country doubled in number from 1870 to 1900 and redoubled by 1950. The 1980 census revealed a total population of 226,500,000. It is expected to reach the 300,000,000 mark before the end of the century. The proportion of rural population to this total population has fallen for 200 years. From 54.3 percent in 1910, it dropped to about 25 percent in 1980. Since 1950 the decline has been absolute as well as relative. Consequently, since 1910 there has been a steady increase in the percentage of the population living in urban areas, with the exception of the 1930–40 decade, when urban and rural increases were about equal. The 1920 census was the first to report an urban majority, when the percentage of urbanites stood at 51.2.

However, urban growth during the last few decades has been uneven. In the Northeast, the urban population has increased at a slightly faster rate than in the rural areas, but the greatest increases in urban areas have taken place in the West and the South. Population growth has also affected other aspects of American life; for example, the problems of air and water pollution are clearly related to population expansion. But there is some evidence that this population growth is currently slowing down, and there is even a long-range possibility that the American population will become stabilized in several decades. In the meantime, the total population is expected to increase substantially. As projected at present, this increase will occur primarily in metropolitan areas. The prospect is that our urban majority—which has existed for many years—will continue to grow both in terms of numbers and as a proportion of the total population.

Obviously, what happens, or does not happen, in urban America is of cardinal importance to the well-being of the country. Since the process of urbanization has been such an important development in America, we shall examine the process and its political consequences in more detail.

Urbanization has proved to be a key concept in American political development. During the early years of the nation, when the economy was primarily agrarian, it was reasonable to assume that the great crop regions would constitute sectional units. From this perspective, political conflict was viewed as a series of contests among wheat areas, cotton regions, and so on.

But the diversification of economic interest diluted the theory of sectionalism, especially following the Civil War period. The weakening of sectional blocs came from the multiplication of economic interests within the regions. These alterations in the previous economy were related in one way or another to increasing urbanization, as finance, manufacturing, and distribution tended to be centered in the cities.

The erosion of sectionalism is especially visible in the South, where rapid urbanization has resulted in changes that occurred decades earlier in the northern cities. Whole new business classes were created that had more in common with their northern counterparts than with southern sectional interests. This attitude was particularly evident in such burgeoning industrial and regional centers as Atlanta and Houston. Southerners began to act, politically, more like people in other sections of the country, with profound political consequences. Not only has the structure of historic agrarianism been undermined in the South and elsewhere, but the class basis of politics has been changed. The influence of labor unions in politics, for instance, has been directly related to urbanization.

All aspects of the governmental process are affected by urbanization. New problems are created, which in turn require the creation of new governmental agencies. The national party system was affected as the Democratic party became more and more dependent on urban support. In national Democratic affairs, party leaders in New York, Boston, Chicago, and other large cities assumed more prominent roles, and the metropolitan vote became increasingly pivotal in presidential elections.

Urbanization developed a politics based on class. As the principal voting behavior studies have shown, there is today a close correlation between class and party preference. In the metropolitan areas, party cleavages tend to follow class lines. Insofar as the recent in-migration to the cities consists of low-income blacks and Hispanics, the net effect should be to reinforce and perhaps strengthen the Democratic party organizations.

## Sunbelt-Frostbelt Conflict

The issues of regional growth in the United States are complex and varied. Recently, population shifts have pointed to the growth of the sunbelt and the decline of the frostbelt. The 1980 census reported 169 cities with populations above 100,000. During the 1970s 26 cities achieved that population, while 11 fell below it. Most of the cities passing the 100,000 population were in the South and West. (See Appendix A)

TABLE 1.2
Cities Over 100,000 Population
By Region, 1970 and 1980

| Region | Total of Cities with 100,000 plus | Total of Gainers | Total of Losers |
|---|---|---|---|
| UNITED STATES | 169 | 93 | 76 |
| Northeast | 23 | – | 23 |
| North Central | 39 | 8 | 31 |
| South | 60 | 46 | 14 |
| West | 47 | 39 | 8 |

Source: Bureau of the Census, *U.S. Department of Commerce News* (Washington: June 3, 1981), p. X.

While it is true that most large cities in the Northeast and North Central areas lost population, while cities like Houston, Los Angeles, San Jose, San Diego, El Paso, and Austin all gained people, generalizations can be misleading. During the 1970s a new regionalism emerged, dividing the warmer sunbelt states from the cooler frostbelt states. This division is not fixed by any government agency, nor does it have any official sanction. Rather it emerged from the energy crisis of the early 1970s coupled with some very cold winters in the North. In a more economical and political sense, the sunbelt-frostbelt conflict is a product of a new industrial growth in aerospace, defense, oil, natural gas, computers, tourism, and real estate. These industries, in turn, developed their own interest groups to help promote their economic well-being and that of the warmer areas of the country. The members of Congress and the governors of these states have also helped to perpetuate this regionalism by seeking additional federal funds to accommodate their burgeoning populations.

The sunbelt is usually thought to contain eighteen states: Virginia, North and South Carolina, Georgia, Florida, Tennessee, Alabama, Mississippi, Louisiana, Arkansas, Texas, Arizona, New Mexico, Colorado, Utah, Nevada, Hawaii, and California. These states have benefited in the past ten to fifteen years from increasing numbers of people moving to warmer climates as well as many new industries, which have numerous skilled and semiskilled jobs to offer.[16]

In an urban sense, however, more needs to be analyzed than just population shifts and average yearly snowfall. Houston, Phoenix, and Los Angeles may have warm climates and abundant job opportunities, but are they, for example, any better managed than Minneapolis, Milwaukee, or Baltimore? Cities like Cincinnati, Buffalo, Pittsburgh, and Seattle have revitalized their downtown areas to attract shoppers and people interested in cultural activities, while a number of sunbelt cities have few if any attractions of this nature in their central core areas.

The thirty-two so-called frostbelt states have numerous problems, such as outmoded manufacturing facilities, deteriorating physical plants, high costs of services, and declining tax bases. As Dye and Garcia showed in their study, the older cities of the Northeast and North Central areas provide more services to their citizens than do the newer cities of the South and Southwest. This not only increases their expenditures, but makes them more attractive places for lower-income people who have less discretionary income with which to buy services.[17] The financial burden on the city grows, and the cycle continues to repeat itself.

The frostbelt-sunbelt dichotomy is of limited value in trying to understand the dynamics of urban politics and administration. At the state level, where data on income, education, federal grants, and job development are more accessible, perhaps the frostbelt-sunbelt dichotomy is of greater use. In the political wars between the two, the frostbelt states have held their own politically and economically. However, as population shifts and reapportionment is implemented, sunbelt states and their cities may become more powerful. It is also possible that in the near future the rapid increase in population and industry will produce in the sunbelt cities the same urban problems of crime, health, welfare, education, and pollution that characterize the frostbelt cities of the 1980s.

## Some New Perspectives on Urban Politics

Over the years many U.S. historians have pictured American history as the continuing creation of a "consensus" among hitherto dissimilar groups of people. The motto, "From many, one," has been taken almost as a historically accurate prophecy. Ever higher unities have emerged from lesser diversities.

From the consensus historians, the great majority of political scientists

have taken their lead in the interpretation of American political developments. Political struggle has generally been viewed not as an end in itself but
as a necessary means for establishing a new level of agreement. In every
case, the emphasis was on the achievement of a compromise solution following intensive bargaining. In terms of political philosophy this view is called
"pluralism," and in terms of party competition it may be characterized as
"brokerage politics."

In recent years, a small minority of historians has come to question the
tenets of the consensus school. Some political scientists have also come to be
skeptical of the consensus interpretation of political conflict. As they assess
the evidence, the importance of consensus in contemporary politics has been
exaggerated. By the same token they conclude that the prevailing orthodox
interpretation downgrades fairly severely the part played by conflict in modern American politics.

During the last twenty years, urban political life has undergone vast
changes. The 1960s began in a peaceful manner, with scholars such as Banfield, Meyerson, and Dahl examining the patterns of influence and power in
American cities.[18] By the mid-1960s, riots had broken out in hundreds of
cities, large and small. Cities with progressive mayors who attracted both
federal grants and foundation dollars were subject to riots and disorders
along with cities that had developed reputations for indifference and insen-
sitivity to the needs of their citizens.

Several things resulted from the riots of the 1960s. First, the federal
government began developing new programs for urban areas, funded through
grants-in-aid. The programs grew dramatically in numbers and in dollars.
Second, citizen groups began demanding a greater voice in local government
decision-making. This took the form of new mechanisms for citizen participation and greater decentralization of local government agencies. Third, citizens began demanding greater sensitivity to their needs on the part of urban
bureaucrats as well as a greater quantity and quality in urban service delivery. Each of these issues tended to heighten the conflict between citizens and
local government officials.

During the early years of the 1970s these conflicts became intense.
Federal grants-in-aid continued to grow, and the battles over program control and dollars highlighted the 1970–75 period. The economic recession in
1973–74 and the ensuing financial disaster in New York City helped to focus
all interested parties on the fact that an era of resource scarcity and inflation
was upon us.

The growing inflation rate and spiraling interest rates prompted the
Carter administration to tighten the federal budget and reduce the rate of
growth in federal aid to states and localities. Cities that had become quite
dependent on federal grants for part of their revenue began to feel the
squeeze and tried to put pressure on Washington. Late in the Carter administration it became clear that the days of new social programs and increased
federal grants were numbered. Local governments began tightening their
budgets by cutting their programs and reducing the number of employees.

The Reagan administration cut the federal budget for domestic programs shortly after coming into office. In its second year it cut domestic

spending once again and eliminated or consolidated a number of grant programs targeted for local governments. Local governments had no choice but to reduce their work forces, thus adding to an already increasing national unemployment figure.

The rapid changes in urban political life over the past twenty years have also changed our thinking about cities. The consensus viewpoint has been replaced by the conflict approach. In the past ten years we have also begun to place a greater value on the role of management in local government. Good urban managers are essential to building consensus, but they are also critical in managing conflict situations, whether they arise from distrust, alienation, fiscal retrenchment, or organizational decline.

This conflict approach to urban problems is heightened by the fragmented nature of urban areas, which leads to competition among groups for limited resources. Douglas Yates has labeled this process "street-fighting pluralism," which is characterized by chaos, competition, and alliances. The actors know one another as well as their goals, strengths, and weaknesses. The battle lines are drawn, the conflict on one level or another is continuous, and the elected officials as well as the top administrators are constantly drawn into the fray with little hope that any one set of actors can control the processing of issues and bring order out of chaos.[19]

It is important, therefore, for students of urban politics to understand the formal structure and processes of urban political systems. In many instances these structures and rules help to determine who gets what in the resource allocation process. However, conflict still occurs behind the scene. This conflict is engaged in by many actors seeking to alter the distribution of goods and services within the political system.

Many of these actors are new entrants into the urban political system. Citizen associations, single-issue neighborhood organizations, and articulate individuals have all become actors in the system, wielding different amounts of power at different times on different issues.

Behind the scenes, one can also find non-governmental actors such as the business community. In some cities business executives and corporations exercise a great deal of power, much of which is not part of the traditional public policy agenda. Who has power in the system and how it is exercised is the subject of the next chapter.

# NOTES

1. Noted in Jane Jacobs, *The Economy of Cities* (London: Jonathan Cape, 1970).
2. See Lewis Mumford, *The City in History* (London: Penguin Books, 1966), p. 11.
3. Ibid., p. 23.
4. Ibid., p. 109.
5. H. J. Dyos, "Agenda for Historians," in H. J. Dyos, ed., *The Study of Urban History* (London: Edward Arnold, 1968), pp. 1–46. Dyos would also add "cultural setting" as a fifth factor.
6. See Leo F. Schnore, "Problems in the Quantitative Study of Urban History," in H. J. Dyos, *Urban History*, pp. 189–208.
7. Press release, Office of the Mayor, New York City, dated May 27, 1971.

8.  Edward C. Banfield, *The Unheavenly City Revisited* (Boston: Little, Brown, 1974), p. 22.
9.  T. D. Allman, "The Urban Crisis Leaves Town and Moves to the Suburbs," *Harper's,* December, 1978, pp. 41–56.
10. Allman, "Urban Crisis," p. 55.
11. *Whither or Whether Urban Distress* (Washington: U.S. Department of Housing and Urban Development, 1979), p. 2. A response to the article "The Urban Crisis Leaves Town."
12. *Whither or Whether,* p. 42.
13. Sam Bass Warner, Jr., *The Private City: Philadelphia in Three Periods of Its Growth* (Philadelphia: University of Pennsylvania Press, 1968), p. x. The three periods are 1770–1780, 1830–1860, and 1920–1930.
14. Ibid.
15. *Standard Metropolitan Statistical Areas and Standard Consolidated Statistical Areas: 1980* (Washington: Bureau of the Census, October, 1981), p. 1.
16. David C. Perry and Alfred J. Watkins, eds., *The Rise of the Sunbelt Cities* (Beverly Hills: Sage Publications, 1977). Also see Richard M. Bernard and Bradley R. Rice, eds., *Sunbelt Cities: Politics and Growth Since World War II* (Austin, Texas: University of Texas Press, 1983).
17. Thomas Dye and John Garcia, "Structure, Function and Policy in American Cities," *Urban Affairs Quarterly* 13 (September 1978): 103–22.
18. Edward C. Banfield, *Political Influence* (New York: Free Press, 1961); Martin Meyerson and Edward C. Banfield, *Politics, Planning and the Public Interest* (Glencoe, Ill.: Free Press, 1955); and Robert A. Dahl, *Who Governs? Democracy and Power in an American City* (New Haven: Yale University Press, 1961).
19. Douglas Yates, *The Ungovernable City: The Politics of Urban Problems and Policy Making* (Cambridge, Mass.: MIT Press, 1977), p. 34–37.

# 2. DECISION-MAKING IN LOCAL GOVERNMENT: WHO HAS POWER?

One of the most important questions confronting students of urban politics is "Who has the power in local government?" After all, if cities are in crisis, as many commentators suggest, then public officials and citizen activists need to determine who has the power to make decisions to change these unacceptable conditions. This issue is important because it enables us to look behind the formal structures of local government and discern the roles of less visible political actors. We can ascertain if there are people and organizations behind the scenes who play an important role in the decision-making process.

Furthermore, an understanding of the decision-making process in local government can tell us how democratic or fair the city is in allocating its resources. If the political process appears to respond to a small number of influential business executives representing the corporate elite, then it is a relatively closed political system responding to the few. If, on the other hand, the system appears to be open and responsive to a range of diverse interests, then it is considered more democratic.

Strange as it may seem, there is still no agreement among academicians as to who exercises the most power in local government. Even worse is the inability of the major academic disciplines to agree on a methodology for ascertaining who makes decisions in local government. In other words, we not only don't know who makes decisions in local government, but we have not yet determined how to find the answer to this important question.

## THE SOCIOLOGIST'S APPROACH

After decades of field research, sociologists found that, in the cities they studied, business elites controlled the decision-making process. A discussion of several of these studies follows. In the late 1920s and early 1930s, two Columbia University sociologists, Helen and Robert Lynd, published the pioneering studies in the field of urban decision-making. Their books, *Middletown* and *Middletown in Transition*, were the result of several years of field research in Muncie, Indiana.[1] The Lynds did not set out to conduct a decision-making study of Muncie; rather, they were intent upon recording and analyzing the trends and patterns of life in an "average" American city. Their aim was "to present a dynamic, functional study of the contemporary life of this specific American community in light of the trends of changing behavior patterns observable in it during the last thirty-five years."[2]

The Lynds concerned themselves with six major areas of life in Muncie.

1. Getting a living
2. Making a home
3. Training the young
4. Using leisure time
5. Engaging in religious practices
6. Engaging in community activities

Using several graduate students to help them collect data, the Lynds began to draw a profile of life in Muncie. The publication of their first study hardly touched upon political power. However, by the time *Middletown in Transition* was published it was clear from their research that Middletown was controlled, in all important respects, by the "X Family." Using a social anthropological approach, the Lynds found that the city's most important family dominated the business class of Middletown and, through that class, maintained its influence in education, housing, religion, and government. In other words, a business elite ran the community, but the X Family dominated that elite.

The ruling elite hypothesis was also put forth by social science researchers such as C. Wright Mills, Ferdinand Lundberg, and G. William Domhoff.[3] Domhoff's study is worth reviewing as an example of the sociological approach. His thesis is that the American upper class is a governing class.[4] As a starting point, therefore, it is necessary to demonstrate the existence of an upper class. Using the *Social Register* of twelve major American cities as his leading index, Domhoff asserts that the listing of a person in one of these volumes demonstrates his or her upper class membership. Other criteria for such membership include social institutions such as private schools and exclusive clubs. On the basis of such indices, Domhoff concludes that the American upper class consists of less than 1 percent of the total population.[5]

The relationship between a "governing class" and a "power elite" is said to be straightforward.[6] A governing class is "a social upper class which owns a disproportionate amount of the country's wealth, receives a disproportionate amount of the country's yearly income, and contributes a disproportionate number of its members to positions of leadership."[7] But not all members of this top social group concern themselves with power. Some may while away their lives riding to hounds, entertaining mistresses, or drinking with members of the international jet set. Other members of the upper class will, of course, busy themselves with governmental or corporate affairs.

The power elite, on the other hand, is defined as those who are "in command positions in institutions controlled by members of the upper (governing) class."[8] "Any given member of the power elite may or may not be a member of the upper class. The important thing is whether or not the institution he serves is controlled by members of the upper class."[9]

From here on, Domhoff's objective is to show that members of the upper class control or dominate major corporations, foundations, universities, and the executive branch of the federal government.[10] In contrast, the power elite (members of the American upper class and their high-level employees) does not control but merely influences Congress, most state governments, and local governments.[11] Why this aspect of American political life escapes control by the upper class is not clear from Domhoff's account. Presumably, such dominance may not be worth the effort.[12]

While Domhoff relied on the *Social Register* as his first step in identifying the upper class, it is possible to use other indices to get similar results. Lundberg, for instance, stresses directorates in key corporations. From membership lists he then creates tables of interlocking directorships. Certain key individuals appear with regularity in powerful non-corporate institutions such as the prestige universities, the great foundations, and important church and charitable organizations. Lundberg, like Domhoff, uses the position of an individual in society as the starting point in the search for who has power. The lists of those who are powerful, while not identical, are largely overlapping.[13]

Even though their published works enjoyed wide circulation and drew an enthusiastic readership, Mills, Lundberg, and Domhoff ran into pointed shoals of scholarly criticism. For example, the thesis of a national governing elite was held to be so nebulous as to be virtually unresearchable. Many said that there was no way of proving or disproving the stated conclusions. All three authors were charged with confusing position with power, and it was stressed that many persons with a high social position are virtually without influence or power. A third general criticism was that the national elitist school failed to distinguish between the possibility that there might be several competing elites. If there were several such groups, might not the competition among them really serve popular and democratic purposes after all? Finally, critics pointed out that even if there were a national elite, most people are more concerned with the question of power in their own communities. From this perspective, critics asked, is it possible for there to be competing elites in the cities even if there is no competition at the national level?

Interest in this question was not new, for community power studies predate the national studies by a decade. But the writings of people like Mills served to spur on the search to locate power at all levels of American life, including the local community. Research in this field obviously held advantages over research at the national level, for it was possible to observe personal behavior at first hand. Often, the researcher could be a participant-observer. Meetings of officials were more frequent and more accessible. Interviews and polls were more feasible on a local than on a national basis. And in terms of expense, of course, a locally conducted scientific inquiry offered more for one's money than one on a national scale. For these reasons, the emphasis of the elitists tended to shift from national to community investigations. The result has been the proliferation of a large and important group of studies dealing with community power.

In the years following the appearance of the Lynds' studies, scores of books on American communities have been written. Of such works, the most influential study to arrive at elitist conclusions has unquestionably been *Community Power Structure,* Floyd Hunter's famous analysis of decision-makers in Atlanta.[14] Published in 1953, the Hunter investigation has served as the archetype for a whole school of community studies. Its methodology has been widely imitated, and its findings have been replicated in numerous instances. Because of the overriding importance of the Atlanta study, its main findings warrant summarization.

Hunter tells us that his project grew out of an intense feeling of dissatisfaction with the existing knowledge as to how the governors and the governed communicated with each other.[15] In the belief that a case study of leadership and power relationships in an actual city would help clarify the communication process, he decided to study the situation in Atlanta, which he referred to as Regional City.

It was Hunter's first task to find out who in Atlanta held power. In order to pursue this question, he employed a reputational method. "In Regional City," he says, "the men of power were located by finding persons in prominent positions in four groups that may be assumed to have power connections."[16] The groups were identified with business, government, civic associations, and "society." "From the recognized, or nominal, leaders of the groups mentioned, lists of persons presumed to have power in community affairs were obtained."[17] Using a process of "judges" to determine leadership rank, and also a system of self-selection, some 40 persons in the top levels of power in Atlanta were selected from more than 175 names.[18]

What people do for a living locates them in a community. On this basis, the occupational breakdown of the forty leaders fell into certain clusters. Eleven of the forty were directly associated with the activities of large commercial enterprises. Seven persons were in banking and investment operations, the second largest category. In the "service" category were five lawyers and one dentist. Five persons had major industrial responsibilities. Government personnel were represented by four persons. Two labor leaders, representing very large unions, made the listing. The remaining persons were classified by Hunter as "leisure personnel," persons with social or civic organization responsibilities but no day-to-day professional concerns. Of these persons, one was a woman who spent little time in Atlanta but who contributed $100,000 annually to charitable purposes in the community.[19]

Though the very top policymakers differ in many respects, they have certain common characteristics. For example, Hunter indicates that they tend to have expensive offices, frequent similar social clubs, and reside in the best residential district of the city.[20] The professionals, used as a contrasting group in the study, cluster in a different residential district.[21] Comparisons of this type are made among the other segments of the forty leaders.

But above all else, the leaders are persons of power status. "They are persons of dominance, prestige, and influence. They are, in part, the decision-makers for the total community."[22] Further, "They are able to enforce their decisions by persuasion, intimidation, coercion, and, if necessary, force."[23]

It would be an error to assume that the power personnel represent a "true pyramid of political power." Though they are dominant economically, and influential politically when they want to be, they have no continuing and permanent mechanism for transmitting their views to the various legislative bodies of the area. On some political issues the power group is simply not interested in the outcome.

Atlanta has a large black community next to the heart of the business and commercial districts. It is a substandard, segregated community, but it is functional. It provides a substantial labor force for the total community, and it is organized. In terms of power, "The Negro community represents a sub-structure of power as well as a sub-community."[24]

Yet the relationship between the black leaders and the decision-makers in the larger community is "superficial."[25] As a result, communication between the smaller and the larger community was incomplete and sporadic.

Certain other aspects of community power were underscored in the Atlanta study.[26] Contrary to popular belief, the policymakers did not operate clandestinely behind the cloak of nightfall. In real life, "The men of power usually operate openly with one another and on equal terms."[27] Another important consideration is the process of selection. On this, Hunter comments, "As it presently stands, leaders are for the most part self-selected."[28] When it comes to planning that relates to government activity, the policy-making group is apprehensive. It shows this apprehension by accepting reports of planning experts but making sure that the reports gather dust in agency files. In short, the recommended programs are stopped before any implementation can be undertaken.[29]

Even though many of the top leaders of Atlanta are fearful regarding the directions of social change, their fears to date have been more imaginary than real. On most of the important issues, the policymakers are united, and this is a reason for their collective strength. So far as their own basic value systems are concerned, the leaders are in nearly total agreement.[30]

In his concluding essay, Hunter returns to the role of government in a community controlled by a business elite. Only government, he contends, is big enough to provide for social planning that will take into account the interest of both the upper and lower structures of power. Expressing his faith in the democratic process, Hunter sees the possibility of reform of structural arrangements through changes in the process of selecting leaders. He would like the citizen, in relation to community participation on the level of policy decision, to have a "voice in determining who would be at the top."[31]

Hunter's study triggered scores of decision-making studies by sociologists in the next few years. These decision-making studies of local government have been remarkably similar in their methodology and their findings. Using a reputational technique—asking people who they think are the most important decision-makers or who has the reputation for power—they have almost without exception found an elitist governing structure heavily populated by prominent business executives. This pyramidal power structure is often referred to as the power elite.

## THE POLITICAL SCIENCE APPROACH

For many years the elitist model espoused by sociologists was the accepted model for understanding how decisions were made in local government. Over the past twenty years, however, this model has been challenged by political scientists who have found that power was not as concentrated nor decision-making as closed as the sociologists had concluded. The two models are now thought to be of equal value in explaining urban decision-making.

Of the many decision-making studies that support a pluralist model, the most influential has been Robert Dahl's 1960 study of New Haven, Connecticut.[32] Because Dahl was one of the first political scientists to conduct a decision-making study of local government, his work has been consistently used as a departure point for numerous other studies conducted by political scientists. For this reason a discussion of his methodology and findings is essential.

Dahl begins by noting that in any American democratic political system—including that of New Haven—knowledge, wealth, social position, and other resources are unequally distributed. This being so, the general question arises as to whether it is even remotely likely that the "people" can rule. But if the people, even in popular government, do not seem to be in a position to make decisions, who does make them? In order to reduce this broad query to manageable proportions, Dahl proposes to launch more specific inquiries relating to the distribution and patterns of influence and to the activities and characteristics of leaders.[33] He is also interested in learning whether his approach to community power will throw light upon the problem of change and stability in a democratic system generally.

In the New Haven investigation, the emphasis is placed upon decision-making in the community. This inquiry, in turn, is focused on three specific issue-areas: urban redevelopment, public education, and political nominations. These areas were chosen because Dahl felt they were significant and data were available for in-depth examination. Decisions in the first two of these areas "require formal assent of local government officials at many points."[34] While the third area, nominations, is only quasi-governmental, it is included because it is reasonable to assume that whoever controls nominations has influence over the elected officials.

Dahl posits several hypotheses relating to the distribution of influence in the three control areas. After studying the leaders in these areas, Dahl concludes that only a small number of people have direct influence "in the sense that they successfully initiate or veto proposals for policies."[35] On the other hand, in critical or close elections, the voters have great indirect influence on the decisions subsequently made by the elected leaders.

To know the distribution of influence does not by itself give sufficient information to answer the question of who governs. It is also essential to know something about the patterns of influence. For analytical purposes, it is useful to imagine two situations. In the first, the leaders in every issue-area could be assumed to be substantially identical and to agree on the policies they want. It could be further assumed that they come from the same social stratum. Given these assumptions, there would, of course, be an elite with presumably ample power to make all the important community decisions if it wished. What we have here is the elitist hypothesis.

But a rival supposition is also logical. If the various leaders differ from issue-area to issue-area and also among themselves, power is not held by a united elite. The power of one leader would be offset or checked by the power of another. In terms of supporting their leaders, the citizens would have choices not available under elitist rule. So the inquiry next turns to the questions of what strata furnish the leaders and the extent of their agreement or disagreement.[36]

At this point in the New Haven study the strength of the pluralist position emerges. Of the fifty different persons identified as leaders in the three issue-areas, only three "initiated or vetoed policies in more than one issue-area."[37] These were Celentano and Lee—two mayors—and Logue, one of the top leaders in redevelopment. The same specialization of influence was found to exist among the sub-leaders. So far as background was concerned, the leaders did *not* come from a single homogeneous stratum of the community. On the contrary, they manifested considerable ethnic, religious, and economic diversity.[38]

The two conclusions regarding patterns of influence were these:

> First, a leader in one issue-area is not likely to be influential in another. If he is, he is probably a public official and most likely the mayor.
> Second, leaders in different issue-areas do not seem to be drawn from a single homogeneous stratum of the community.[39]

Dahl also found that all citizens possessed some political resources, but on many occasions they chose not to use them, allowing these resources to lie idle. When threatened, however, these citizens could mobilize their resources and exert influence on political leaders. Dahl cites a case of the developer who tried to construct metal frame houses that residents felt would be incompatible with the character of their neighborhood. Residents mobilized and began to exert political influence. As a result, the city halted construction of the controversial project. Dahl cited this example to show that power was more widespread than traditional elitist theory had implied.[40]

These findings add up to a rejection of the Hunter elitist thesis. However power is exercised in New Haven, it is not managed by a covert elite of the top economic stratum.[41] Other aspects of the study have important implications for political theorists, but the central thesis is that power is located not in one but in several groups, depending on the issue. New Haven, Dahl concludes, is a "pluralistic democracy."[42]

Studies in other cities confirmed Dahl's pluralistic findings in New Haven. In Chicago, for instance, Banfield found that, contrary to popular belief, political issues were not controlled by the political machine. In several case studies Banfield found that Mayor Richard Daley was able to maintain control of the city only by carefully "brokering" the demands of various interest groups. Daley often waited for groups to raise political issues before placing them on the public agenda. Once much of the conflict was resolved, Daley would assist those he deemed worthy of his support by placing the power of the machine behind them. Therefore, even in Chicago in the 1940s, and under Daley in the 1950s, a pluralist picture of decision-making was much more evident than an elitist one.[43]

## CRITIQUES AND OTHER APPROACHES

### Critique of the Elitist Model

While sociologists continue to maintain the validity of their elitist conclusions, political scientists are equally vigorous in affirming their pluralist model. One major critique of the sociological approach came from Nelson W. Polsby, who worked as a research assistant to Dahl on the New Haven study. Polsby, in a book and several articles, criticized the theory, data collection and analysis, methodology, and conclusions of more than half a dozen sociological studies of decision-making.[44] The major thrust of the Polsby argument was that the reputation for power does not necessarily equal the actual exercise of power. He recommended that researchers conducting decision-making studies use primary documents and interviews in order to determine the actual behavior of the actors involved in the political process.

### Critique of the Pluralist Model

The political scientists, using the decision- or issue-oriented approach, have repeatedly found that decision-making in cities is pluralistic. However, their research has been subject to review, and the critiques of their work are important to students of urban affairs. Critics have argued that a researcher could not generalize about the distribution of power and influence in the community by analyzing only a small number of issues. Dahl, for example, used only three issues in drawing inferences about power and its distribution in New Haven. Pluralists also tend to define power only as it is used by public actors or public agencies. There is little acknowledgment or analysis of the role of private actors in local decision-making. Pluralists select issues for examination in which overt conflict is observable. This approach assumes that if no conflict is occurring, then power is not being exercised. It fails to account for the possibility that bureaucratic inertia or citizen group inaction could be a passive technique for exercising power.[45]

In a more recent study of how power is distributed in New Haven, Domhoff reexamined Dahl's data as well as uncovered additional evidence unavailable to Dahl. Contrary to Dahl's findings, Domhoff concluded that a business elite did exercise great influence over the outcome of important issues, such as downtown redevelopment in New Haven.[46]

Other critiques have been leveled at the pluralists, citing their failure to account for factors such as indirect influence, anticipated reactions, and undetected political manipulations. Critiques of a more general nature are directed towards the whole field of local government decision-making. One of these states that decision-making studies are static, not dynamic, and therefore no matter how sophisticated the research methodology, the most optimistic conclusion we can draw is that this is how power was distributed and how decisions were made during a particular time period. In other words, one cannot project the conclusions of an individual case study to either another city or to the same city at another time.

Another general critique of local government decision-making studies centers on the dynamics of external forces on the city's decision-makers. Few, if any, of the major studies have dealt extensively with the impact of county, state, and federal government actions on local government. As cities have become increasingly desperate for additional funds, other levels of government have come forward with aid. With that aid have come rules, regulations, and guidelines, which in some cases preempt decision-making by local officials. The extent of this reduction in local autonomy is extremely difficult to assess.[47]

## Non-Decision-Making

One of the most serious critiques of the pluralist approach was presented by Bachrach and Baratz in 1962. Bachrach and Baratz suggested that there had recently emerged a "neo-elitist" position on community power studies that relied heavily on the concept of non-decision-making. Non-decision-making occurs when organized groups are able to confine decision-making to relatively safe issues and keep issues that threaten their interests out of the political arena.[48]

First, the neo-elitists argue that the pluralists misunderstand the way power is exercised in local government. Neo-elitists believe that non-elites have their values set for them by elites. These values are transmitted by the elites to the non-elites using both overt and covert techniques. Consequently, non-elites are often not even aware that they have major differences with the elite. This type of false consensus limits conflicts and major community issues to those that do not threaten the elites, namely, safe issues.

Second, the neo-elitists claim that pluralists are best able to assess power when conflict is occurring. However, on many issues non-elites sense that despite their disagreements with elites there is nothing to be gained from conflict, since they lack the resources to win. In these instances the elites are powerful enough to create the phenomenon of "anticipated reactions." To the public or the researcher, there is no conflict, no real issue; therefore, decision-making or issue analysis employed by political scientists is useless. A community group that wants a new junior high school in its area learns to read cues. If money is scarce, political power weak, and student members declining, it is not likely that the request will be greeted enthusiastically. Rather than fight a losing battle, the community elects to conserve its political resources by anticipating the reactions of local elected officials and not raising the issue.

In other words, relative influence cannot be measured solely in terms of who initiates and who vetos proposals. There is a broad area where the exercise of power might limit or prevent an issue from being actively contested. Under these circumstances, decision-making would have to be analyzed by keeping in mind that in certain situations individuals act or do not act in anticipation of the sanctions that might befall them.

Third, pluralists, as stated above, focus on decisions in the public or governmental arena. This raises questions about issue selection and saliency. Some issues may die or be resolved before ever reaching the governmental decision-making agenda. The resolution of some of these issues may, in fact, propel a whole new set of issues onto the public agenda. Take, for example, the mayor who only introduces legislation that has a high probability of being passed by the council. Controversial legislation is not introduced; consequently, the mayor's legislative record appears very effective when in fact it may not have addressed any of the important issues confronting the city.

Bachrach and Baratz inspired a number of urban scholars, who in the 1960s began to ask questions about the efficacy of specific groups in society. The Kerner Commission report on the urban riots of the 1960s heightened this interest with its detailed account and analyses of distrust, powerlessness, and violence among many inner-city residents.[49] Still, it did not take long for critics of the neo-elitists to appear. Richard Merelman argued that Bachrach and Baratz, in criticizing the pluralists, had not offered alternative methodologies that would allow researchers to discover how power was distributed and exercised in local government.[50]

A good example of non-decision-making is reported by Crenson, who studied the steel industry in Gary, Indiana. Crenson points out that Gary was late in implementing air pollution controls due to the power U.S. Steel derived from its position as the town's major employer. U.S. Steel did not want to pay the costs of fitting its smokestacks with scrubbers. Yet, according to Crenson, had pluralists studied Gary they would not have found any overt evidence of U.S. Steel's role, since the giant corporation did not actively or publicly lobby the Mayor or the Council. The point is that U.S. Steel did not have to engage in this political activity. U.S. Steel's position concerning costly air pollution devices in the Gary mills was common knowledge. It was also obvious that U.S. Steel could cut back production, and consequently employment, if it wanted to. In other words, U.S. Steel did not have to exert a great deal of pressure publicly. Non-decision-making in the form of anticipated reactions occurred as U.S. Steel's presumption of power was sufficient to delay the imposition of strong air pollution controls.[51]

The debate between political scientists and sociologists has continued for over twenty years with very little resolution of the differences in methodology or the conclusions resulting from the studies. Besides the pluralist, elitist, and non-decision-making models, there is at least one other approach purporting to show how decisions are made in local government. This is called revisionist theory.

## Revisionist Theory

Revisionist theory grew out of the turmoil of the 1960s, which prompted many practitioners and academics to reassess their traditional thinking about power relationships and decision-making patterns in American cities. Not satisfied with either the pluralist or elitist models, many of these critics subscribed to the Bachrach and Baratz thesis on non-decision-making.[52]

While these critics did not necessarily believe that one unified elite ruled a city, neither did they believe that power was as widespread as the pluralists claimed. They saw in the civil disorders of the 1960s a new set of problems that had not been addressed by earlier researchers. These problems centered around the ability of certain interest groups (banks, insurance companies, and realtors) to consistently exercise power in such a way that they continually maintained a favorable position in the decision-making structure. Furthermore, these groups were able to impact upon the system sufficiently to prevent specific issues from being placed on the public agenda.[53]

Pluralists have never denied that bias exists in the system, but they have contended that it is less pervasive than the revisionists assert and more dispersed throughout the system, so as not to be cumulative. Revisionists focused their attention on the bias built into the system and sought to find out which groups were advantaged and disadvantaged by this bias.[54]

Revisionist theory is supported by several case studies. Lipsky, in his study of the rent strike movement in 1964–65 in New York City, found that organized protests still provided only marginal resources for the poor. Furthermore, the object of the protest movement can still find ways to resist the protest and thwart the demands of the poor. This was accomplished by refurbishing one house in the area or issuing implied threats of eviction if the strikers did not relent. In the end, the rent strike achieved virtually nothing for the tenants.

In Newark, Parenti found it impossible for citizens in a black ward to obtain a traffic light on their corner despite years of protest and the accumulation of hundreds of signatures. In a nearby white ward, residents were able to secure such a light in less than a month with fewer than fifty signatures.

For both Lipsky and Parenti, pluralism is not an accurate picture of how politics is played in city government. The poor do not get their demands met, and pluralism does not describe power in the lower-income communities, where very little power exists.[55]

## Summary and Conclusions

The study of local government decision-making is a complex and important component of the study of urban politics. Fifty years of research and several hundred studies conducted by thousands of social science researchers have not satisfactorily answered the questions of how decisions are made in local government or who makes them. Even more discouraging, there continues to be disagreement over how to find the answers to these questions.

How power is distributed and exercised in local government is important to our understanding of what type of political system we live under. There is still a great deal of controversy about how open our political systems are. Even pluralists recognize that business interests are very active in our cities, and decisions made by corporate executives have a tremendous impact upon life in the city. Decisions about plant relocations or branch office moves affect jobs, taxes, and services. Similarly, decisions by banks and insurance companies on when and where to invest their capital can have a major impact upon an urban or metropolitan area.

While open political systems may be the ideal, it is important to remember that covert decisions made by private actors can often have a much greater effect on a neighborhood or ward than deliberations in the city council chamber. Furthermore, even under fairly closed political systems there are many issues on which the elite decision-makers disagree. This often encourages coalition building and helps to open up the system a little more.

We have looked at several different approaches to understanding decision-making in local government. These approaches have shown us that some political systems are more open and responsive than others, and this helps us to determine who makes decisions about the allocation of resources in urban areas. The next chapter examines the formal structures of local government and helps us to understand who gets what in urban politics.

## NOTES

1.  Robert S. and Helen M. Lynd, *Middletown* (New York: Harcourt, Brace, 1929), and *Middletown in Transition* (New York: Harcourt, Brace, 1937). Also see Theodore Caplow et al., *All Faithful People: Change and Continuity in Middletown's Religion* (Minneapolis: University of Minnesota Press, 1983).
2.  Lynd and Lynd, *Middletown*, p. 6.
3.  G. William Domhoff, *Who Rules America?* (Englewood Cliffs, N.J.: Prentice-Hall, 1967); C. Wright Mills, *The Power Elite* (New York: Oxford University Press, 1956); and Ferdinand Lundberg, *America's 60 Families* (New York: Vanguard Press, 1937).
4.  Domhoff, *Who Rules America?*, p. 3.
5.  Ibid., p. 7.
6.  Ibid., p. 9.

7. Ibid., p. 9.
8. Ibid., p. 10.
9. Ibid., p. 10.
10. Ibid., p. 11.
11. Ibid., p. 11.
12. Ibid., pp. 132–137.
13. Lundberg, *America's 60 Families*.
14. Floyd Hunter, *Community Power Structure* (Garden City, New York: Anchor Books, 1963). The book was originally published in 1953.
15. Ibid., p. 1
16. Ibid., p. 11.
17. Ibid., pp. 11–12.
18. Ibid., p. 12.
19. Ibid., p. 13.
20. Ibid., pp. 14–19.
21. Ibid., p. 22.
22. Ibid., p. 24.
23. Ibid., p. 24.
24. Ibid., p. 110.
25. Ibid., p. 139.
26. Ibid., p. 139.
27. Ibid., p. 178.
28. Ibid., p. 227.
29. Ibid., p. 234.
30. Ibid., p. 241.
31. Ibid., p. 253. Hunter's recent study of Atlanta confirmed his earlier findings. *Community Power Succession: Atlanta's Policymakers Revisited* (Chapel Hill: University of North Carolina Press, 1980).
32. Dahl, *Who Governs?* Also see Raymond Wolfinger, *The Politics of Progress* (Englewood Cliffs, N.J.: Prentice-Hall, 1974); Robert Presthus, *Men at the Top: A Study of Community Power* (New York: Oxford University Press, 1964); and Robert E. Agger, Daniel Goldrich, and Bert E. Swanson, *The Rulers and the Ruled: Political Power and Impotence in America* (New York: John Wiley and Sons, 1964).
33. Dahl, *Who Governs?*, pp. 7–8
34. Ibid., p. 103.
35. Ibid., p. 163.
36. Ibid., p. 165.
37. Ibid., p. 181.
38. Ibid., p. 183.
39. Ibid., p. 183.
40. Ibid., pp. 192–199.
41. Ibid., p. 185.
42. Ibid., p. 305.
43. Banfield, *Political Influence*. Another pluralistic view of city politics is presented in Wallace S. Sayre and Herbert Kaufman, *Governing New York City* (New York: W. W. Norton, 1963).
44. Nelson W. Polsby, *Community Power and Political Theory* (New Haven: Yale University Press, 1963). Also see Nelson W. Polsby, "Three Problems in the Analysis of Community Power," *American Sociological Review* 24 (December 1959): 796–803; and Raymond Wolfinger, "A Plea for a Decent Burial," *American Sociological Review* 27 (December 1962): 841–847.
45. See Thomas Anton, "Power, Pluralism and Local Politics," *Administrative Science Quarterly* 7 (March 1963): 425–457; and "Rejoinder to Robert Dahl's Critique of Power, Pluralism and Local Politics," *Administrative Science Quarterly* 8 (September 1963): 257–268. Also see David Ricci, *Community Power*

and Democratic Theory: The Logic of Political Analysis (New York: Random House, 1971), chaps. 7–10; and Philip J. Trounstine and Terry Christensen, Movers and Shakers: The Study of Community Power (New York: St. Martins Press, 1982), chap. 2.

46. G. William Domhoff, Who Really Rules?: New Haven and Community Power Reexamined (Santa Monica: Goodyear Publishing Co., 1978), chap. 5.

47. Arthur Vidich and Joseph Bensman, Small Town in Mass Society (Princeton: Princeton University Press, 1958).

48. Peter Bachrach and Morton S. Baratz, "The Two Faces of Power," American Political Science Review 56 (December 1962): 947–952. Also see Bachrach and Baratz, Power and Poverty: Theory and Practice (New York: Oxford University Press, 1970), pp. 43–46.

49. Report of the National Advisory Commission on Civil Disorders (New York: Bantam Books, 1968), pp. 203–282.

50. Richard M. Merelman, "On the New-Elitist Critique of Community Power," American Political Science Review 62 (June 1968): 451–460.

51. Matthew Crenson, The Un-politics of Air Pollution: A Study of Non-Decision-making in the Cities (Baltimore: Johns Hopkins Press, 1971), pp. 55–82.

52. Bachrach and Baratz, "The Two Faces of Power."

53. Clarence N. Stone, Robert K. Whelan, and William J. Murin, Urban Policy and Politics in a Bureaucratic Age (Englewood Cliffs, N.J.: Prentice-Hall, 1979), pp. 197–198.

54. E. E. Schattschneider, The Semi-Sovereign People (New York: Holt, Rinehart and Winston, 1960).

55. See Michael Lipsky, Protest in City Politics (Chicago: Rand McNally, 1972); and Michael Parenti, "Power and Pluralism: View from the Bottom," Journal of Politics 32 (1970): 501–530.

# 3. FORMAL STRUCTURE AND LEADERSHIP STYLE

## FORMAL STRUCTURE AND POLICYMAKING

It is important to understand the formal structure of local governments in America. The formal structure and powers are established in laws, charters, and constitutional provisions. The political and administrative leaders of local governments are guided or constrained in their actions by the formal powers delegated to the city or the county. Many political issues never reach the public agenda because of legal restraints in the documents governing local government powers. Political concerns such as tax rates, bond issues, and type of government are often seen as procedural issues with legal implications that require negotiations with state officials for approval.

The formal rules and structure of government often determine who gets what from the political system. Groups that understand the budget process have a better appreciation for timing their campaigns to affect issues being discussed by decision-makers. The same could be said for those who understand the amount of discretion devolved to bureaucrats in field offices.

Citizen groups who understand the amount of power exercised by the mayor and other political leaders will know whether or not to seek mayoral assistance in obtaining a federal grant, a national convention for the city, or advice on a city-suburban neighborhood squabble. Similarly, knowledge about a council-manager form of government and the role and powers of the manager as a trained professional, will assist businessmen and neighborhood organizations in making decisions about who will and will not be likely to respond to political pressure.

### Formal and Informal Power

No two cities in the United States have governmental forms so similar that they will process a given issue in exactly the same manner. Therefore, it is important to study the formal structure of local government because it affects the policymaking process, which in turn determines who gets what from city hall. Any technique for organizing local government will advantage some groups in the community and disadvantage others. Over time, some groups learn to work the system better than others. The groups who feel disadvantaged often attempt to make changes in the pattern of local government to reduce their perceived disadvantages and to change their prospects for success. Since change in the American political system occurs incrementally, minor modifications rather than large scale reorganizations have been the pattern.

Structural arrangements in local government do have an impact upon the issues being processed by the political system. Local government structure will affect the strategies and tactics of groups trying to influence the system. However, knowledge of the governmental structure alone is rarely sufficient to a full understanding of how decisions are made in local government.[1]

The distribution of legal power and authority recorded in the charter and laws of a local government is often not reflective of the pattern of distribution of actual influence in that community. In some strong-mayor cities, appointed advisory boards and commissions make the political life of the mayor miserable. Similarly, there are council-manager cities in which the council appoints boards and commissions that act independently of the manager.

There are several reasons for this apparent discrepancy between legal and actual power. Many legal powers granted to local officials in charters and laws are, in fact, shared powers. The concept of checks and balances is honored at the local level, and powers delegated to a specific official or branch of government are often checked by someone else in the system. This is a common problem in the appointment of senior administrative personnel, who often think they will have a greater degree of unchecked power than they really have.

Furthermore, some actions delegated to local officials require state administrative or legislative authority. The local government, in these instances, acts almost as an agent of the state and shares power for the function performed. With the growth of the federal grant-in-aid system, local governments found themselves performing many more functions in concert with federal administrative agencies. The local government administered the federally financed program, but was subject to rules and regulations promulgated by Washington. Federal grants, state laws, and constitutional requirements have made the structure of local government much more complex than in earlier years.

The delegation of formal authority does not always determine the amount of power that will be exercised. A city may have the legal right to perform a function, but faced with opposition, the city might choose not to exert its full authority. For instance, a city could impose a car towing ordinance for illegally parked cars to relieve overcrowding in a commercial area. But the city might choose not to implement it because the policy will be costly and time-consuming and might offend merchants who want the illegally parked customers to patronize their stores. In this case the city might elect to moderate its position and attempt to achieve a reasonable solution among the parties involved. To an outsider, the city might appear weak and indecisive.

An interesting example of the difference between formal and informal power was seen in the city of Chicago under Mayor Richard Daley. The formal structure of Chicago is a classic weak-mayor government, but any outsider relying solely on the city charter for guidance would be seriously misled. Daley, by centralizing political power in the Democratic party, which he headed, and by mobilizing corporate power to support him in exchange for favorable considerations, was able to broker the major political and administrative decisions in Chicago for two decades.[2]

Occasionally, public issues are tied in knots by citizens who feel the city has mistreated them or has violated legal or administrative procedures. Law suits filed by citizens are a very effective strategy for limiting the political authority of local officials. During the 1960s and early 1970s, citizen groups were successful in tying up in the courts numerous freeway projects and environmental quality issues.

The legal powers granted to local officials in city charters or state legislation or constitutions occasionally are ambiguous and leave room for discretion. The interpretation of these laws and regulations leaves a wide area for policy implementation. This, in turn, creates variations in the use or nonuse of delegated authority.

Bureaucrats do not always follow through on the orders issued by politicians. Lowi has found that bureaucrats are quite adept at insulating themselves from mayoral control by virtue of their civil service position and unionization. Savas and Ginsburg pointed out that numerous changes were required in the civil service system if New York City was to have a responsive bureaucracy. Finally, Lipsky analyzed the range of discretionary power available to street-level bureaucrats in interpreting program guidelines and administering programs on a day-to-day basis. Through this discretion, street-level bureaucrats, in effect, gave direction to ambiguous legislation and often decided who would receive the program benefits.[3]

Finally, there is the prospect that even when a local government elects to use its legal authority, this power may be ignored. Pickets can refuse to leave a street corner, and teenagers might continue to gather in a park after its legal closing time. Public officials find some subordinates who arrive late, leave early, abuse sick leave agreements, and tend to personal business during work hours. None of these actions may produce severe consequences, but they are all examples of legal municipal authority that is not complied with by citizens. In each case there is a threat of sanctions, but these will be applied selectively and in varying degrees, depending upon the local government involved. A good example is the issue of housing code violations. Each city has laws and rules governing the safe and sanitary conditions of housing. On the surface it appears that vigorous enforcement of these laws would end unsafe and unsanitary housing in America's cities. Years of trial and error have shown the more likely result of such enforcement is housing abandonment, high court costs, and limited upgrading of housing stock. Selective enforcement, using different techniques in different cities, has proved to be a much more effective strategy than generally invoking the legal power of the city.

## Dillon's Rule and the Limits of City Government

The basic distribution of governmental powers in the United States is set forth in the United States Constitution. The Tenth Amendment states specifically that all powers not conferred on the federal government are "reserved" to the states or to the people. Since cities and other local governments are not even mentioned in the Constitution, the legal assumption is that they fall under the jurisdiction of the states. This is another way of saying that there is no inherent right of a subdivision of the state—whether it be a county, a city, a borough, or a township—to exercise local governmental powers. Such powers must be conferred on the local unit by the state, either through the state's constitution or by statute.

The legal position of municipal corporations—and other subdivisions as well—was given its classic formulation in a remarkable statement by Judge John F. Dillon (1831–1914), a famous jurist and legal commentator, in a work first published in 1872. Dillon's Rule reads as follows:

> It is a general and undisputed proposition of law that a municipal corporation possesses and can exercise the following powers, and no others: First, those granted in express words; second, those necessarily or fairly implied in or incident to the power expressly granted; third, those essential to the accomplishment of the declared objects and purposes of the corporation,—not simply convenient, but indispensable. Any fair, reasonable substantial doubt concerning the existence of power is resolved by the courts against the corporation, and the power is denied.[4]

In this formulation, Judge Dillon went far beyond asserting that municipal corporations possess only those powers delegated by the state. He also says that such powers as have been granted must be very strictly construed by the courts. When it is recalled that the very existence of a municipal corporation is determined by an action of the state, it is clear that, under American law, such a corporation is legally dependent upon the state.

It is true that there have been occasional challenges to Dillon's Rule, but most of them have not been successful. However, the present constitutions of New Jersey and Michigan are explicit in declaring that constitutional and statutory provisions concerning local government should be liberally construed. Legal theory holds that the power to grant incorporation to the inhabitants of any urban area is legislative in nature and may not be delegated. Yet the practice today is considerably different.

Formerly, any community wishing to incorporate itself would petition the colonial assembly, or later the state, which could, if it wished, pass a specific statute of incorporation. But as the country expanded and the number of such requests reached a total that made legislative action inconvenient, other devices were invented. Today state legislatures assign the task of incorporation to other agencies, usually to the chief legislative and administrative agency of the county. If and when certain statutory requirements are met, the agency is empowered to proceed with the act of incorporation. The fiction of legislative action was maintained by assuming that the county was merely performing an administrative, not a legislative act.

So the present day procedure is basically this: A stated, significant percentage of the residents of an area, through petition or referendum, must indicate that they favor incorporation. The petition must state the precise area of the proposed corporation. In some states a particular level of population density must exist before consideration of the petition. If the county agency accepts the petition, the agency then appoints a set of interim officials or provides for the immediate election of permanent officials. The incorporation is then made a matter of public record. This is evidenced by the granting of a charter, which becomes, in a sense, the constitution of the municipality.

## City Charters

Today there are several forms of city charters, all of which are drafted by the state legislatures, except in the case of home rule cities. Until about 1850, the normal practice was for a legislature to incorporate a city by passing a special act. But, as we have noted, the process became cumbersome and other methods were adopted. The objective was not only to obtain a more efficient process, but also to obtain a higher degree of uniformity among the charters. So, as an improvement over the passage of specific charters, the states began to adopt general charters of incorporation. While this dealt with the efficiency problem, it failed to come to grips with the requirements of uniformity.

As a result, the states today for the most part grant *classified* charters. The idea, clearly, is to make meaningful distinctions among cities that may differ vastly in socioeconomic aspects. Commonly, the basis for classification is population, although the assessed value of taxable property is sometimes used as well. If a city's population changes rather dramatically, does it automatically move from one category to another? The general answer is no. The change from one classification to another is not automatic, but depends on some prescribed formal procedure. States also impose different service requirements and grant different powers to each class of city. Even though the system of classes is to protect a city from arbitrary treatment, a state will occasionally single out a major city, such as Boston, Baltimore, or New York, for special action if there is only one very large city in the state.

Some states give their cities a choice in which they may opt for one or another plan of city charter. The most common plans are the mayor-council form, the commission form, and the council-manager form. These will be dealt with in the ensuing discussion of forms of city government. In the meantime, certain other aspects of city government warrant some brief analysis.

## Home Rule

Though the term *home rule* is open to a variety of interpretations, the basic difference between the charters analyzed so far and a home rule charter is that an ordinary charter may be changed by the state legislature at any time, but a home rule charter may not. A home rule charter, drafted originally by the municipality, grants the municipal corporation a high degree of independence with regard to charter changes and revisions.

Broadly considered, there are two general types of home rule charters. When the state legislature permits a city to draft its own charter, the consequent action is termed legislative home rule. Under this procedure, the legislature, of course, retains the power to cancel or revise the existing home rule charters. But in practice, cities with this type of home rule have enjoyed a rather lasting and effective independence.

Because the second type of home rule charter comes from authority granted in the state constitution, it is called constitutional home rule. What this means is that the legislature has been prohibited by the constitution from prescribing the form of government those cities shall have. As a consequence, a city may adopt whatever form of charter it believes best meets its needs, regardless of the sentiments of the legislature. The first use of constitutional home rule occurred in Missouri in 1875, when the constitution was amended to make home rule available for the two largest cities of the state.

While it is easy to understand that the concept of home rule is appealing, its practical effectiveness should not be overestimated. Constitutional home rule does not free a city from the state government. Much state action, in scores of ways, continues to affect the city, and general acts of the legislature remain applicable. Furthermore, the lines of demarcation of the powers of the two units of government are usually unclear and are eventually reconciled, if at all, either in the courts or through political compromises.

In some ways home rule is a misnomer, since no state grants to its cities all the powers they need for self-governance. Even home rule cities are generally constrained by state-imposed taxing, borrowing, and regulatory decisions.

## FORMS OF CITY GOVERNMENT

In the United States, there are three principal forms of city government. They are the mayor-council plan, the commission plan, and the council-manager plan. Adapted from the earlier English model, the mayor-council plan is the most traditional and common of the forms now in use. Of those cities with a population of more than five thousand, more than half are reported to operate under the mayor-council system.

## Mayor-Council Government

Under the mayor-council plan, the main agencies of government are an elected council and an elected mayor. In theory, the council is the policy-determining body, and the mayor is the chief executive. In actual practice, a strong mayor may ride herd over a weak council. The plan is characteristically American in that it retains the much-cherished separation of powers, pitting one branch against another. It should be emphasized in this connection that the council members are elected on one section of a ballot and the mayor is elected on another. The mayor represents a city-wide constituency, while the council represents, as a rule, individual districts. This electoral system means that voters often have to vote for one candidate for mayor and only one candidate from their district or ward for the city council. This system is often referred to as a short ballot since it reduces the voter burden by requiring the voter to obtain information about a limited number of candidates. The alternative to this is a long ballot, which is required in cities that use nonpartisan or at-large electoral systems, where there are many candidates to choose from on the ballot. These systems are discussed in Chapter 5.

At present, nearly all city councils are unicameral, or one-chambered. But up until recent decades it was common for the councils to be bicameral. And it can be argued that New York City today, with a city council and a board of estimate, still represents a version of the earlier bicameral system of municipal government.

Called councilmen or aldermen, council members are chosen by popular vote, usually for a term of two or four years. Nomination is ordinarily by primary election. In some cities, both the primary elections and the general elections are nonpartisan, although often this is an extremely thinly disguised fiction.

As mentioned above, the most common practice calls for the election of council members by wards or districts. But in some cities (for example, Philadelphia, New York, and Washington, D.C.) some council members are chosen from councilmanic districts and some from the city at large.

In any election based on the winner-take-all principle (i.e., the person who gets the most votes carries the district), there is bound to be a distortion between the percentage of seats held on the council by the majority party and the percentage of all popular votes for candidates for that party. In order to overcome this obvious problem, some cities have adopted proportional representation (P.R.) in council elections. The system used in America is called the Hare plan, named after its inventor, an English barrister.

Under this plan, a voter ranks the candidates numerically in order of preferences. Once a candidate achieves the quota necessary for election to the council, his or her surplus votes are transferred and added to those of the next-ranked candidate on each ballot who has not to that point achieved the quota needed for election. Because of this characteristic, the plan is also referred to as the "single transferable vote" system. As the transferring of votes continues, nearly every voter helps elect some persons to the council, even though the council members elected may not have been those of the voter's first choice. Inaugurated in 1915 in Ashtabula, Ohio, the plan continues to operate successfully in a number of cities, including Cambridge, Massachusetts. From 1938 to 1949, a form of P.R. was used in New York City. The individual boroughs served as the election districts, and party designations appeared on the ballot. The abandonment of P.R. in New York City apparently came about because under the system an occasional Communist was elected from Brooklyn. This was more than the civic conscience of the majority of New York City's voters could bear, and the retention of P.R. was defeated in a popular referendum.[5]

Councils meet regularly on a weekly or monthly basis. In some cities, the mayor is the presiding officer; in others, the council president presides. In the latter case, there is apt to be continual and often acrimonious rivalry between the two officials. As with most legislative bodies, a good deal of the real work is done in the standing committees.

In their legislative capacity, councils give most of their attention to financial and regulatory matters. They regulate such fields as health, traffic, building standards, and zoning. They may let contracts and authorize public improvements. In its legislative functioning, a council can pass an ordinance, which becomes local law, or a resolution, which is usually an action on an administrative matter.

In many cities council members are constrained by the fact that their jobs are part-time and low paying. In these cities, council members cannot devote the necessary time to city affairs. Many city councils are plagued by a lack of professional staff. Hence, in numerous cities council members are dependent upon mayoral initiatives and executive branch recommendations and analyses on policy issues. In these cities the most active council members are those whose occupations (lawyers, housewives, academics, retirees) allow them to commit the necessary time to council duties.

As state government tends to parallel the federal, the powers of the mayor tend to parallel those of the governor. He or she appoints and removes officials (often with the consent of council) and has the power to veto and to make recommendations. A very strong mayor may get a good deal of authority not specifically spelled out in the charter through the adroit use of public relations techniques, approbation by the mass media, and support from powerful interest groups and alliances. In addition, in most of the larger cities there has been created in recent years a position of managing director (the titles vary), an official directly responsible to the mayor for the day-to-day management of affairs. This position is not to be confused with that of a city manager, who, as we shall see, is responsible to the council. If there is a managing director, the mayor is thereby freed to give attention to activities other than administration—and many a mayor is more skilled in public relations or politics than in administration.

Mayoral assistants, or Chief Administrative Officers (CAOs), have very different responsibilities in each city. While they perform a variety of tasks, their primary functions tend to be in the areas of budgeting, fiscal affairs, and personnel matters. They are often charged with the responsibility of supervising departments, thus freeing the mayor to engage in more long-range policymaking.

Upon election to office, mayors often confront the appointment of a CAO as one of their first tasks. At that juncture the mayor must choose between a person with a strong administrative background, who may be politically neutral, or a close personal or political ally, who may lack the administrative skills and experience to manage the city on a day-to-day basis. Occasionally a mayor is fortunate enough to find someone who is both politically and administratively acceptable. Too often, the big city mayor finds one of his or her first decisions to be a choice between loyalty or expertise in the appointment of a CAO.

In some cities the CAO is not appointed by each individual mayor but is either a career civil servant or an appointee who serves an extended fixed term. In these cities the CAO is a valuable source of administrative continuity, providing a new mayor with much-needed knowledge about the budget, the administrative process, and the power realities within city hall. However, it is also possible that a new mayor may distrust a CAO who served in the administration of a predecessor.

San Francisco, in 1931, was one of the first cities to install a CAO. Los Angeles, Philadelphia, Boston and New Orleans all have created positions that in many ways resemble a CAO. New York City established the position during the Wagner administration (1954–66). However, it came under severe criticism during the Lindsay administration and was formally abolished under Mayor Abraham Beame. Beame, however, soon created a Deputy Mayor's position, which embodied many of the powers of the original CAO under Wagner.[6]

## Strong-Mayor–Council

It is important to distinguish between two types of mayor-council governments: the weak-mayor type and the strong-mayor type. As the term indicates, the weak-mayor type gives the mayor relatively unimportant administrative powers as compared to those of the council. Under the strong-mayor plan, the mayor has formidable administrative powers, and the powers of the council are correspondingly diminished. In most of the larger cities the trend, in recent years, has been to increase the administrative powers of the mayor and to decrease those of the council. From the point of view of public administration, this makes good sense, for it lets the public know where responsibility should be placed for good or bad civic performance.

During the colonial period, colonial governors appointed mayors in many municipalities outside of New England. The mayors were often selected from among the men who served as aldermen or councilmen. These were experienced officials who were influential members of the community and who were held in high esteem by the citizens in their communities.

The mayors served one-year terms, but were often reappointed, which added to their experience and their influence. The use of the one-year term provided the colonial governors with a check on the power of the mayor. At the end of the year mayoral performance was assessed, with reappointment dependent upon the colonial governor's evaluation. Should a mayor become too influential or too independent of the governor, reappointment was denied and a new member of the community was appointed to fill the position for a year.

Few of the mayors were paid, but in the larger jurisdictions, being mayor carried a good deal of prestige. Mayors presided over council meetings and had the power to vote on issues, but they could not exercise a veto. In contemporary terms they were truly weak mayors.

After the Revolutionary War and the drafting of the Constitution, many new local charters were drafted that provided for the popular election of the mayor. While these charters reflected the concepts of checks and balances and separation of powers, by 1820 the majority of mayors were still elected by councils, not by the electorate. During the first quarter of the nineteenth century, the powers of the mayor were not expanded.

For the next fifty years, 1825–1870, mayoral power did not change markedly. The country still regarded its colonial experience under George III as sound enough reason to minimize and check executive power whenever possible. During this period councils grew in importance, and their workloads increased tremendously.

By 1850, however, an enormous increase in municipal functions had occurred. The city councils, their committees, and a limited staff were incapable of legislating for and administering local government at the same time. Rather than investing additional powers in the local executive office of the mayor, the councils sought relief from the state legislature. The legislatures responded sympathetically, since they did not want to increase executive power either. The result was a series of boards, agencies, and commissions created by the legislature that effectively diminished much of the local council's control over policymaking and implementation.

Some of these boards and commissions, which were given functional responsibility for policy in areas such as education and law enforcement, were part of the local government, and their members were elected by the local citizenry. Others had their members appointed by state officials and were almost completely controlled by the state. Vestiges of this nineteenth century arrangement can still be found in some cities in the eastern and mid-eastern regions of the United States.

As the country emerged from the Civil War it became clear that the extraordinary amount of legislative and administrative authority vested in the legislative branch of local government had gotten out of hand. The legislative branch had grown considerably, and its ability to function effectively had been impeded. By 1870 a movement to curb the powers exercised by state legislatures was underway. State constitutions were amended, or new ones were drafted, restricting legislative power over local affairs. Laws that had authorized state boards and commissions to control local government administrative functions were repealed. New local charters were drafted, which for the first time provided for significant increases in the powers of the mayor. The 1870–1880 period marks the beginning of strong mayoral government in the United States.

Mayors were given the power to appoint administrative personnel, and a decade later they were empowered to remove appointed officials. As mayors added to their powers the right to veto legislation and to prepare and present local government budgets, the locus of power shifted from the council to the Mayor's office.

However, local government did not automatically grant unlimited power to the mayor. Many city charters included the classic checks and safeguards against the unwholesome use of executive power. Councils can be empowered to confirm the mayor's appointments as well as to limit the power of removal. Councils usually control the appropriation process and can request audits and investigations of executive department activities. Finally, councils can restrict purchasing authority and contracting procedures.[7]

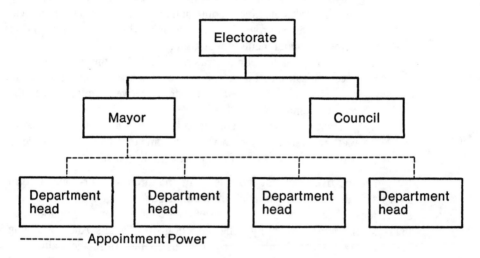

FIGURE 3.1
Strong-mayor Structure

City charters vary as to how much power they give the mayor's office. Among the cities that are considered to have a strong-mayor–council form of government are New York, Detroit, Philadelphia, Cleveland, Boston, Baltimore, Pittsburgh, and St. Louis.

## Summary

The strong-mayor–council form of government has been found most often in large cities, primarily because of its emphasis on political leadership and the need for someone to mediate among the contending interests for the city's resources.

The major strengths of the strong-mayor–council form are:

1.  Use of the short ballot reduces voters' burdens by limiting the number of key elected officials and focusing voter attention on these few candidates.

2. Administrative authority is concentrated in a single official of government who is responsible for all administrative decisions throughout the government.
3. A strong mayor provides political leadership, a necessary requirement for effective local government.
4. The structure allows for great latitude in hiring competent administrators and firing incompetent ones.

The weaknesses of the strong-mayor–council form of government are:

1. Mayors have to be elected before they can implement their policies. To do so they incur political debts and obligations to political parties, interest groups, and individuals. These are often repaid in terms of appointments, favors, etc.
2. The mayor, as top administrator, is elected by the voters. Experience indicates that few trained, experienced administrators are elected to the office, and administratively we are often left to the mercy of amateurs.
3. The structure fails to separate politics from administration. Complete separation is not feasible, but some effort should be made to separate policymaking from policy implementation.

Yet the overwhelming popularity of the strong-mayor–council form over its rivals comes not so much from administrative as from political considerations. Cities, especially big cities, want their mayors to be public figures of considerable visibility. The attraction of Atlanta's Andrew Young and San Francisco's Dianne Feinstein stems mainly from their ability to attract public attention. Psychologically, the mayor is viewed as the local counterpart of the governor or the president. Who handles the park system is not very important as long as the parks are reasonably well run. Because the commission and council-manager plans have failed to meet these leadership standards, they have generally not been successful in the very largest American cities.

Big-city mayors also reflect demographic changes. In April 1981, voters in San Antonio—the nation's ninth most populous city—chose Henry Cisneros as mayor. This made him the first Mexican-American to be elected as mayor of a major city in the USA. San Antonio's heavy Mexican-American base of population provides Cisneros a strong mayoral position.

## Weak-Mayor–Council

It is easy to classify mayor-council governments as being either weak or strong. However, that assigns many cities, which defy clear categorization, to one or the other category. In fact, numerous cities don't meet the definition of strong or weak mayor.

The position of the mayor as chief administrator is very weak. Several reasons account for this. First, the council exercises extensive administrative authority through the appointment and removal of department heads. Sec-

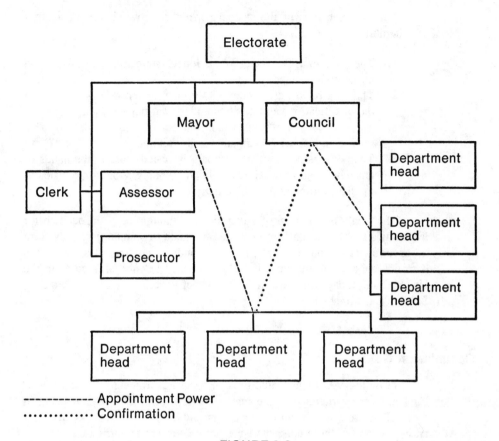

FIGURE 3.2
Weak Mayor Structure

ond, the council is responsible for the preparation and presentation of the budget, which it then is responsible for adopting. Third, administrative authority and responsibility have been delegated to a number of boards and commissions, the members of which have been elected by the voters, making the members relatively independent of the mayor. Fourth, there are independent boards and commissions mandated by state law, which are responsible more to state officials than to local officials such as the mayor.

It is difficult to find many advantages associated with the weak-mayor form of government. Some have argued that it is a more democratic system, since there are so many independently elected officials directly responsible to the electorate. Another advantage of this system is that it provides numerous checks and balances against potential misuse of administrative power. Finally, it is felt that the large number of elected officials provides numerous access points to government for the less influential and less organized members of the community.

The disadvantages of the system appear to outweigh the advantages considerably.

1.  The weak-mayor system is no longer supported by reform and major civic groups.
2.  The long ballots are a deterrent to many voters who seek to learn the qualifications and positions of the various candidates.
3.  There is no one official responsible for city administration. This leads to a lack of coordination and direction.
4.  The administration of government is vested more in the hands of amateurs than professionals, which probably reduces the efficiency of government and the quality of city services.

The weak-mayor form of government is thought to be inadequate for large cities today and much more suited to smaller communities. This form of government is found mostly in rural southern communities where the demands on government are relatively modest. The only large cities in the United States today with weak-mayor forms of government are Los Angeles, Seattle, and Minneapolis.

## Commission Government

Prior to 1900 almost all forms of local government outside of New England were variations on the mayor-council form. The key concepts in these plans were a separation of powers and a system of checks and balances. However, these concepts were not a deterrent to corruption.

During the latter half of the nineteenth century a number of cities experimented with new forms of government, one of which was the commission form. In the 1860s and 1870s Sacramento, New Orleans, Mobile, and Memphis responded to corruption, inflation, and bankruptcy by installing a new, but relatively short-lived, governmental system that was the forerunner to the commission form of government instituted in the twentieth century.

Perhaps the most sustained example of the use of commission government to rectify financial problems occurred in Washington, D.C. In 1871 Congress, responding to a number of conflicting demands as to how Washington should be governed, created a territorial government with strict limits on indebtedness and taxation. During the ensuing three years, Washington embarked upon an ambitious public works and beautification plan that far exceeded the financial capacity of the District of Columbia or the amounts agreed to by Congress in cooperating in the project.

By 1874 Washington's Board of Public Works had spent excessive sums of money, leaving the city heavily in debt. Congress did not take long to declare the territorial government a failure and to arrange for all of its debts to be repaid. A board of three commissioners was appointed to oversee the governance of the District. This three-member commission form of government remained in operation until 1967.[8]

Commission government probably began in the Galveston charter of 1901, and the circumstances of its development are interesting. In September of 1900 a disastrous flood engulfed Galveston, Texas. The city government, operating under a mayor-council plan, quickly proved itself totally unable to deal with the emergency situation. At the request of a group of imaginative Galveston citizens, the Texas legislature, by a special act, granted the commission form of charter. So successful was the new government in Galveston that it was widely imitated. Houston requested and received a similar type of charter in 1905. The peak of popularity for the commission form of government was probably reached about 1917, at which time some 500 cities were operating under the plan. Since that time, the number of adoptions has been small, and there have been frequent abandonments. The plan has always had its greatest appeal in places of less than 50,000 population, probably because its structure is fairly well adapted to the administration of smaller municipalities.

The Galveston Plan concentrated all powers of municipal government in one body—a commission. Three of the five members were appointed by the governor and two were popularly elected. As a body, they functioned as a city council. A mayor-commissioner presided over the council and served as the ceremonial head of the city. The mayor could vote on legislation but had no veto power or legislative authority not delegated to the other commissioners.

Ordinances, budgets, contracts, and many appointments had to be approved by a majority of the commissioners. Each of the commissioners was placed in charge of a department of government and could make minor appointments independently. The mayor-commissioner was not assigned to a department, but, rather, was responsible for general supervision of all administration.

Houston and Des Moines refined the plan by adding features such as a mayoral veto, appointive and removal powers for the mayor, a merit system for public employees, and nonpartisan elections. Allowing for some variation in detail, the essential features of commission government are the same everywhere. Usually the plan provides for a body of from five to seven commissioners, who are the only elected officials of the city. Normally, they are chosen at large and, most frequently, on a nonpartisan ballot in both primary and general elections. As a group, they form the commission and are responsible for both policy formulation and legislation in the municipality.

The key feature of the plan is that each commissioner serves as head of one of the administrative departments. This means that the separation of powers doctrine is abandoned, since obviously both administrative and legislative powers rest in the same hands. In some cities the commissioners are elected to head specific departments; in others actual assignment is determined by majority vote of the commissioners themselves. One of the commissioners will be given the title of mayor through one of several possible routes. But however the mayor is selected, he or she is merely the titular head of the city. Aside from presiding over meetings and greeting visiting dignitaries, the mayor has the same authority as any other commissioner.

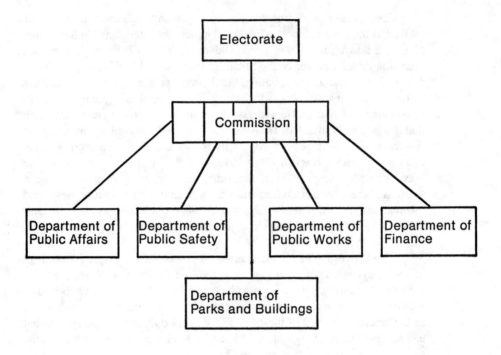

**FIGURE 3.3**
**Commission Structure**

The advantages of the commission plan are thought to be the following:

1.  It is a very simple plan. Powers of government are all concentrated and, therefore, voters can hold the elected public officials accountable.
2.  The short ballot, meaning fewer elected officials, allows for greater voter knowledge of the candidates and their positions.
3.  Elimination of separation of power and checks and balances makes it easier for elected officials to respond to the needs of the people.
4.  Nonpartisan, at-large election of the commissioners reduces the power of the political organizations in the election process.

The disadvantages of the plan are numerous.

1.  Under this plan, the electorate chooses commissioners who are department heads as well as legislators. Voters rarely elect capable administrators, who need to be appointed on the basis of experience and merit.
2.  There is a failure to provide a check on public spending. The elected commissioners who appropriate the funds are also the ones who spend the money in their roles as department heads. There is

little incentive under this system to carefully scrutinize the budget requests of other departments since efficiency and enthusiasm are often rewarded by retaliation from other commissioners.

3. The plural executive form of government tends to create deadlocks and unyielding factions because of a lack of leadership and a generally acceptable negotiator.

4. There is no separation between policy determination and policy implementation. Commissioners view one another's programs with sympathy in order to insure passage of their own.

5. The plan may be too rigid. Since each commissioner heads a department, it makes administrative reorganization or realignment extremely difficult.

Because of the serious problems plaguing the commission form of government, it has enjoyed little popularity in the United States in recent years.

## Council-Manager Government

The origin of the council-manager form of government is uncertain, but it is known that Staunton, Virginia, was the first city to install a manager in 1908. Staunton was impressed with the commission plan of Galveston and Houston and probably would have established a commission government except that the Virginia Constitution required a mayor-council government for all cities the size of Staunton. For Staunton to adopt the commission government would have necessitated a constitutional amendment.

The Virginia Constitution did provide for city councils to create by ordinance those offices necessary to conduct the affairs of government. The Staunton city council, therefore, created the position of a general manager with extensive administrative authority. This experiment proved to be quite successful.

At the same time that Staunton was experimenting with a manager, Richard Childs, a businessman and head of the National Short Ballot Organization, was trying to end the pattern of corruption in cities by reducing the number of elected officials and, consequently, the size of the ballot. Childs felt the machines maintained their control over city government by putting together a slate of candidates and coercing their followers to vote for it. Childs was interested in uniting the short ballot movement with the commission plan of government.

After the success of Staunton's government became known, Childs and his followers became very interested in the manager concept and shortly thereafter modified it to create the council-manager form of government. The short ballot movement was swept along with the crusade for reform of local government. Childs later became president of the National Municipal League, a leading reform organization of the time. From this vantage point, Childs was able to promote the concept of council-manager government through numerous speeches and the publication of the League's booklet, the *Model City Charter,* which extolled the virtues of the council-manager plan.[9]

The first effort to produce a council-manager plan occurred in Lockport, New York, in 1911. While the New York state legislature rejected the plan, it did represent the first time that a classic council-manager form of government had been seriously contemplated. The Lockport plan received a great deal of publicity and became the model from which other cities implemented their own council-manager plans. The following year Sumter, South Carolina, received a charter from the state and began to advertise for a city manager. In the next few years several cities followed Sumter's lead, and the council-manager plan became a reality.

In 1914, a natural disaster similar to the one that befell Galveston occurred in Dayton, Ohio. A flood ravaged the city, and the local government proved to be totally incapable of dealing with the crisis. Faced with the crisis, a charter committee, which had been formed to study alternative governance mechanisms, recommended a council-manager form of government. Business leaders spearheaded the movement, and the voter-approved charter made Dayton the first city of over 100,000 to install the manager plan. By 1920 over 100 cities had adopted the plan, and its growth continued as the council-manager plan became a critical component of the reform movement in local government.

Council-manager government has become the second most popular form of government in the United States today. This is particularly true in cities with populations between 5,000 and 50,000. More than 40 percent of cities over 5,000 are council-manager cities, but most of the largest cities in the country have not adopted the council-manager plan. Only San Diego, Dallas, Kansas City, San Jose, Oklahoma City, Cincinnati, San Antonio, and Phoenix have elected to use it. The largest city to ever adopt and then abandon the plan was Cleveland.

The council-manager plan was intended to overcome the deficiencies of the commission plan by providing for a professional city (or county or town or borough) manager who operates directly under the supervision of the council. Normally, the council itself is not very large. It is common to elect council members at-large, but some plans employ election by wards or districts. In a great many of the council-manager cities, election is nonpartisan.

As in the commission plan, the separation of powers is discarded in favor of a fusion of executive and legislative powers. But there is, in fact, a very effective separation of functions. The council, of course, performs the legislative function, but the council members themselves do not carry on the administrative work of the municipality. For this purpose the council appoints a manager who is directly in charge of the department heads and supervises their performance. The council, in brief, performs two main functions: it legislates, and it appoints a manager.

Again, as with the commission plan, the council-manager plan provides for a mayor. But the office is purely titular and ceremonial, and the mayor possesses no appointive or veto powers. Usually, the mayor is chosen by the council from among its own membership.

The essential relationship in the council-manager plan is that between the council and the manager. This is a difficult relationship to describe, for

## TABLE 3.1
## Cumulative Distribution of U.S. Municipalities

| Classification | All cities | Cities 2,500 & over | Cities 5,000 & over | Cities 10,000 & over | Cities 25,000 & over | Cities 50,000 & over | Cities 100,000 & over | Cities 250,000 & over | Cities 500,000 & over | Cities over 1,000,000 |
|---|---|---|---|---|---|---|---|---|---|---|
| Total, all cities | 6,957 | 6,598 | 4,328 | 2,589 | 1,060 | 447 | 170 | 57 | 23 | 6 |
| **Population group** | | | | | | | | | | |
| Over 1,000,000 | 6 | 6 | 6 | 6 | 6 | 6 | 6 | 6 | 6 | 6 |
| 500,000–1,000,000 | 17 | 17 | 17 | 17 | 17 | 17 | 17 | 17 | 17 | |
| 250,000–  499,999 | 34 | 34 | 34 | 34 | 34 | 34 | 34 | 34 | | |
| 100,000–  249,999 | 113 | 113 | 113 | 113 | 113 | 113 | 113 | | | |
| 50,000–   99,999 | 277 | 277 | 277 | 277 | 277 | 277 | | | | |
| 25,000–   49,999 | 613 | 613 | 613 | 613 | 613 | | | | | |
| 10,000–   24,999 | 1,529 | 1,529 | 1,529 | 1,529 | | | | | | |
| 5,000–    9,999 | 1,739 | 1,739 | 1,739 | | | | | | | |
| 2,500–    4,999 | 2,270 | 2,270 | | | | | | | | |
| Under 2,500[1] | 359 | | | | | | | | | |
| **Geographic region** | | | | | | | | | | |
| Northeast | 1,942 | 1,826 | 1,282 | 749 | 263 | 100 | 23 | 6 | 3 | 2 |
| North Central | 2,018 | 1,936 | 1,235 | 746 | 288 | 111 | 39 | 14 | 6 | 2 |
| South | 2,038 | 1,936 | 1,167 | 654 | 252 | 114 | 61 | 23 | 8 | 1 |
| West | 959 | 900 | 644 | 440 | 257 | 122 | 47 | 14 | 6 | 1 |
| **Metro status** | | | | | | | | | | |
| Central | 431 | 431 | 431 | 431 | 390 | 272 | 143 | 57 | 23 | 6 |
| Suburban | 3,679 | 3,591 | 2,541 | 1,546 | 548 | 175 | 27 | | | |
| Independent | 2,847 | 2,576 | 1,356 | 612 | 122 | | | | | |
| **Form of government** | | | | | | | | | | |
| Mayor-council | 3,766 | 3,683 | 2,074 | 1,099 | 400 | 176 | 75 | 35 | 18 | 6 |
| Council-manager | 2,513 | 2,287 | 1,840 | 1,243 | 587 | 248 | 87 | 20 | 5 | |
| Commission | 178 | 177 | 137 | 102 | 48 | 17 | 8 | 2 | | |
| Town meeting | 419 | 370 | 219 | 100 | 6 | 1 | | | | |
| Rep. town meeting | 81 | 81 | 58 | 45 | 19 | 4 | | | | |

[1]Limited to municipalities recognized by the International City Management Association as providing for the council-manager plan or providing for a position of overall general management.

Source: International City Management Association (Washington, D.C.: *The Municipal Year Book 1983*), p. XVI.

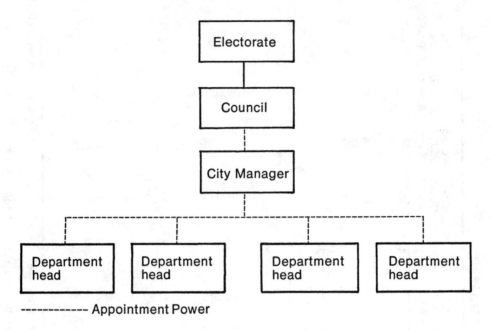

FIGURE 3.4
Council-manager structure

it varies from city to city and from personality to personality. It might appear that the line between policy formulation by the council and policy execution by the manager is a clear and obvious one, but this is not the case. The most successful managers have always been initiators of policy, even if only in subtle ways. Most council members look to the manager for leadership. Yet this leadership cannot be exercised in a way that is offensive to the council, for the manager serves at the pleasure of the council. The manager may be discharged by the council at any time—that is a basic part of the arrangement.

What are the advantages of the council-manager plan? In the first place, it has great administrative strength. Administrative responsibility is centralized in the hands of one official. There is also a great emphasis on professionalism, and the managers have themselves developed a national association and supportive publications. The practice has been for successful managers to begin in small or medium-sized municipalities and move from them to larger cities. Though the risks are obviously high, the salaries are usually generous. Many a person has made a lifetime career as a manager.

The plan has two other advantages worth mentioning. All powers of government are concentrated in the council. The voters know who to hold responsible for public policymaking. While there is no separation of legislative and administrative powers, there is a separation of the appropriating and spending power.

There have also been criticisms of the council-manager plan, chiefly on two grounds. One criticism focuses on the relative unresponsiveness of the manager's office. Not having to face the public in a general election, a manager does not have to be as responsive to citizens' demands as does an elected mayor. The appointed manager is more free to follow his or her professional managerial training. However, defenders of the manager plan note that though the office is not elective, as long as the manager is held accountable to a publicly elected body, the city council, the prerequisites of popular control in a democracy are fulfilled.

The second common objection to the plan is that it often fails to provide for adequate political leadership. There is probably some validity to this argument as applied to the largest cities. As we noted in discussing the strong-mayor–council plan, the largest cities appear to want as their chief executives persons who are vigorous, effective, and visible leaders. Under these conditions, the day-to-day supervision given by a manager under the council-manager system can be entrusted to a city director appointed by the mayor and responsible only to the mayor.

The council-manager plan has also been criticized because some cities choose local officials as managers after one or two bad experiences with outside professionals. This often leads to sacrificing professional competence and elevating partisan or personal considerations.

Many cities find it difficult to find well-trained and experienced managers who meet their criteria for employment. A case can be made that there are not simply not enough qualified city managers to go around. Furthermore, the smaller cities find this an expensive plan to implement. Qualified managers require decent salaries commensurate with their training and experience. In many cities under 10,000 in population the council-manager plan loses its appeal when compared with the commission or mayor-council plan, which use local officials.

Nonetheless, the council-manager plan continues to increase its popularity in the smaller cities; it has been adopted by numerous boroughs and townships and by a few counties. It also has the great advantage of being easy to understand, at least in principle. Anyone who understands the relationship of a superintendent of education to an elected board of education automatically understands the basis of the council-manager plan, for the relationship in the two cases is identical.

## MAYORAL LEADERSHIP STYLE

Once we viewed governmental structure as the sole or dominant factor in determining how policy was made and who received benefits from the system. Formal governmental structure remains important in urban politics because it is one component of a very complex system of policymaking. Contemporary research has helped us to broaden our understanding of urban policymaking. Today we are much more concerned with leadership style in assessing urban policy and the process that produces it.

Two important aspects of the mayoral leadership–policy relationship need to be discussed. First, in analyzing the political actors in the urban environment much more attention is being paid to the behavior of individuals and groups and less to the formal structures outlined in city charters. In fact, a growing body of literature is beginning to question whether or not cities are governable, by mayors or managers, regardless of the formal structure of the city government.

Pressman, in his study of the mayor's office in Oakland, California, suggested that in order to exercise leadership and be able to influence the various groups in the city, a mayor would require several resources. These included:

1.  sufficient financial and staff resources
2.  city control of social program areas, e.g., education, housing, and job training
3.  mayoral jurisdiction in social program areas
4.  high enough salary to enable the mayor to be a full-time executive
5.  sufficient staff support for the mayor—planning, speech writing, and politicking
6.  access to friendly media
7.  political organizations, including a political party that could be mobilized to help the mayor achieve specific goals[10]

Pressman pointed out that while these resources were important, political structure, social factors, and mayor personality should not be disregarded. In Oakland all of these factors influenced mayoral leadership. The mayor was lacking almost all of the requirements Pressman established for effective leadership, and he tended to be a private man who shunned conflict whenever possible. Pressman concluded that the mayor could not establish goals and mobilize his political forces to influence the outcome of important policy issues.[11]

In a similar vein, Douglas Yates has proclaimed the American city to be ungovernable. Citing excessive decentralization, too much dependence on state and federal government for policies and funding, and a failure of the mayor and the top administrative echelon to effectively manage their bureaucracies, Yates sees the city as incapable of governing itself.

> Given its present political organization and decision-making process, the city is fundamentally ungovernable. By ungovernable I mean that the urban policy-making system is incapable of producing coherent decisions, developing effective policies, or implementing state or federal programs.[12]

Yates minimizes the importance of government structure on the outcome of policy. He suggests that the way cities process issues usually affects the policy outcomes. Believing American urban policymaking to be highly fragmented, unresponsive, and erratic, he sees it as inevitable that policies designed to assist cities will have the same characteristics. He labels this fragmented and decentralized urban predicament as one of "street-fighting pluralism."[13]

A second factor to be considered in analyzing policy outcomes in cities is the issue of mayoral style. Kotter and Lawrence developed a depiction of mayoral styles based upon their observation of mayors in twenty cities. The five styles are labeled caretaker, executive, ceremonial, individualist, and entrepreneur. Each of the styles is different from the others in explaining how and why mayors behave as they do and what factors determine a mayor's chances to succeed or fail.[14]

The five different styles of mayors are described as:

1. Ceremonial—focuses on personal appeals to existing networks in the city.
2. Caretaker—focuses on short-term issues, a troubleshooter. Mayor has a limited impact on the city.
3. Individualist—focuses on personal appeals instead of trying to develop networks. Makes a few changes in the city.
4. Executive—very project-oriented and uses all existing networks for support.
5. Entrepreneur—uses all networks in the city and has a major impact on the city.

Kotter and Lawrence developed their framework of mayoral behavior showing the environment in which mayors operate. The framework was based on three interrelated processes. (1) Mayors must set the political agenda by deciding what it is they want to do. (2) Mayors must mobilize resources by building and maintaining networks that can be called upon as needed. (3) Mayors must use their resources to implement their policies and accomplish the tasks on their agenda.

The behavior of the mayor is affected by four variables that determine the mayor's ability to process the policy issues on his or her agenda. These variables are: the personality of the mayor, which provides the executive with certain skills and orientations; the formal structure of government, which provides varying amounts of power; the distribution of power in the community, which determines the kinds of resources available; and the city environment, which presents the mayor with the full range of problems and issues.[15]

The Kotter and Lawrence typology, when applied to contemporary urban politics, indicates that most big-city mayors are caretaker, ceremonial, or individualist mayors. The changing nature of power relationships, which have become much more dispersed and fragmented, means that mayors have greater difficulty setting clearly defined, long term agendas and mobilizing networks to help them implement policies. This accounts for the few mayors who might be labeled executives or entrepreneurs.[16]

A similar study was conducted by Cunningham when he compared the mayors in Cleveland, Chicago, Pittsburgh, and New Haven in the 1960s. He analyzed their performances in mobilizing and utilizing scarce resources to combat urban problems. Cunningham developed a set of seven traits of mayoral leadership or style against which the four mayors were compared. The traits were: originality, risk-taking, initiative, energy, openness, organizational ability, and promotional ingenuity. Cunningham concluded that Mayor

Lee of New Haven was the most entrepreneurial, followed by Mayor Barr in Pittsburgh. Mayors Daley in Chicago and Locher in Cleveland ranked lowest, leading the author to suggest that several other traits besides ethnicity and party loyalty should be considered in the selection of urban mayors.[17]

A different approach to understanding mayoral leadership was suggested by Levine in his study of three mayors trying to manage their cities during periods of racial conflict. Case studies of Stokes in Cleveland, Hatcher in Gary, and Seibels in Birmingham were used to analyze the implications of conflict on mayoral leadership. Levine pointed out that racial conflict is an issue of much greater severity than conflicts traditionally analyzed in studies of mayoral leadership. Analysts who assess mayoral performance by using traditional pluralistic models may find their work limited by the failure to differentiate between types of conflict and strategies employed to resolve them.[18]

## Summary and Conclusions

Knowledge of the formal powers and structure of local government is important in explaining the variations that exist in urban America. Power is distributed and exercised differently in local governments, and this is particularly true with respect to the powers given to the mayor in relation to the council and the bureaucracy.

We have seen that much of the history of the development of local government in the United States was based on the fears that Americans shared about strong executives. It took almost 100 years for cities to invest the office of mayor with enough power for it to be called a strong-mayor form of government. The strong mayor had numerous strengths, including political leadership, appointive powers, and budgeting control. However, weaknesses were noted where mayors incurred political debts in getting elected, failed to separate politics from administration and were burdened with having an elected official serve as the top administrator in the city.

An alternative to the strong-mayor form of government was thought to be the council-manager form of government, with its commitment to experienced employees, accountability, and professional administration. However, the council-manager cities often lacked political leadership. Many cities found it difficult to recruit well-trained managers, and some smaller cities found the plan to be much more expensive than a mayor-council or commission form of government.

The commission form of government is another alternative, but it is no longer widely used and has decreased in importance in the past fifty years. Currently it is used most often in the South and in rural areas.

The amount and type of power a mayor exercises is not always a product of the formal powers associated with the office. One of the strongest mayors in contemporary urban history, Richard Daley of Chicago, technically operated under a weak-mayor structure. Therefore, it is important to observe *how* a mayor exercises power and what leadership style he or she employs rather than drawing conclusions derived from the formal or legal powers of the office.

Kotter and Lawrence found several mayors who were "ceremonial." Other mayors have overcome and expanded the powers and boundaries of their offices. Daley is an oft-cited case, but others are Richard Lee in New Haven and Kevin White in Boston.

More recent literature is focusing on the behavior and personality of the mayor as a way of understanding the political and administrative policies of a city. However, Pressman reminds us that the mayor must mobilize certain resources to be able to process issues regardless of his or her ambition, style, and personality. Failure to do so will often prevent the mayor from becoming a leader in the policymaking process.

# NOTES

1. For a good discussion of the relationship of political structure to public policies, see Brett W. Hawkins, *Politics and Urban Policies* (Indianapolis: Bobbs-Merrill, 1971); and Robert L. Lineberry and Edmund P. Fowler, "Reformism and Public Policy in American Cities," *American Political Science Review* 61 (September 1967): 701–16. Also see Raymond Wolfinger and John Osgood Field, "Political Ethos and the Structure of City Government," *American Political Science Review* 60 (June 1966); and Thomas Dye and John Garcia, "Structure, Function and Policy in American Cities," *Urban Affairs Quarterly* 13 (September 1978): 103–22.

2. For a discussion of the Chicago political system see Edward C. Banfield, *Political Influence* (New York: Free Press, 1961); Martin Meyerson and Edward C. Banfield, *Politics, Planning and the Public Interest* (Glencoe, Ill.: Free Press, 1955). Also see Milton Rakove, *Don't Make No Waves—Don't Back No Losers: An Insider's Analysis of the Daley Machine* (Bloomington: University of Indiana Press, 1974); and Mike Royko, *Boss: Richard J. Daley of Chicago* (New York: E. P. Dutton, 1971).

3. These issues are discussed in chapter 7. See Theodore J. Lowi, "Machine Politics—Old and New," *The Public Interest* 9 (Fall 1967): 83–92; E. S. Savas and Sigmund G. Ginsburg, "The Civil Service: A Meritless System?" *The Public Interest* 32 (Summer 1973): 70–85; and Michael Lipsky, *Street-Level Bureaucracy: Dilemmas of the Individual in Public Services* (New York: Russell Sage Foundation, 1980).

4. John F. Dillon, *Commentaries on the Law of Municipal Corporations*, 5th ed. (Boston: Little, Brown, 1911), vol. 1, sec. 237.

5. See Belle Zeller and Hugh A. Bone, "The Repeal of P.R. in New York City—Ten Years in Retrospect," *American Political Science Review* 62 (December 1948): 1127–1148.

6. Sigmund G. Ginsburg, "The New York City Administrator: A Critical Eulogy," *National Civic Review* 64 (October 1975): 451–58.

7. Much of the historical information in this chapter comes from W. B. Munro, *The Government of American Cities* (New York: Macmillan, 1918).

8. For a discussion of the creation of the territorial government and the three member commission see Constance McLaughlin Green, *Washington, Village and Capital, 1800–1878* (Princeton: Princeton University Press, 1962), pp. 325–62.

9. For an analysis of this period in American urban history see Richard S. Childs, *Civic Victories* (New York: Harper and Row, 1952); and John Porter East,

Council-Manager Government: The Political Thought of Its Founder, Richard S. Childs (Chapel Hill: University of North Carolina Press, 1965).

10. Jeffrey L. Pressman, "Preconditions of Mayoral Leadership," American Political Science Review 66 (June 1972): 512.

11. Ibid., p. 522.

12. Douglas Yates, The Ungovernable City: The Politics of Urban Problems and Policy Making (Cambridge, Mass.: MIT Press, 1977), p. 5. For a discussion of the limits of city politics see Paul E. Peterson, City Limits (Chicago: University of Chicago Press, 1981).

13. Yates, The Ungovernable City, pp. 6, 33–37.

14. John P. Kotter and Paul R. Lawrence, Mayors in Action: Five Approaches to Urban Governance (New York: Wiley Interscience, 1974).

15. Kotter and Lawrence, Mayors in Action, pp. 105–21.

16. See Clarence N. Stone, Robert K. Whelan, and William J. Murin, Urban Policy and Politics in a Bureaucratic Age (Englewood Cliffs, N.J.: Prentice-Hall, 1979), p. 170.

17. James V. Cunningham, Urban Leadership in the Sixties (Waltham, Mass.: Lemberg Center for the Study of Violence, 1970).

18. Charles H. Levine, Racial Conflict and the American Mayor (Lexington, Mass.: Lexington Books, 1974). Also see Myron A. Levine, "Goal-Oriented Leadership and the Limits of Entrepreneurship," The Western Political Quarterly 33 (September 1980): 401–16.

# 4. MACHINE POLITICS

Political machines are an important part of American urban history. Throughout much of the nineteenth century, and through the first half of the twentieth century, many large cities in the eastern part of the United States were controlled by political machines. Most notable were those of New York City, Philadelphia, Boston, Jersey City, and Albany. While most of the political machines have ceased to exist, there are still some cities where machines control political activity or at least play a prominent role in political life. Chicago and Albany are two contemporary examples.

The political machines historically showed us how power was distributed and exercised in a number of urban areas. The machines were fairly successful in controlling political decision-making, which tended to upset many middle-class business interests. Shortly after the turn of the century, the successes of the machines caused a backlash, and groups of people who were not reaping rewards from them or who were being disadvantaged by them set out to reform local politics.

Like many others who are negatively affected by politics, these reformers sought to change the formal and informal structure of government so as to reduce the power of the political organization and open up the system to a larger number of participants. The reform movement, as we shall see in the next chapter, was successful in curbing machine power by changing the rules within which politics was played. These changes in the pattern of urban politics have affected cities up to the present by helping to decide who gets what from the political system.

## MACHINE POLITICS

A political machine is a party organization that depends crucially upon inducements that are both specific and material. . . . A machine like any other organization offers a mixture of material and non-material inducements in order to get people to do what it wants them to do.

Banfield and Wilson, *City Politics*[1]

Senator Plunkitt is a straight organization man. He believes in party government; he does not indulge in cant and hypocrisy and he is never afraid to say exactly what he thinks. He is a believer in thorough political organization and all-the-year-around work, and he holds to the doctrine that, in making appointments to office, party workers should be preferred if they are fitted to perform the duties of the office. Plunkitt is one of the veteran leaders of the organization; he has always been faithful and reliable, and he has performed valuable services for Tammany Hall.

Charles F. Murphy, onetime leader of Tammany Hall, in 1905.[2]

The political machine has many of the characteristics of a brokerage arrangement. There is the exchange of votes for a variety of rewards, both tangible and non-material. There is also a political leader or boss who dominates the system and serves as the broker who must make the ultimate decision concerning how favors will be bestowed.

## The Brokerage Style

The traditional urban political system (and it is undergoing changes, as we shall note) is characterized by a brokerage system of politics. In a manner somewhat similar to a commodities exchange, sales and purchases are handled by specialists operating under carefully specified procedures. No one is required to engage in the acquisition, trading, or selling of the commodities, but a person choosing to do so thereby agrees to accept the rules and regulations of the exchange.

As is true in other aspects of life, the so-called traders are unequal in the resources at their disposal; some are far more powerful than others. In fact, the ownership of the commodities tends to be highly concentrated. A few people own a great deal, and many individuals possess only a small fraction of the total.

In the brokerage system, the broker is always a key figure. As a person who brings buyers and sellers together—for a fee, of course—the broker is in a position to affect the play of the game in numerous ways. Without the broker's presence, in fact, the game could not take place at all. There would be chaos, followed, no doubt, by some sort of dictatorial arrangement to counteract anarchy. So the broker is necessary. Above all else, the broker endlessly supervises bargaining, trading, and negotiating, with the result that all parties may have at least the illusion that the best arrangement possible under the given circumstances was consummated. The deals that are made—the decisions—come about not as the result of abstract appeals to justice or freedom, but in response to the realities of the marketplace.

In its political manifestation, the brokerage system is built around a leader and the leader's organization. Persons or interests desiring to arrange a political accommodation must do so through the cooperation, intervention, and assistance of the dominant political group. In working out a solution to a problem—for example, whether a community group, a factory, or a school gets the use of a particular parcel of land—the political organization provides the means and the milieu for the bargaining among the different interests. There is a quid pro quo, a trade-off, as in the commodities exchange system.

Brokerage politics places a high premium on organization, as Charles F. Murphy rightly noted in his paean to Plunkitt. And, conversely, disloyalty to the organization is the cardinal sin. In Plunkitt's words: "There's no crime so mean as ingratitude in politics, but every great statesman from the beginnin' of the world has been up against it."[3]

In Plunkitt's time (1842–1924), the role of the political organization was quite clearly defined. Indeed, up to the outbreak of World War II, this role was well understood even when deplored, as by the early twentieth-century upper-class reformers. Only in recent times has the position of the organization seemed ambiguous.

Banfield, in his study of the Daley organization in Chicago, shows how that organization did not initiate policies of its own to advance its goals in redevelopment, housing, etc. By initiating policies, the political organization stood to make enemies and thereby lose support. Instead, the organization waited for other actors and groups to reach a consensus, then the machine assisted the parties to achieve their agreed-upon goals, earning the obligation of all concerned, a "broker's fee." This entitled the machine to ask the various parties for favors later.[4] In this sense the machine was nonideological, content to watch the interplay among actors and wait for issues to surface and be brought to the machine for arbitration.

## Golden Age of the Machine

From the founding of the first New York Society of Tammany in 1785 until the present, the tactics, antics, and personalities of the Democracy of New York have delighted journalists, scholars, and presumably the voting public. Even the Indian symbolism of the Society—a Grand Sachem, twelve lesser Sachems, the use of an Indian calendar in correspondence—pleased an electorate in search of political trimmings in a drab, republican country.

Starting as a patriotic society, Tammany rapidly developed into a private political club. Toward the end of George Washington's administration, it became the principal exponent in New York City of Jefferson's doctrines. Under the leadership of Aaron Burr, the first real leader of the Society, the Republicans (Jeffersonians) carried New York State in 1800. By 1815, Tammany obtained complete control of the state as well as of the city.[5]

The Golden Age of Tammany took place following the Civil War, when it was under the leadership of William M. Tweed. The son of a prosperous chairmaker, Tweed entered politics as a volunteer fireman, became better known, and then joined in ward politics. Working his way up in the Democratic organization, Tweed became a Sachem of the Tammany Society and in 1857 was elected to the New York County Board of Supervisors. He then sold his chairmaking business and devoted his full time to politics.

In 1859 the first Tweed Ring, based on the County Board of Supervisors, was founded for the purpose of controlling for the Democrats the appointment of inspectors of elections. Subsequently, the Tweed Ring enlarged its sphere of operations. In 1861 Tweed was elected chairman of the Tammany General Committee. Shortly thereafter, he was chosen Grand Sachem and became known as "the boss." In 1863, he became Deputy Street

Commissioner, a post that permitted him to recruit thousands of followers. In 1868, he became a state senator, a position that made it possible to give personal supervision to the operations of the state legislature in Albany. In 1870, Tweed secured from the legislature a new charter for New York City. Reported to have cost around a million dollars in bribes, the charter was worth every penny: it relieved the ring of accountability to any state governmental authority.

By 1870 the fortunes of the Tweed Ring were on the decline. The immediate causes of the exposure of the operations of the Tweed Ring were accidental. In December, 1870, Watson, one of the chiefs of the Finance Department, was fatally injured in a sleigh-riding accident. He was succeeded by a new man, and in the subsequent job turnovers Matthew J. O'Rourke became county bookkeeper. O'Rourke amassed considerable evidence of fraud and presented his evidence in the summer of 1871 to the *New York Times*. The charges were printed in full, and the collapse of the ring was under way.

Tweed himself was arrested and held on $1 million bail. After being indicted for a felony, he was removed as Grand Sachem. In November, 1873, he was found guilty on three-fourths of 120 counts and sentenced to Blackwell's Island. After a year's imprisonment, he was released because of a legal technicality. He was promptly tried again, but managed to escape while on a visit from the penitentiary. For two days he hid in disguise in New Jersey, and later he reached Florida, from where he escaped in a fishing smack to Cuba, and finally to Spain.

But it was not possible for Tweed to escape New York justice. Upon the request of the United States Secretary of State, Hamilton Fish, Tweed was arrested by Spanish authorities and returned to the United States on the man-of-war *Franklin*. Sent to the Ludlow Street jail, he occupied the warden's parlor at a cost of $75 per week. While dying, he said to the matron's daughter: "Mary, I have tried to do good to everybody, and if I have not, it is not my fault. I am ready to die, and I know God will receive me." His hearse was followed by only eight carriages—a decidedly unimpressive number. The remaining members of the ring fled the country or were imprisoned. It is estimated that the total plunderings of the Ring amounted to about $200 million.

As the archetype of the classical machine, the Tammany Society was imitated in large cities throughout the country. But toward the end of the nineteenth century, the machine came under increasing attack. There was, as we shall see in the next chapter, a concerted effort by reformers to take politics out of municipal government. Secondly, there was an effort to bolster city government through devices like merit civil service, professionalization, and the impartial administration of the law, all of which weakened the machine.

A high peak in the mortality rate of traditional machines occurred during the years 1947–51. On June 17, 1947, Frank Hague resigned as mayor of Jersey City. His successor and nephew, Frank Hague Eggers, was defeated in the election of May 10, 1949, by a rival ticket headed by John V. Kenny.

In November, 1949, City Clerk John B. Hynes defeated James M. Curley in a bitter battle for the Boston mayoralty. The Republicans lost Philadelphia in the 1950 gubernatorial race by 75,000. In the next year they lost control of the city itself, as the Democratic candidate for mayor of Philadelphia, Joseph S. Clark, Jr., won by more than 100,000 votes. The Democratic party lost the New York City contest for mayor in 1950 to Vincent Impellitteri, an Independent. All in all, it was a bad season for the political machine.

The ouster of the McFeely organization in Hoboken, N.J. in 1947 illustrates the mood of the period. Located across from lower Manhattan on the New Jersey side of the Hudson River, Hoboken in 1947 was a city with a dimly romantic past and a depressing present. It was characterized by wharves, factories, warehouses, bookie parlors, 254 bars, and bleak blocks of ancient brownstone houses. Some 50,000 people lived in its one square mile.

For twenty-two years Bernard McFeely had been undisputed boss of the city. The son of a butcher, he had quit school at the age of nine. He had driven a dump wagon, and later left that job for ward politics. After becoming top man in the Democratic organization, McFeely made his brother Edward chief of police and his nephew Thomas superintendent of schools. At one time, seventy-nine McFeelys were on the city payrolls.

There was nothing very complicated about McFeely's methods. Prior to his reign, the city paid $36,000 a year for garbage disposal. Under the new regime the McFeely Contracting Company was awarded the business, and the annual price rose to $112,000. Contractors found they could not get permits unless the company did their hauling for them. An old Sunday-closing law was enforced against theater owners unless they contributed $600 a year to the organization. For saloon owners, the price of staying in business was $200. On the average, the machine collected $100,000 a year and spent $15,000 a year on elections. McFeely himself handled the funds. Although his salary never topped $5,000, his wealth in 1947 was estimated at $3 million.

In addition to fees assessed against various kinds of business operators, the machine exacted 3 percent salary kickbacks from city employees. The machine received the cooperation of the AFL leaders who controlled the votes of the dock workers. There was a working alliance with Jersey City's Mayor Hague.

Despite all of this activity, prosperity seemed to bypass Hoboken during the McFeely years. The population fell by one-fifth, taxes soared, and no outsider prophesied a happy future for the city. Unlike most bosses, McFeely himself staged no circuses. Nor did he make any public speeches—his grammar was simply too atrocious. A bachelor, he lived in a frame house across from an automobile scrap yard. He never went to Florida, or to Europe, or to the horse races. He hated Italians (persons of Italian ancestry comprised 65 percent of the population), and did his best to make their lives miserable.

On May 13, 1947, a reform ticket defeated the organization. Three principal factors caused the downfall. The state, for the first time in Hoboken's history, had installed and actually used voting machines. Some policemen, who were World War II veterans, opposed the machine candidates and were successful. Veterans and others simply got out the anti-McFeely vote. The magnitude of the upset was shown in the composition of the new city commission: three persons of Italian descent, one Irish policeman McFeely had persecuted, and one CIO union leader. What took place in Hoboken also occurred, in less dramatic fashion, in other cities across the nation—it was a period of general municipal housecleaning.[6]

## THE MACHINE TYPE: NATURE, FUNCTIONS, SOCIAL BASE

The traditional urban political machine has been studied in depth, and from the wealth of studies some general observations as to its nature have emerged. Of all the investigations undertaken during the last three decades, one of the very best remains Dayton D. McKean's 1940 appraisal of the Hague organization in Jersey City.[7] Because the main points developed by McKean have a wide applicability, they are cited with the understanding that what was true of the Hague machine in its heyday is more or less typical of the style of machines in general.

For the Hague organization, the cardinal tenet was self-interest. What was good for the organization was assumed to be good for Jersey City, Hudson County, New Jersey, and, ultimately, the nation. With reference to Mayor Hague, McKean states: "The central principle of this thinking is that what benefits the political organization is desirable and therefore right; what damages it is undesirable and therefore wrong."[8] A philosophy of this sort has the virtue of making it quite simple to establish operational priorities. Moral considerations that might trouble some people can be dismissed as being irrelevant.

In line with this conviction, decision-making in the Hague machine was confined to the uppermost echelon. The concept of grassroots democracy in the sense of ideas flowing upward for execution and implementation was alien to the mayor's thinking. Writes McKean, "The nature of political leadership, as he [Hague] conceives it, leaves little room for the formation of policy anywhere except at the top of the organization; while the party workers keep the citizens in line by all the variety of means at the disposal of a well-built machine, the leader decides what is good for the people."[9]

Had he been aware of the Hague organization, the great German sociologist Max Weber would have admired its dedication to the bureaucratic principles of discipline, hierarchy, and line of command. City commissioners or legislators under Hague's control were expected to vote as they were instructed and to present a united front toward the outside world.[10] "Complete obedience is necessary from the bottom to the top; officials are not supposed to have ideas on public policies, but to take orders."[11] Successful though this tactic was in producing solidarity in the ranks of the organization, it failed lamentably to produce strong individuals who could appeal to voters in other sections of New Jersey.

So far as spoils, patronage, and taxes were concerned, Mayor Hague was consistent with his basic principles. Patronage appointments and spoils were considered fundamental facts of political life. It should be noted, however, that the machine had its puritanical side. Brothels were not tolerated in Jersey City, nor was burlesque. But the city was generally considered to be the national headquarters for horse-racing gambling.[12] On taxes, McKean notes, the Hague attitude was straightforward. "The Mayor's position on the question of taxes is clear and consistent. He favors a continually increasing public revenue."[13] How the funds were raised did not matter to the mayor.[14]

Did the leaders of political machines have any characteristics in common other than political success? This question was posed by J. T. Salter in his 1935 study of the then-dominant Republican organization in Philadelphia. After noting that no two politicians were alike, Salter listed certain attributes of the successful ones. They are those who "(1) stick everlastingly at it, (2) know that the kingdom of heaven is taken by violence, (3) live decades among their people and learn to judge their wants, (4) have a flair for getting along with people, (5) have problem-solving ability, and (6) understand that politics is the science of the possible."[15] Surely George Washington Plunkitt would have agreed!

If machines performed no function other than to enrich themselves, it seems unlikely that they would have remained for so long on the political scene. In fact, such organizations serve a variety of purposes that society—or some elements of society—wants fulfilled. It has long been realized that the boss fulfills the function of providing some measure of centralized direction in the largely decentralized administration of American municipalities. Given the vast formal dispersion of power among the mayor, the council, and scores of boards and agencies, someone has got to serve as a unifying force. When the official apparatus of government could not so operate, it became the historical function of the boss to provide the needed centralized leadership. Even the rise of strong-mayor local governments has not obviated the need for unofficial methods of bringing about centralized direction. In many cases, the mayor has taken on this function not because of his position as mayor, but because of his additional strength as machine boss. The power of Mayor Richard J. Daley in Chicago, for instance, rested both on his legal base as mayor and, even more importantly, on his extra-legal base as party chief. In combination, these bases of support made it possible for Daley to control the Chicago municipal government with a firm hand.

But machines also fulfill social functions that other agencies in society tend to neglect. Even where the services provided by the machine and by other agencies may be identical, as in certain types of welfare referral, the machine often provides its services in a more satisfactory manner. For the subgroup receiving these services, this difference in style or manner may be all-important. In his famous essay on the functions of political machines, the sociologist Robert K. Merton observed that the politician may be closer to understanding the needs and doing something about them than the "impersonal, professionalized, socially distant and legally constrained welfare worker."[16]

One might, of course, choose another illustration to make the same point. What Merton is emphasizing is that the "deprived classes" constitute one subgroup "for whom the political machine satisfied wants not adequately satisfied in the same fashion by the legitimate social structure."[17] The best example of this comes from Plunkitt's own experiences in his district. Plunkitt made it a point to know, and know the needs of, everyone in his district. He and his co-workers helped residents by getting them jobs, finding housing, obtaining licenses, paying rent, getting coal for heat, and attending weddings, funerals, and block parties.[18]

A second subgroup identified by Merton is that of "business." Here the political organization provides "those political privileges which entail immediate economic gains."[19] Big businesses seek, of course, political dispensations that will enable them to increase their profits. The machine provides a degree of economic security. If guarantees needed to limit competition and maximize profit cannot be obtained through conventional channels, then they are obtained through the efforts of the machine.

The relationship between the machine and local businesses was important to the growth of many cities. Businesses sought, and were granted, clearances and quick city action on zoning, planning, and development, which enabled them to develop property and build new businesses. The relationship proved to be mutually beneficial; business got preferential treatment and made profits, while the machine received money and jobs it could distribute in exchange for votes and power.

A third subgroup whose needs may be met by the machine consists of those whose social mobility has been blocked. For such persons the machine provides a means for getting ahead that would otherwise not exist. One thinks immediately of Irish and other immigrant groups. Denied access to satisfactory niches in the economic and social structure, they turned to politics and were notably successful. Another subgroup would include the professional criminal. Viewed in functional terms, the racketeer or gambler "has basic similarities of organization, demands and operation to the subgroup of the industrialist, man of business or speculator."[20] From the economic point of view, "legitimate" and "illegitimate" businesses are about the same. "Both are in some degree concerned with the demand."[21] For both groups, the function of the machine is to prevent undue interference from government.[22]

Salter, in his Philadelphia study already referred to, also stresses the service nature of the machine. The party organization resolves such "fellow-creature wants" as jobs, food, and shelter.[23] Even if the machine of today is of less importance in these areas than in Salter's time, Salter's conclusion remains valid: "The party is, basically, an intermediary between the citizen and the state."[24] The party is a service institution, "and service means favors."[25]

Besides the sociological functions noted by Merton and the service functions underscored by Salter, a third type of function has been stressed by Harold F. Gosnell. After a careful study of Chicago politics from the late 1920s to the mid-1930s, Gosnell was struck by the conciliating role of the

Democratic machine. He asserts: "Some of the submerged groups may not be so appreciative; but the fact remains that during the years 1930–36 the city was comparatively free from violent labor disputes, hunger riots, and class warfare."[26] While Chicago had plenty of troubles during the great economic crisis of the period Gosnell studied, "on the credit side of the ledger should be placed the success of the bosses in softening class conflicts."[27]

The essential mass base of the traditional machine was the immigrant population. The reason is that the machine rendered certain services that an immigrant clientele considered important. In exchange for these services, this clientele gave its electoral support to the organization. So long as immigration was a continuing process, it was possible for the machine to replenish its strength indefinitely. With the virtual cessation of large-scale European immigration during the 1920s, this source of machine strength gradually dried up. "It was the succeeding waves of immigrants that gave the urban political organizations the manipulable mass bases without which they could not have functioned as they did," notes Elmer E. Cornwell, Jr.[28] But since the 1920s there have been two additional forms of migration. Blacks from the rural south and Hispanics have moved in a steady stream to northern and western population centers. Thus, the migrant base for urban organizations continues to renew itself.

When viewed through a socioeconomic lens, the traditional machine appears as a lower-class based organization. It is from this class that its principal support has always come. This is the case today in cities such as Chicago, where machine-type politics remains the norm. Throughout the 1970s, however, the Chicago machine has begun to experience a change in the traditional support the lower-income black wards have provided. There has been a trend for some of these wards to vote for more ideological black candidates. In the 1983 Democratic mayoral primary, a black congressman defeated the incumbent mayor as well as the son of former Mayor Daley in a close race. To put the matter differently, machine-type politics thrives in a lower-class milieu while reform-type politics flourishes in a middle-class environment. Given this condition, one would expect changes in the type of politics as the socioeconomic culture undergoes change.

## The Machine at Work

Political machines could be identified by several characteristics. First, there was an element of central control. The boss or his associates made all of the major decisions that had an impact upon the party. Therefore, the chain of command was clear, and everyone understood the power relationships.

A second characteristic involved the use of material incentives—jobs, housing, food, clothing, etc. The machine used incentives to encourage and reward party workers so they would turn out the vote. Victory at the polls allowed the machine to replenish its supply of rewards and to distribute them again at the next election. The cycle of rewards for votes, which generated more rewards, was crucial to the continued existence of the machine. The cycle continued as long as people put little or no value on their right to vote, or as long as the value of what the machine offered exceeded the value people placed on their vote.[29]

Another characteristic of the machine was its lack of ideology. The machine existed to service voters and was rarely concerned with the political ideology of people who needed favors. If the machine could satisfy a need, it probably had won over a voter, and that was an important source of power that surpassed the political leanings of the client.

As we saw in the Daley machine example, an organization that pursues policy goals of its own tends to make enemies. Hence, the pursuit of goals is at variance with the machine's primary objective: to control votes and maintain its own power. It will not expend influence to achieve policy or ideological goals.

A fourth characteristic of the machine was its ability to organize the territory. Many machines were organized in a classic pyramidal fashion. Wherever possible, block captains were selected to minister to the needs of their constituents on a daily basis. This might include such services as providing food, shelter, or clothing for an unfortunate family. Block captains reported to and took all their unsolvable problems to the precinct captain, who was charged with the oversight responsibility for several blocks. The precinct captains, in turn, reported to ward leaders or chairmen, each of whom had responsibility for several precincts. The ward leaders reported directly to the boss or the boss's close assistants.

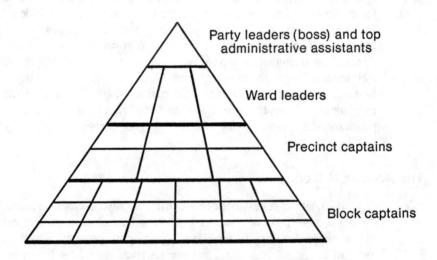

FIGURE 4.1
Political Machine Organization Chart

A final characteristic of the political machine was its ability to develop close personal relationships and to sustain them. The block captains tried to know everyone on their block. They attended weddings and funerals and took note of as many birthdays and anniversaries as they possibly could. The machine also provided access to city jobs, government contracts, and licenses for businesses. It fixed tickets, posted bail, and provided a host of personal services without asking embarrassing personal questions or requiring the filling out of numerous forms. This caring, personal relationship led to a great feeling of loyalty on the part of the local residents, which the machine was able to convert into votes on election day.[30]

The political machine would probably not have been possible without the arrival of the immigrant on our shores. The successive waves of immigrants provided the political leaders and their organizations with the mass of potential voters without which they could not have operated. The machine in many respects dominated the lives of these immigrants through housing, jobs, education, and numerous other favors. As the immigrants settled into the cities of the eastern seaboard, they found that the machine controlled their social and economic mobility. Since the machine was the primary source of many jobs and other favors, the machine was able to control how fast individuals might rise socially or economically.

Richard Hofstadter analyzed the importance of the immigrant to the political machine in his book *The Age of Reform*.[31] Hofstadter argued that up to approximately 1880, the United States could be characterized as rural, Yankee, and Protestant. The immigrants who came to America in the early and mid-nineteenth century had little impact on American social, cultural, and political life.

The industrialization and urbanization of the United States generated a new wave of immigration that lasted forty years, from 1880–1920. The majority of these immigrants were from poor, rural settings. Their background, religion, traditions, and customs made it very difficult for them to be assimilated into American society. In addition, the Yankee Protestants were bigoted and intolerant of the ethnic and religious backgrounds of the immigrants, which also slowed the process of assimilation.

These immigrants arrived on American shores with intense personal needs. The difference between these needs of the immigrants and the typical middle-class values of the Yankee Protestant natives helped to spawn two different systems of political ethics, which have dominated urban politics for most of the twentieth century.

The political organizations that were beginning to dominate the large eastern and mid-eastern cities were strengthened considerably by the increased powers being vested in strong-mayor–council forms of government at this time. However, the persistence of weak-mayor governments with fragmented powers, coupled with the huge increase in the number of immigrants settling in cities, was thought by many to be the catalyst for the continued development and growth of political machines.

The immigrants would have been important to the political organization solely by virtue of their sheer numbers. However, the immigrants of the 1880-1920 period were particularly well suited to fit into the political organizations emerging in the large cities for three reasons. First, for the most part they were unfamiliar with our political system. Concepts of representation and democracy were alien to them, and few big city political leaders were interested in teaching the immigrants anything but how to vote for their party candidates.

Second, most of the immigrants were fleeing authoritarian political systems. Not only were they unfamiliar with democratic principles, but they were accustomed to living under autocratic rule, where they had few freedoms but many rules to guide them in their daily lives. This characteristic was also of great political value to a well-organized political party that thrived on order, rules, discipline, and loyalty.

Third, the immigrants arrived here with intense personal needs. There were virtually no private or government agencies to assist them in housing, employment, or starting a business. The block and precinct captains were only too happy to learn of new arrivals in their area who needed help. They assisted the immigrants in many ways to adjust to life in the U.S. and to settle in their communities. All they asked in return was the promise at some future date to vote for the candidates the block and precinct captain asked them to.

For a new arrival in this country with a rural background, this must have appeared to be one of the best bargains imaginable. The trade of a "negligible" item like a vote for material goods and services necessary to survive was a trade few could afford to pass up.

The advent of increased powers for mayors, coupled with millions of immigrants arriving in our country and settling in large cities, was the formula that launched and perpetuated the political machines. The Progressive Era, which developed in the beginning of the twentieth century, was in many ways a protracted conflict between the political bosses, party professionals, and immigrant masses who had secured power in the urban areas, and moralistic leaders of Protestant reform who realized they had lost control of their cities.

## Decline of Machine Politics

The decline of the political machines in American urban history was the result of a series of unrelated events that occurred over several decades. Each of these factors helped to dissolve the important but fragile balance in the incentive-vote relationship between the political organization and its constituents.

The changes initiated by the reform movement (discussed in the next chapter) took a long time to evolve. However, once they were adopted, a number of them adversely affected the political machine.

One of the most damaging reforms from the standpoint of the machine was the use of merit systems to hire, promote, and fire local government employees. The Pendleton Act, passed in 1883, was the beginning of a civil service system at the national level. New York State adopted a similar law a decade later, and local governments began to implement them shortly thereafter. Today almost every city in the country uses the principles, if not the legal requirements, of a merit system for public employment.

The impact of this reform on political machines was devastating. Patronage, which was in many cases the key reward offered in exchange for votes, was eroded. Without jobs to offer, it became increasingly difficult for block and precinct captains to keep their voters satisfied. After all, if voters could obtain government jobs on the basis of experience or skill, then they were less likely to have to rely upon the candidate of the political organization to get or keep their jobs.[32]

The reformers were also successful in changing many of the rules that governed local political life. Council-manager government and at-large and nonpartisan elections were some of the other devices used by the early twentieth century reformers to erode the power of the political machine. Each of these reforms struck at the heart of the political machine. Council-manager government weakened the power of the political organizations and created the position of a professional, "non-political," city manager. The at-large elections reduced the ward-based parochial interests that were at the center of the bargaining and vote trading arrangement of the political machine. Elected council members viewed politics on a citywide scale rather than on a ward level and could base their decision on what was good for the city as a whole. Nonpartisanship reduced the name and party recognition that was so important to the machine. Without party designations on the ballot, voters had fewer cues to follow and might easily be swayed by the candidate's personality.

The New Deal of Franklin Roosevelt relied upon many of the big city political organizations to deliver services and programs to the needy during the Great Depression. However, as federal and state governments began to establish these programs on a permanent basis, the needy came to rely less upon political organizations and more on local government agencies. This meant that political organizations were not only being bypassed by state and federal programs, but these programs were now competing with the political organizations in the distribution of goods and services to the needy. In some cases the aid went directly to the needy from the federal government. This nationalization of social welfare programs continued to grow for almost fifty years, until the Reagan administration successfully ended the growth pattern in a historic budget battle in Congress.

As mentioned above, the life blood of the political machine was the successive waves of immigrants pouring into the country between 1880-1920. In the 1920's, federal policy drastically curtailed immigration to this country. With the potential source of its votes cut off, the machine watched as earlier immigrants climbed the political, social, and economic ladder out of the ghettos and into middle-income and middle-class respectability. With no immigrants to replace the second and third generation immigrants of earlier times, the machine lost its natural supply of voters. The arrival of blacks and Hispanics in the inner city to replace the immigrants did not succeed in perpetuating the machine. Replacing the immigrants with a different set of minority groups was not easy. (The many problems that resulted are discussed in a later chapter.)

The advent of World War II created many problems for the political machines. Jobs were plentiful, and salaries were good. Just about everyone who wanted to work could do so, and at a decent wage. This had a negative impact on the patronage available to the machines.

Once the war was over, the situation for the machines worsened. The nation began a huge conversion to peacetime production, which created many new and good-paying jobs. On top of this was the beginning of the suburban boom, with many residents abandoning their city apartments and buying suburban homes, made particularly attractive by federal financing and insurance programs.

A final factor contributing to the decline of the machines was the change in media habits and social life. The rise in television viewing made it more difficult for the block and precinct captains to establish and maintain a close personal relationship with local residents. Now, if he came to visit, he was likely to be intruding on the family's television viewing. This media also made the public more politically informed and aware, further lessening the politician's role. No precinct leader now can claim, as Plunkitt once did, to intimately know all the people in his or her district. Also, the availability of other forms of entertainment—movies, theatre, and weekend trips—meant that citizens were no longer dependent on political clubhouses for meetings, picnics, dances, and sports for their entertainment. The machine once filled an important social function that is now being met by other institutions.

All of these factors helped to reduce the power of the machine and to hasten its decline, if not its demise. But political machines have not disappeared altogether from the urban landscape. Chicago and New Haven, and the states of Indiana and New York, have well-developed political organizations that exhibit many of the characteristics of political machines. Wolfinger has pointed out a number of political jurisdictions where patronage for positions is still quite common in political life.[33]

The Chicago machine's survival in light of these factors is instructive. Mayor Daley, recognizing the decline of numerous personal benefits, altered his organization's incentive system by making increased use of public works in the form of freeways and buildings and by exempting thousands of jobs from the civil service system, thereby retaining them for patronage purposes.

However, the future of the Chicago machine is uncertain. The organization Daley built has not been as loyal to his successors as it was to him. Furthermore, for the time being, the job of mayor has been separated from that of Cook County Democratic party chairmanship, thereby reducing the power potential of the mayor.

In the 1983 Democratic mayoral primary the political leadership of the machine was splintered. Some leaders supported incumbent Mayor Byrne, while others lined up behind challenger Richard M. Daley, son of the former mayor. The failure of the party leaders to coalesce behind one candidate ultimately cost them the election. Harold Washington, a black candidate, focused his attention and resources on organizing and mobilizing the black wards in the city. By vastly increasing voter registration and working hard for a huge black voter turnout, Washington was able to defeat the disorganized machine in a three-way race in the primary. Washington then was able to mobilize enough voter support to win a narrow victory in the general election.

The Chicago political machine suffered another setback that makes its future rather precarious. In 1976 the Supreme Court, in *Elrod* v. *Burns,* decided that the newly elected Democratic sheriff in Cook County, Illinois, had acted improperly when he fired two of his non-civil service employees because they were not members of the Democratic party, did not support the party, and were not sponsored for their positions by party leaders.[34] By protecting public employees from discharge based upon what they believe, the court dealt the Chicago patronage system a serious blow. How the Chicago political system elects to operate in the light of the *Elrod* decision might well determine its ability to perpetuate itself as one of the few remaining big city political machines.

There are some who see a whole new form of patronage developing through the use of contracts. In the early 1970s, New York Mayor John Lindsay convinced the Board of Estimate that, in order for New York to retain the Yankee baseball team, Yankee Stadium would require a $24 million facelifting. The Board of Estimate approved the money and also approved a Lindsay request for an additional $2 million to rehabilitate the neighborhood around the stadium.

By 1973, the cost of the renovation had escalated to almost $50 million. This additional funding was approved by the City Council, despite the fact that the city of Pittsburgh had just completed building a new stadium for $45 million.

Mayor Lindsay left office at the end of 1974, and in 1975 Mayor Abraham Beame informed the City Council that the cost had escalated to $57 million. Three months later he would revise his estimate upward to $66 million, still claiming the city was getting a bargain.

A renovated Yankee Stadium finally opened in 1976 at a cost of $101 million. The year before, Pontiac, Michigan, had built a brand new domed stadium for 80,000 people at a cost of $60 million. The $2 million for neighborhood improvement around the stadium was finally deleted from a severely reduced city budget.

The political fallout following the Yankee Stadium renovation showed an interesting pattern of interactions among city council members, construction company executives, garage owners, local Bronx politicians, and officials from the Mayor's office.[35] It also pointed up the fact that cities with loose contracting and procurement policies and regulations can provide political leaders with a vehicle for delivering rewards in exchange for political favors. Even a mayor committed to reform like Lindsay sensed the value in working with Democratic political leaders in the Bronx on the Yankee Stadium project. Reform cities, as we shall see in the next chapter, tend to have tighter regulations and controls governing contracts, bids, and procurements.

Though less open today than in the earlier years of the century, the practice of awarding jobs to party workers through the use of private employers holding contracts from the city obviously continues. This was the sort of alliance between government and business that early twentieth century urban reformer Lincoln Steffens so vigorously exposed. Today, the arena is much broader, for it also includes alliances with particular unions as well as with contractors. It is not at all a question of graft, as it would have been during the Tammany period of the late 1800s. It is rather a question of knowing on which side the bread is buttered and acting accordingly. No one had to order construction workers to vote time after time for the reelection of Nelson Rockefeller to the governorship of New York State. It was obvious that he was the most dedicated sponsor of large-scale construction projects since the pharaohs of ancient Egypt.

## The Machine Evaluated

The study of political machines in American urban history has fascinated students and scholars alike. There is something attractively roguish about the Plunkitts, Hagues, and Tweeds. Few deny that their methods were antidemocratic and their actions often corrupt and illegal. However, it is also thought that political machines were quite effective. The feeling is that machines were well organized to obtain feedback from citizens in order to determine their needs. Once this was accomplished, the machine, through its highly decentralized delivery system, would be able to satisfy citizen needs and thereby continually replenish its good will, which it would convert to votes on election day. Moreover, the political machines were there to help the immigrants when no other institutions were willing to help or capable of providing help.

Furthermore, political machines relied heavily on the cooperation of the business community. Many of the scandals involving political bosses were directly related to their involvement with big business. These corrupt practices drained millions of dollars from city programs and projects that could have benefited the poor and newly arrived immigrants.

On paper, the machine appeared to be very well organized and tightly run. In fact, much of the success of the machine was attributable to the chaos associated with local government fragmentation and stalemate. The machine was able to get things done for people because it concentrated on a minimal number of high visibility requests, and it did not have to process these through normal bureaucratic channels. By pulling together the diverse and splintered elements of government to provide services or favors for residents, the machines gave the appearance of being highly organized.

The machine has also been criticized because of the limited benefits blacks derived from it in the 1960s. Most of the black wards solidly supported the Chicago machine, but Mayor Daley made few serious efforts to advance the cause of integration. In fact, Daley tended to concentrate low-income minority housing in specific areas of the city and even used freeway construction to isolate black ghettos, thereby retaining the support of whites who worked for the machine. The machine responded to specific demands by building swimming pools and housing rather than trying to solve major problems like racial discrimination.[36] In all fairness, there are some who feel that blacks who supported the Daley organization were quite content to receive the material benefits of jobs, housing, and swimming pools in lieu of the less tangible benefits associated with civil rights.

More recently, some scholars have even begun to question how effective the machine was in exchanging services for votes. Kenneth Mladenka conducted a study in Chicago in which he found that the pattern of service distribution was more a product of factors such as population shifts, technological change, and professional standards than it was of rewards for past political support.[37] He claimed there was little evidence that service distribution in Chicago was used as a resource to reward friends and punish opponents.

The debate over political machines continues in every course in urban politics. The machines evolved from a combination of the persistence of weak and fragmented governmental structure and the arrival of millions of immigrants seeking help for personal needs. There can be no doubt that the machines played a great role in the development of contemporary urban politics. They were also an important factor in cushioning the culture shock for the newly arrived immigrants. But perhaps the greatest testimonial to their effectiveness was seen in the need for the reformers to organize themselves in an effort to change local government so they could eliminate the machine from American cities.

# NOTES

1. Edward C. Banfield and James Q. Wilson, *City Politics* (New York: Vintage Books, 1963), p. 115.
2. William L. Riordan, *Plunkitt of Tammany Hall* (New York: E. P. Dutton, 1963), pp. xxvi.
3. Ibid., p. 33.
4. Edward C. Banfield, *Political Influence* (New York: Free Press, 1961).
5. The principal source on Tammany Hall is Gustavus Myers, *The History of Tammany Hall* (New York: Boni & Liverright, 1917). See also, Edwin Patrick Kilroe, "Saint Tammany and the Origin of the Society of Tammany or Columbian Order" (Ph.D. thesis, Columbia University, 1913).
6. The sources on Hoboken and the McFeely machine are *Life Magazine,* May 22, 1947, and *Time Magazine,* May 26, 1947.
7. Dayton David McKean, *The Boss: The Hague Machine in Action* (Boston: Houghton Mifflin, 1940).
8. Ibid., p. 268.
9. Ibid., p. 270.

10.  Ibid., p. 271
11.  Ibid., p. 271.
12.  Ibid., p. 218.
13.  Ibid., p. 278.
14.  Ibid., p. 279.
15.  J. T. Salter, *Boss Rule, Portraits in City Politics* (New York: Whittlesey House, 1935), p. 9. For an interesting analysis of Mayor Daley and his organization, see Mike Royko, *Boss: Richard J. Daley of Chicago* (New York: E. P. Dutton, 1971).
16.  Robert K. Merton, "Some Functions of the Political Machine," pp. 72–82 of a longer article, "Social Theory and Social Structure," in *American Journal of Sociology* (1945). The section of the article relating to machines is reprinted in Garold W. Thumm and Edward G. Janosik, eds., *Parties and the Governmental System* (Englewood Cliffs, N.J.: Prentice-Hall, 1967), pp. 25–32. The citation is at p. 27 of the Thumm and Janosik collection.
17.  Merton, "Some Functions of the Political Machine," p. 27.
18.  Riordan, *Plunkitt of Tammany Hall*, pp. 25–28.
19.  Merton, "Some Functions of the Political Machine," p. 27.
20.  Ibid., p. 29.
21.  Ibid., p. 30.
22.  Ibid., p. 31.
23.  Salter, *Boss Rule*, p. 18.
24.  Ibid., p. 18.
25.  Ibid., p. 224.
26.  Harold F. Gosnell, *Machine Politics: Chicago Model* (Chicago: University of Chicago Press, 1937), p. 183.
27.  Ibid.
28.  Elmer E. Cornwell, Jr., "Bosses, Machines and Ethnic Groups," *The Annals* 353 (May, 1964): 27–39.
29.  For a discussion of how patronage was used by the machine see James Q. Wilson, "The Economy of Patronage," *Journal of Political Economy* 69 (August 1961): 369–80.
30.  Riordan, *Plunkitt of Tammany Hall*, pp. 27–28. Also see Martin Shefter, "The Emergence of the Political Machine," in *Theoretical Perspectives on Urban Politics*, ed. Willis Hawley et. al. (Englewood Cliffs, N.J.: Prentice-Hall, 1976), pp. 14–44.
31.  Richard Hofstadter, *The Age of Reform* (New York: Vintage Books, 1955).
32.  See Wilson, "The Economy of Patronage," and Raymond E. Wolfinger, "Why Political Machines Have Not Withered Away and Other Revisionist Thoughts," *Journal of Politics* 34 (May 1972): 365–398. Both of these articles discuss the impact of patronage on political organizations.
33.  Raymond E. Wolfinger, *The Politics of Progress* (Englewood Cliffs, N.J.: Prentice-Hall, 1974), pp. 87–92. Also see Wolfinger, "Why Political Machines Have Not Withered Away" and Wilson, "The Economy of Patronage."
34.  *Elrod* v. *Burns*, 427 U.S. 347 (1976).
35.  For a discussion of the use of contracts as a political weapon see Jack Newfield and Paul Du Brul, *The Abuse of Power: The Permanent Government and the Fall of New York* (New York: Penguin Books, 1978), chap. 5. Also see Murray Schumach, "Lindsay Plots Own Political Moves," *New York Times* (February 11, 1973), pp. 1, 39.
36.  See Royko, *Boss: Richard J. Daley of Chicago;* and Bill Gleason, *Daley of Chicago* (New York: Simon and Schuster, 1970).
37.  Kenneth R. Mladenka, "The Urban Bureaucracy and the Chicago Political Machine: Who Gets What and the Limits to Political Control," *The American Political Science Review* 74 (December 1980): 991–998. Two other studies that support the view that bureaucrats use routinized decision patterns in which

political decisions are minimized are Frank S. Levy, Arnold J. Meltsner, and Aaron Wildavsky, *Urban Outcomes: Schools, Streets and Libraries* (Berkeley: University of California Press, 1974); and Robert Lineberry, *Equality and Urban Policy* (Beverly Hills: Sage Publications, 1977). A recent study of Chicago politics indicates that the machine was catering to an expanded set of voters who highly prized the efficient delivery of services. See Esther R. Fuchs and Robert Y. Shapiro, "Government Performance as a Basis for Machine Support," *Urban Affairs Quarterly* 18 (June 1983): 537–549.

# 5. REFORM POLITICS

Political machines exercised a great deal of power in American urban political life. In doing so they often reaped many financial rewards, which angered people outside the machine's network. Where the machine's political and economic power became excessive, groups of individuals banded together in an effort to "reform" the system, which they felt disadvantaged them. The reformers were successful in changing many of the rules of local political and administrative life, thus reducing the power of the machines and speeding their decline. The changing rules had an impact on the redistribution of power and the determination of who gets what from the political process.

To understand contemporary urban politics in America one has to be familiar not only with the historical evolution of the forms of local government in the country, but also with the political application of these forms as they emerged from the struggle between the political machines and the reformers. This struggle has had a lasting influence on the structure of city government today. In many cities the reformers won, and reform institutions dominate. Knowing the origins of the reform movements and who the reformers were, we can better evaluate the operation of reform institutions today.

## THE REFORM MOVEMENT

The idea that an entrenched in-group ought eventually to be thrown out of office and replaced by an out-group—the principle of "throw the rascals out"—is, of course, as old as American city politics. Often the principle is accorded more recognition by out-of-power partisan candidates than by the electorate. In the case of Philadelphia, for instance, the Republican organization controlled the city for an uninterrupted period of sixty-eight years. The GOP dominance was ended only in 1951. For the past generation the Democratic organization has been in control.

In rotations of this sort, the shift of power was, and was intended to be, from the hands of one party organization to those of its rival. It remained for the reformers to introduce the concept that politics as such should be removed from municipal government. The reformers left a very marked imprint on the structure of American city governments, although they were less successful in changing the behavior of the electorate. Yet enough of their work was sufficiently enduring so that one may speak of reform politics as the alternative to the more widely publicized machine politics. Both types may currently be observed in operation in urban America.

The reform movement coincided with and grew out of the loss of political power by the old elite that had controlled northern cities prior to the Civil War.[1] Outgunned by the new dominant class of businessmen and entrepreneurs who wanted special favors from local government, outvoted by the new immigrant groups, and outraged by the newly formed political machines, the old elite retreated to the community service organization. This kind of organization included hospitals, charitable groups, and civic-reform associations. Today it includes foundations. From this strong point it launched its appeals for municipal reform and called for a politics serving the public, or general interest, instead of the various private interests.

In calling for a politics of the public interest, the reformers assumed that the task of local government was basically a technical matter; the best informed citizens would establish policy, and qualified technicians would carry out its administration. Because the reformers concentrated on fundamentals, political parties were held to be superfluous and evil—at least, for municipal government. For the same reason, it was felt that group competition on the part of interest groups should be held to an absolute minimum. The principal strategy was to put into office "those best qualified to serve."

The programs of the National Municipal League (discussed later in this chapter) served as models for the reformers. With its emphasis on nonpartisan elections, the city manager plan, and the short ballot, the League provided patterns and standards that were avidly followed wherever the reformers could set the style of local government. They were notably successful in smaller and middle-sized cities. While the larger cities adopted features from the municipal program of the League, they never accepted the total program.

In their evaluation of the Reform movement, Banfield and Wilson were struck by several "anomalies":

1. "Although reformers have lost most of their battles for power, they have in the main won their war for the adoption of particular measures of structural and other change."[2] All cities have adopted a good deal of the reform program.
2. "Although reform has won its war, victory has not yielded the fruits for which the reformers fought."[3] The reformers expected to gain efficiency and eliminate corruption. In general, modern city governments *are* a good deal more efficient than they used to be. At the same time, they continue to be plagued with repeated scandals over housing contracts, welfare and poverty programs, and gambling operations. In addition, the elimination of patronage positions has had unanticipated results. In Philadelphia, as a case in point, the reform Democratic officials—Joseph Clark and Richard-

son Dilworth—soon found they needed patronage in order to keep their own organization together. In this they were not very much different from the Republicans they ousted in 1951.

3.   "Although reform measures have not produced the effects that the reformers have anticipated (and have indeed often produced opposite ones), those desired effects are being produced by other causes."[4] That city government is much more honest than it was a generation ago is not an achievement of the reformers. As Banfield and Wilson see it, the measures and improvements that have occurred "are both effects of a common cause: the steady diffusion in our culture of the political ideal of the Anglo-Saxon Protestant middle-class political ethos."[5] In other words, changes in municipal government have come about because of changes in the political culture.

In an absolute sense, both reform and machine classifications of politics should be regarded as "pure" or "ideal" types. Winnetka, Illinois, and Scarsdale, New York, may indeed display "pure" types of reform politics, but they are exceptional. At the same time, Hoboken, New Jersey, and Chester, Pennsylvania, may have been brilliant examples of the machine type, but, again, they are unusual in this respect. For the most part, the cities of America include elements of both political types, yet the blend is rarely perfect; one type usually is dominant and the other correspondingly subordinate. In the Philadelphia of Mayor James H. J. Tate, the style of government was distinctly of the machine type, as was the case in the Chicago of Mayor Richard J. Daley. While machine politics still survives in Chicago in a somewhat modified form, it should be pointed out that former Mayor Jane Byrne initially ran against the machine slate of candidates. Mayor Byrne was no reformer; in fact, she had been quite willing to govern with the assistance of machine politicians and to attempt to reassert the dominance of the machine, even though she was opposed to some factions within it. The government of New York in the Wagner era emphasized machine style politics, while the second administration of John Lindsay (elected as a Liberal candidate) stressed the reform style. Mayor Koch, who rose to political prominence by building a reform organization to fight the political bosses, has imposed his own style of reform government on the city during his two terms as mayor. Highly decentralized Los Angeles, in the traditional sense, hardly seems governed at all. Yet Los Angeles has adopted many features proposed by the reformers. Former Mayor Samuel Yorty talked a great deal about reform but accomplished little during the 1960s and early 1970s. His successor, Tom Bradley, has made Los Angeles a much more reform-minded city, despite numerous obstacles emanating from the state constitution, the city charter, and local and state laws.

## Theory of Good Government Reforms

In an effort to recapture local government from the clutches of the political bosses, the reformers sought basic modifications in the political system. These were primarily in the structure and in the manner of selecting public officials.

The reformers attacked the machines and their political bosses on a variety of fronts, but the persistent catchwords of the movement were economy and efficiency. The reformers believed they could do it better and cheaper. They espoused four major concepts to improve the quality of local government.

1. The public interest should be served.
2. Politics should be separated from administration.
3. Experienced administrators should be hired to manage local government.
4. Scientific management principles should be applied to local government.

These concepts were implemented through a campaign to modify the structure of local government and the techniques used for electing public officials.

The reformers believed that the public interest was not being served by the narrow, partisan considerations of the political organizations in power. They felt that the public interest could be defined objectively, and, therefore, public policy could be used to benefit all citizens equally. Citywide projects would take precedence over ward, community, or neighborhood projects, since these types of projects presumably benefited more citizens.

The reformers never precisely stated how individuals or governments could accurately assess the public interest. Lacking this precision, it was only a matter of time before their own private interests came to be linked with the public interest. The importance of this concept cannot be minimized. There is hardly a "reform" oriented candidate running for office in any large city who does not invoke the "public interest" in his or her campaign.

In a democratic political system, the public interest is usually hard to ascertain. Since public policy is usually the result of contending political forces battling in the public arena, there are always winners and losers. The losers often feel that the public has been cheated. The winners believe that the public has been served by their efforts. This scenario is repeated on most public policy issues.

Part of the reason the reformers clung so tenaciously to the concept of the public interest was their belief in human nature and the feeling that good people would always surface to produce good policy. It is no surprise, therefore, that the reformers greatly minimized the role politics should play in the policymaking process. The reformers wanted politics separated from administration in local government. They reasoned that if the public interest could be defined objectively, then the really important function of local government was administration. Politics was not necessary in the efficient implementation of public interest policies.

It followed logically from the first two concepts that administrators were of greater value than politicians in the reform model of politics. Good administrators were people with training and experience in their respective fields. Proven experts were to be recruited to manage the business of local government. These administrators would be recruited from around the country and subject to the regulations of the newly emerging local government civil service systems.

The reformers subscribed to the principles of scientific management being espoused by Frederick Taylor, a mechanical engineer who, early in the twentieth century, spent much of his time trying to improve worker productivity. Local government, the reformers felt, should be run like a business corporation. The techniques and principles of scientific management used in business should be applied to local government. This would also reduce the need for political leaders and political organizations to process public issues and provide an opportunity for the scientific managers to take control and run government according to accepted principles. According to the reformers, efficient government could be reduced to a question of mechanics.

## Results of the Reform Movement

The structural reforms necessary to implement the major concepts of the reform movement were numerous.

### Council-Manager Government

This form of government has been discussed previously, but its major principles are worth repeating since they are reflective of the reform model espoused by the National Municipal League in its Model City Charter. The manager form of government is based on a belief that capable and public-spirited citizens should run for office so they can work in the public interest. The council members should be elected to office in nonpartisan, at-large elections. Administration of city government is delegated to a trained executive who is to manage the city like a corporate executive. Administrative authority, therefore, is concentrated in the city manager. Under this system of government the council is held politically responsible, while the manager is to be a neutral administrator, shunning political involvement and acting only in accord with the principles of professional urban management.

### Nonpartisanship

Nonpartisanship means that candidates run without party designations next to their names on the ballots, but it does not mean there will be an absence of factional groups or political interests involved in local elections. All elections are partisan in the sense that there will always be groups or interests involved.

Nonpartisanship has other implications for local government as well. First, it tends to weaken local political parties, which are the foundation upon which the national political party system is built. Nonpartisanship also impedes recruitment of candidates for office. Parties often establish channels of recruitment based upon past performance in political campaigns. This becomes very difficult under nonpartisan elections, where independent candidates and well-known citizens are often encouraged to run for office. This, in turn, makes it more difficult to raise funds without the recognizable party names for easy identification. Active political parties help to relieve confusion at election time by publicizing issues of importance to their candidates and thereby giving cues to the voters.

Secondly, nonpartisan elections tend to encourage issue avoidance. Candidates are not necessarily identified with positions on issues, since they run independently of state, county, or national party policy. This leads candidates to seek out the middle ground on most issues and to avoid mentioning the really controversial issues, if possible. In this way, candidates tend to maximize support with middle-of-the-road positions while minimizing their loss of votes by avoiding tough issues.

The role of the media is usually enhanced during the campaign. When candidates avoid discussing controversial policies, the media tend to publicize these in an effort to draw out the candidates. The result is a campaign where voters get a great deal of information about important policies from the media, but not as much as they should from the candidates.

A third consequence of nonpartisanship is that minority groups are disadvantaged under this electoral form. Without party labels and normal party recruitment channels, few minority candidates will be put forward by civic organizations and special interest groups. These groups need to broaden their appeal under this form of election and minority candidates are likely to produce the broad-based coalition to achieve victory.

A fourth consequence of nonpartisanship is that it frustrates protest voting, whereby the outs replace the ins. Without party labels it is more difficult to identify and to hold elected officials accountable on their positions on specific issues.

Fifth, nonpartisan cities, with a lack of party discipline, might find a governing consensus hard to develop. Council members view themselves as having been elected independently of one another, and the normal ties of party affiliation are absent. Furthermore, with an independently elected mayor, the same lack of discipline could apply as the mayor attempts to build a working consensus on issues. Council members feel little or no loyalty to the mayor, and the party is unable to impose its will since it lacks the normal resources to punish and reward candidates and elected officials.[6]

Sixth, without active party organizations there are no mechanisms for getting out the vote. Therefore, middle- and upper-class voters, who traditionally have high turnouts on election day, will further exaggerate the class bias in voting because lower-income voters will not be encouraged to vote by local party workers. This problem is exacerbated in many communities where nonpartisan elections for school boards are held at separate times from other elections. This reduces voter turnout and leads to middle-class and teacher union dominance in the elections.

TABLE 5.1
Cities Having Nonpartisan Elections

| Classification | No. of cities reporting (A) | Cities having nonpartisan elections | |
|---|---|---|---|
| | | No. | % of (A) |
| Total, all cities . . . . . . . . . . . . | 4,008 | 2,813 | 70.2 |
| **Population group** | | | |
| Over 1,000,000 . . . . . . . . . | 3 | 2 | 66.7 |
| 500,000–1,000,000 . . . . . . . | 12 | 9 | 75.0 |
| 250,000–  499,999 . . . . . . . | 24 | 16 | 66.7 |
| 100,000–  249,999 . . . . . . . | 93 | 69 | 74.2 |
| 50,000–   99,999 . . . . . . . | 223 | 159 | 71.3 |
| 25,000–   49,999 . . . . . . . | 458 | 322 | 70.3 |
| 10,000–   24,999 . . . . . . . | 993 | 663 | 66.8 |
| 5,000–    9,999 . . . . . . . | 1,026 | 697 | 67.9 |
| 2,500–    4,999 . . . . . . . | 1,176 | 876 | 74.5 |
| **Geographic division** | | | |
| New England . . . . . . . . . . . . | 187 | 101 | 54.0 |
| Mid-Atlantic . . . . . . . . . . . . | 611 | 69 | 11.3 |
| East North Central . . . . . . . | 839 | 540 | 64.4 |
| West North Central . . . . . . | 456 | 421 | 92.3 |
| South Atlantic . . . . . . . . . . | 546 | 484 | 88.6 |
| East South Central . . . . . . . | 237 | 180 | 75.9 |
| West South Central . . . . . . | 438 | 373 | 85.2 |
| Mountain . . . . . . . . . . . . . . | 216 | 182 | 84.3 |
| Pacific Coast . . . . . . . . . . . | 478 | 463 | 96.9 |
| **Form of government** | | | |
| Mayor-council . . . . . . . . . . | 2,042 | 1,191 | 58.3 |
| Council-manager . . . . . . . . | 1,854 | 1,540 | 83.1 |
| Commission . . . . . . . . . . . . | 112 | 82 | 73.2 |

Source: International City Management Association (Washington, D.C.: *The Municipal Year Book* 1982), p. 181.

## Ward vs. At-Large Systems

Another structural reform sought by the reformers was to change the geographical base of the candidates from wards or districts to at-large voting systems. The political machine bosses favored wards or districts since it allowed them to capitalize on a strong, decentralized political organization. By compartmentalizing the city, the machine was able to control the small geographical areas by expending sizeable resources when and where they were needed. The information necessary to achieve this was usually available from the block and precinct captains in each ward.

The ward system has several advantages for residents. First, in moderate to large cities there is a tendency for people of similar socioeconomic and cultural interests to live in the same general areas. If election wards or district lines are drawn with these goals in mind, then it is possible to elect a council that is more representative of the residents than under an at-large electoral system.

Second, under a ward system there is usually a short ballot. Thus, voters have fewer candidates to choose from than in the lengthy at-large ballots, where it is often difficult to collect information about all the candidates.

Third, voters have an opportunity to vote for candidates whose stand on local issues is better known. Moreover, these candidates are more familiar with the specific problems and issues confronting their district.

Some disadvantages of the ward system have also been cited. First, single-member districts provide for representation of some interests but do not provide for proportional representation of multiple interests, since not all citizens with similar interests are found together in a city.

Second, special emphasis is placed on the interests of the citizens in specific geographical districts. These rather narrow, parochial interests may not be in the best interests of the city as a whole.

Third, ward systems are very compatible with the political style of the machine, which is based upon brokerage politics. Ward politics involves gerrymandering to maintain political boundaries conducive to machine electoral victories. Elected ward representatives also quickly learn the art of trading votes for favors and programs. This bargaining process often determines how and when issues are processed at city hall.

The reformers perceived the importance of the wards to the political machine and sought to restructure the electoral system, substituting at-large elections for the ward system. The reformers supported their proposals by arguing that political issues in an at-large system are focused at the citywide level. There is far less of the selfish community-based interest politics, and the elected council members have a broader vision of the city's needs and resources. There is also a greater possibility of electing council members of higher quality, since quality is not randomly distributed by ward.

Critics of the reform-sponsored at-large system argue that at-large elections in partisan cities usually produce one-party councils. This is the situation in many mayor-council cities today, and as a result of a one-party vote, minority groups are often unrepresented or underrepresented on the local councils.[7]

A good example of the problem was publicized in 1973, when the Fifth U.S. Circuit Court of Appeals in New Orleans ruled that the at-large electoral system in Mobile, Alabama, excluded blacks, was unresponsive to blacks, and had demonstrated a pattern of discrimination. Mobile's black population was 35 percent, but a black had never been elected to the city council. In 1976 District Court Judge Virgil Pittman ordered Mobile to convert to a ward-based election plan. Other southern cities that had adopted a ward-based system—Dallas and Montgomery, Alabama—had elected blacks to the city council almost immediately.[8]

However, in 1980 the U.S. Supreme Court overturned Judge Pittman's order on Mobile's electoral system, stating that for the original ruling to

TABLE 5.2
Types of Electoral Systems

| Classification | No. of cities reporting (A) | At large system | | Ward or district system | | Combination system | |
|---|---|---|---|---|---|---|---|
| | | No. | % of (A) | No. | (A) | No. | % of (A) |
| Total, all cities . . . . . . . . . . . . | 4,089 | 2,721 | 66.5 | 595 | 14.6 | 773 | 18.9 |
| **Population group** | | | | | | | |
| Over 1,000,000 . . . . . . . . . . | 3 | 0 | 0.0 | 1 | 33.3 | 2 | 66.7 |
| 500,000–1,000,000 . . . . . . . | 12 | 4 | 33.3 | 2 | 16.7 | 6 | 50.0 |
| 250,000– 499,999 . . . . . . . | 25 | 13 | 52.0 | 3 | 12.0 | 9 | 36.0 |
| 100,000– 249,999 . . . . . . . | 95 | 48 | 50.5 | 15 | 15.8 | 32 | 33.7 |
| 50,000– 99,999 . . . . . . . | 226 | 134 | 59.3 | 20 | 8.8 | 72 | 31.9 |
| 25,000– 49,999 . . . . . . . | 463 | 294 | 63.5 | 61 | 13.2 | 108 | 23.3 |
| 10,000– 24,999 . . . . . . . | 1,012 | 662 | 65.4 | 122 | 12.1 | 228 | 22.5 |
| 5,000– 9,999 . . . . . . . | 1,048 | 706 | 67.4 | 151 | 14.4 | 191 | 18.2 |
| 2,500– 4,999 . . . . . . . | 1,205 | 860 | 71.4 | 220 | 18.3 | 125 | 10.4 |
| **Geographic division** | | | | | | | |
| New England . . . . . . . . . . . . | 185 | 100 | 54.1 | 22 | 11.9 | 63 | 34.1 |
| Mid-Atlantic . . . . . . . . . . . . | 625 | 455 | 72.8 | 109 | 17.4 | 61 | 9.8 |
| East North Central . . . . . . . | 857 | 463 | 54.0 | 152 | 17.7 | 242 | 28.2 |
| West North Central . . . . . . | 467 | 203 | 43.5 | 132 | 28.3 | 132 | 28.3 |
| South Atlantic . . . . . . . . . . | 555 | 425 | 76.6 | 43 | 7.7 | 87 | 15.7 |
| East South Central . . . . . . . | 243 | 202 | 83.1 | 12 | 4.9 | 29 | 11.9 |
| West South Central . . . . . . | 451 | 300 | 66.5 | 62 | 13.7 | 89 | 19.7 |
| Mountain . . . . . . . . . . . . . . | 223 | 146 | 65.5 | 41 | 18.4 | 36 | 16.1 |
| Pacific Coast . . . . . . . . . . . | 483 | 427 | 88.4 | 22 | 4.6 | 34 | 7.0 |
| **Form of government** | | | | | | | |
| Mayor-council . . . . . . . . . . | 2,111 | 1,199 | 56.8 | 438 | 20.7 | 474 | 22.5 |
| Council-manager . . . . . . . . | 1,878 | 1,422 | 75.7 | 157 | 8.4 | 299 | 15.9 |
| Commission . . . . . . . . . . . . | 100 | 100 | 100.0 | 0 | 0.0 | 0 | 0.0 |

Source: International City Management Association (Washington, C.C.: *The Municipal Year Book* 1982), p. 181.

stand the plaintiffs would have to show that the at-large system of government was intentionally designed to exclude blacks. In 1982 the U.S. Supreme Court appeared to retreat from its position in the Mobile case when it upheld a lower court ruling forcing Burke County, Georgia, to end its at-large system of electing commissioners. Even though no clear-cut case of discrimination was proven, no black had ever been elected commissioner, despite the fact that blacks constituted over 53 percent of the county's population.

Another criticism is that at-large elections usually entail long ballots, a severe burden for the voter. This obstacle can be overcome by staggering the terms of the council members.

At-large elections also tend to increase the cost of both primary and general elections for the candidates. Candidates have to campaign and advertise city-wide instead of concentrating on their local wards. This discourages some candidates whose fundraising capabilities are marginal.

## Other Structural Reforms

### Civil Service and Merit Systems

The establishment of civil service commissions and the adoption of a merit system of employment were also major structural changes sought by the reformers. Since patronage was one of the most important rewards distributed by the machine, one way to weaken the machine was to reduce or eliminate as much patronage as possible. This was accomplished by placing as many city jobs as possible under the civil service system. This meant that job descriptions were written, a formalized and public recruitment system was established, and qualifications for each position were determined. Applicants filed their credentials for job openings, and the city had an opportunity to hire the best qualified candidate.

The merit system did not completely eliminate patronage, but it dramatically reduced the number of jobs available for distribution by the political organization. The arguments for efficiency and economy associated with the movement for a merit system were very persuasive, and city after city began to adopt these principles as standard personnel procedures. As we shall see in the next two chapters, the creation of the civil service system produced many problems concerning accountability and the bias of civil servants towards their clients.

### City Planning Commissions

The reformers also strongly supported the creation of city planning commissions. Having watched the political machines use their inside knowledge to obtain economic advantage, the reformers recognized the need to implement an orderly process where once chaos and corruption reigned. The key to achieving this was to establish a professional, non-political planning commission that would make decisions on the orderly growth and development of the city in an objective manner. As an alternative to what existed in large American cities in the early twentieth century, this was a sound and rational proposal. Once again, the reformers had found a persuasive argument to improve the quality of life in cities at the same time as they eroded some of the power of the political machine. However, we have seen that the planning profession has its own biases, and while planning commissions are often nonpartisan in nature, their decisions on highways, schools, and buildings have an impact on neighborhoods and communities.

*Direct Primary*

The reformers also found that political machines used party conventions to select their candidates, thus effectively shutting out the public from the nominating process. To counter this, reformers fought to institute the direct primary, which allowed the voters an opportunity to select their candidates. The movement towards primaries and away from party conventions opened up the political process and reduced the stranglehold the political machines once had on the nominating process. However, in primary voting, as in election day voting, there is a much higher turnout among the middle class. This reform also contributed to middle- and upper-class control of local government.

*Initiative, Referendum, and Recall*

To open up the system still further, and to weaken the grip of the machine on the political system, the reformers proposed adding to each city's charter the initiative, the referendum, and the recall. The initiative permits a legally designated number of citizens to draft a piece of legislation or a charter amendment to be put on a ballot for approval or disapproval by the voters. The referendum allows a prescribed number of voters to petition for a public vote on a piece of legislation that has already been passed by the council. Voters have an opportunity to overturn a bill passed by their representatives. The recall permits a prescribed number of voters to collect names on a petition requesting the recall, or removal from office, of an elected official before his or her term expires.

In an effort to guarantee representation on the council in proportion to voting strength, some cities have adopted proportional representation in council elections. (See the discussion of proportional representation in Chapter 3, page 39.) The results are said to have produced a calibre of councilmen higher than that under the district system.[9]

## THE REFORM TYPE: NATURE, FUNCTIONS, SOCIAL BASE

In order to realize their ideals of good government, the civic reformers supported certain concrete measures. These included, as we have discussed, the initiative, referendum, and recall; the direct primary and proportional representation; nonpartisan municipal elections held in odd-numbered years; the council-manager form of government; and at-large elections. The objective of these proposals was to destroy the political machines and return governing power more directly to the people.[10]

The National Municipal League, founded in 1894, served as the intellectual center for the reform movement. The League adopted its first municipal program in 1900. In its current version, this program may be found in the latest (1941) version of the Model City Charter. The Charter continues to stress the council-manager form of municipal government, nonpartisanship, and election by proportional representation.[11]

Even though the reformers emphasized certain common objectives, the movement itself has assumed several different forms. James Q. Wilson has identified five types of reform movements: citizens' associations, candidate screening committees, independent local parties, blue ribbon leadership factions, and intraparty reform clubs.[12]

A citizens' association usually operates outside the party structure. It performs such functions as reviewing the record of elected officials and making recommendations regarding expenditures and taxes. The League of Women Voters is an illustration.

Candidate screening committees, prominent in certain nonpartisan cities, examine prospective candidates, make recommendations, and raise funds for the persons they endorse.

Reform movements occasionally assume the form of an independent local party. One such party was the Fusion party, which helped elect mayors of New York City in 1901, 1913, and 1933 by forming a temporary alliance with the Republicans. A more continuing type of local party is the independent good government organization, of which one of the most famous examples is the City Charter Committee in Cincinnati. In every sense this is a permanent, local party.

A blue ribbon leadership faction sometimes emerges when a reform movement occurs within the ranks of a major party. Here the emphasis is on purging the existing party leadership. In such cases, the objective is to oust machine-oriented leaders and replace them with a reform-oriented elite. Often there is a very pronounced class difference between the two contending factions. The Clark-Dilworth seizure of power in the Democratic party in Philadelphia during the early 1950s illustrates the blue ribbon type of reform.

Finally, there is the intraparty reform club. Members of these clubs consider themselves amateurs when compared to the professional politicians. Reform clubs tend to be issue-oriented and, relative to the regular organizations, somewhat ideological. Reform Democratic clubs are scattered throughout the Upper West Side of Manhattan and in Greenwich Village in New York City. They also exist in other big northern and midwestern cities.[13]

Unless one has had personal involvement in reform politics, it is difficult to appreciate the fervor the movement generates. In her excellent case study of Toledo, Jean L. Stinchcombe recaptures the dedication of reform politics in that city during the last seventy years. Under such colorful figures as Samuel M. "Golden Rule" Jones and Brand Whitlock, the reformers took control of Toledo early in the century. In spite of continuing challenges, the movement has succeeded in dominating Toledo municipal politics until the present time.[14] In the process, it must be added, the original enthusiasm of the reformers has given way to a good deal of weariness and lassitude. But the *forms* devised by the movement remain embedded in municipal politics and government.

In Toledo, and elsewhere, one of the lasting contributions of the reform movement has been nonpartisanship. Thomas R. Dye notes that over
three-fourths of America's cities use the nonpartisan ballot to elect local
officials.[15] Nonpartisan local elections are held in large as well as smaller
cities. In the former category are found Boston, Chicago, Cincinnati, Detroit, Los Angeles, Milwaukee, San Francisco, and Seattle. There appear to
be several distinct types of political systems in the various nonpartisan cities.
In one type, for example, the parties operate quite openly, with the exception
that party designations do not appear on the ballot. Chicago is an illustration.
In another type of local political system, the parties disguise themselves
behind other formal organizations. Where this occurs, as in Detroit and Dallas, no one is deluded by the deception. In the smaller cities, there tends to
be a third type of nonpartisanship, in which the parties play no role at all in
local contests.[16]

Political scientists have long been interested in the effects of nonpartisanship on the vitality of the political parties. While some consequences
have been identified, it is difficult to establish firm general relationships. In
some cities, nonpartisanship does not seem to have affected the vitality of
party politics—Boston, Chicago, and Detroit are examples. In other cities,
such as Toledo, the effect seems to have been the reverse. Given the present
state of information on the subject, it is necessary to examine a particular
city over time in an effort to judge the relationship. The general belief is that,
all things being equal, nonpartisanship ought to weaken the local base of the
national and state party organizations.

There is a good deal of hard evidence, and therefore more agreement,
as to the social base of the reform movement as a whole. One careful student
of municipal politics, Duane Lockard, has concluded that "efforts to initiate
or to maintain 'nonpolitical' operations in municipal government tend to
divide communities along class-status lines with upper-class elements favor-
ing and lower-class elements opposing these procedures."[17] But a problem
arises. If there are more lower-class than upper-class voters, why have the
cities adopted so many elements of the reform program supported by the
upper class? Lockard's answer is that a much higher proportion of upper-
class voters goes to the polls in all elections, including referenda. Thus, the
strength of the upper-class group proportionately is magnified.[18]

As has been emphasized in this analysis, the reform movement was
highly successful in getting many of its specific proposals accepted by
municipal governments. But what have been the general consequences in
terms of public policy? This is, after all, the substantive result—the pay-off
—that the reformers wished to achieve.

In an effort to come to grips with this question, Robert L. Lineberry
and Edmund P. Fowler made a careful study of spending and taxing in 200
American cities. They found that reformed cities do, in fact, tend to spend
less and tax less than unreformed municipalities. Even more significant was
the finding regarding the responsiveness of the two kinds of cities to the
composition of their populations. "The more reformed the city, the less
responsive it is to socio-economic cleavages in its political decision-mak-

ing.''[19] Reformed cities are relatively unresponsive in their tax and spending policies to distinctions in income, education, and ethnic characteristics of their populations. In contrast, the unreformed cities take these factors into account when arriving at such decisions. Another way of looking at this is to note that reformism tends to diminish the impact of ethnicity, education, home ownership, and religion in city politics. Unreformed cities (those with mayor-council governments, partisan elections, ward as opposed to at-large constituencies) reflect in their public policies a more pronounced response to socio-economic divisions.[20]

In her study of Toledo, Jean Stinchcombe was able to test certain hypotheses about reform politics against the actual record. She had posited the hypothesis that the ''compatibility of reform institutions with middle-class civic ideals would encourage participation by business leaders.''[21] But this proved to be false. In actual fact, ''the community participation of executives is confined to good works and isolated issues of direct concern to business.''[22]

Another hypothesis tested in the Toledo study was that the reform movement would enhance the influence and interests of business and middle-class groups at the expense of lower-class and minority groups. However, ''this hypothesis is not completely true. Although the roles of lower-income groups have been restricted, the participation of other groups has not increased.''[23]

Finally, Mrs. Stinchcombe weighs the values of reform against the needs of Toledo and finds an unbridgeable chasm between the two.[24] ''The values of reform,'' she declares, ''are in fact antithetical to the character of the large industrial city.''[25] Abstract reform ideals are of little use when it comes to resolving such issues as racial discrimination in education, housing, and employment. Toledo does not have a political machine, but neither does it have effective political leadership. ''Toledo's experience,'' she concludes, ''suggests that the ethos and institutions of reform can have debilitating consequences in populous, industrial cities.''[26]

More studies of the Toledo kind are needed in order to develop a body of high-level generalizations applicable across the country. But it is clear that reform politics has not turned out to be the panacea its founders had expected. Nor have the structural changes engineered by the reformers brought about any basic changes in the rules of the game.

The reform movement has been characterized by another observer as being a distinctly middle-class movement that was driven by the upper classes. The movement for municipal reform was led by important business executives and professionals who formed a good-government coalition to achieve their goals. There was very little involvement on the part of small business operators, skilled and unskilled workers, or white-collar employees.

The movement for reform in municipal government, therefore, constituted an attempt by upper-class professionals and large business groups to take formal political power from the previously dominant lower- and middle-class elements so that they might advance their own conceptions of desirable public policy.

Reformers, therefore, wished not simply to replace bad men with good; they proposed to change the occupational and class origins of decision-makers. Toward this end they sought innovation in the formal machinery of government which would concentrate political power by sharply centralizing the process of decision-making rather than distribute it through more popular participation in public affairs.[27]

The great paradox of local government reform centers on the concepts of democratization and centralization. The reformers sought to break the power grip the machines exerted on local government by making government more open and accessible to all citizens. In trying to achieve this, however, the reformers instituted a number of changes in municipal government that had the opposite effect. Many of these reforms effectively excluded the lower-class immigrants from municipal jobs where decisions affecting their lives were being made. In this respect the machine proved to be infinitely more democratic in assessing the needs of citizens and responding to them.

As the reform movement succeeded in changing local government structure and professionalizing the bureaucracy, it also removed the government further from the people. This centralizing trend made it increasingly difficult for the urban bureaucracies to deliver the quantity and quality of services required by the agencies' clients, since the bureaucracies had become white and middle-class, while the clients were black or Hispanic and lower income. Bureaucracies not only became unresponsive and nonrepresentative, but, as they became more insulated from popular control, they were less accountable. The advent of the civil service system in many large cities resulted in local governments that were "well-run but ungoverned." Each functional bureaucracy controlled its own turf by establishing professional norms and guidelines that often were at odds with client needs and even thwarted efforts by local elected officials to impose controls. The reformed bureaucracies became "independent islands of power" capable of derailing the plans of even a strong mayor.[28] As we will see in Chapters 6 and 7, many of the problems of contemporary urban America stem from these early twentieth century conflicts between the machines and the reform movement.

## Impact of the Reform Movement

Like many other aspects of urban politics, the reform movement has had both successes and failures. One thing can be agreed upon: the reform movement has had a dramatic and lasting impact on American cities.

The reform movement was not universally adopted across the country. In the larger and older cities, particularly those with large immigrant populations, resistance to the reform proposals was strongest. Reformers had their greatest successes in implementing their program in middle-sized cities that were growing rapidly and where the population was relatively homogenous and had achieved a higher education level.[29]

Second, there has been a much greater emphasis on background, training, and experience in the selection of department heads for local government agencies. This has, in most cases, added to the professionalism of the departments and upgraded the quality of administration by increasing the standards for performance.

However, critics have suggested that this professionalization of the bureaucracy has also depersonalized the administration and impeded the delivery of urban services. The more-exacting civil service standards made entry into the public service much more difficult for ethnics and minorities. This path of upward social and economic mobility was being closed; as a consequence, ethnics and minorities came to be underrepresented in the bureaucracy. Since these were the groups with the greatest service needs, their lack of representation has created numerous agency-client conflicts.

Third, since reform groups minimized the importance of politics in local government, it was no surprise that bureaucratic power increased at the expense of legislative power as a result of the reform movement. To the reformers, impartial and objective administration of government was to be preferred to legislative bargaining and compromising. The impact of this approach was seen in a reduction in accountability for locally elected officials.[30] This lack of accountability was also a result of nonpartisanship. As mentioned above, nonpartisanship reduced party discipline and, consequently, made it more difficult for citizens to hold political leaders accountable.

Fourth, the reformers did not hinder the machines greatly in those cities where they were able to institute only a few structural and electoral reforms. However, where changes were effected, over time their cumulative impact was substantial. Even in those cities where the machines continued to win elections, their power was drastically diminished to the point where it was difficult to govern. The rising tide of unionism and the shift of power to the bureaucrats were two factors that cut deeply into the political power of the machine.

A fifth impact of the reform movement was the increase in fragmentation in metropolitan areas. The reformers tended to favor the autonomy of suburban governments, which increased the number of government units. In addition, they solved the problem of initiating new services or resuscitating inefficient ones by creating autonomous special service districts. (A special district is an autonomous service delivery organization that is usually unifunctional. Most special districts collect taxes or user fees to finance their operations. The most common form of special district in the United States is the school district.) The growth of special districts not only added to government fragmentation and proliferation, but it also removed service delivery further from control of locally elected officials, thus reducing accountability and helping to exacerbate the conflicts between agencies and their clients.[31]

## Conclusions

The rules governing urban political life in many cities were changed drastically as a result of the reform movement. The changes initiated by the reformers rearranged a number of political relationships by increasing the power of some actors while decreasing the power of others.

In many respects the reformers "cleaned up" local government and helped to return some of its integrity. They accomplished this by pressing for reforms that depoliticized decision-making, reduced corruption, and increased the quality and credentials of the people who came to work for local government. These reforms were not without their drawbacks. Some observers have pointed out that cities that adopted the reform proposals often lacked strong leadership, provided little accountability between the bureaucrats and their clients, and developed a bureaucratic class bias against lower-income minority citizens.

These criticisms have prompted some people to suggest that urban governments need a second reform movement. Such a reform movement would be designed to modify some of the inequities that have emerged in bureaucratic accountability, agency-client conflict, city council representation, and decentralization of political power. These issues are the subject of the next two chapters.

## NOTES

1. The account follows generally from Edward C. Banfield and James Q. Wilson, *City Politics* (New York: Random, 1963), pp. 138–150.
2. Ibid., p. 148.
3. Ibid., p. 148.
4. Ibid., p. 149.
5. Ibid., p. 150.
6. See Eugene C. Lee, *The Politics of Nonpartisanship* (Los Angeles: University of California, 1960). Also see Charles R. Adrian, "Some General Characteristics of Nonpartisan Elections," *American Political Science Review* 46 (September 1952): 766–776; and Charles R. Adrian, "A Typology of Nonpartisan Elections," *Western Political Quarterly* (June 1959): 449–58.
7. For a discussion of this issue, see Clinton B. Jones, "The Impact of Local Election Systems on Black Political Representation," *Urban Affairs Quarterly* 11 (March 1976): 346–56. Also see Albert K. Karnig, "Black Representation on City Councils: The Impact of District Elections and Socioeconomic Factors," *Urban Affairs Quarterly* 12 (December 1976): 223–242; and Banfield and Wilson, *City Politics*, pp. 94, 95, 307, 308.
8. *Zimmerman* v. *McKeithen*, 485 F.2d 1287, 5th Circuit (1973).
9. Banfield and Wilson, *City Politics*, p. 44; and Joseph F. Zimmerman, *The Federated City: Community Control in Large Cities* (New York: St. Martin's, 1972), pp. 74–79, 91–92, and 96–97.
10. For an elaboration of the reformers' objectives, see Jean L. Stinchcombe, *Reform and Reaction: City Politics in Toledo* (Belmont, Calif.: Wadsworth, 1968), p. 27.
11. The history of the National Municipal League and the details of the Model City Charter are skillfully summarized in Thomas A. Flinn, *Local Government and Politics* (Glenview, Ill.: Scott, Foresman, 1970), pp. 136–141. The League itself publishes a substantial library of technical materials.
12. James Q. Wilson, "Politics and Reform in American Cities," in *American Government Annual, 1962–63* (New York: Holt, Rinehart and Winston, 1962), pp. 37–52.

13. For an interesting study of nonprofessionals in politics, see James Q. Wilson, *The Amateur Democrat* (Chicago: University of Chicago Press, 1963).
14. Stinchcombe, *Reform and Reaction,* especially the concluding chapter.
15. Thomas R. Dye, *Politics in States and Communities,* 4th ed. (Englewood Cliffs, N.J.: Prentice-Hall, 1981), pp. 271–72.
16. For a detailed account of the kinds of nonpartisan political systems, see Dye, *Politics in States and Communities,* pp. 271–76.
17. Duane Lockard, *The Politics of State and Local Government* (New York: Macmillan, 1963), p. 247.
18. Ibid., pp. 247–52.
19. Robert L. Lineberry and Edmund P. Fowler, "Reformism and Public Policies in American Cities," *The American Political Science Review* 61, 3 (September 1967): 701–16. Citation at p. 714.
20. See also the discussion in Dye, *Politics in States and Communities,* pp. 380–81.
21. Stinchcombe, *Reform and Reaction,* p. 229.
22. Ibid., p. 229.
23. Ibid., p. 231.
24. Ibid., p. 321.
25. Ibid., p. 321.
26. Ibid., p. 223.
27. Samuel P. Hays, "The Politics of Reform in Municipal Government in the Progressive Era," *Pacific Northwest Quarterly* 55 (1964): 157–69.
28. See Theodore J. Lowi, "Machine Politics—Old and New," *The Public Interest* 9 (Fall 1967): 83–92.
29. Raymond Wolfinger and John Osgood Field, "Political Ethos and the Structure of City Government," *The American Political Science Review* 60 (June 1966): 306–26. Also see Thomas R. Dye and Susan A. MacManus, "Predicting City Government Structure," *American Journal of Political Science* 20 (May 1976): 257–71.
30. Lowi, "Machine Politics—Old and New," pp. 83–92.
31. John J. Harrigan, *Political Change in the Metropolis,* 2nd ed. (Boston: Little, Brown, 1981), pp. 111–12.

# 6. CITIZEN PARTICIPATION AND DECENTRALIZATION

On August 11, 1965, a Los Angeles police officer named Lee Minikus, acting on a tip from a truck driver, pursued and stopped a young black man named Marquette Frye for speeding, driving without a license, and driving while intoxicated. By the time Minikus and his partner had arrested Marquette Frye an angry crowd had gathered, and before the night was over, the Watts district of Los Angeles was engulfed in a series of street riots. By the next morning millions of Americans across the nation knew that Watts was the name of a small section in south-central Los Angeles. Many Americans also surmised that neither race relations nor politics in urban areas would ever be the same again.[1]

In 1966 riots erupted in Cleveland and Chicago, and in 1967 they spread across the country and flared up in both large and small urban areas. Large cities such as Newark, Milwaukee, Detroit, Houston, Cincinnati, Phoenix, and Atlanta experienced burning, looting, and violence; but so did smaller cities such as Tampa, Florida; Plainfield, New Jersey; Paterson, New Jersey; New Haven, Connecticut; Grand Rapids, Michigan; Jackson, Mississippi; and Cambridge, Maryland.[2]

During the first nine months of 1967, 164 disorders were recorded by the National Advisory Commission on Civil Disorders. Eight of these were classified as major in terms of their violence and damage, while 33 were classified as serious but did not reach the level of violence or damage sustained in the other riots.[3]

The importance of the urban riots of the late 1960s to an understanding of contemporary urban politics cannot be minimized. These outbreaks of discontent and distrust reverberated throughout city governments and helped to pave the way for the election of several young, enthusiastic mayors—Carl Stokes in Cleveland, John Lindsay in New York, Kevin White in Boston, Kenneth Gibson in Newark, and Richard Hatcher in Gary.

The increase in the demand for citizen participation in local government signaled the end of an era when citizens were willing to continue playing traditional roles in politics. The urban riots of the 1960s were an example of changing attitudes. Disgruntled citizens were less willing to express their unhappiness through the traditional channels of voting, complaining, and letter writing. More non-traditional styles began to emerge in the form of direct participation—sit-ins, picketing, and mass demonstrations. The citizens engaging in the protest activities felt that their views were not being adequately represented in local decision-making. More active citizen participation was one means of increasing their involvement. This increased activity helped to redistribute some of the political resources in the city and gave citizen groups more power than they had previously exercised.

The riots of the mid-1960s were not the sole cause of the increasing unhappiness of citizens with their local government. Racial discrimination, police brutality, lack of trust in government, unsanitary and unsafe housing, and heightened expectations in the form of government promises and programs were contributing factors as well. In addition, the federal government encouraged and subsidized citizen participation in a number of programs at the local level, giving citizens the feeling that the federal government was supportive of their efforts to have a voice in local policymaking.

This chapter and the next analyze four areas in which city politics and administration have changed as a result of the emerging urban problems of the 1960s and early 1970s. These problems led to demands to increase citizen participation in government, to decentralize decision-making in cities, to hold urban bureaucrats more accountable for their actions, and to equalize service delivery among neighborhoods. While all four of these areas are interrelated to some extent, they will be examined individually.

## CITIZEN PARTICIPATION

Citizen participation became one of the most hotly debated issues in urban politics in the 1960s. The issue, however, is as old as democracy itself. It surfaced during the era of the Greek city-states, where it was believed that every citizen should be allowed to participate in decision-making. This concept, sometimes referred to as primary democracy, is practiced in relatively small political jurisdictions where all citizens can have a voice in decision-making. New England town meetings and citizen group associations are typical of this type of citizen participation.

With the few exceptions mentioned above, American government has never functioned as a primary democracy. Because of our size and number we have a republican form of government in which elected representatives speak and vote for their constituents. During the 1960s serious doubts were raised in many urban areas about how representative of minority views elected council members were. This, in turn, led to efforts to find other techniques for citizen involvement in the political and administrative process.

### Citizen Participation 1960–Present

The 1960s was a turbulent decade in American urban history. Never before had so much attention been focused on the cities and their problems.

Several events helped to highlight the plight of the cities during this period. In his 1960 campaign for the presidency, John F. Kennedy had spent a good deal of time in West Virginia seeking to win that state's votes in the Democratic primary. During his numerous trips to the state, he was impressed with the incredible amount of poverty he witnessed and was determined to do something about it once he became president. Soon after taking office Kennedy assigned a number of staff people to study the problem and bring him policy suggestions about how to alleviate poverty in the country. According to Daniel P. Moynihan, former Kennedy aide and now Senator from New York, the poverty issue would have become the focal point of the 1964 legislative agenda in Congress had Kennedy lived.[4]

A second event that propelled the poverty issue to the front of the legislative calendar was the publication in 1962 of Michael Harrington's book, *The Other America*.[5] In his work, Harrington carefully detailed the condition of 40–50 million Americans who were living at or below the poverty level. Furthermore, Harrington argued, this group was virtually invisible, since no one was paying attention to their plight. This book helped to mobilize people both within and without the Kennedy administration to develop programs to assist the poor.

The culmination of this concern for poor people occurred in 1964, during the Johnson administration, with the passage of the Economic Opportunity Act, the keystone of Johnson's War on Poverty. The act authorized Community Action Programs in Title II-A. These programs were to be implemented by Community Action Agencies, which were charged with achieving three objectives in their urban communities:

1. Provide and improve public services to the poor.
2. Mobilize public and private resources to help alleviate poverty.
3. Involve the poor as much as possible in implementing programs in their communities.[6]

A third factor that helped to focus our thinking on urban areas was the speed with which urban riots broke out across the country. Isolated precipitating incidents that triggered riots in New York in 1964 and Los Angeles in 1965 quickly became a torrent as Newark and Detroit exploded in 1967. In April, 1968, in the wake of Martin Luther King's assassination, another round of riots erupted, and there was no longer any doubt that America's cities had become one of the most serious problems in the country's history.

The National Advisory Commission on Civil Disorders was charged with examining what had happened, why it happened, and what could be done about preventing further violence. In the section of the report on why it happened, the Commission cited three components of white racism that were mainly responsible for the riots: pervasive discrimination and segregation, black migration and white exodus, and black ghettos. In addition they cited three other factors which, when coupled with racism, helped to create the incendiary situation that triggered the riots:

1.  Frustrated hopes—primarily derived from the achievements of the civil rights movement and civil rights legislation and unfulfilled promises of both.
2.  Legitimization of violence—generated mostly by whites who hated and thus terrorized blacks during the civil rights movement in flagrant disregard of statutory and constitutional guarantees against abuse.
3.  Powerlessness—resulting primarily from a feeling of being politically and economically exploited by whites and not being able to gain access to the power centers of government to effect change.[7]

A fourth factor that helped to focus the nation's attention on urban problems was the election of black mayors in a number of large American cities. Carl Stokes in Cleveland, Richard Hatcher in Gary, Kenneth Gibson in Newark, and Walter Washington in Washington, D.C., all helped to establish new role models for aspiring blacks and demonstrated that, where blacks were able to mobilize their resources and vote in blocks, it was possible to achieve goals democratically. These articulate young black mayors began speaking out on urban problems; and they were supported by mayors like Kevin White in Boston, John Lindsay in New York, Joe Alioto in San Francisco, and Jerome Cavanaugh in Detroit. In the 1970s black mayors were also elected in Atlanta, Detroit, and Los Angeles. Urban problems now were fixed on the nation's political agenda by virtue of having elected executives who repeatedly dramatized the problems of the cities.

The final factor that publicized the urban condition in the 1960s was the rapidly growing belief that despite all the social legislation, the national government commitment, and the huge sums of money expended, nothing substantial was happening to improve the lives of low-income, minority, inner-city residents. In fact, some critics viewed the War on Poverty and many of the urban-oriented social programs as having a deleterious effect on poor people, since they raised expectations far beyond what could be achieved.[8]

These factors all helped to highlight for residents of inner cities the need to organize themselves to influence the actors and institutions that affected their lives. The variety of techniques by which citizens began this process came to be known as citizen participation.

## Definitions of Citizen Participation

A precise definition of citizen participation is difficult to arrive at. Jean and Edgar Cahn view citizen participation in terms of citizens having enough information to participate in initial decisions on the allocation of resources and creation of institutions that will affect their lives.[9] Others, like Milton Kotler, see participation as being linked to neighborhoods and local self-rule, where residents share power and participate in the performance of certain municipal functions.[10] Finally, there is a definition offered by Sherry Arnstein, who writes:

Citizen participation is a categorical term for citizen power. It is the redistribution of power that enables the have-not citizens, presently excluded from the political and economic processes, to be deliberately included in the future. It is the strategy by which the have-nots join in determining how information is shared, goals and policies are set, tax resources are allocated, programs are operated, and benefits like contracts and patronage are parceled out. In short, it is the means by which they can induce significant societal reform which enables them to share in the benefits of the affluent society.[11]

In the 1960s bureaucrats, elected officials, and citizens were all searching for something more than definitions to resolve the often heated conflict over the allocation of power at the local level. Citizen participation became a rallying cry for many urban residents in the 1960s, and they sought to broaden the scope of the term beyond the mere involvement in local decision-making. For many citizens the term implied opening up the whole structure of government and providing for a redistribution of power and authority. Whereas bureaucrats viewed citizen participation as a static concept, many residents in the communities saw it as a strategy for changing their lives. Bureaucrats attempted to treat citizen participation as a one-time aberration that would pacify angry citizens and quickly pass like a fad. Citizens quickly dispelled this notion by arguing that citizen participation needed to become an ongoing process for all issues on a continuing basis. In other words, local government officials saw citizen participation as an end, something to give to the community to appease them and to satisfy federal guidelines, while citizen activists viewed it as a means of opening up the process of government decision-making. Citizens sought to establish it as an ongoing component of the political process.

## What Is Citizen Participation?

Just about every article, monograph, report, and book that deals with citizen participation asks this question. The routine answers indicate that citizen participation runs along a continuum from voting to violence, with a number of variations in between. These include: letter writing, interest-group activity, organizing community groups, testifying before the city council, lobbying, picketing, non-violent demonstrations, and obstructionist tactics such as sit-ins.[12] Citizen participation became a major issue in urban politics in much the same way as decentralization. With all of the contending forces trying to manipulate the concept of citizen participation to meet their needs, confusion prevailed.

Title II of the Economic Opportunity Act called for "maximum feasible participation" of the local residents in Community Action Agencies. A number of citizens began to organize themselves to take over the boards of community-based organizations. In many instances problems arose because the community organizations being funded were either developing programs that the city opposed or because inexperienced personnel were receiving funds and not administering programs in a competent manner. In Chicago a neighborhood gang was able to obtain poverty funds to develop youth programs in a church. It was alleged that members of one gang were using federal money to buy weapons. Mayor Richard Daley was incensed that young, unemployed gang members should be receiving federal funds to run community-based programs that he felt could better be administered by city agencies. Similar problems arose with Child Development in Mississippi and the Black Arts Theater in Harlem. Congress, which was becoming increasingly apprehensive about some of the community action programs, began holding hearings to determine the extent of city hall discontent.

In 1967 Congress, apparently responding to numerous local government officials unhappy with their federally funded poverty programs, passed the Green Amendment, named after congresswoman Edith Green of Oregon. The Green Amendment gave local government officials the option of taking over control of the community action agencies, provided that a third of the board members represented the poor. In this way Congress hoped to eliminate some of the more distasteful programs and return much of the responsibility for oversight to mayors and council members.[13]

Understanding what Congress, city hall, and community activists meant by citizen participation became increasingly difficult. In 1969, Sherry Arnstein, an urban consultant, published an article entitled, "A Ladder of Citizen Participation," which helped to clarify what all actors meant when they talked about citizen participation.[14] In her article Arnstein developed a typology of eight levels, ranging from nonparticipation to citizen power.[15] (See Figure 6.1).

1. *Manipulation* Citizens are appointed to advisory boards and committees so they can be educated or coerced by local officials. Rather than citizen participation you have public relations.

2. *Therapy* Powerlessness is synonymous with an illness. Citizens are brought together to discuss ways of changing their behavior rather than changing the behavior of public officials whose actions have often caused the problem at hand. Citizens feel they are very active in decision-making but are, in effect, being conned. Public housing tenant meetings are a good example.

3. *Informing* Citizens are made aware of their rights, responsibilities, and options in a one-way flow of information from government officials to citizens. This information usually comes too late to be effective, and there is no prospect for bargaining or compromising. Model Cities planning meetings in the 1960s were reflective of this level.

4. *Consultation* This can be an important component of citizen participation. Citizen opinions are solicited through surveys, hearings, and neighborhood meetings. However, if no process is established for incorporating these views into policy decisions then consultation becomes a superficial technique. Many of the early urban renewal programs used this technique.

5. *Placation* Some poor residents of the community are picked to sit on police, education, housing, or health boards. These people

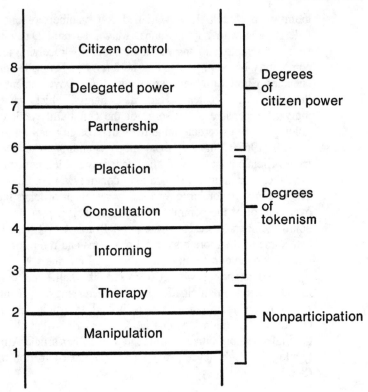

FIGURE 6.1
Eight Rungs on a Ladder of Citizen Participation

Source: Reprinted by permission of the *Journal of the American Institute of Planners,* volume 35, number 4, July, 1969.

    are not accountable to their constituents and are likely to be out-voted on any of the boards where they are represented. City Demonstration Agencies (CDAs) created under the Model Cities Program were examples of this approach.

6. *Partnership*  Power is shared between citizens and local officials. This is arrived at through negotiation, so both parties understand their responsibilities in the decision-making process. Neither party can alter these arrangements unilaterally. Both citizens and government officials are accountable to their respective constituencies. The policy-making committee of the Philadelphia CDA was an example of partnership after citizens were given five of the eleven seats on the committee.

7. *Delegated Power*  In some situations negotiations between citizens and officials result in citizens achieving the balance of power in decision-making. At this level it is the public officials who seek to initiate discussions on new programs and policies. Several

Model Cities programs in Dayton, Hartford, and St. Louis were cited by Arnstein as having achieved this step on the ladder.

8. *Citizen Control*  Here, residents exercise control over a program or an organization, including decisions that affect how the program or organization can be changed. Neighborhood corporations where access to funds was unimpeded were the best examples of citizen control.[16]

The Arnstein typology is important because it shows that not all forms of participation involve power sharing between citizens and bureaucrats. In fact, the types of participation at the bottom of the ladder—manipulation and therapy—can benefit the bureaucrats by allowing them to manipulate or co-opt citizens into participation with no modification in agency goals or behavior. In many community action programs, potentially critical and activist citizen leaders were co-opted or neutralized because they were brought inside the decision-making process. In other cases, citizen leaders determined that it was more important for them to remain outside of the government in order to accurately reflect the views of community residents. In these instances the community leaders continued to push for more power sharing arrangements, which Arnstein labeled "degrees of citizen power."

The Arnstein typology has been used by numerous community organizations as a guide in their negotiations with city officials. It has helped many interested parties to negotiate with a common understanding of how much power was being redistributed and how it was to be exercised.

## Measuring Citizen Participation

One area where many problems arose was the issue of measuring participation. Research has shown that people with higher socioeconomic status (higher income, better jobs, and higher educational achievement) are more likely to participate in both social and political activities than are people of lower socioeconomic status.[17] Most of the federal programs discussed above were designed to involve low-income, inner-city, minority residents who the Congress and federal bureaucrats felt had been excluded from involvement in local decision-making for too long. When programs were implemented and citizen participation mechanisms were in place, it was felt, neighborhood residents would seize the opportunity to become involved. The results were quite mixed. While no federal officials or legislation specified what the optimal level of participation should be, it was evident from early programs that formal mechanisms for involving citizens were not reaching even minimal expectations.

Early in the poverty program, neighborhood residents were asked to elect representatives to serve on the Community Action boards. The results were dismal and allowed critics to assert that the poor were not interested in participation and did not want to help determine their future. The turnouts in selected cities were: Philadelphia 2.7 percent, Los Angeles 0.7 percent, Boston 2.4 percent, Cleveland 4.2 percent, and Kansas City, Mo. 5 percent.[18]

Others commented that these were new programs that proposed democratic techniques for achieving desired objectives, and it would take time for poorer and less-educated citizens to fully comprehend the potential power being placed at their disposal.

Some defenders of citizen groups saw elements of conspiracy in the low voter turnouts. They viewed the low turnouts as the natural result of poor scheduling of meetings and lackluster efforts to spread information about meetings and elections. Meetings held during normal working hours excluded all residents of the neighborhood who worked. Tacking notices on trees or sending them home with schoolchildren represented a "scatter gun" method for reaching all potential residents. Roland C. Warren summed it up well at a conference:

> Never again should we ask the slum residents of 150 American cities to come out to endless rounds of frustrating meetings, to be lectured on what a splendid opportunity they have to improve their neighborhoods if they will only participate responsibly in decision making; never again should we expect them to jump through the same old participation hoops, with the help of the same old professional people at their elbows telling them why this or that innovation is impractical; never again should we promise them the improvement of conditions of living in 150 cities for 575 million dollars a year. It is an insult to their own intelligence and integrity.[19]

Citizen participation is very difficult to measure without precisely stating what it is we want to achieve. Citizen participation under certain circumstances can be successful if large numbers of people attend meetings regardless of the outcome of the issue. In other instances, a small number of knowledgeable and persistent individuals can be very effective in achieving desired results, but they will appear elitist to outsiders because large numbers of community residents are not participating.

Two of the more publicized programs of the 1970s—Revenue Sharing and Community Development Block Grant (CDBG)—have been analyzed on several occasions to determine how effective they were in meeting their citizen participation requirements.

In the CDBG program, both the Brookings Institution Study and the HUD internal review concluded that the required levels of citizen participation were being met. This differed somewhat from the survey conducted by ACIR and the International City Management Association, in which they found many cities were not fulfilling the requirements for public hearings. In reviewing the impact of citizen participation on CDBG programs, HUD and Brookings both found that citizen involvement was influencing the level of social service expenditures as well as the programs and activities selected for action. Still, HUD's review found high levels of dissatisfaction with the citizen participation program because it was unable to generate greater involvement of lower-income citizens. Those who did participate felt that many cities and counties could have paid more attention to the comments and suggestions made by the neighborhood residents.[20]

In the Revenue Sharing bill, passed in 1972, citizen participation was not a major priority. This was changed, with greatly strengthened provisions added to the 1976 reenactment. Caputo and Cole surveyed chief executive officers of cities over 50,000 during 1973 and 1974. They found that an "unexpectedly large number of cities have experienced some degree of citizen participation during their General Revenue Sharing decision making processes."[21]

The General Accounting Office (GAO) and the National Science Foundation (NSF) conducted or funded several studies of General Revenue Sharing (GRS). In a number of cases the impact of citizen participation was a major issue analyzed by the studies.

The NSF-funded studies found some positive results from citizen participation activities. One study found more citizen participation in large cities; active groups in the GRS process usually had been funded by earlier federal programs, and the use of public hearings helped public officials to better understand the needs of local residents. However, it was also determined that after the first year the number of public hearings declined, indicating that public involvement in GRS decisions might also diminish.[22]

The federal involvement in citizen participation has not always helped us to understand this issue, but it has taught us a number of things about this extremely complex subject. First, we have learned that the federal government does not have any better definition of citizen participation than state and local officials, neighborhood residents, or interested scholars. As a result, different agencies requiring the implementation of citizen participation processes do not prescribe a uniform set of standards for doing so.

Second, agencies are required to monitor citizen participation activities on a regular basis to determine if they are being implemented according to the law or the regulations. Moreover, government agencies such as GAO, NSF, and the Office of Revenue Sharing have conducted or funded numerous studies to monitor citizen participation activities.

Third, citizen participation requirements have not always been greeted enthusiastically by state and local government officials. Federal officials monitoring from above and neighborhood residents applying pressure from below have helped to insure that the rights of citizens to participate have not been flagrantly violated.

Fourth, neither the federal government nor the state and local governments have been successful in trying to measure citizen participation in an effort to make it more effective. The diverse nature of the programs, localities, public officials, and citizen groups have made the task virtually impossible.[23]

## The Federal Government and Citizen Participation

The federal government has been involved in citizen participation activities in local government for a number of years. The most publicized of these activities was the "maximum feasible participation" clause of the Economic Opportunity Act of 1964. However, several other federal programs required citizen participation even before the War on Poverty was launched. Three of the most notable were the Urban Renewal Program, the Workable

Program for Community Improvement, and the Juvenile Delinquency Demonstration Projects.

This earlier type of citizen participation was quite different from that of the 1960s, in which citizen participation became much more radical as liberals and civil rights activists pushed for more social reform. Most of the participation in these earlier programs was in the form of commissions, bureaus, and agencies made up of urban professionals. Planners, bankers, lawyers, ministers, business executives, and educators populated the citizen advisory bodies. Most of these advisors were white, middle-class, and nonresidents of the communities where the programs were to be implemented.

> A major purpose of this kind of citizen involvement, in the view of many federal and local officials, was often to promote community understanding of a controversial project and to build popular support for its implementation. Another objective was therapy or self-help, in the sense that public representatives would be able to articulate needs and to assist in shaping remedial measures for affected areas.[24]

Two years after the War on Poverty began, the Johnson administration initiated the Model Cities Program, which expanded the practice of federally mandated citizen participation. Instead of requiring "maximum feasible participation," the Model Cities Program called for "widespread citizen participation" in community action programs. These programs were centralized in city hall, but neighborhood organizations could, in some cases, approve or veto grant proposals that affected their areas. The usual process was to elect citizens to Model Cities Commissions, which in turn would become the negotiating agent between the city and the residents.

During the 1970s citizen participation requirements in federal legislation began expanding at a rapid rate. Each of the following programs required the responsible agencies to hold hearings, involve citizens, or "seek consultation with affected parties" in implementing the mandates of the act:

Coastal Zone Management Act (1972)

Headstart Economic Opportunity and Community Partnership Act (1974)

Resource Conservation and Recovery Act (1976)

Housing and Community Development Act (1974)

Federal Water Pollution Control Act Amendments (1972)

Regional Development Act (1975)

Federal mandates for citizen involvement reached their peak, in one respect, in the General Revenue Sharing legislation passed in 1972 and reenacted in 1976.[25] The original act covered almost *39,000* units of government and required recipients to publish reports on planned and actual use of their revenue sharing funds. State and local governments were required to follow the same procedures in expending revenue sharing funds as they did in expending their own funds. This meant public hearings, public notices, and, in some cases, open meetings. Many citizen groups complained to the Office of Revenue Sharing that the public hearings were being held late in the process—after the major decisions were made. To remedy this, the 1976 reenactment legislation required both a proposed-use hearing, early in the decision process, and a budget hearing later in the process, when all points of view had been heard, but prior to the final decision on budget allocations.

In 1979 the Advisory Commission on Intergovernmental Relations (ACIR) released a report analyzing the scope and involvement of the federal government in mandating citizen participation activities at the state and local level.[26] ACIR reported that 31 percent, or 155 of 498, federal grants to state and local governments required some form of citizen participation. These 155 programs accounted for over 80 percent of federal grant expenditures in FY 1977.

## Summary

Citizen participation has had an impact upon local government activities and officials. Mayors, county executives, and city managers have become involved in helping to implement the process of citizen participation in their communities. This has meant working closely with their own executive branch personnel as well as with citizen groups in the communities.

Building a trust relationship between citizens and government is an important factor in developing a citizen participation program. However, increased citizen participation can represent a threat to the administrative and political power of the bureaucrats. As citizens become more involved in decision-making, bureaucrats become less powerful in the amount of administrative discretion they exercise. Furthermore, as citizen participation opened up the process of government, neighborhood residents have gained greater access to information about programs and policies and have been able to discuss and negotiate issues with bureaucrats and elected officials with more knowledge and confidence than in the past. Bureaucrats have slowly come around to understanding that they need to produce information in a manner that is readable by lay people as well as by professionals capable of understanding the technical aspects of the reports.

Bureaucrats have also viewed the rising tide of citizen participation as a potential threat to their job status, promotion, policy development responsibilities, and accountability issues. Fearful that dissatisfied citizens might blame bureaucrats for their problems, the bureaucrats responded by closing ranks and reducing contacts with citizens. Many of these problems have been overcome with the help of mayors and council members who reduced tensions and smoothed over rough transition periods.[27]

Council members have also found themselves faced with a dilemma concerning citizen participation. Some elected council members viewed citizen participation as a new means for communication with constituents and as a device for improving relations with numerous citizen groups in their communities. Other council members have seen citizen participation as a threat to their power base and a technique that markedly slows up the process of government decision-making. This latter group of council members sometimes saw themselves as being held hostage by a small group of well-organized, highly vocal citizens who threatened to oust the council member each time he or she voted against the group's interest. The council members, for their part, could never be sure of who really spoke for the community and how representative these highly vocal citizen leaders were.

Because citizen participation has become an ongoing process in many local governments, it has changed as programs, people, and issues changed. For this reason we will probably be unable to resolve some of the arguments for and against citizen participation that have contributed to much of the debate in urban politics over the past twenty years.

The major arguments advanced for developing a meaningful citizen participation program can be summarized as follows:[28]

1. CP is consistent with democratic theory. It increases the numbers of people participating in decision-making, which means more citizens have access to more and better information. It increases the alternatives for sound decision making.
2. CP helps to develop leaders from the community who might otherwise not have emerged to espouse a cause.
3. CP creates both political and social networks that are essential to building a community.
4. CP is psychologically rewarding for those who participate. It reduces feelings of powerlessness and creates feelings of efficacy.
5. CP makes local government appear more legitimate to neighborhoods and their residents. People believe they have access to government and that officials will listen to their point of view.
6. CP creates a feeling of pride in a program or a project once it is completed.

The major arguments against citizen participation are:[29]

1. CP, under the best of circumstances, is likely to only make a small impact upon the physical planning and development of the city.
2. CP tends to heighten interest in local issues to the detriment of citywide concerns.
3. CP is never completely, and often not fairly, representative of the range of community interests. Single issues with short life spans tend to be favored, while most individuals avoid participation and involvement.
4. CP creates many problems while it is trying to solve others. Competition among factions in the community often increases when CP mechanisms are being established.
5. Organizing citizens into groups for action is not universally accepted by local officials. Once organized and operating, these groups slow down the process of government, which further alienates public officials.

## DECENTRALIZATION

One of the strongest pressures applied by community groups upon city officials was the movement to locate local government offices out in the neighborhoods, to make government more visible and more accessible. The concept describing this citizen demand was called decentralization of government.

The movement for decentralization stirred up a number of controversies between local public officials and community leaders. The decentralization movement began from a feeling that too many decisions in city government were being made in central offices downtown by officials who were unaware of or insensitive to the needs of residents in the neighborhoods. In some places the demand for decentralization appeared confused, since in some large geographic areas, such as Los Angeles and Orange Counties in California, the county government had been decentralized for decades. In other smaller political jurisdictions the problem centered on specific services and their accessibility. In these communities the demand for decentralization was directed at local officials who responded that services such as law enforcement, fire protection, and education—the very ones being criticized by community leaders as ineffective and unresponsive—had historically been decentralized.

By the late 1960s it became apparent that the concept of decentralization meant quite different things to local public officials and neighborhood groups. In essence, the concept of decentralization focused on how power was to be distributed and exercised in the urban political community. It took the political actors at the local level a decade to reach a common understanding of what was at issue and how it could be resolved. In the 1980s there are still numerous political jurisdictions where the issues of political and administrative decentralization have not been resolved.

## Types of Decentralization

Decentralization takes many different forms and is viewed in different ways by the various political, administrative, and community actors in the city. One way of classifying decentralization is to establish a typology that categorizes the range of decentralization possibilities according to how much power is devolved.

### Geographical

Geographical decentralization usually occurs when a local government agency, mayor, or city manager decides to locate an agency field office closer to the clients being served. In many cases the agency will lease an abandoned store. This type of office contains only a few staff people, whose main function it is to receive complaints and pass them along to the responsible departments. The field office staff has no political or administrative power with which to exercise discretion. These offices are usually city grievance centers, or complaint centers. Citizens entering the office fill out forms describing their complaints and are told they will hear from the appropriate agency in the near future. If the plaintiff receives a response, and a serious effort is made to redress the grievance, then the word will quickly spread about the satisfactory service and other clients will begin to use the office. If the complaint goes unanswered, or there is an unsatisfactory response, this information is also likely to circulate throughout the community. If several community residents experience similar dissatisfaction, this is often followed by declining interest in the services of the field office.

## Administrative

Administrative decentralization involves the transfer of several people to a field office. These can be either from a government agency or from several agencies. The major difference between geographical and administrative decentralization concerns the administrative discretion vested in the field employees. Unlike employees in a geographical arrangement, these employees are empowered to make administrative decisions and can exercise some discretionary power where policy and program implementation is concerned. A parole officer might allow a parolee out of the state for a short period of time to attend a funeral, or an administrator might exercise discretion in determining the eligibility for a vocational rehabilitation program. In administrative decentralization some administrative power and discretion has been devolved to the field office, but the majority of power remains with the main office officials. Examples of administrative decentralization would be "little city halls" or multiservice centers. Little city halls were a response to the recommendations in the Kerner Commission Report. They are agency branch offices that attempt to improve the delivery of services to neighborhoods as well as to establish better relations with community residents. Both Kevin White in Boston and John Lindsay in New York established little city halls throughout their cities. However, both mayors retained power over the services by vesting control with their own officials and not with neighborhood residents.[30]

Multiservice centers usually occupy large facilities and provide a fairly complete in-house array of services to a specific neighborhood. In the late 1960s and early 1970s Baltimore and Chicago established a number of multiservice centers, some of which were very successful in meeting citizen needs.[31]

## Political

Political decentralization implies a shift in power and authority from city or county agencies to recognized community groups. Elected and/or appointed officials of the community will participate with public officials in the development and implementation of policy. In political decentralization there is an implied parity of power between the community and the city.

Neither can impose its programs on the other, and occasionally a veto power is granted to the community. Political decentralization is characterized, in theory, by consensus and cooperation rather than conflict, but it also represents a new set of power relationships, which many of the actors require time to adjust to. An example of this sharing of power occurs when a local community group screens candidates for principal of the local school and the superintendent selects one of the candidates recommended by the community board.

### Community Control

The last category in the typology, and the one in which there is the greatest shift in power from government agency to community group, is called community control. Under community control there is a devolution of power to a community-selected subunit of government that makes policy, allocates resources, vetoes unwanted government intrusions, and exercises a great deal of autonomy over a specific territorial unit. Ideally, such a unit should raise its own revenues from which to allocate resources in making policy decisions. Unfortunately, few, if any, inner city areas have the wealth to provide a tax base sufficient for service delivery. Hence, few urban communities have attained financial as well as political autonomy.

Milton Kotler, who wrote one of the first books on neighborhood government with a prescription for community control, left the issue of finances ambiguous. Kotler suggested funding from three sources: taxation, foundations, and gifts, none of which are realistic for large-scale units or for neighborhoods over a long period of time.[32] In fact, the ideal community control example is the incorporated middle-class suburban community. Many of these jurisdictions exercise both the financial and political autonomy so avidly sought but rarely attained by numerous lower-income, minority communities.[33]

The decentralization typology illustrates the range of techniques available to local governments considering a reallocation of political and/or administrative power. It also helps to define some of the areas of conflict between community groups and government officials seeking to reach accommodation on decentralization issues.[34] Community groups seeking to increase their power through decentralization have usually sought either the political or community control type of decentralization. Local government officials trying to minimize any shift in power away from their agencies were willing to discuss decentralization as it was embodied in the geographical and administrative types. From the mid 1960s through the late 1970s, decentralization was frequently on the political agenda of many large city governments. For most of this period, community groups and government officials were discussing different interpretations of the same management concept, since each actor realized that any form of decentralization was likely to increase the power of one group at the expense of the other.[35]

## Other Models of Decentralization

Other typologies of decentralization emerged as scholars began to study this politically volatile issue. Eric Nordlinger examined the little city halls established by Boston Mayor Kevin White. Nordlinger created four models to explain the ratio of control in public services between bureaucrats and community groups. His four models were called status quo, representational, bureaucratic, and neighborhood.[36]

In the status quo model there is no decentralization, since both the delivery of services and political control are highly centralized. In the representational model political and administrative decision-making are still centralized, but clients representing different areas of the city are represented on

Decentralization of Political Control ⟶

| Decentralization of Delivery of Services | Status Quo Model<br><br>*Examples:*<br>  Autonomous bureaucracies<br>  Functional fiefdoms<br>  Little city halls | Representational Model<br><br>*Examples:*<br>  Client representation<br>  Little city halls |
| --- | --- | --- |
| | Bureaucratic Model<br><br>*Examples:*<br>  Decentralized schools in<br>    New York since 1969;<br>    Detroit since 1970<br>  Little city halls | Neighborhood Government Model<br>*Examples:*<br>Neighborhood corporations<br>Community action agencies<br>Model city councils<br>Demonstration school districts<br>  in New York 1967–69 |

FIGURE 6.2
Categories of Citizen Control and Decentralization
Source: Eric Nordlinger, *Decentralizing the City: A Case Study of Boston's Little City Halls* (Cambridge, MA: MIT Press, 1972), p. 9.

the policymaking bodies for each service. In the bureaucratic model political decision-making remains centralized, but most of the routine administrative tasks are decentralized to field or branch offices, increasing their autonomy and discretion in meeting the needs of clients in their areas.

Finally, there is the neighborhood government model, where both political and administrative decision-making are devolved to designated community groups who are in charge of delivering specific services to clients. This last model is rarely found operating in the United States.

One of the more intricate typologies of decentralization has been proposed by Professor Henry J. Schmandt. He defines decentralization "as a mechanism—an institutionalized governmental arrangement—for the achievement of certain end values. It involves the allocation of authority and responsibility to lower territorially based echelons of the established bureaucracy or to geopolitical levels lower than the large municipality or school district."[37] Schmandt then develops five models of decentralization: exchange, bureaucratic, modified bureaucratic, developmental, and governmental.

The exchange model stresses information, advice, and interaction. It represents a communications model, which ideally should have a two-way flow of information. Plans and policies are made available to residents in local government field offices. Once citizens have had an opportunity to review these documents, their comments and suggestions are transmitted back to the administrative agencies and up the administrative ladder to the decision-makers. The best examples of the model were the mini-city halls established in New York during the Lindsay administration, the poverty program information and referral centers, and urban ombudsmen programs that were initiated in the 1960s and 1970s.

The bureaucratic model involves the delegation of authority to civil servants working in the neighborhoods. This can be either functional by department or territorial, with several services clustered in a single area or district office. In the functional arrangement the use of authority remains fairly static within the department. In the territorial system a district or service manager, who reports to either a top elected or appointed administrative officer, is given responsibility for all these services in an area.

The modified bureaucratic model is similar to the bureaucratic model except that civil servants in the field have responsibilities both to their superiors and, to a lesser extent, to the organized interests in the community. In this model citizen groups exercise much more influence in planning, implementation, personnel decisions, and monitoring of programs. Residents gain some measure of control over programs and people affecting their lives.

The developmental model uses the neighborhood as the basic unit of control. In this model a community development or neighborhood corporation is chartered by the state or federal government but is controlled by the local residents. The Bedford-Stuyvesant Corporation in New York City is an example of such a corporation. The corporation assumes all responsibilities for service delivery as well as economic development and physical rehabilitation activities. The corporation also contracts with city agencies to administer a number of service facilities such as health centers, day care programs, and social service intake centers.

In this model, power has shifted from the local government to the citizens who control the corporation. The local citizens produce and consume both public and private goods. The people chosen to manage the corporation must be capable of servicing the needs of the community while working closely with the local bureaucracy to obtain management contracts for service facilities. In addition, the corporation managers must continuously work with foundations and government agencies on all levels to obtain funding for their programs.

Local residents determine their needs and establish the level and quality of services they deem acceptable for their community. The corporation is given the power to make these decisions, while government agencies devolve certain administrative functions to the corporation. The agencies, however, still exert considerable influence over the corporation with respect to these services and can abrogate the management contracts in order to retain control in instances where the agency feels the corporation has been inefficient or incompetent.

The developmental model appears to be the one preferred by the Reagan administration in its effort to increase neighborhood "capacity-building." Reagan's goal was to allow communities to develop the capability to solve their own problems, not to increase their power or voice in decisions of city-wide bureaucracies.

The final model in the Schmandt typology is the governmental model, in which legally defined subunits of the city are recipients of legally devolved powers. These urban subunits take on many of the political and administrative characteristics of suburban governments. An example occurred in Washington, D.C., in 1967, when the school system created an independent school in the Adams-Morgan area and endowed it with powers to hire its own teachers, determine its own curriculum priorities, purchase its own supplies, and establish its own local school board. A similar experiment was initiated later in southeast Washington, D.C.

While this model devolves the most power to subunits of government, it still faces some of the traditional problems of organizational life. Bureaucracy is essential to any organization's existence, and community groups often learn this the hard way. Thinking their newly won powers will help them eliminate or reduce bureaucracy, they are shocked to find out they have to recruit staff, set pay scales, establish criteria for evaluation and promotion, prepare job descriptions for employees, and maintain both personnel and financial records.[38] Bureaucracy rarely disappears; it just takes on a local orientation. As the neighborhood organization grows and expands its area of operation, it becomes more bureaucratic and seeks to perpetuate itself.

One of the most important consequences of the governmental model was the recruitment and development of local residents into the community organizations. A number of these people quickly displayed leadership abilities and were moved into positions of importance. This process produced a more legitimate organizational structure in the eyes of the local residents and assisted numerous community organizations over the difficult period when they were establishing themselves in the community.

A summary of Schmandt's typology is depicted in Table 6.1, in which Schmandt has related each of the models to the goals often espoused for decentralizing local government.[39]

TABLE 6.1
The Impact of Decentralization Models and Goal Achievement

| Models | Goals | | | | |
|---|---|---|---|---|---|
| | Efficiency | Responsiveness | Participation | Resident Control | Political Mobilization |
| Exchange | High | Low | None | None | None |
| Bureaucratic | High | Low | None | Low | None |
| Modified Bureaucratic | High | Medium | Low | Medium | None |
| Development | High | High | Medium | High | Low |
| Governmental | High | High | Medium | High | Low |

Source: Table I (p.32) in "Decentralization: A Structural Imperative" by Henry J. Schmandt from *Neighborhood Control in the 1970's: Politics, Administration and Citizen Participation* edited by George Frederickson (Chandler). Copyright © 1973 by Harper & Row, Publishers, Inc.

## Other Views of Decentralization

In his book, *Neighborhood Democracy,* Douglas Yates examined seven decentralization experiments in New York and New Haven.[40] Yates suggested that all political systems were characterized by some degree of decentralization and that these characteristics could be ordered according to their degree of decentralization. Yates then identified nine different types of decentralization. These are:[41]

1. Self-help organizations
2. Advisory boards
3. Neighborhood field offices and little city halls
4. Ombudsman structure
5. Multiservice centers
6. Model Cities programs
7. Community corporations
8. Neighborhood health corporations
9. Community school boards

Using the characteristics and types of decentralization, Yates constructed a matrix showing a scale of decentralization in neighborhood experiments. From this matrix Yates drew some generalizations about patterns of decentralization. First, community control has not been successfully implemented in any of the experiments he examined. Second, the degree of power exercised in these different experiments varies inversely with the number of functions and services performed by the local unit. Power tends to become fragmented in the less focused, general purpose governments.[42]

## Arguments for and Against Decentralization

The different typologies tell us as much about the complexities of decentralization as they do about the political and administrative issues in implementing a decentralized system. Several reasons are given for why local governments and citizen groups attempt to develop a decentralized system.

| | Self-help organizations | Advisory boards | Field offices and little city halls | Ombudsmen | Multi-service centers | Model cities | Community corporations | Neighborhood health corporations | Community school boards |
|---|---|---|---|---|---|---|---|---|---|
| 1) Intelligence gathering | | + | + | + | + | + | + | + | + |
| 2) Consultation and advisory planning | No formal powers | + | + | + | + | + | + | + | + |
| 3) Program administration | | | + | + | + | + | + | + | + |
| 4) Political accountability | | | | Sometimes | Sometimes | + | + | + | + |
| 5) Administrative accountability | | | Sometimes | + | + | + | + | + | + |
| 6) Authoritative decision making A) Some | | | | | + | + | + | + | + |
| B) Shared | | | | | | | + | + | + |
| C) Dominant | | | | | | | | | |
| 7) Resources A) Some | | | | | | + | + | + | + |
| B) Shared | | | | | | | | + | + |
| C) Dominant | | | | | | | | | |

FIGURE 6.3
A Scale of Decentralization in Neighborhood Experiments

Source: Reprinted by permission of the publisher, from *Neighborhood Democracy: The Politics and Impacts of Decentralization,* by Douglas Yates, (Lexington, Mass.: Lexington Books, D. C. Heath and Company, Copyright 1973, D. C. Heath and Company).

1. Decentralization improves communications between citizens and government officials by establishing a two-way feedback system so information flows freely in both directions.[43]
2. It improves service delivery systems. By bringing government closer to the people, government officials can better determine the quantity and quality of services needed. Government is more responsive.[44]

3. It redistributes power to the subunits in the city without decentralization, too much power resides in city hall.[45]
4. Psychologically, it is good for city-community relations. People feel that government is closer to them and they can have a greater impact on government to better their lives.[46]
5. Decentralized government is more democratic. People know their government officials and can gain access to them in their field offices.[47]
6. Decentralization involves a number of locally-oriented people and produces an indigenous leadership class in the community.[48]

A number of empirical studies have drawn mixed conclusions about the validity of the arguments for decentralization. Yates, in his analysis of the New York and New Haven experiments, found several reasons to contest the arguments for decentralization.

First, he found that decentralization had little impact on increasing representation or internal democracy within different decentralized arrangements.[49]

Second, Yates found that decentralization did not achieve the oft-stated intention of mobilizing the neighborhood's resources and expanding the neighborhood's power in other political arenas. According to Yates, few of the neighborhood leaders sought to expand their power bases by running for elective office, and few were involved in an intensive campaign to mobilize resources in the true sense of the word. Most of the leaders, according to Yates' study, remained service-oriented and consequently, did not think in terms of broad-based resource development.[50]

Third is the efficacy hypothesis, which states that decentralization of government will decrease the powerlessness felt by community residents. Yates concludes that decentralization does not automatically increase feelings of efficacy among community leaders. However, the large number of variables involved in trying to test this hypothesis produced a wide range of scores on the political efficacy scale.[51] Richard Cole, on the other hand, found evidence that participation increases trust and confidence in government.[52] Two other researchers analyzed national survey research data to see if decentralization reduced feelings of alienation and found little to support this claim.[53]

Those who oppose decentralization within cities and counties have generally agreed on their criticisms. First, before decentralizing, political jurisdictions should attempt pilot projects. However, because this issue has been so volatile for the past twenty years, it has not been feasible to attempt pilot projects at a time when political emotions were running high.

Second, decentralization would disperse the departmental expertise and reduce the economies of scale in the department. These arguments have been countered by those who claim that in spite of all the experts in city or county hall, services have been inadequate or ineffective. By moving these experts into the field, they suggest, perhaps service quality will improve. Furthermore, not all aspects of department activity are subject to economies of scale. In fact, many departmental activities might cost less if they were administered by field offices rather than the headquarters. This system exists already in many urban police departments and school systems.

Third, decentralizing city services might exacerbate racial and ethnic rivalries and encourage poor treatment for minorities. Some low-income city and county residents argue that these rivalries already exist and might be reduced if these people had more access to service agencies. Moreover, since many minorities already feel dissatisfied with public service, it is doubtful that they will experience worse treatment at the hands of a locally directed service operation.

Another argument voiced in opposition to decentralization is that standards of service could disappear and opportunities for corruption might increase. There is no evidence to support the claim that centralized management, with its oversight and auditing functions, has reduced the opportunities for corruption to publicly acceptable levels. Nor, for that matter, have standards been maintained at such a high level that decentralization would seriously impair the current record.[54]

Perhaps the most publicized decentralization effort was the attempt in 1968 by the New York City Board of Education to establish three experimental school districts controlled by local residents. One of these districts was Ocean Hill-Brownsville. Because the type of decentralized control to be exercised by the local school board was not completely agreed to by all the parties concerned, conflicts quickly arose. The local school board began hiring community residents to work in their schools, but the residents were not members of the United Federation of Teachers. Union members working in the Ocean Hill-Brownsville district transferred to other schools. The union objected, and, when a negotiated settlement could not be reached, the teachers went on strike. Police officers eventually had to be called in to quell disturbances and maintain law and order. The Ocean Hill-Brownsville controversy was one of the first indications of how difficult it was going to be to introduce the more radical forms of decentralization.[55]

## Decentralization Today

What is the state of decentralization today? Much of the acrimony of the 1960s and 1970s has faded and been replaced by a more cooperative spirit. Decentralization has undergone a minor revolution, with many cities and counties in the United States having several government agencies that have decentralized to some degree. The majority of the decentralization programs implemented in the past fifteen years have been administrative rather than political, raising the question of whether citizens have, in fact, achieved the devolution of power they sought.

Most efforts to decentralize today are not focused on sharing political power as they were in the 1960s, nor are they directed towards increased neighborhood participation in decision-making. Decentralization has taken the form of restructuring and reorganizing local government to improve communications, monitor services and employees, reduce lead time in delivering services, and bring local government closer to its clients by locating government offices in their communities.

## Conclusions

Decentralization of local government has many consequences for political actors in the system. In most cases decentralization has meant a loss of some power for local executives. As power has been devolved to field offices, executives have had to learn to manage urban areas under a new set of political and administrative arrangements. One problem that arose immediately concerned who was responsible for the actions of city employees. Even though many functions had been decentralized to subordinate officials in the field, when a serious problem arose all interested parties quickly turned to the mayor or chief administrative officer for action. In New York under Mayor Lindsay, community school issues and snow removal problems wound up in the Mayor's office, as did police-community issues under Mayor Rizzo in Philadelphia. It seems that no matter how much power was decentralized, in time of crisis, even a geographically specific one, the mayor was held accountable for finding an acceptable solution.

In some cases decentralization has been initiated by mayors in an effort to circumvent bureaucratic indecision, delay, and red tape. By establishing government outposts in the communities, mayors have forged strong alliances with community leaders. In New York under John Lindsay and Boston under Kevin White, this voluntary decentralization of government reaped strong political rewards for the mayors but tended to alienate the bureaucracy, which felt the mayors had relinquished too much power (any power would have been too much in the late 1960s) without receiving any tangible considerations in return.

Understandably, bureaucrats have not shown a great deal of enthusiasm for most forms of decentralization. Implicit in many decentralization schemes was a loss of power in policymaking and control over how programs were implemented. This struck at the heart of professionalism by undercutting those who had been trained to make policies and who had the experience to coordinate, implement, and monitor programs. With few exceptions, bureaucratic response to decentralization was cool.

In addition, some forms of decentralization posed apparent threats to the basic principles of the civil service system in many local governments. In the more radical forms of decentralization, where there were marked shifts of power from city hall to community-based organizations and service centers, bureaucrats feared a serious erosion of their recently acquired powers. With more and more involvement of community residents in policymaking and implementation, bureaucrats saw that standards for recruitment, hiring, firing, and promotion of workers could be seriously undermined. They were also fearful that federally funded programs that inspired decentralization might disrupt long-established pay scales by ignoring seniority, experience, and overtime provisons.

There was also the question of the allegiance of newly-hired community workers in field offices. Would these employees view themselves as local government employees working in outreach offices, or would they assume the role of community leaders on loan to the government?

Finally, there was the issue of fragmentation. City- or county-wide decentralization created many of the same problems that plagued metropolitan areas with large numbers of local governments. Decentralization increased the number of units each agency, the council, and the executive had to deal with in making and implementing policy. More leaders had to be consulted and accommodated in the bargaining process, and this inevitably delayed the policymaking process. The multiple number of field offices and administrative and political leaders increased the difficulties in coordinating programs and hindered long-range planning for city or county programs.

Few local governments have successfully dealt with the management problems posed by decentralization. The most serious problem remains largely unresolved. That is, how to devolve meaningful power and administrative authority to field offices while at the same time retaining a substantial element of policymaking and oversight control. The problem is not new, and, as has been pointed out, numerous techniques of decentralization have been attempted. This issue will surely be one of the critical problems facing local government managers in the 1980s.

## NOTES

1. For a detailed account of the Watts riot, see Robert Conot, *Rivers of Blood, Years of Darkness* (New York: Bantam Books, 1967).
2. *Report of the National Advisory Commission on Civil Disorders* (New York: Bantam Books, 1968), chap. 1.
3. *Report of the National Advisory Commission,* pp. 5–7.
4. Daniel P. Moynihan, *Maximum Feasible Misunderstanding* (New York: Free Press, 1969).
5. Michael Harrington, *The Other America* (New York: Macmillan, 1962). Also see Dwight MacDonald, "Our Invisible Poor," *New Yorker,* January 19, 1963, pp. 81–132.
6. For a discussion of the politics surrounding the creation of the Economic Opportunity Act, see Moynihan, *Maximum Feasible Misunderstanding*; Richard W. Boone, "Reflections on Citizen Participation and the Economic Opportunity Act," *Public Administration Review* 32 (September 1972): 441–456; and John C. Donovan, *The Politics of Poverty* (New York: Pegasus, 1967). For an account of the first few years of the poverty program, see Joseph A. Kershaw, *Government Against Poverty* (Chicago: Markham Publishing Company, 1970).
7. *Report of the National Advisory Commission on Civil Disorders,* pp. 203–206.
8. See Moynihan, *Maximum Feasible Misunderstanding,* chaps. 5–8, and Kershaw, *Government Against Poverty.* Also see Richard A. Cloward and Frances Fox Piven, *The Politics of Turmoil: Poverty, Race and the Urban Crisis* (New York: Vintage Books, 1965); and Kenneth B. Clark and Jeannette Hopkins, *A Relevant War Against Poverty: A Study of Community Action Programs and Observable Social Change* (New York: Harper and Row, 1968).

9. Edgar S. and Jean Camper Cahn, "Citizen Participation" in *Citizen Participation in Urban Development*, ed. Hans B. Spiegel (Washington: NTL and National Education Association, 1968), pp. 218–222.

10. Milton Kotler, *Neighborhood Government: The Local Foundation of Political Life* (Indianapolis: Bobbs-Merrill, 1969). Also see James V. Cunningham and Milton Kotler, *Building Neighborhood Organizations: A Guidebook* (Notre Dame, Indiana: University of Notre Dame Press, 1983).

11. Sherry R. Arnstein, "A Ladder of Citizen Participation," *Journal of the American Institute of Planners* 35 (July 1969): 216. Reprinted by permission of the *Journal of American Institute of Planners,* volume 35, number 4, July, 1969.

12. See Edgar S. Cahn and Barry A. Passett, eds., *Citizen Participation: Effecting Community Change* (New York: 1971). Also see Praeger "Curriculum Essays on Citizens, Politics, and Administration in Urban Neighborhoods," *Public Administration Review* 32 (October 1972). Several articles in this special issue discuss different types of citizen participation. Also see Stuart Langton, ed., *Citizen Participation Perspectives* (Medford, Mass.: Tufts University, 1979).

13. It is interesting to note that not many local governments acted upon the Green Amendment. In the first six months only about 5 percent of the eligible CAAs were placed under city hall control.

14. Arnstein, "A Ladder of Citizen Participation," pp. 216–224.

15. Ibid., p. 217.

16. Ibid., pp. 218-223. Reprinted by permission of the *Journal of the American Institute of Planners,* volume 35, number 4, July, 1969.

17. Lester Milbrath, *Political Participation* (Chicago: Rand McNally, 1965). Dale Rogers Marshall, "Who Participates in What?" *Urban Affairs Quarterly* 4 (December, 1968): 201–224. Also see Walter Grove and Herbert Costner, "Organizing the Poor: An Evaluation of Strategy," *Social Science Quarterly* 50 (1969): 643–657.

18. Lillian Rubin, "Maximum Feasible Participation, The Origins, Implications, and Present Status," *Poverty and Human Resources Abstracts* (November-December 1967).

19. Roland C. Warren, "The Model Cities Program: Assumptions-Experience-Implications," paper presented at the Annual Forum Programme, National Conference on Social Welfare, Dallas, May 17, 1971.

20. See U.S. Department of Housing and Urban Development, *Citizen Participation in Community Development* (Washington: U.S. Government Printing Office, 1978). Richard P. Nathan et al., *Block Grants for Community Development* (Washington: The Brookings Institution, 1977). For data from the ACIR-ICMA survey see *Citizen Participation in the American Federal System,* pp. 146–50. A good compilation of case studies on the Community Development Block Grant program can be found in Paul R. Dommel and Associates, *Decentralizing Urban Policy: Case Studies in Community Development* (Washington: The Brookings Institution, 1982).

21. David A. Caputo and Richard I. Cole, "The Impact of Citizen Participation on the Expenditure of General Revenue Sharing Funds," paper presented to the Northeast Political Science Association meeting at Saratoga Springs, New York, November 1974, p. 7.

22. Edie Goldberg, "Citizen Participation in General Revenue Sharing," in *The Economic and Political Impact of General Revenue Sharing,* ed. Thomas Justin (Ann Arbor, Mich.: Institute for Social Research, 1976), pp. 165–182. Also see Comptroller General of the United States, *Revenue Sharing: Its Use By and Impact Upon Local Governments* (Washington: U.S. General Accounting Office, April 1974).

23. Two efforts in this area are Judy B. Rosener, "Citizen Participation: Can We Measure Its Effectiveness?" *Public Administration Review* 38, no. 5 (September/October 1978): 457–463; and Nelson Rosenbaum, "Evaluating Citizen Involvement Programs,"in Langton,*Citizen Participation Perspectives,*pp. 82–86.

24. Carl W. Stenberg, "Citizens and the Administrative State: From Participation to Power," *Public Administration Review* 32, no. 3 (May/June 1972): 191. For an analysis of some of the early community action programs, see Peter Marris and Martin Rein, *Dilemmas of Social Reform: Poverty and Community Action in the United States*, 2nd ed. (Chicago: Aldine Publishing Company, 1973), chaps. 1 and 7. Also see *Citizen Participation in the American Federal System* (Washington: Advisory Commission on Intergovernmental Relations, 1979), pp. 109–111.

25. Public Law 94-488, Section 7.

26. *Citizen Participation in the American Federal System*, chap. 4.

27. S. M. Miller and Martin Rein, "Participation, Poverty, and Administration," *Public Administration Review* 30, no. 1 (January/February 1969): 15–24. Cities like Milwaukee, Baltimore, Washington, D.C., and Columbus, Ohio are examples of successful efforts in this area.

28. Most of these arguments have been gleaned from a series of readings on the subject of citizen participation. See "Curriculum Essays on Citizens, Politics, and Administration in Urban Neighborhoods," *Citizen Participation in the American Federal System*, chaps. 1–3; Langton, *Citizen Participation Perspectives*, section 2; Cahn and Passett, *Citizen Participation: Effecting Community Change*, part I; and Spiegel, *Citizen Participation in Urban Development*.

29. The arguments against citizen participation can be found in numerous writings. See James Reidel, "Citizen Participation: Myths and Realities," *Public Administration Review* 32, no. 3 (May/June 1972): 211–220; Edgar S. and Jean Camper Cahn, "Maximum Feasible Participation: A General Overview," in *Citizen Participation: Effecting Community Change*, ed. Edgar S. Cahn and Barry A. Passett (New York: Praeger, 1976), pp 9–16; and Alan Altshuler, *Community Control: The Black Demand for Participation in Large American Cities* (New York: Pegasus, 1970).

30. *Report of the National Advisory Commission*, pp. 32–33; and Eric Nordlinger, *Decentralizing the City: A Study of Boston's Little City Halls* (Cambridge, Mass.: MIT Press, 1972).

31. See Howard W. Hallman, *Neighborhood Government in a Metropolitan Setting* (Beverly Hills: Sage Publications, 1974), chap. VII.

32. Kotler, *Neighborhood Government*, pp. 52–54.

33. David C. Perry, "The Suburb as a Model for Neighborhood Control," in *Neighborhood Control in the 1970s*, ed. George Frederickson (New York: Chandler, 1973), pp. 85–89. Also see Matthew Crenson, *Neighborhood Politics* (Cambridge, Mass.: Harvard University Press, 1983), and Howard Hallman, *Neighborhoods: Their Place in Urban Life* (Beverly Hills: Sage Publications, 1984).

34. This typology was analyzed with respect to the Service Area System in Washington, D.C. See Bernard H. Ross and Louise G. White, "Managing Urban Decentralization," *The Urban Interest* 3, no. 1 (Spring, 1981): 82–89. Also see Douglas Yates, *Neighborhood Democracy* (Lexington, Mass.: D. C. Heath, 1973), pp. 24–30.

35. Henry J. Schmandt, "Municipal Decentralization: An Overview," *Public Administration Review* 32 (October 1972): 573.

36. Nordlinger, *Decentralizing the City*, p. 9.

37. Henry J. Schmandt, "Decentralization: A Structural Imperative," in *Neighborhood Control in the 1970s*, ed. George Frederickson (New York: Chandler, 1973), p. 19.

38. For a discussion of these problems, see Bernard H. Ross, "The Management of Neighborhood Organizations," *South Atlantic Urban Studies* 4 (1979): 32–42.

39. For a discussion of all the models, see Schmandt, "Decentralization: A Structural Imperative," pp. 17–35.

40. Douglas Yates, *Neighborhood Democracy* (Lexington, Mass.: D. C. Heath, 1973).
41. Yates, *Neighborhood Democracy,* pp. 28–30.
42. Yates, p. 30.
43. Joseph F. Zimmerman, *The Federated City: Community Control in Large Cities* (New York: St. Martin's, 1972), pp. 43–47.
44. Almost all the literature on the Ocean Hill-Brownsville school conflict in New York City advocates this virtue of decentralization. See Maurice Berube and Marilyn Gittell, *Confrontation at Ocean Hill–Brownsville* (New York: Praeger, 1969). Also see Marilyn Gittell, "Decentralization and Citizen Participation in Education," *Public Administration Review* 32 (October 1972): 670–686.
45. Kotler, *Neighborhood Government.*
46. Kotler, *Neighborhood Government;* and Alan Altshuler, *Community Control* (New York: Pegasus, 1970).
47. This argument has been raised by almost every proponent of decentralization.
48. See Saul D. Alinsky, *Reveille for Radicals* (Chicago: University of Chicago Press, 1946); and Moynihan, *Maximum Feasible Misunderstanding.*
49. Yates, *Neighborhood Democracy,* pp. 81–83. Also see Anthony Downs, *Neighborhoods and Urban Development* (Washington: The Brookings Institution, 1981).
50. Ibid., pp. 102–103.
51. Ibid., pp. 103–107.
52. Richard Cole, *Citizen Participation and the Urban Policy Process* (Lexington, Mass.: D. C. Heath, 1974), pp. 106–111.
53. Robert K. Yin and William A. Lucas, "Decentralization and Alienation," *Policy Sciences* 4 (September 1973): 327–336.
54. A good test would be to check the housing code violations reported, scandals involving contracts awarded for city projects, and misuse of public funds by city officials. In most of these situations centralized management has not been sufficient to maintain very high standards.
55. See Mario Fantini and Marilyn Gittell, *Decentralization: Achieving Reform* (New York: Praeger, 1973); Mario Fantini, Marilyn Gittell, and Richard Magat, *Community Control and the Urban School* (New York: Praeger, 1970); and Berube and Gittell, *Confrontation at Ocean Hill-Brownsville.*

# 7. URBAN BUREAUCRACY AND SERVICE DELIVERY

## BUREAUCRACY

We have already discussed the reform movement and its impact upon the structure of urban government. In an effort to rescue government from the clutches of the machine, the reformers sought to professionalize the bureaucracy by instituting a civil service system and establishing standards for employment based on experience and training. By requiring experience and training or education as a prerequisite for holding a job, the reformers were, in fact, changing the nature and composition of local bureaucracies. Since many first and second generation immigrants did not have the qualifications to fill these jobs, they were systematically excluded from a number of local government agencies—planning, finance, engineering, etc. Where once they could have been appointed because they had been loyal and hardworking party members, they soon found themselves relegated to less prestigious jobs, such as in fire, police, and public works departments. The impact of this policy was seen in the growing middle-class composition (and in many cases biases) of service providers in agencies such as schools, planning, renewal, and welfare. By the mid-1960s many large city agencies were composed of administrators who were very different in background, age, race, and attitude from the clients they were serving, who were younger, poorer, and from minority groups.

However, it should be pointed out that the professionalization of the bureaucracy helped to clean up the patronage system and reduce favoritism in the awarding of jobs. The bureaucracy began to develop a set of standards in implementing policy, as well as a core of program experts.

A second impact of the reform movement that affected urban bureaucracies was the changing nature of the linkage between the agency and its clients. In the early twentieth century the political machine established a decentralized communication and administration system, which allowed agency personnel to monitor problems in the city and to respond to them wherever possible. This occurred because the political leaders and their organizations had a vested interest in providing services to citizens who worked and voted for the political organization.

The nature of this relationship changed dramatically as the early twentieth century reforms were instituted. Political machines began to lose their power, and reform-minded administrators were no longer beholden to the remaining machines for their jobs. As a result, the strong ties that linked the citizen, the political organization, and the service bureaucracy became unraveled. Citizens found fewer and fewer responsive bureaucrats who fully understood their needs, and bureaucrats provided services to all eligible clients without regard to their potential impact on the local political organization.

As the agency-client linkages dissolved, the decentralized nature of local government was transformed. More power became centralized in the bureaucracy, which was becoming increasingly alienated from the citizens it was supposed to service.

As the reform movement became more entrenched and the political machines lost their hold on the citizenry, administrative power began playing an increasingly important role in local politics. The deterioration of traditional pathways of power—political parties—almost made it inevitable that the balance of political power would begin to shift toward the bureaucracy.

> Modern bureaucracies thus contain the same competitive, self-serving urges that motivated the traditional political machines. Whereas the ward bosses pursued their career goals by promoting the particular interests of neighborhood and ethnic groups, modern administrators pursue their career goals by promoting the particular interests of departmental and professional specialty groups.[1]

## Bureaucratic Power

It could be argued that appointed administrators and career bureaucrats wield more power in making and implementing policy than any other group of actors involved in local political life. However, the size and the impact of bureaucracy varies from city to city. Large bureaucracies tend to be more impersonal and less sensitive to citizen inquiries. Small bureaucracies tend to be more personal and accessible.

The sources of bureaucratic power, therefore, are varied and numerous. First, much of the legislation passed by local elected bodies is skeletal in nature and requires bureaucratic agencies to develop rules, regulations, and guidelines to implement policies. The authority delegated to the bureaucrats carries with it a great deal of administrative discretion. While there is a strong effort made to adhere to the intent of the legislation, it is also true that certain established administrative rules and operating procedures make it easier to implement a program in one way rather than another.

Second, bureaucrats are regarded as the repositories of knowledge and expertise on the specific programs of their agencies. In many cases these administrators have helped to draft the legislation, have testified before the council or board of supervisors, have helped to draft guidelines within which the program is to be administered, and have monitored and evaluated the progress of the program once it has become operational. Bureaucrats are often criticized because the rules and regulations they operate under are thought to hinder innovation and reduce productivity. It is also true that civil service rules and regulations allow top government officials to withstand the unwholesome pressures of interest groups.

Since appointed department heads and elected officials come and go in local government, it is the top career bureaucrats who help to provide the administrative continuity. These bureaucrats retain both the institutional and the programmatic memory necessary to keep government functioning even though the top elected and administrative leadership experiences a rather high turnover rate.

Third, bureaucrats not only provide information and advice during the policy formulation stage, but they are often active in helping to mobilize outside client groups. These groups have a vested interest in the programs of the agency. When bureaucrats sense they are not able to exert enough pressure to influence the important actors on resource allocation decisions, they often quietly pass the word to client groups that external pressure might be welcome and appropriate.

Fourth, bureaucrats are occasionally confronted with policy or administrative decisions with which they strongly disagree. Their duty is to implement the policy regardless of their personal preferences, since it was developed by democratically elected or legally appointed officials. However, bureaucrats have learned the art of prolonging the decision-making and consultation process, slowing everything to a standstill. In a process that moves haltingly to begin with, this strategy can often be fatal to a program or an administrative reform.[2]

## Characteristics of Bureaucracy

In his writings on bureaucracy, the German sociologist Max Weber developed a set of characteristics that helped describe the phenomenon of large-scale organizations. To Weber, bureaucracy was a way of organizing large groups of people to accomplish specific tasks. These large organizations all possessed the similar traits of hierarchy, specialization, and impersonality.[3]

Regardless of the tasks performed (park maintenance or TV manufacture) or the environment in which the organization operated (private vs. public), Weber believed there was an "ideal type" of organization that included the following characteristics:

1. hierarchy
2. recruitment and promotion based on competence, not patronage
3. use of rules and regulations
4. fixed areas of official jurisdictions
5. development of a career system
6. impersonality in the performance of one's duties

Weber had mixed feelings about bureaucracies. He found them to be efficient and a much-needed way for society to function. However, he was also aware that bureaucracies were very protective of their power and repositories of important information vital to the policymaking process. An examination of some of these characteristics of bureaucracy helps to explain the problems client groups experienced in trying to deal with urban bureaucracies.

*Hierarchy*

Hierarchy connotes a relationship between people that defines their role and influence in the organization. The pyramid exemplifies this concept by showing large numbers of workers at the bottom and progressively fewer workers at each higher level in the organizational hierarchy. The few direct the many by preparing and issuing directives and orders, which carry the necessary legitimacy to be implemented. The orders and directives are usually widely distributed and well known within the organization. If it is a public organization, then many outsiders are also aware of the orders and directives. For example, the decision by a local government to implement a flextime system (whereby employees can work according to their own schedules as long as they work the prescribed number of hours per week), will be of great importance to many people in the community. People such as day care directors, food suppliers, contractors, school officials, and nearby local governments will want to examine their patterns of interaction with the local government in order to be as compatible as possible with the new work schedules.

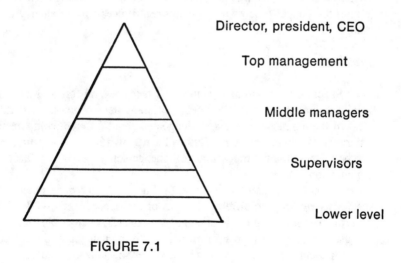

FIGURE 7.1

Hierarchy is also characterized by many control patterns emanating both from written rules and from customs and practices. It does not take a new employee long to determine if his or her superiors are amenable to such items as plants, radios, and sculpture in the office area. Either the written rules or the accepted norms and practices will be quickly made known to the new employee.

It is also true that, with few exceptions, all employees work in a hierarchical organization. The higher one rises in an organization, the greater is the responsibility. The rise to a position of prominence often means that an employee has displayed desirable job skills, and he or she is rewarded with a higher salary.

All organizations are hierarchical. This means that the U.S. Postal Service, the IBM Corporation, the Catholic Church, the City of Rochester, and the American University all have this characteristic in common. In some organizational arrangements, client dissatisfaction generates immediate concern and action, but this was not the case with local governments in the 1960s and 1970s. Individuals and organized groups repeatedly attempted to deal with local agencies by stating their grievances at the only access point available to them—police officer, school teacher, welfare worker, or health specialist. These officials, however, were on the lowest level of the pyramid. They were either new employees or employees of longer tenure who, for a variety of reasons, had not risen to a position of greater responsibility in the agency's hierarchy. These entry-level workers did not make decisions affecting overall agency policy. They were instructed, formally and informally, to implement policy according to the rules and regulations of the agency. Since they could not change policy, they bore the brunt of client anger and hostility toward the agency and its policies. It took a number of years for client groups to learn how to use elected officials to their advantage in dealing with the bureaucracy. This was accomplished through more citizen involvement in both the budget process and appointment process of top agency administrators.

*Specialization*

Specialization within organizations takes several forms. First, there is specialization of knowledge, where different people working in different areas of the organization are knowledgeable about different components of a program or an issue. As organizations have grown in size and complexity, it has become virtually impossible for one person to know all facets of an organization's operations.

Second, there is specialization by function. Each department includes specialists working on different aspects of the department's work. A health department, for example, included not only nurses, doctors, and technicians, but also special departments for mental health, prenatal care, disease control, and outpatient care. This division of labor, or specialization, means that very few people have a thorough knowledge of how the health department is organized and how it is servicing its clientele.

Bureaucratic needs to specialize and to divide up tasks led to increased client dissatisfaction. This characteristic of the bureaucracy encouraged greater impersonality and routinization and created organizations that could service only portions of clients' needs. Specialization increases the need for better coordination, which can only come about through the imposition of strict rules and formalized procedures. This, in turn, makes a bureaucracy appear rigid to the client and further exacerbates agency-client relations.[4]

Thus, large urban bureaucracies often find themselves in a bind. When they utilize sound management techniques and divide complex tasks into smaller, specialized units, they sacrifice the ability to effectively coordinate their programs. Moreover, specialization often precludes an agency's dealing with the total client, although that is usually the mandate under which all bureaucrats work.

Hahn and Levine summarized the bureaucratic obstacles posed by specialization.

> Labor and functional specialization in large bureaucracies breeds impersonality and routinization. Narrow productivity norms encourage bureaucrats to find ways to simplify, control and ration services. They develop routine actions and standard operating procedures rather than tailoring services to fit the unique needs of each particular client. Since specialization also increases the need for coordination, a strong emphasis on rules and rigidly defined procedures tends to develop in professionalized agencies. Attempts by professionals to improve the way their agency handles clients are stifled as professionals learn that following the rules has many rewards.[5]

*Professionalism*

Professionalism implies that an employee has had some formal training or education before being hired. It also connotes a set of methods or code of conduct and practices that have been developed, accepted and utilized.[6]

Professionalism also encompasses several other factors. There is a good deal of mobility among professionals in the same field. They confront the same problems on a daily basis and tend to apply the same solutions. For example, a civil engineer or an urban planner in Richmond, Virginia, can move into a similar position in Nashville, Tennessee, with a minimal amount of training and orientation.

The growth of professions and professionalism has been enormous in the past twenty years. The greatest increases have been in the larger cities and the more specialized government departments. The services that have shown the highest degree of professionalism in local government are education, engineering, and social work. This is a result of city employees' having earned college degrees and, in some cases, having been certified by state or local boards. In the mid-range are police officers and fire fighters, with highway workers and office clerical help at the lowest end of the scale of professionalism.

In many ways the professions extend beyond the specific local governments in which they work. The professional associations to which these employees belong provide links among the members across the country. Members of professional associations attend the same conferences, read the same journals, and work on the same federally funded programs.

In some cases the clients of these agency personnel are also linked nationally. The National Welfare Rights Organization was just such an organization. When funding of programs is threatened by elected officials, bureaucrats can contact client groups and urge them to mobilize in support of continued funding, increased resources, or specific programmatic changes.

But professionalism also created problems in agency-client relations. One of the primary concepts underlying professionalism concerns career advancement and development. As members of a profession, these bureaucrats have norms, goals, and concerns that are a product of their background, education, and peer influences. In order to advance, they have to be successful, and the best way to achieve success is to service agency clients as efficiently and as effectively as popssible. Many bureaucrats are able to do this through a device known as "creaming." They service those agency clients who appear most likely to be able to respond to the agency's services. Clients with the greatest needs are likely to receive modest assistance. Employment training and criminal justice are two areas where creaming has been used extensively. Since the public sector does not reward bureaucrats for finding more customers, creaming becomes an important strategy in some agencies. Resources are targeted carefully, and there is good public relations value for the agency with favorable client relations.[7] An interesting study of the agencies that assist the blind found that many agencies treated some clients as more "worthy" than others since they were deemed to be closer to becoming self-sufficient. Similar situations exist in education, training, and rehabilitation programs.[8]

Professionalism among bureaucrats also manifests itself in the middle-class biases that crept into services they were delivering. Because some of these bureaucrats had difficulty understanding problems related to broken homes, teenage pregnancy, and welfare families they were unable to administer these programs in an equitable and sensitive manner. As a result, many needy clients were intimidated into not requesting services because they felt themselves completely out of the mainstream of American life.[9] Professionalism may also decrease responsiveness to citizens. Some professionals deem it to be more responsible and important to follow the norms established by their peers in the profession than to "give in" to citizen demands. The decision to arrest prostitutes working an area is less the result of citizen complaints than it is of the prevailing norms operating in the local precinct at that time.

Finally, there is the mismatch between client and agency needs. Bureaucrats become accustomed to working regular nine-to-five business hours out of their downtown headquarters. Clients became disenchanted with these procedures, since they often could not get to a government agency until after work or on the weekends. Furthermore, the downtown offices were out of the way, making them expensive and inconvenient for most clients who lived in low-income neighborhoods. Decentralization and extended working hours were hotly debated issues between agency bureaucrats and their clients in the 1960s and 1970s.

## Rules and Regulations

Two different types of rules and regulations pertain here. First are the formal rules and regulations that are decreed by top policymakers, which have the force of law when implemented in client relations. Second, informal rules of behavior are established by the bureaucrats themselves and may or may not have any relationship to the formal regulations of the agency. These informal rules are created according to unknown criteria, without any citizen involvement, and are handed down from veterans to newcomers over time.[10] Everyone involved understands the game, and newcomers are discouraged from changing the rules and upsetting the predictable patterns of work habits in the agency.

1.  If you follow the rules you reduce your chances of ever getting into trouble.
2.  A clever bureaucrat can insure his or her success by mastering the rules of the agency.
3.  Some bureaucrats use rules as a protective shield. They hide behind them whenever they are confronted with an unusual or an extraordinary request.
4.  Rules can be used by bureaucrats as bargaining tools or weapons in order to gain an advantage over an opponent or to punish someone.[11]

Rules and regulations have their place in all bureaucratic organizations. When carried to extremes, however, rules and regulations become burdensome and have provided obstacles to normal work routines in local government agencies. In certain routine functions, overconformity to the rules becomes the norm. Workers who perform these tasks day in and day out become attached to the process, and, as a result, conforming to the rules becomes the goal rather than a means of effectively servicing the clients.[12]

Several problems arise from this excessive attention to rules. First, the literal interpretation of these rules can so distort the issues that the objectives to be accomplished by the rules are undermined. Rules against loitering in parks or shopping centers are created to reduce petty crime or to enhance the shopping environment. But teenagers, who are most often affected by these rules and regulations, become discouraged if there are no alternative outlets for their energies, such as recreation or community centers, and often rebel against police authority by refusing to move.

Second, some clients will persist in having their cases or needs reviewed as exceptions. Bureaucrats will avoid the decision by passing it on to their superiors, who may, in turn, pass it even further up the hierarchical ladder. The decision process is delayed, clients are unhappy, and paperwork is increased.

Third, the literal application of rules requires the categorizing of clients by groups. Clients see their needs in individual terms and seek personal attention, which conflicts with the rules. Clients become unhappy and accuse bureaucrats of being insensitive to their needs.[13]

The development of decision rules to help bureaucrats implement programs is another way of guaranteeing a relatively secure and predictable organizational environment. This also reduces the exceptions to the rules and makes a bureaucrat's job reasonably stable. In the Oakland, California, study the researchers found that bureaucrats employed the "laissez-faire" approach or the "Adam Smith rule," which says, "when a customer makes a 'request,' take care of him in a professional manner; otherwise leave him alone."[14]

In Oakland the researchers found that the decision rules appeared reasonable on the surface but actually contained hidden biases. The library system, which tended to allocate its resources to the high circulation branches, was discriminating against communities with low circulation, which were located in lower-income areas of the city. Consequently, the libraries in the lower-income neighborhoods did not have the resources to provide new materials to their clients even though tremendous demographic changes were occurring in their areas.

A similar situation arose in the allocation of resources to city streets. The heavily traveled streets received more resources than the less traveled streets. The research team found this decision to be beneficial to commuters who used these streets to get to and from work, some from outside of Oakland. The less traveled streets were not repaired adequately to keep them at a satisfactory operational level. Thus, bureaucratic decision rules, which are in many ways an important asset in bureaucratic life, often contain hidden elements of bias that can perpetuate inequity.[15]

*Impersonality*

Another characteristic of bureaucracy, as Weber noted, is the tendency towards impersonality. Bureaucrats perform their jobs in an impersonal manner regardless of the special concerns of their clientele. In part this impersonality results from several of the other factors associated with bureaucracy. Job specialization, professional training, and formal and informal rules and regulations all contribute to a feeling of impartiality and neutrality in the provision of services. Bureaucrats feel discouraged in trying to be sensitive or innovative in dealing with clients because the bureaucracy is structured to allow large numbers of people to be processed in the most expeditious manner possible. If a bureaucrat attempts to differentiate among clients according to needs, an endless stream of forms and exceptions have to be obtained for each client. Few bureaucrats are dedicated enough to pursue this course on a regular basis. It is much easier to follow the rules and imitate their peers, thus not calling attention to themselves.[16]

## Analyzing Bureaucrats and Bureaucracies

The importance of the bureaucracy in the politics and administration of local government cannot be overestimated. Not only is the bureaucracy sometimes referred to as the fourth branch of government, but at the local level its importance is magnified by the fact that its employees are in daily contact with the clients they serve. Programs and policies decided by a council can be implemented rather quickly. In a relatively short period of time, field workers can begin reporting back on how clients are responding to the changes. This relatively quick feedback is unmatched on any other level of government and places unusual demands and burdens upon local bureaucrats. Changing the hours of a health center or opening a new field office are good examples.

The unique position of local government bureaucrats has prompted many scholars to examine urban bureaucracy. A few of the more important studies are worth reviewing.

In 1967 Theodore Lowi, a political scientist, wrote an article based upon his observations of municipal bureaucracies in New York and other large cities. He argued that those large urban bureaucracies had replaced the old machines and were now running the cities in much the same fashion as the old machines had. He labeled these newly-emerged large urban bureaucracies, the "new machines."[17]

The reform movement had created the professionalized bureaucracies in order to eliminate the stranglehold the political machines had on the cities. But the bureaucracies have now become machines themselves. In weakening and, in many cases, destroying the local political parties, the reformers had succeeded in transferring power from the political party to the service bureaucracy. According to Lowi, "The Legacy of Reform is the bureaucratic city-state."[18]

Citing the 1961 mayoral election in New York as one of great significance, Lowi discusses how Mayor Robert Wagner carefully assembled his slate of running mates for president of the city council and comptroller just as a machine politician would have done. The only difference was that Mayor Wagner selected candidates from among career civil servants. Instead of looking to the Democratic party as his power base, Mayor Wagner established his base in the city bureaucracy.

Many of the city agencies were organized by ward, precinct, or district. The agency heads were extremely powerful and semiautonomous because such a large share of their budgets came from federal and state sources. With New York's agencies growing in strength and importance, Lowi commented, "bureaucratic agencies are not neutral; they are only independent."[19]

Another interesting analysis of urban bureaucracies was undertaken by Michael Lipsky, who coined the term "street-level bureaucrats." In several of his writings Lipsky analyzed these unique bureaucrats, who "are those men and women who in their face-to-face encounters with citizens, 'represent' government to the people."[20]

The street-level bureaucrats examined by Lipsky included police officers, school teachers, and welfare workers. The work of these employees was characterized by several factors that differentiated them from other bureaucrats.

1. They are called upon regularly to interact with clients or citizens in doing their jobs.
2. There is a high degree of independence afforded to these employees, which is manifest in the discretion they can exercise in making decisions. This discretion could have a significant impact upon the citizens they interact with.[21]

The characteristics of their jobs also provide different kinds of stress for the street-level bureaucrats, which are not found among employees processing drivers licenses or authorizing the purchase of office supplies. Lipsky observed three different kinds of stress among the street-level bureaucrats.

1. *Inadequate Resources*  Street-level bureaucracies lack sufficient resources to do their required tasks. Police forces are understaffed, welfare caseworkers are overloaded, and classrooms are overcrowded. Under these conditions street-level bureaucrats often make hasty decisions, using limited information in order to process people and problems as quickly as possible.
2. *Threat and Challenge to Authority*  Many street-level bureaucrats work under, or think they work under, conditions that are physically or psychologically dangerous. Some, like police officers, fear death, while others, like social workers or teachers, travel through or to hostile neighborhoods to work.
3. *Contradictory or Ambiguous Job Expectations*  Many bureaucrats are unsure of what is expected of them in the performance of their jobs. Besides the formal rules and regulations, there are also pressures for action suggested by peers, superiors, clients, media, and friends.[22]

In order to deal with their unique position in local government and the stress that accompanies their jobs, street-level bureaucrats develop mechanisms and strategies for coping. In an effort to reduce organizational complexity and to compensate for inadequate resources, the street-level bureaucrats often develop routines and stereotypes that help them to simplify their work tasks and allow them to use shortcuts in decision-making. Categorizing clients and reading cues in the neighborhood are two devices adopted by street-level bureaucrats. Police officers scour communities looking for telltale signs that a crime is being committed. Teachers categorize students by behavior, dress, and records, based upon stereotypes formed from previous classes.[23]

An examination of street-level bureaucrats and their impact upon agency-client relationships leads to several inferences about this pattern of delivering urban services. First, for individual clients the quantity and quality of the services they receive is often determined by the behavior and attitudes of the street-level bureaucrats. Second, these street-level bureaucrats enjoy a considerable degree of autonomy in the performance of their duties, since it is extremely difficult for the central office of each agency to constantly monitor the activities of this scattered network of employees, many of whom move from place to place in the course of their jobs. Many street-level bureaucrats perform their jobs in the field, completely isolated from direct supervisory review, e.g., teachers in classrooms, outreach social workers in the home, police officers in patrol cars, and housing inspectors in individual apartments.

Third, better control over the activities of street-level bureaucrats could be sustained, but at a very high cost. Performance measures for all facets of their jobs would have to be developed and agreed to. Actual behavior would have to be monitored and compared to the performance measures. Finally, the agency would have to be willing to impose and capable of imposing sanctions on those employees who did not meet the standards. Needless to say, the smaller the office and the fewer the number of people who work outside, the easier this task becomes. For street-level bureaucrats, economically and administratively it is virtually impossible to implement this type of control system. To the degree that such a system cannot be implemented, the control of street-level bureaucrats is diminished and their autonomy increased.[24]

## SERVICE DELIVERY

The primary purpose of urban bureaucracies is to deliver public services to citizens. Over the past twenty years we have come to understand that the way bureaucrats deliver services often determines how that service will be viewed by clients and whether or not it will meet its stated objectives. Executives can propose good or bad laws, and councils and boards can pass good or bad laws, but the tactics and the competence displayed in implementing the programs are the responsibility of the bureaucracy. The success or failure of most urban programs rests with the bureaucrats.

Douglas Yates summed up the transition from the 1960s to the 1970s succinctly. He commented,

> After a decade of protest and demands for participation and community control, urban government appears to be entering a new era. Now that the "urban crisis" has been discovered, debated, and in some quarters dismissed, government officials and academic analysts alike have increasingly come to focus on "service delivery" as the central issue and problem of urban policy-making.[25]

The problems of service delivery appear simple to remedy: deliver more of what the citizens want in a more economical and effective manner. However, as more citizens have become concerned and interested in the question of service delivery, the underlying problems in providing public services have become better publicized. As urban areas try to respond to all of the service needs emanating from industrialization and urbanization, they confront the realities of inflation, higher taxes, declining tax bases, and soaring interest rates.[26] Citizens want more from government, but they are reluctant to pay for it. The payment for services is separated from the delivery of services. Therefore, as long as clients do not directly pay for each service, they want more of them.

Responsiveness by urban bureaucracies to needs and demands of citizens is not as easy to accomplish as it first appears. There are several intervening factors, besides fiscal issues, which inhibit the swift and desired response by bureaucrats to service needs of clients. First is the issue of government contacts. Most citizens do not contact city agencies concerning the quality of service delivery. Without strong community organizations or local political parties, the individual citizen is unlikely to "take on the bureaucracy."[27]

If citizens do not contact local government agencies, does this mean they are generally satisfied with the quantity and quality of the services they receive? Most of the survey data collected indicates a majority of citizens are satisfied with their local services. In 1970 the Urban Observatory Program sponsored a ten-city survey—Albuquerque, Atlanta, Baltimore, Boston, Denver, Kansas City (Missouri), Kansas City (Kansas), Milwaukee, Nashville, and San Diego—to determine citizen attitudes towards urban service delivery. Most citizens surveyed appeared satisfied with their services, but there were variations by race, class, education, and service.[28] In other smaller-scale studies we have learned that respondents generally view taxes as too high, but at the same time they would like to see more tax dollars diverted to education, public safety, and health care. This clearly states the urban bureaucrats' eternal paradox.

Second, from our discussion of urban bureaucracy it is also possible to discern certain obstacles citizens perceive in the provision of services. Most urban services have been organized to operate according to prescribed rules and regular patterns. This eliminates the need for bureaucrats to respond differently to each individual client contact. Consequently, clients whose needs differ from the prescribed rules have a difficult time in their encounters with bureaucrats.

Citizen groups who periodically contact local agencies to complain about services are unlikely to have a major impact on the service system. Urban bureaucracies are not going to change rules for every community complaint. Furthermore, the regularized rules are a defense behind which some bureaucrats choose to hide. Whether the issue is garbage pickup, road repair, or snow removal, there is a regular pattern to the provision of the service, which is often cited to answer complaints about why services are not better, faster, or cheaper.

The level of services a community receives is largely determined by the administrative decisions made within the agency. These internal decisions establish the guiding principles for delivering services, and community inputs are treated as information for future consideration, but rarely affect the level of bureaucratic responsiveness. Occasionally citizen groups may succeed in stimulating a bureaucracy to become more responsive by altering its service delivery rules. However, this is not likely to happen very often.[29]

A third factor inhibiting the smooth delivery of services concerns the ability of city-wide bureaucracies to provide flexible service levels to meet the varying requests of different neighborhoods. Governed by rules and regulations, urban bureaucracies have not been able to overcome the centralization that makes them less flexible and more remote from their clients.[30]

## Explaining Service Delivery

Like other subareas of urban politics, the issue of service delivery has developed its own set of terms, some of which are not clearly understood by all of the actors. Three terms used with great frequency in service delivery are *efficiency, effectiveness,* and *equity.* The first two are so common they have been adopted by almost all candidates for local office, who repeatedly use them in their campaign speeches. Furthermore, as agency administrators are called upon to make more public appearances, these terms have become part of their vocabulary in discussing the services their agencies provide to citizens. Not only are efficiency and effectiveness used with little care for precision, but sometimes they are used interchangeably by flustered public officials who grasp for terms to satisfy angry citizens, inquiring constituents, or local reporters.

Efficiency measures are concerned with costs. How can a unit of government maximize its output from a specific allocation of resources? What is the cost of each unit of goods or services an office, agency, department, or the city as a whole produces? Efficiency measures tell us how much it costs to collect one ton of garbage, keep a police officer on the beat, treat a drug overdose patient in an emergency ward, and operate a city bus on a per-mile basis. Efficiency measures do not tell us *how well* we do any of the above, but only how much it costs to perform the service. Consequently, efficiency measures tend to ignore issues of equity.

Effectiveness measures are concerned with objectives. Is the governmental unit responsible for delivering the service meeting its objectives? Effectiveness measures are goal-oriented and focus on analyzing outcomes regardless of the costs or resources. Are health care services more readily available? Are elementary-school test scores higher? Has crime been reduced in the central business district? Are public housing units all receiving heat and hot water?

One could argue that the history of urban America from 1964 onward could be analyzed in terms of the concepts of efficiency and effectiveness. Since the budget process plays such a paramount role in the politics and administration of local government, it is not surprising to find most local officials thinking, planning, developing, and analyzing programs in terms of efficiency criteria. In other words, government officials think in terms of how many services they can provide for the amount of money allocated. The opposite approach would be to ask how much money and other resources are required for a program to meet its stated objectives. Occasionally local officials do ask their elected leaders this question, and the responses are invariably "funds are tight," "we can't raise taxes," or "do the best you can."

On the client side, issues are not often viewed in efficiency terms. The payment and the receipt of services are usually independent of one another. Therefore, clients and geographically-based citizen groups usually wonder why an agency cannot provide a better quality of services. When they are told it costs too much, their response ranges from "who cares?" to "take the money from somewhere else." Clients, in other words, are results- or goal-oriented, since they do not automatically relate their tax payments to the provision of the specific service being criticized.

The disputes between efficiency-minded local officials and effective-ness-oriented citizen groups have abated somewhat. Many local governments made a concerted effort to monitor and improve the quality of the provided services. Others began involving citizen leaders in the decision-making process so that the views of the clients were incorporated into the programs.

In a number of cities, the local government opened branch offices or little city halls to better monitor the performance of both programs and em-ployees. New York, Boston, and Washington pioneered in this effort, with the results proving only moderately successful.

Of greater importance has been the weakened economy. As govern-ments on all levels entered a period of cutback management and budgetary constraints, the concern with efficiency in the provision of services in-creased. The few advances that had been made toward an effectiveness-orientation were shelved in favor of budgetary cuts, reductions in force, and job freezes.[31]

The third term, *equity,* presents similar problems for understanding urban service delivery. Levy, Meltsner, and Wildavsky, in their study of Oakland, suggested three different approaches to the concept of equity.[32] First, equity could mean *equal opportunity*. All citizens would receive the same level of service regardless of their needs or the amount of taxes they paid. Under this system there would be no redistributive impact arising from government services, and, since everyone received the same quantity, it would enhance a system that operates primarily on decision rules and routini-zation. Trash collection, snow removal, and environmental protection are services that represent this type of equity.

A second interpretation of equity is labeled *market equity*. Citizens receive services in rough approximation to the amount of taxes they paid. The more taxes paid, the more services received, just as if one purchased these services in a private service system. In this system there is no adjust-ment for need. Upper-middle-class suburbs provide a good example, since their higher tax base provides more and better services to their residents.

A third approach is called *equal results*. In this system, agencies are instructed to allocate resources so that citizens are in approximately equal status after funds have been expended and services provided. The amount of taxes paid by citizens is unrelated to the services they receive, but people with greater service needs receive proportionately more in services than they would under either of the other two approaches. Most social service pro-grams reflect this type of equity.

A fourth possibility, not raised in the Oakland study, is *equal access,* which opens up the political and administrative system to allow all interested parties equal access to the decision-making process. Organizational ability, timing, resources, and strategy then become key factors in working the system to provide the quantity and quality of services each group deems necessary. Some groups will win and some will lose, but all will have had an equal opportunity to influence the political and administrative process. Low-income and minority groups would have access to the political system in determining how resources are allocated to their communities. Higher-income residents in the community tend to favor the equal opportunity approach and, under certain conditions, the market equity approach. Lower-income residents almost always favor the equal results approach, but they have, in the past, also been very active in pursuing the equal access system.

Given these four approaches and the persistent complaints about specific services, how do we explain the different allocation of resources and the varying levels of satisfaction with urban services? Is there a conscious effort to discriminate against certain groups or geographical areas in the city, or are differences better explained by a subtle or subconscious bias unintentionally imposed on the service delivery system? The answer to some of these questions can be found in an interesting study of urban service delivery in San Antonio conducted by Robert L. Lineberry.[33]

In his study, Lineberry suggested there were five possible explanations for how public policy affected the distribution of services in San Antonio. For each of these explanations Lineberry developed a hypothesis. The five explanations were: race, class, power elite, ecological, and decision rules.

The underclass hypothesis suggests that there is either a conscious or an unconscious effort to distribute services in such a way that all disadvantaged groups are discriminated against. These groups can be separated into racial, economic, or political categories. Each one of these categories can be tested empirically.

1. *Race*  There is a belief among many that differences in urban service delivery were the result of racial discrimination. In the case of San Antonio this meant census tracts that were heavily populated by Chicanos, not blacks.
2. *Class*  This explanation focused on a broader spectrum of the population than race. It included all of the economically disadvantaged groups in the area—blacks, Chicanos, and poor whites—and suggested they received inadequate services because they were poor, not because of race or ethnic background.
3. *Power Elite*  People in positions of power were able to direct rewards to people and areas of their choosing. The powerholders were more likely to assist their friends, since it was in their own interest to do so. This help took the form of contracts, appointments, and tax advantages.
4. *Ecological*  This hypothesis is less conspiratorial than the others and can be more easily tested using quantitative data. Instead of analyzing political, racial, ethnic, and economic factors, the eco-

logical hypothesis focused on age, population density, and other geographical factors as determinants of how and when services were delivered. In this way, a researcher could ascertain if specific areas of the city were receiving favored treatment.

5. *Decision Rules* The decision-rules hypothesis was discussed previously. It concentrates on bureaucrats and the conflicts inherent in their jobs that affect the quality of service delivery. These include rules and regulations that routinize bureaucratic work and make it predictable. It also includes the wide discretion available in implementing programs, which heightened unpredictability in interactions between teachers and parents and police officers and gang leaders.[34]

Lineberry's conclusions about service delivery in San Antonio were consistent with the earlier findings of Levy, Meltsner, and Wildavsky in Oakland. In the Oakland study, the authors found little evidence to support the hypothesis that urban services were consistently provided at lower levels to lower-income communities and at higher levels to higher-income communities. This was true in some instances, but not in others. In some cases there was no evidence that any one group benefited.[35]

Lineberry concluded that the underclass hypothesis, which asserted that the poor, the powerless, and minorities received fewer services and poorer quality, was not supported by the data. Each of the hypotheses had been tested, and none could explain much of the variation in the distribution of services in San Antonio. Of the five tested, the ecological hypothesis was best able to explain some of the variations.

> The private Santa Claus delivers his largesse in rough correspondence to family incomes. The public Santa Claus is not much more equal in his allocation, but his largesse is only weakly related to socio-economic status. Ecological factors carry us somewhat further than considerations of power and status. Age and density of neighborhoods are, on the whole, more closely tied to their service levels than are the class, racial and political characteristics of their residents.[36]

## Problems of Urban Service Delivery

We have examined some of the different concepts that help to define equity in service delivery, and we have reviewed the major hypotheses that might explain how and why services are delivered to different areas of a city. None of these approaches, however, has provided us with a clear understanding of the nature of service delivery.

Before local government agencies can deliver services to consumers they must have a reasonably good idea of what it is the clients want. This process of receiving information and converting it into programs is complex for several reasons. First, people of similar interests and backgrounds tend to cluster together in neighborhoods. Within these neighborhoods, however, are subareas that have different needs and require different levels and kinds of service. Where services are delivered in a uniform manner, numerous inequities will result. Some residents will not receive the services they need, while others will find services being offered that they do not want or cannot use.[37]

In Berkeley, California, two researchers examined which parts of the city tended to use which public services the most. They found that low-income neighborhoods used police, welfare, and health services more than high-income neighborhoods did. The latter, however, used libraries and summer camps more frequently than did the lower-income communities.[38] This type of information becomes useful only if local governments are able to adjust service delivery levels to reflect these use patterns. The equity concerns mentioned above often come into play at this point, and political and administrative bargaining are necessary to resolve conflicts. This rarely results in a pattern of service delivery that meets the needs of all residents of a community.

A second problem affecting the equitable distribution of services is that most public services are collective goods. Clean air and water, paved sidewalks, and street lights are all services used by citizens living in similar geographical areas. All citizens avail themselves of these services, even though some do not feel they are high priority services and others fail to see the value received for the dollars expended. No individuals are excluded from using the collective goods, but neither is use predicated upon individuals paying for their costs.[39]

Third, when groups of people organize to apply pressure on government to change or improve services, new issues arise for consideration. Because of a number of factors discussed in the section on bureaucracy, it is difficult to make major changes in service delivery patterns in the short run. Furthermore, when changes do occur, it is often through a complex set of changes in law, rules, behavior, and perhaps elected and administrative personnel. The actions taken by a variety of individuals are hard to trace in an effort to determine the true impact of pressure for change exerted by organized community groups.[40] Bureaucrats are also wary of community groups that sporadically apply pressure for change. Local government officials can never be certain of the extent to which these groups represent the sentiments of the whole community.

One effort to assess the impact of geographically-based intermediary groups on the distribution of urban services was carried out in Chicago by Bryan Jones. In this study, Jones attempted to determine if organized community groups and locally-based political parties could affect service delivery. Jones reasoned that intermediary groups were interested in solving community problems. These groups might encourage citizens to increase their demands on agency bureaucrats with the goal of transforming demands into changed service patterns. He also hypothesized that urban service agencies might be more receptive to service appeals from geographical areas where party and community groups were well organized.

It is also possible that organized groups and local party organizations might help neighborhoods in the provision of services. This would have a much greater impact on service delivery than would be possible in areas with weak or nonexistent intermediary groups.

Using data on citizen complaints, agency outputs, and the impact of services upon specific neighborhoods, Jones investigated the enforcement of building codes in Chicago. He found that the influence of the political party organization was felt at all stages of the political process affecting service delivery. In all stages of the process—citizen contact stage, output stage, and impact stage—it was the ward-based party organization that had a significant effect. At the same time, there was very little evidence to indicate that organized community groups had an impact in any of the three stages.[41]

> Community organizations, with their small paid staffs and volunteer labor, cannot provide the day-to-day incentives that are necessary to keep government agencies constantly in touch with citizens.[42]

## Clients and the Bureaucracy

Lipsky points out that the relationship between street-level bureaucrats and their clients is different from most other agency-client relationships. Street-level bureaucrats service nonvoluntary clients, that is, clients who have no alternative sources to turn to for their services. Therefore, these clients cannot penalize the agency for poor service and "vote with their feet" by going to another provider for assistance. As Lipsky states, "street-level bureaucracies usually have nothing to lose by failing to satisfy clients."[43]

Another aspect of agency-client relations that affects the delivery of services is the cost of obtaining the service by the client. Using a rational model, we might assume that a potential client will continue to make an effort to receive an agency's services until the client determines that the costs involved outweigh benefits to be received.

Some of the costs imposed upon clients are high and deliberately introduced. Agency personnel may make clients wait a long time or verbally abuse them in the course of their meetings. We have already mentioned the costs involved in the implementation of rules and regulations that curtail the activities of agency clients. In other cases, costs to clients are incurred because agencies are unable to alter their routines to meet the changing needs of society and their agency's clients.[44] Two good examples of these problems were the length of time it took urban educational systems to begin providing a second language to non-English-speaking school children and the reluctance of local police departments to estabish police-community relations units to provide a non-authoritative link with the neighborhood.

The relationship between street-level bureaucrats and clients is a complex one. The clients of urban service bureaucracies are the consumers of the agency's services as well as the raw material being processed. The health department exists to provide health care and other services to its clients. But the health department makes the final determination on who is eligible to be a health department client. Without clients there would be no need for a health department. In other words, the street-level bureaucrats and the clients have a highly reciprocal relationship.[45]

Other costs are also associated with client entry into the service system. Application forms are complicated and take a long time to fill out. This process is worsened by numerous agencies that are understaffed or inadequately staffed and must, as a consequence, deny potential clients the time and answers they need to process their applications.

There are also psychological costs involved in being a client. Not only do the clients want to mask the fact that they are clients, but the street-level bureaucrats feel superior to their clients and can intimidate them. People using a health center may not want others in the neighborhood to know they are sick. Welfare recipients and families awaiting public housing may not want neighbors to know they require such services.

Two other costs imposed upon clients are time and information. Clients often wait a long time before receiving services. Because they are relatively powerless actors in the system, with few if any resources, they are unlikely to complain. The information possessed by street-level bureaucrats is another powerful weapon in manipulating the delivery of services, according to Lipsky. Some clients are given adequate information to help them work the system to their advantage. Other clients are denied elementary information with which to gain entry into the system.

Information can also be provided in such a manner that it is too confusing and too complex for the client to understand. Planning agencies in the late 1960s repeatedly made their master, sector, and function plans available to citizens, who could barely comprehend what was being provided to them. It wasn't until the citizen groups were able to hire their own planners that the information provided became valuable enough for them to use in dealing with city agencies.[46]

Because of the high costs of services to clients and the inadequate staffing, some clients are turned off and fail to avail themselves of services they are entitled to. Bureaucrats impose many of these costs on clients as a way of rationing services to reduce their work load as well as to have the clients conform to the agency conception of who they are.

> A public service bureaucracy does not distribute goods among clients, but distributes clients among goods. The work of the bureaucracy consists of categorizing and processing people as a precondition to their receiving benefits —not unlike an ordinary factory where materials are processed as a precondition to their sale. In this sense, the clients of a public service bureaucracy play the role of the organization's raw material: the real work of the employees is remolding clients to define their relation to the agency as consumers.[47]

## Measuring the Quality of Urban Services

One of the gray areas of urban service delivery concerns the issue of the quality of the services local governments provide. If residents in an area are unhappy with specific services they might voice their discontent by citing isolated cases of service failure, poor management, or surly employees. These personal grievances are not the most precise inputs from which department heads or city managers are able to make changes in patterns of service delivery. In order to adjust departmental activities and programs, local government managers need fairly accurate and continuous data about the impact of the services they are providing.

David Morgan has identified several performance measures used by local government officials to help them monitor and evaluate their agency's services. First are workload measures, which are similar to efficiency measures discussed above. Workload measures focus on quantity or volume of services provided and are made more sophisticated by relating these output measures to the input measures required to achieve the output. For example, a crude measure of service quality would be the number of infant deaths recorded at birth or the number of police arrests for burglary. Establishing a ratio tells us more about the relationship of prenatal services for pregnant mothers to infant mortality or the increase in the police education program designed to reduce burglaries. These measures help local government managers understand service performance over time but usually do not lend themselves to short-term responses to deficiencies in service provision.[48]

A second performance measure would be the use of effectiveness measures to assess services. Does the new alignment of school districts provide a better racial mix in each school as well as reducing the length of bus trips to and from school each day? Is the use of a new water hose by the fire department increasing water pressure and reducing wear and tear on fire fighting equipment? As mentioned above, effectiveness can be established by both government officials and citizen leaders to assess how well local agencies are meeting their job objectives. In other words, are client groups satisfied with their services?

Productivity measures are a third approach to assessing service delivery. Productivity measures include both efficiency and effectiveness. This approach uses total resources, dollars, labor, supplies, and public education costs involved in delivering the service. Using productivity measures stimulates local government managers to use several measures to assess the quality of an agency's services.[49]

A final approach to performance measures emanates from a series of studies conducted by the Urban Institute. The Urban Institute recognized the limitations placed upon performance measure studies that restricted themselves to departmental recordkeeping as a source of data on service delivery. Recognizing that quality measures and citizen satisfaction assessments could not be obtained from traditional departmental records, Harry Hatry and his associates proposed a number of additional measures to be used in gathering field data about services.

First was a systematic inspection of the physical features associated with a specific service. Snow removal and garbage pickup are two good examples of how this works. Departmental recordkeeping would indicate which streets had been cleared and provide crude measures of how well this had been accomplished. Several cities, such as New York and Washington, have begun using inspectors to randomly check city streets against predetermined criteria. These on-site inspections helped to supplement the basic information collected from traditional channels.[50]

A second device for measuring service performance is the use of sample citizen surveys to assess client satisfaction and the level of citizen involvement. These surveys must be administered on a fairly regular basis—at least once a year—to be of any value. The wording of the questionnaires is crucial, since valuable data can be gleaned from the responses on hours of operation, safety, courtesy, comprehensiveness of services, and adequacy of the facilities. Health, recreation, library, athletic, and cultural activities are well-suited to this type of data collection. The data collected over a period of time can be compared and analyzed against performance measures being used by the department.[51]

The use of linked records is an additional technique for obtaining information about service performance. In this system, clients have been traced through more than one agency in an effort to evaluate the quality of a variety of services they have used. Persons arrested by the police are tracked through the courts, prison, and parole systems to ascertain what impact connected or linked services have had on them. The same type of system can also be employed in the health and welfare fields, where clients often come into contact with more than one agency.[52]

Hatry's final approach is merely to make better use of the data already collected by local government agencies. By altering data collection techniques to provide agencies the option of receiving data by race, age, sex, geographical area, income level, or ethnic origin, the possibility exists for more sophisticated analysis leading to better targeting of services to client groups in need.

A system similar to this was established in Washington, D.C., in 1970 by executive order of the mayor. The District of Columbia was divided into nine service areas, each of which was to report data on all services to a central office. The data was to be analyzed and disseminated to the operating departments, which were to make program and policy decisions based upon this data.

Each ward had a Service Area Committee (SAC) to operate in the area while solving problems and making recommendations to the departments about needs in the community that were not being met. Two coordinating bodies were established to monitor the SAC activities and to link the mayor and the departments in a concerted effort to improve service quality throughout the city. The effort was marginal at best because of political and administrative problems related to changes some agencies wanted to implement while other agencies opposed them. Lack of strong mayoral leadership also weakened the program.[53]

## Alternative Techniques for Delivering Services

From our discussions of bureaucracy and service delivery, it is apparent that some of the problems affecting urban service delivery are caused by the overt and deliberate actions of bureaucrats who are not sensitive to client needs. However, it is equally clear that certain characteristics of the bureaucracy and patterns of bureaucratic behavior have unintentional, negative consequences for clients with service needs. The reality of how a bureaucracy and citizens interact has prompted some academics and practitioners to investigate alternative techniques for delivering services to clients.

One proposal is called coproduction, in which the quantity and quality of services available to neighborhood residents is determined by the efforts of both the service providers and the clients. In an era of fiscal constraint and service cutbacks, ideas like coproduction became increasingly important. Citizens who complain about high crime rates, dirty streets, or unacceptable reading levels in the schools have the option of working to improve this service. In many urban and suburban neighborhoods citizens fearful of rising crime rates have begun street patrols to monitor activity in their communities during peak crime hours. Communities also make their areas safer by turning on outside lights when the sun sets to help deter crime. Neighborhood cleanliness is not just a result of trash collections by the sanitation department. Local communities that engage in anti-litter practices invariably are cleaner than communities where no similar efforts are made, regardless of the quality of trash collection in the city. Parents who volunteer to assist in remedial reading programs in the schools are helping to coproduce an important service that can improve the quality of their children's education.[54]

Even if only small increases in service quality are achieved in individual services, the results can be dramatic when multiplied by the number of services a local government provides. Active involvement by citizens in coproduction also produces financial savings for local agencies. In some cases the savings can be substantial, and departments recognizing this fact aggressively seek ways to expand coproduction activities with citizens within the legal and professional limits allowed.[55]

Some have viewed coproduction efforts as a "rip-off," where citizens supply the time and labor, in addition to their tax dollars, to improve service quality. However, it can be argued that citizens decide how and when to participate, what needs they would like met as a result of their efforts, and which policies affecting their neighborhoods should be changed.

> Coproduction is a broad form of citizen participation, directly impacting on service delivery, while simultaneously satisfying such traditional participatory functions as enabling citizens to express their preferences, inducing official and producer responsibility, and serving as an instructive information-gathering device for citizens.[56]

A second alternative for delivering urban services is to contract with private companies to provide the services. In almost every urban area the local government agencies have a monopoly or a near-monopoly position in service provision. The upper-middle- and upper-income residents often have a choice as to whether or not they should rely upon government services to satisfy their needs. In cases where they find local government services lacking, they enter the market and privately purchase, at their own expense, services necessary to meet their needs. This might require a community to hire its own security guards to patrol the streets as a deterrent to crime or an individual family to pay the tuition at a private school so their child can receive the education the parents feel is necessary. The other option is to "exit," or move to an area where services are more desirable and meet more of their needs. This is a feasible but costly alternative sometimes, even for the rich.

Lower-middle- and lower-income groups rarely have the resources to enter the private market and purchase the services they require to meet their needs. Their neighborhoods are patroled by local police officers, and their children attend the local public schools. Therefore, a large segment of the population cannot penalize the service providers, since there are no viable alternatives for them, and moving to a more suitable community is usually too costly to be seriously contemplated. Poor services are not rewarded, but, unlike in the private sector, neither are they penalized. Citizens are left with the only option available, voicing their discontent to government.

> The inefficiency of municipal services is not due to bad commissions, mayors, managers, workers, unions, or labor leaders; it is a natural consequence of a monopoly system. *The public has created the monopoly, the monopoly behaves in predictable fashion, and there are no culprits, only scapegoats.*[57]

Aside from the fact that monopolistic service agencies do not provide alternatives, they are exempted from the competitive pressures that require private producers to be responsive, effective, and efficient. Failure to achieve these goals in the private sector is tantamount to disaster, but in the public sector the lack of incentives to produce satisfactory results often is concealed in a maze of political and administrative decisions and pronouncements that may be irrelevant to the service under question.

The debate over public and private provision of services has often been heated, with few persuasive arguments emerging. On the one hand, public agencies acting as monopolies have been accused of being inefficient and unresponsive. On the other hand, the private sector chafes at regulation and may be reluctant to undertake a number of services because costs are high and profits modest. Transportation, education, public safety, and health care are examples of such services. In the case of education and public safety, citizens can choose a private alternative if they are willing to pay the substantial costs. In the field of mass transportation, the private sector has had a difficult time making a satisfactory profit, and public agencies have had to take over many public transit systems and provide the service.

In recent years, a number of studies have been conducted comparing public and private agency provision of services. The two services where these studies have been conducted most frequently are trash collection and fire protection. In his studies of numerous cities, Savas has repeatedly found that private trash collection firms offer services similar to or better than public agencies of government. The New York City Sanitation Department collected trash at a cost of $39.71 per ton, while private firms working in the city were collecting trash at less than half that cost. In another case, Savas found a private firm collected trash three times per week in a suburban New York community at less than half of what city trash collection cost for twice-weekly pickups. Municipal sanitation in New York City costs more for several reasons. The sanitation workers are unionized; therefore, they receive higher pay and more fringe benefits than non-union workers. Also because of unions, it is difficult to implement productivity measures that might reduce the work force. Finally, civil service protected workers, and public monopolies do not have any incentives to be efficient, since their clients have few if any service alternatives and service employees do not have to compete with others to retain their jobs. Similar differences between public and private service agencies have been reported in fire protection, licensing, and inspection services.[58]

While private contracting appears to have many advantages over public agency provision, there is no great rush by local governments to contract out services. Recent surveys indicate that some local governments are becoming more involved in contracting, particularly in refuse collection and equipment maintenance. There seems to be agreement that in many areas private firms can provide services at a high level and a lower cost to citizens. Some of these services are administrative or housekeeping and do not involve direct agency-client relationships. Two authors have speculated that the reluctance of local governments to convert more services to private contracting is a result of employee opposition, fear of corruption, and obstacles envisioned to active citizen involvement.[59]

If and when more evidence of cost savings and increased effectiveness of private provision of services is produced, local government officials will have to rethink some of the traditional arguments in favor of public provision. Increasing pressure on local taxpayers coupled with reduced federal funding might prove to be the catalyst to a growth in private contracting.[60]

A final set of options relate to the possibility of establishing a neighborhood-based service delivery system. To achieve this, local governments would have to devolve power to numerous neighborhood institutions, which would then provide services to their local constituents. This neighborhood system is predicated on the assumption that there would still be a metropolitan level that would provide many areawide services such as sewage disposal, water supply, and air and water pollution control.

Neighborhood organizations would be allowed to provide services in any one of several ways: (1) develop their own service delivery system, (2) purchase services from other political jurisdictions—city, county, state, or neighborhood, (3) coproduce services with other neighborhood jurisdictions, (4) create a self-governing special district or development corporation, or (5) contract with private firms for the purchase of services. Each neighborhood unit would decide upon the appropriate option based on citizen preferences for services, community resources, costs, and quality desired.[61]

Schemes for neighborhood delivery of services have surfaced periodically as a panacea to many of the service delivery problems mentioned above. Few of these proposals have been enacted, and these few have proved only moderately successful. In an era of scarce resources, new ideas about improving the quantity and quality of urban services are likely to increase. The test for urban managers in the 1980s will be to design and pilot new ideas for greater efficiency and effectiveness in delivering urban services.

These new ideas will have to be coupled with performance measurement systems that are economical, fair, and accurate, and the whole process will require the active involvement of elected officials, administrators, and citizens if local governments are to meet the needs of their residents.

As Lineberry has noted, the distribution of urban public services is characterized as one of unpatterned inequality. Change in this system will be slow, but necessary if we are to increase the quality of life in urban America.

The issues of decentralization, citizen participation, urban bureaucracy, and service delivery are complex, important, related, and highly political. We have seen these issues surface as a result of the urban riots in the 1960s and 1970s. For fifteen years citizen groups, bureaucrats, and elected officials have negotiated and bargained on techniques and strategies for making local government more responsive to citizen needs. These efforts have focused on trying to decentralize some of the decision-making processes and devolving more power to the communities.

However, not all of these issues can be attributed to the urban riots. The reform movement had a major impact on the structure and operation of local government. By professionalizing and centralizing local government, the reformers took decision-making away from the political organizations and, in many instances, the people.

The dominance of bureaucratic power and the increase of bureaucratic decision rules have given rise to many unintended and occasionally negative consequences. Lineberry noted that decision rules caused unequal service delivery between neighborhoods. Lipsky pointed out that street-level bureaucrats responding to established decision rules often make decisions not in the best interests of their clients. Bureaucrats in larger, more bureaucratic cities have been criticized for waste, inefficiency, fraud, and lack of responsiveness to citizen demands. These negative characteristics of large bureaucracies have made local officials much more aware of the need for change and innovation in the administrative branch. These reform efforts, designed to increase bureaucratic performance and productivity, are implemented sometimes at the expense of equity concerns, and often at the expense of access and participation by citizens.

The movement for greater involvement by citizens and for reform of the bureaucracy is as much a reaction to reform as it is a result of poor living conditions. To understand the changes occurring throughout urban America today, students need to understand the relationship of machine politics to the reform movement and the relationship of reform politics to contemporary urban administration.

## NOTES

1. Clarence N. Stone, Robert K. Whelan, and William J. Murin, *Urban Policy and Politics in a Bureaucratic Age* (Englewood Cliffs, N.J.: Prentice-Hall, 1979), p. 143.
2. David R. Morgan, *Managing Urban America: The Politics and Administration of America's Cities,* 2nd ed. (North Scituate, Mass.: Duxbury Press, 1983), pp.

80–83. Also see Francis E. Rourke, *Bureaucracy, Politics, and Public Policy*, 3rd ed. (Boston: Little, Brown, 1984), chaps. 2–4.

3.  H. H. Gerth and C. Wright Mills, eds., *From Max Weber: Essays in Sociology* (New York: Oxford University Press, 1946), pp. 196–204.

4.  Robert K. Merton, "Bureaucratic Structure and Personality," *Social Forces* 18 (May 1940): 562.

5.  Harlan Hahn and Charles H. Levine, eds., *Urban Politics: Past, Present and Future*, 2nd ed. (New York: Longman, 1984), p. 17.

6.  See Robert K. Merton, "Bureaucratic Structure and Personality," in *Social Theory and Social Structure*, ed. Merton (New York: Free Press, 1957); and W. Richard Scott, "Professional Employees in a Bureaucratic Structure: Social Work," in *The Semi-Professions and Their Organization*, ed. Amitai Etzioni (New York: Free Press, 1969), pp. 119–22.

7.  For a discussion of this concept see Stone, Whelan, and Murin, *Urban Policy and Politics*, pp. 319–324.

8.  Donald A. Schon, "The Blindness System," *The Public Interest* 18 (Winter 1979): 24–39.

9.  Frances Fox Piven and Richard A. Cloward, *Regulating the Poor: The Functions of Public Welfare* (New York: Pantheon Books, 1971), chaps. 4–5.

10. Joseph Wambaugh has written several novels about police officers depicting this type of behavior. See *The Blue Knight, The New Centurions*, and *The Black Marble*, all available in paperback. To date, no exciting novel has been written about sanitation workers.

11. Stone, Whelan, and Murin, *Urban Policy and Politics*, p. 322.

12. Merton, *Social Theory and Social Structure*. Also see Anthony Downs, *Inside Bureaucracy* (Boston: Little, Brown, 1967).

13. Demetrios Caraley, *City Governments and Urban Problems* (Englewood Cliffs, N.J.: Prentice-Hall, 1977), p. 262; and Downs, *Inside Bureaucracy*, p. 100.

14. Frank Levy, Arnold Meltsner and Aaron Wildavsky, *Urban Outcomes: Schools, Streets and Libraries* (Berkeley: University of California Press, 1974), p. 229. Also see Kenneth R. Mladenka, "The Urban Bureaucracy and the Chicago Political Machine: Who Gets What and the Limits to Political Control," *The American Political Science Review* 74 (December 1980): 991–998; Bryan D. Jones, Saadia R. Greenberg, Clifford Kaufman, and Joseph Drew, "Service Delivery Rules and the Distribution of Local Government Services: Three Detroit Bureaucracies," *Journal of Politics* (May 1978): 332–368.

15. See Levy, Meltsner, and Wildavsky, *Urban Outcomes*.

16. Most of the literature on citizen participation cited above discusses impersonality as a major reason for wanting agencies decentralized and more community residents involved in the delivery of services.

17. Theodore J. Lowi, "Machine Politics—Old and New," *The Public Interest* (Fall 1967): 83–92.

18. Ibid., p. 86.

19. Ibid., p. 86.

20. See Michael Lipsky, "Toward a Theory of Street-Level Bureaucracy," in *Theoretical Perspectives on Urban Politics*, ed. Willis Hawley et al. (Englewood Cliffs, N.J.: Prentice-Hall, 1976) p. 196; and Michael Lipsky, "Street-Level Bureaucracy and The Analysis of Urban Reform," *Urban Affairs Quarterly* 6 (June 1971): 391–409.

21. Lipsky, "Toward a Theory," p. 197.

22. Ibid., pp. 198–201. Also see Michael Lipsky, *Street-Level Bureaucracy: Dilemmas of the Individual in Public Services* (New York: Russell Sage Foundation, 1980), chaps. 3–6.

23. Lipsky, "Toward a Theory," pp. 201–204; and Lipsky, *Street-Level Bureaucracy*, chaps. 7–10. Also see Jeffrey M. Prottas, "The Power of the Street-

Level Bureaucrat in Public Service Bureaucracies," *Urban Affairs Quarterly* 13 (March 1978): 285–313.

24. See Prottas, "The Power of the Street-Level Bureaucrat," pp. 288–89. Also see Lipsky, *Street-Level Bureaucracy,* pp. 15–25 and chap. 4.

25. Douglas Yates, "Service Delivery and the Urban Political Order," in *Improving Urban Management,* ed. Willis D. Hawley and David Rogers (Beverly Hills: Sage Publications, 1976), p. 147.

26. David Greytak, Donald Phares, with Elaine Morley, *Municipal Output and Performance in New York City* (Lexington, Mass.: D. C. Heath, 1976), p. xvii.

27. For a discussion of participation activities by citizens see Sidney Verba and Norman Nie, *Participation in America* (New York: Harper and Row, 1972); Kenneth Mladenka, "Citizen Demand and Bureaucratic Response," *Urban Affairs Quarterly* 12 (March 1977): 273–290; Peter K. Eisinger, "The Pattern of Citizen Contacts with Urban Officials," in *People and Politics in Urban Society,* ed. Harland Hahn (Beverly Hills: Sage Publications, 1972), pp. 43–69; and Marilyn Gittell et al., *Limits to Citizen Participation: The Decline of Community Organizations* (Beverly Hills: Sage Publications, 1980).

29. York Wilbern and Lawrence Williams, "City Taxes and Services: Citizens Speak Out," *Nation's Cities* (August 1971), pp. 10–23. Also see Wayne Hoffman, "The Democratic Response of Urban Governments: An Empirical Test with Simple Spatial Models," in *Citizen Preferences and Urban Public Policy,* ed. Terry N. Clark (Beverly Hills: Sage Publications, 1977), pp. 29–50.

30. Douglas Yates, *The Ungovernable City: The Politics of Urban Problems and Policy Making* (Cambridge, Mass.: MIT Press, 1977), pp. 63–64.

31. See Charles H. Levine, Irene S. Rubin, and George G. Wolohojian, *The Politics of Retrenchment: How Local Governments Manage Fiscal Stress* (Beverly Hills: Sage Publications, 1981).

32. Levy, Meltsner, and Wildavsky, *Urban Outcomes,* pp. 16–17.

33. Robert L. Lineberry, *Equality and Urban Policy: The Distribution of Municipal Services* (Beverly Hills: Sage Publications, 1977).

34. Lineberry, *Equality and Urban Policy,* chap. 3.

35. Levy, Meltsner, and Wildavsky, *Urban Outcomes,* chap. 3.

36. Lineberry, *Equality and Urban Policy,* p. 147.

37. Richard C. Rich, "Equity and Institutional Design in Urban Service Delivery," in *The Politics and Economics of Urban Services,* ed. Robert L. Lineberry (Beverly Hills: Sage Publications, 1978), p. 122.

38. Charles Benson and Peter Lund, *Neighborhood Distribution of Local Public Services* (Berkeley: Institute of Government Studies, University of California, 1969).

39. Rich, "Equity and Institutional Design in Urban Service Delivery," p. 126.

40. For a discussion of some of the influences that affect service distribution see Bryan Jones and Clifford Kaufman, "The Distribution of Urban Public Services: A Preliminary Model," *Administration and Society* 6 (November 1974): 337–360.

41. Bryan D. Jones, "Party and Bureaucracy: The Influence of Intermediary Groups on Urban Public Service Delivery," *American Political Science Review* 75 (September 1981): 689.

42. Jones, "Party and Bureaucracy," p. 699.

43. Lipsky, *Street-Level Bureaucracy,* p. 55.

44. Stone, Whalen, and Murin, *Urban Policy and Politics,* p. 318.

45. Jeffrey Manditch Prottas, *People Processing: The Street-Level Bureaucrat in Public Service Bureaucracies* (Lexington, Mass.: D. C. Heath, 1979), pp. 1–7.

46. For a discussion of the costs of services to clients see Lipsky, *Street-Level Bureaucracy,* pp. 88–94; and Jeffrey Manditch Prottas, "The Cost of Free Services: Organizational Impediments to Access to Public Services," *Public*

*Administration Review* 41 (September/October 1981): 527–532. For an interesting analysis of four case studies of how clients interact with agencies see Prottas, *People Processing,* chaps. 1–4. A much more optimistic view of agency-
client relations is presented in Charles T. Goodsell, *The Case for Bureaucracy:
A Public Administration Polemic* (Chatham, N.J.: Chatham House, 1983).

47. Prottas, "The Power of the Street-Level Bureaucrat in Service Bureaucracies,"
    p. 289.
48. Morgan, *Managing Urban America,* pp. 47–49.
49. Ibid., p. 156.
50. For a discussion of performance measures see Harry P. Hatry, "Measuring the
    Quality of Public Services," in *Improving Urban Management,* pp. 13–18.
51. See Kenneth Webb and Harry P. Hatry, *Obtaining Citizen Feedback: The
    Application of Citizen Surveys to Local Government* (Washington: Urban Insti-
    tute, 1973). Also see Nicholas Lovrich, Jr., and G. Thomas Taylor, Jr.,
    "Neighborhood Evaluation of Local Government Services: A Citizen Survey
    Approach," *Urban Affairs Quarterly* 12 (December 1976): 197–222.
52. Hatry, "Measuring the Quality of Public Services," pp. 16–17.
53. For analysis of this system and its problems see Bernard H. Ross and Louise G.
    White, "Managing Urban Decentralization," *The Urban Interest* 3 (Spring
    1981): 82–89.
54. For a discussion of coproduction of services see Roger B. Parks et al., "Con-
    sumers as Coproducers of Public Services," *Policy Studies Journal* 9 (Summer
    1981): 1001–1011; and Stephen L. Percy, "Conceptualizing and Measuring
    Citizen Coproduction of Safety and Security," *Policy Studies Journal* 7
    (Special Issue 1978): 468–492.
55. Rich, "Equity and Institutional Design in Urban Service Delivery," p. 128.
56. Rick K. Wilson, "Citizen Coproduction as a Mode of Participation: Conjec-
    tures and Models," *Journal of Urban Affairs* 3 (Fall 1981): 40.
57. E. S. Savas, "Municipal Monopoly," *Harpers Magazine* (December 1971), p.
    55. For a discussion of the exit and voice options see Albert O. Hirshman, *Exit,
    Voice and Loyalty: Responses to Declines in Firms, Organizations and States*
    (Cambridge, Mass.: Harvard University Press, 1970); and Robert L. Bish and
    Vincent Ostrom, *Understanding Urban Government* (Washington: American
    Enterprise Institute, 1973).
58. See E. S. Savas, "Municipal Monopolies Versus Competition in Delivering
    Urban Services" in *Improving the Quality of Urban Management,* p. 483; and
    Roger Ahlbrandt, "Efficiency in the Provision of Fire Services," *Public
    Choice* 16 (Fall 1973); 1–15. Also see E. S. Savas, "How Much Do Govern-
    ment Services Really Cost?", *Urban Affairs Quarterly* 15 (September 1979):
    23–42; and E. S. Savas, *Privatizing the Public Sector: How to Shrink Govern-
    ment* (Chatham, N.J.: Chatham House, 1982).
59. Patricia S. Florestano and Stephen B. Gordon, "Private Provision of Public
    Services: Contracting by Large Local Governments," *International Journal of
    Public Administration* 1 (1979): 307–327; and Florestano and Gordon, "A Sur-
    vey of City and County Use of Private Contracting," *The Urban Interest* 3
    (Spring 1981): 22–30.
60. Some of this evidence can be found in E. S. Savas, "Intercity Competition
    Between Public and Private Sector Service Delivery," *Public Administration
    Review* 41 (January/February 1981): 46–51.
61. Rich, "Equity and Institutional Design in Urban Service Delivery," pp. 134–
    136.

# 8. METROPOLITAN AMERICA: CITIES AND SUBURBS

## METROPOLITAN AREAS

A chief—probably the chief—characteristic of modern urban America is its very high degree of metropolitanization: the centering of the urban population in metropolitan areas. The term *metropolitan area* is a loose one and is used to refer to any large concentration of urban dwellers who evidence a high degree of economic interdependence and social interaction. This particular use of the expression disregards government boundaries and emphasizes instead the common social and economic interests of the population.

A more precise definition has been devised by the federal government, a definition that makes it possible to contrast one metropolitan area with another in a meaningful way. The definition also reminds one that government in metropolitan areas is highly fragmented. Too often, studies of urban politics tend to concentrate on the central cities, leaving out in large measure the politics of suburbia. In this chapter, we first take a look at metropolitan areas and then give some specific attention to the problems of suburbia.

As we shall see, the notion of a metropolitan area emphasizes the degree of interaction and interdependence of the residents of those areas. Yet, there exists no government which is capable of acting to advance the interests of the entire metropolitan area. Instead, the governmental power and authority of the metropolitan area are fragmented and unevenly distributed. Each political jurisdiction is given the right to rule over its own area without taking into account how its actions will affect the residents of neighboring communities.

## SMSAs and MSAs

The concept of the *Standard Metropolitan Statistical Area (SMSA)* was developed to give government and industry a basis for comparative research. A definition has been created by the United States Bureau of the Budget and has been used extensively by the Census Bureau. The term was adopted for

TABLE 8.1
Distribution of Population in Metropolitan and Nonmetropolitan Areas: 1950 to 1980
*(Reflects areas as defined at each census)*

| Area | 1950[1] | 1960 | 1970 | 1980 |
|---|---|---|---|---|
| POPULATION (MILLIONS) | | | | |
| United States | 151.3 | 179.3 | 203.2 | 226.5 |
| Inside SMSA's ................. | 84.9 | 112.9 | 139.4 | 169.4 |
| Central cities .............. | 49.7 | 58.0 | 63.8 | 67.9 |
| Outside central cities .................... | 35.2 | 54.9 | 75.6 | 101.5 |
| Outside SMSA's ............... | 66.5 | 66.4 | 63.8 | 57.1 |
| PERCENT OF U.S. | | | | |
| United States .......... | 100.0 | 100.0 | 100.0 | 100.0 |
| Inside SMSA's ................. | 56.1 | 63.0 | 68.6 | 74.8 |
| Central cities .............. | 32.8 | 32.3 | 31.4 | 30.0 |
| Outside central cities .................... | 23.3 | 30.6 | 37.2 | 44.8 |
| Outside SMSA's ............... | 43.9 | 37.0 | 31.4 | 25.2 |

[1]Including Alaska and Hawaii.
Source: 1980 Census of Population, Bureau of the Census, October 1981, p. 1

TABLE 8.2
Population Growth in Metropolitan Areas: 1950 to 1980 (in Percent)

| Area | 1940–1950[1] | 1950–1960 | 1960–1970 | 1970–1980 |
|---|---|---|---|---|
| United States ................. | 14.5% | 18.5% | 13.3% | 11.4% |
| Inside SMSA's .................... | 22.0% | 26.4% | 16.6% | 10.2% |
| Central cities[2] ................... | 14.0% | 10.7% | 6.4% | 0.1% |
| Outside central cities........................ | 35.5% | 48.6% | 26.8% | 18.2% |
| Outside SMAS's ................. | 6.1% | 7.1% | 6.8% | 15.1% |

[1]Including Alaska and Hawaii.
[2]Data for central cities and outside central cities do not include any revisions for annexations or other boundary changes during the decade.
Source: 1980 Census of Population, Bureau of the Census, October 1980, p. 1

use in the 1960 census. Based on certain criteria we shall look at in a moment, the Bureau of the Budget (now the Office of Management and Budget) has been able to establish precise geographical boundaries with the advice of an interagency Federal Committee on Standard Metropolitan Areas.

The principal objective in setting up standard definitions was to "make it possible for all Federal statistical agencies to utilize the same boundaries in publishing statistical data useful for analyzing metropolitan problems."[1] In clarifying this, the bureau added: "The general concept of a metropolitan area is one of an integrated economic and social unit with a recognized large population nucleus."[2]

How does one go about determining whether or not a particular area qualifies as an SMSA? The bureau's definition of the term is all-important:

> The definition of an individual standard metropolitan statistical area involves two considerations; first, a city or cities of specified population to constitute the central city and to identify the county in which it is located as the central county, and second, economic and social relationships with contiguous counties which are metropolitan in character, so that the periphery of the specific metropolitan area may be determined. Standard metropolitan areas may cross State lines, if this is necessary in order to include qualified contiguous counties.[3]

In 1980 the Federal government changed its designation classification from SMSA to Metropolitan Statistical Area (MSA). Using new standards developed by the interagency Federal Committee on Standard Metropolitan Statistical Areas, the Office of Management and Budget implemented a two-stage process for reclassifying metropolitan areas. The process was completed in mid-1983.

The new standards provide a more flexible system for defining metropolitan areas in three different categories: primary metropolitan statistical areas, metropolitan statistical areas, and consolidated metropolitan statistical areas. These areas are further refined into four levels based on population size:

Level A    1,000,000 or more
Level B    250,000–1,000,000
Level C    100,000–250,000
Level D    less than 100,000

Metropolitan statistical areas are relatively freestanding areas and are not associated with other metropolitan statistical areas. These areas closely resemble the old SMSAs. In population areas over 1 million, primary metropolitan areas may be identified. These areas consist of a large urbanized county or cluster of counties that demonstrate strong economic and social links. Primary metropolitan statistical areas are parts of large areas called consolidated metropolitan statistical areas.

## Distribution of MSAs

Because of population growth, the number of SMSAs or MSAs constantly increases. The listing also changes from time to time because the definition of an MSA may be amended. As of June 27, 1983, there existed 335 MSAs (including five in Puerto Rico). The population included within the MSAs amounted to 75 percent of the entire U.S. population of the same date. In terms of land areas of the country, however, these same metropolitan areas accounted for only 16 percent of the total.

Obviously metropolitan areas vary greatly in size. Some, like Enid, Oklahoma, and Lawrence, Kansas, are quite small. Others, like New York, Chicago, and Los Angeles, are very large. Some metropolitan areas spill over state lines; e.g., New York, Chicago, St. Louis, Washington, Philadelphia, and Memphis. In other instances the metropolitan area is contained within a single county; e.g., Miami, Florida; Jersey City, New Jersey; Green Bay, Wisconsin; Galveston, Texas; and Erie, Pennsylvania.

## Metropolitan Fragmentation

One of the most difficult problems confronting people seeking solutions to urban problems is the enormous number of local government units in the country. Table 8.3 makes it easy to understand Congressman Reuss' exasperation when he states, "Nowhere but in America have so few ever been governed by so many."[4] The total represents approximately one local government for every 3,000 U.S. residents.

TABLE 8.3
Scope of the Subnational System:
Number of Governments in the U.S.

| Type of Government | 1962 | 1967 | 1972 | 1977 | 1982 |
|---|---|---|---|---|---|
| Total | 91,237 | 81,299 | 78,269 | 80,171 | 82,688 |
| U.S. Government | 1 | 1 | 1 | 1 | 1 |
| State Governments | 50 | 50 | 50 | 50 | 50 |
| Local Governments | 91,186 | 81,248 | 78,218 | 80,120 | 82,637 |
| Counties | 3,043 | 3,049 | 3,044 | 3,042 | 3,041 |
| Municipalities | 18,000 | 18,048 | 18,517 | 18,856 | 19,083 |
| Townships | 17,142 | 17,105 | 18,991 | 16,822 | 16,748 |
| School Districts | 34,678 | 21,782 | 15,781 | 15,260 | 15,032 |
| Special Districts | 18,323 | 21,264 | 23,885 | 26,140 | 28,733 |

Source: U.S. Bureau of the Census

Students of American national government know that the size and the scope of the federal government and its activities is overwhelming. What they often forget is that the size and the scope of the subnational system is equally impressive and much more complex. A look at the table helps to highlight some of our problems:

Even though the number of governments in the U.S. has decreased by 9,000 in the past twenty years, there are still well over 80,000 units of local government, which is a huge number.

Governmental units have remained relatively constant except for school districts and special districts. Schools have been reduced by half, due primarily to consolidation. Special districts have increased by 50 percent in an effort to find new service delivery mechanisms.

The subnational system represents a highly decentralized administrative system that serves as a check against unwise or autocratic federal policymaking. It also produces fragmentation, duplication, and waste.

The MSAs have over 20,000 local governments, which averages out to more than 70 per MSA. The range is enormous, however, with some MSAs, like New York and Chicago, having over 1,000 while others have fewer than 10. The older metropolitan areas average more local governments than the newer ones. Some researchers have claimed that the number of governments in an MSA is less the result of statutory and constitutional restrictions than it is a product of the city's age and its location in the country.[5]

## Race and Income Imbalance in Metropolitan Areas

One of the outstanding—but not surprising—findings of the 1970 census was the degree of racial polarization found in the largest metropolitan areas. During the 1960s, the trend had accelerated. In the sixty-six largest metropolitan areas, accounting for half the population of the United States, the white population declined 5 percent while the black population went up by 30 percent. The exodus of white residents to the suburbs, coupled with the inflow of black migrants to the central cities, drastically affected the racial composition and distribution in the largest metropolitan regions.

By 1980, the picture had changed again. Blacks increased in both numbers and percentage of total population in the suburbs of the largest urban areas. They were moving with increasing frequency into white suburban areas that for years had been unwilling to accept them. During the 1970s these close-in suburban communities began to experience population declines and economic hardship. For many black families these suburbs still represented a move upward from the decaying inner cities they came from. The result was that many black middle-class neighborhoods began to develop in previously all-white suburbs. In cities such as Los Angeles, Washington, D.C., St. Louis, Baltimore, Atlanta, Newark, and Cleveland, the exodus of blacks to the suburbs was similar to the "white flight" experience of the 1960s.

The Census Bureau reported that in the 38 metropolitan areas with populations over 1 million, the number of blacks living in suburbs increased from 2.3 million to 3.7 million during the 1970s—an increase of 60 percent.

Of course, the integration of the suburbs has not proceeded uniformly. In Washington, D.C., for example, there was during the 1970s extensive black population growth in Prince Georges County, Maryland, but much less black migration to the more exclusive areas, such as Montgomery County, Maryland, and Fairfax County, Virginia. Black migration to the suburbs appears to have increased, but it still does not equal the exodus of whites from central cities to the suburbs.

Interestingly, a different picture emerges when examining the 41 metropolitan areas whose populations fall between 500,000 and 1 million. In these areas the black population rose 25 percent between 1970–1980, from 726,000 to 907,000. Unlike in the largest metropolitan areas, however, here the percentage of blacks in the suburbs fell from 5.3 percent to 3.1 percent. This category included a number of younger cities as well as some southern cities.[6]

In the central cities the changes are more predictable. Of the nation's fifty largest cities in 1970, three (Washington, Newark, and Atlanta) were reported to be more than half black. Another major city, Gary, Indiana, also had a black majority. In percentages, the black population accounted for 71.1 percent of the population of Washington; 54.2 percent of Newark; 52.8 percent of Gary; and 51.3 percent of Atlanta. Of the twelve largest cities, the only one to gain in white population was Los Angeles, where the whites increased by 5.3 percent to 2.17 million. During the 1960–1969 decade, the largest loss of white residents took place in Chicago. This came to 505,000 persons, a drop of 18.6 percent from the total 1960 population.

By 1980 several more cities recorded a black majority. Added to Washington, D.C., Newark, Atlanta, and Gary were Birmingham, Wilmington, New Orleans, Baltimore, Detroit, and Richmond. At the same time this was happening, several cities in the South were reporting a decline in black suburban populations. Among these were Houston, Tampa, Fort Lauderdale, Memphis, Nashville, Charlotte, and Greenville, South Carolina. In many cases these figures tell less about migration than they do about growth. As these cities expanded their boundaries or grew into adjacent areas, their new metropolitan areas soon encompassed larger numbers of whites.

In general one can say that almost every major city outside the South experienced an increase in the number of blacks living in suburbia. The pattern of increase is not even, however. The northern cities experienced their black suburban increases in older, close-in suburbs. Many of the newer suburban areas, located on the fringes of the metropolitan area, showed little or no increases in the number of blacks.[7]

Minorities have a higher birth rate than whites. Therefore, we can expect that more and more central cities will develop black or Hispanic majorities. Recent reports indicate that Hispanics are now the single largest ethnic group in the United States, and by 1990 they will be our largest minority group. It is also estimated that by 1990 Hispanics will comprise 50 percent of California's population and 33 percent of the population of Texas.

There is no reason at present to anticipate a major shift in nonwhite population from the central cities to the suburbs, although there are indications that more middle-class blacks are moving to the suburbs. The reverse flow of whites back to the central cities, a very minor one, seems mostly to consist of upper- or middle-class couples who do not have children, or whose children have left home.

Also unequally distributed in metropolitan areas is poverty. Inside the metropolitan areas, the poor are concentrated in the central cities. The reason for this is very simple: the great majority of nonwhite poor live in the central cities. In 1975, for example, of the 15,348,000 persons living in metropolitan areas who were classified as "poor," some 4,967,000 were black. Very few of them lived in the suburban rings of the great cities. The poor, obviously, cannot afford good, nonsubsidized housing.

In almost every aspect, including better housing and better schools, the suburbs have the advantage over the central cities. Yet there are many qualifications that must be made, since suburbs vary considerably. It is simply a fiction of antisuburban novelists that the suburban population of this country is almost entirely upper-class, white, and "main line" Protestant.

What seems to lead to the confusion here is that, in the aggregate, there are certain significant differences between central cities and their urban fringes. A 1964 census study examined the socioeconomic status for urbanized areas based on measures of occupation, education, and income.[8] Using a four-range scale, the researchers found that proportionally more persons of high status were found in the suburbs. Some 23 percent of the suburban residents were placed in the highest status category, while less than 4 percent were in the lowest. In the central cities only about 14 percent of the population achieved highest status rank and some 9 percent fell into the lowest classification.

Yet when the investigators focused their attention on the middle range of scores rather than the extremes, they found that the supposed urban-suburban wall between "haves" and "have-nots" does not really exist. There is, instead, a substantial overlap. One-fourth of the suburban residents were discovered to be in the lower two of the four categories, while more than one-half of the central city population was in the two highest categories.

In addition to this census study, there is abundant evidence to indicate that class composition varies from suburb to suburb. For example, it has been estimated that about half of all AFL-CIO members live in the suburbs; for those under the age of forty, the figure rises to three-quarters. In short, the suburbs are not the locale of only the rich and the wellborn. They contain, in fact, a broad middle range of American society.

An analysis of the Saint Louis metropolitan area also pointed up the fallacies of the central city–suburban stereotype. Employing the techniques of social area analysis, the study confirmed the general impression that the central city contained more neighborhoods of low social rank, high urbanization, and high segregation than its suburbs. But it was also learned that the governmental boundary between the city and the suburbs was not a social boundary separating the poor from the rich. There were prosperous and poor neighborhoods on both sides of the city line.[9]

In view of such findings, how is one to account for the readily observable suburban-urban disparities? Leo F. Schnore has come up with a reasonable explanation.[10] He concludes that the two basic determinants of differences among metropolitan areas are the size of the metropolitan area and the age of the central city. Given this information, one could account for the differentials that exist within particular metropolitan regions.

## SUBURBIA

The 1970 census confirmed what experts on population had long suspected would eventually happen. This census indicated for the first time that more than half of the population of metropolitan areas was located in the suburbs. The shift in the balance of metropolitan populations from the central cities to their suburbs has had obvious consequences in a large variety of fields, including marketing and distribution of goods, communication of ideas, finance and banking, and governmental services. In focusing attention on the importance of the suburbs generally, the census also suggested their importance in specific sectors, including the political.

From a political point of view, suburbanization was a dominant force in the electoral and governmental processes of the 1970s. This was true at the state level as well as within particular metropolitan areas.

As we have observed earlier, the term *suburb* encompasses a wide variety of actual localities. As far back as 1925, H. Paul Douglass advised his fellow sociologists to distinguish between the "suburb of consumption" —the residential type—and the "suburb of production"—the industrial type.

More recent research has thrown a good deal of light upon the socio-economic differences in American suburbs. These are considerable and cover a very wide range, as the study of 154 suburbs undertaken by Frederick M. Wirt has shown.[11] What emerges from his study is a continuum of suburbs, each with its own socioeconomic composition and its own life-style.

Suburbs, therefore, can no longer be stereotyped as the typical bed-room community. The once-popular commuter or dormitory suburb of the middle-class white family has become but one of several different types of suburbs. Suburbs today can be categorized by economic status, race, age, religion, or proximity to the central city. In addition, there are recreational suburbs, light industrial suburbs, and commercial suburbs, all of which cater to the different needs of their residents and residents in the metropolitan area.[12]

People move to the suburbs, stay there, and raise their children there for a wide variety of reasons. There is both a "push" and a "pull" effect. The push forces are such things as crime in the cities, bad schools, and deteriorating housing. The pull forces include the desire for more space, the wish to own a home, and the attraction of superior suburban schools.

Whether, or to what extent, people who have willingly moved from central city to suburbs have achieved their objectives is not readily determinable. What is clear is that the great social problems of education, housing, crime, health care, drug addiction, and care for the elderly are becoming increasingly more serious in metropolitan areas outside the central cities.

### Political Characteristics of Suburbs

Congressional representation is rapidly shifting in favor of the suburbs. In 1966, 171 members of the House came from rural areas and small towns, while the remaining 264 were from districts that were predominantly metropolitan. Of these metropolitan districts, 110 were located in central cities, 98 were dominated by the suburban areas surrounding the central cities, and 56 districts contained a mixture of central city and suburban populations along with a minority of rural residents.

By 1972, the effects of reapportionment according to the 1970 census were felt. As a result of the 1972 elections, 291 members of Congress came from metropolitan areas and 144 from rural areas. Of the metropolitan group, 100 were from districts dominated by the central city, 129 were from predominantly suburban districts, and 62 represented districts that were mostly composed of central city and suburban voters, with a minority of rural residents.

This shift meant that the suburban portions of metropolitan areas picked up some thirty-one new congressional representatives between 1966 and 1972. For the first time in American history, suburban representation in Congress was greater than that of the central cities. More members of Congress came from suburban areas than from either cities or rural districts.

Taken by itself, the logic of the shift implied the probability of new congressional alliances through the 1970s. On the other hand, there is no evidence at all that the members of Congress from suburban areas constitute anything approaching a bloc, probably because they do not perceive themselves as such.

The trends noted above had accelerated by the time returns from the 1980 census became available. Florida proved to be the biggest winner, with a gain of four seats in the House of Representatives. Texas gained three seats and California two. New York was the biggest loser, with five seats being taken away, but Ohio, Illinois, and Pennsylvania each lost two seats. However, the only state that actually lost population was Rhode Island, which lost less than half a percent.

More than 40 percent of the national population growth was accounted for by just three states: California, Texas, and Florida. Together they gained about 9.25 million people.

*Nonpartisanship*

In contrast to national and state elections, many elections for suburban offices are conducted on a nonpartisan basis. The use of nonpartisan elections is, of course, widespread in the smaller and medium-size communities of the country. As we have seen earlier, nonpartisanship is accepted in theory in some of the largest cities, but in practice politics in such cities (and in many smaller ones) is nonpartisan in name only.

The popularity of the genuine nonpartisan approach is especially noteworthy in the suburbs. Practiced in approximately 60 percent of the suburbs, nonpartisanship may take several forms. Sometimes it is simply a means to add another party to the local scene to show independence from the dominant regional party, as in the Washington, D.C., suburbs. Or it may take the form of inclusion of members of the minority party in local councils, as happens in suburbs in New York and Connecticut. But most frequently, nonpartisanship takes the form of no association at all between local politics and the established parties. Public affairs are considered to be the province of various civic organizations whose goals are said to be "what is best for the community."

In this connection, it should be noted that a large percentage of suburban officials are appointed, not elected. Such people are not likely to have long-range political ambitions, since they presumably do not care whether they are gaining or losing political support. The suburban officials most likely to take a metropolitan-wide perspective are those who expect to run for higher office. The true "locals" are those most likely to resist regional perspectives.

Many communities that are not suburban also emphasize local politics, but it is important to distinguish between the no-party pattern common to suburbia and the one-party localism that occurs in many small towns. Under one-party localism, there is apt to be a good deal of intraparty fighting, as is shown in the primary battles. After the primary, it is expected that the ranks will close and party regularity will prevail. Party, per se, is valued.

In the suburbs, the political ethos is considerably different from that in most small towns. For example, this ethos deplores partisan activity and strives for a politics based on consensus. The ethos also requires that a suburbanite, if qualified, agree to participate in civic affairs. This may include unpaid part-time service, for example on a borough council. There is also the belief that the citizen knows best. Men and women should make up their own minds; they do not need ward leaders and politicians to tell them what to think or how to act.

### Economic Correlates of Suburban Voting Patterns

For some years now, social scientists have noted a close relationship between economic indexes and partisan voting. For example, an association has been found between persons with high incomes and those who vote Republican. Even though psychological factors may depress any one-to-one ratio between economic factors (rent, income, occupation) and voting behavior, the association between the two remains statistically high. In other words, suburban political variety is related to variety in the suburban economic base.

To translate these general propositions into the political behavior of a particular suburb presents obvious hazards, for the propositions are derived from aggregate data. Nonetheless, suburban political leaders have usually assumed the existence of some general correlation between economic characteristics and voting behavior. Their hunches have largely been supported by scientific data.

From a partisan point of view, what does this portend for the suburbs, especially in state and national elections? It is likely that the "exploding metropolis" will to some extent duplicate the patterns in the central city, where there are working-class, mixed, and silk-stocking wards. Since the out-migration consists only in small part of upper-class Republicans and in large part of middle-class and lower-class Democrats, the expectation is that the suburban Republican margins in state and national elections will be progressively reduced. What we do know about political socialization implies that the new migrants to the suburbs will retain their party affiliations, which are largely Democratic. Although there may be some reverse migration of rich Republicans into fashionable city sections, on balance the continuing migration ought to help the suburban Democrats.

## Political Issues of Suburbs

Observers have long noted that much of suburban politics is concerned with family-related issues. In particular, questions concerning the schools and housing attract continuing interest and attention. Of almost equal prominence is the perennial problem of taxes. Occasionally in the limelight are such additional subjects as the police, recreational facilities, and corruption in government. But corruption is much more likely to become an issue at the county level than within a particular suburb. In short, the politics of small communities tends to be focused on local issues. Local government in the suburbs usually pays very careful attention to the interests of its constituents.

### Schools

Everywhere in America, education is a prominent issue in local politics. But it is especially stressed in the residential suburbs since, as we have noted, one of the reasons people have moved to the suburbs is the presumed superiority of suburban over central-city schools. While there is wide variety in suburban school systems, there is no doubt that those found in the more affluent suburbs are at the top of the educational pyramid. Presumably this is because of the high socioeconomic status of the residents.

In the nonpartisan atmosphere of suburban politics, a sharp line traditionally has been drawn between politics and education. The tasks of the citizens were to see that the necessary funds were raised for school operations and to attend PTA meetings from time to time.

In recent years the schools in suburbia have increasingly been the subject not only of public interest but of public controversy. The reasons for this development are clear in a very broad way, but the specifics are hard to deal with unless one considers a particular school system over time. In general, the reasons for discontent stem from money and from dissatisfaction with what the student gets out of attending school.

The financial problem comes partly from the fact that in most states the principal source of revenue for suburban schools has been the local property tax. Dependence on local property taxes means that rich suburbs can spend more money on school systems than the poorer suburbs. This situation has been attacked in the courts, and various moves toward equalization of funding are under way. A second reaction has come from the taxpayers themselves. During the 1960s, the percentage of school bond issues voted down in referenda rose dramatically in spite of comparatively good financial years for most people. The results of the very deep recession in the mid-1970s made earlier taxpayers' resistance look tame by comparison. For example, in March, 1975, 60 percent of proposed local school district budgets in New Jersey were rejected by the voters. This happened even in the affluent suburbs.

In the late 1970s, taxpayers' revolts escalated. In California, Massachusetts, and Prince Georges County, Maryland, voters passed restrictive propositions that curtailed the ability of locally elected officials to arbitrarily raise property taxes to pay for local services. Propositions 13 and 2½ in California and Massachusetts and TRIM in Prince Georges County are just beginning to have a major impact on the provision of services.[13]

Taxpayer revolts are not confined to suburbs, but they do flare up in places like Prince Georges County, where homeowners became outraged by raises in assessments and taxes. Elected officials find that they are restricted in their ability to raise taxes, so they must cut services and reduce the work force. This is the situation that faced the newly elected County Executive in Prince Georges County. While schools have a revered place in the hearts of local residents and elected officials, the school budget is usually sizeable and, therefore, a prime candidate to be cut.

There are, of course, other problems, such as whether or not to recognize a teachers' union, the extent of busing, racial integration, and so on. But it also seems that a large part of parental objections to the management of any suburban school districts is the alleged decline in the quality of the educational product. As a result, there has been, nearly everywhere, a renewed emphasis on basic skills and a reimposition of curricular sequences and requirements. In the depressed 1970s, suburban parents were concerned more over the question of whether their offspring obtain good jobs than over how they spend their leisure hours. This pattern has continued into the 1980s.

*Housing and Land Use*

Problems of housing and land use are generally in the forefront of suburban political controversy. This is not unexpected, since one of the leading reasons for moving to, or living in, the suburbs is comfortable housing with adequate space. These considerations are at the very heart of the concept of suburban living.

When proposals are entertained for changes in land use—for instance, by amending the zoning ordinances to rezone an area from residential to light industrial—the disagreements tend to be very sharp. Such proposals always guarantee a full house at the hearings of the zoning board. This is understandable, because zoning changes have not only economic but also social consequences. Changes in the zoning code have an immediate impact on individual families and property owners. The disruption of existing patterns is viewed in highly personal terms.

Housing and land-use issues are quite often linked, since decisions about the use of land will determine if a developer decides to proceed with plans and what kind of housing will be built. Communities that seek to maintain the value of their housing as well as the racial purity of their neighborhoods have resorted to a number of techniques to protect their investments. Two of the most common strategies have been exclusionary zoning and limited-growth zoning.

Exclusionary zoning took the form of limiting the number of apartments with more than two bedrooms or limiting the use of the land by establishing minimum lot sizes, which were quite large. Both tactics had the effect of limiting or excluding lower-income families, who were not able to purchase an expensive home or to live in a two-bedroom apartment.

One study in the New York area found that over 99 percent of the undeveloped land zoned for residential use was zoned for single-family dwellings, thus excluding those wishing to reside in rental apartments.[14] A much more blatant example was the Black Jack, Missouri, case of the early 1970s. When a church-sponsored organization obtained approval from HUD to construct some moderate-income housing in Black Jack, the local residents responded by swiftly and successfully mounting a drive to incorporate their community and, consequently, take control of their own zoning process. One of their first acts was to pass a zoning ordinance outlawing multiple-family housing units. A local citizens' organization filed suit, charging that the zoning ordinances were blatantly discriminatory and in violation of the 1968 Fair Housing Act. After a succession of trials, the U.S. Supreme Court in 1974 finally upheld a lower court ruling striking down the Black Jack zoning ordinance.[15] Three years later, the Supreme Court refused to strike down an exclusionary zoning ordinance that prohibited a subsidized townhouse development. In this case, the court ruled that local officials in Arlington Heights, Illinois, did not intend to discriminate racially when they passed the ordinance.[16]

Limited-growth zoning issues have become very volatile and, as with other issues of this type, have defied political solution. Once again the courts were required to step in and resolve many of the disputes.

With limited-growth zoning, a political jurisdiction can develop a set of zoning specifications that imposes limits on the amount of growth the community will tolerate. In Ramapo, New Jersey, the political leaders worked out a careful plan for growth and development for a twenty-year period. They agreed to allow development to be phased in gradually, thus assuring that some building permits would be available each year. Developers submitted their proposed plans, which were evaluated against the capital improvements program. The courts upheld the plan and allowed Ramapo to implement it.[17] A similar growth plan was implemented in the small community of Petaluma, California, outside of San Francisco. This limited growth plan specifically provided for low-income housing, and, though initially rejected by the courts, it was eventually upheld by a federal circuit court of appeals.[18]

## FEDERAL IMPACT ON METRO AMERICA

The policies of the federal government have also had a substantial impact on the people and the politics of metropolitan America. The two areas where this impact has been the greatest have been in federal housing and federal highway policy. At the time these policies were being implemented, few people perceived the negative impact they would have on urban America.

### Federal Housing Policy

Federal housing policy had a negative impact on cities in several ways. As millions of veterans returned home after World War II, they married and began to start families, thus encouraging the housing industry to expand rapidly. The key to financing many of these new homes was section 203 of the 1934 Housing Act. This section authorized the Home Mortgage Insurance Program, enabling the newly created Federal Housing Administration (FHA) to insure millions of homes built over the next forty-five years.

The purpose of section 203 was to finance the acquisition of proposed, under-construction, or existing one- to four-family units. FHA would provide insurance up to 80 percent of the value of the property. The combination of a low down payment, a low risk for the developer, and a twenty-five to thirty-year period of relatively small payments helped to make this a very attractive program.

Second, the postwar economy was booming, and millions of young families had money to spend on durable goods such as homes, automobiles, and appliances, which had been in short supply during the war. For this reason, the passage of the GI Bill of Rights in 1944 became extremely important. Under the GI Bill, the Veterans Administration (VA) was authorized to insure home mortgages to veterans. No down payment was required from the buyer under this act.

The combined impact of section 203 and the GI Bill was to make new homes available to many more Americans. It also put the federal government heavily into the mortgage market, where it has remained to this day.

The housing market began to grow, as did the FHA-insured mortgages, which were heavily concentrated in new homes, not apartments, in suburban areas. This trend reduced the percentage of rental units in the nation's housing stock and also excluded from the suburbs segments of the population that could not afford to enter the single-home market.

Title I of the 1934 Housing Act was thought to be the device for eliminating inadequate and unacceptable housing as well as for rebuilding central business districts in the cities. If money was available to help rehabilitate and remodel city homes, it was assumed, the middle- and upper-middle-income residents might remain in the city. The basic premise of the government housing program was undermined when very little money was ever appropriated by Congress to implement the provisions of Title I.

The results are clear. All of the advantages, particularly for young marrieds, pointed to the suburbs. As housing was built, more suburbs flourished. Apartments and less-desirable housing in the central city were left to the new migrants, namely the blacks and Hispanics. The turnover principle of the housing market was in full swing. As more and more middle- and upper-income people fled the city, more older, run-down housing became available for lower-income residents to inhabit.[19]

The commitment of the young marrieds to move to the suburbs was reinforced by the federal tax code. By allowing homeowners to deduct mortgage interest and property taxes from their income taxes, the federal government encouraged and subsidized suburban growth at the expense of inner-city revitalization. White middle-class families were the prime movers to the suburbs. The billions of dollars deducted from taxes each year by middle-class home owners exceeded the amount of money the federal government allocated to subsidized housing for the poor. More recently we have seen how this same tax policy has stimulated the condominium and cooperative apartment conversion movement, which is displacing the elderly and the poor in many cities.

The cities lost much of the next generation of their middle-class and civic, business, and political leaders to the suburbs. Along with the middle class went a high percentage of its disposable income. These dollars were now being spent in suburban shopping malls, movie theaters, and automobile showrooms rather than in downtown retail shops.[20]

The southern migrants who moved into the large urban centers in the post-World War II period could not economically replace the middle-income residents who moved to suburbia. The new arrivals came to the cities of the northeast and north central states seeking jobs, but, for the most part, they possessed limited job skills. Without federal training programs, which did not start until the middle 1960s, the only available option was the apprenticeship-journeyman process in the unions. Since many of the unions were not anxious to expand their membership, particularly with blacks and Hispanics, acquiring the necessary job-related skills was almost impossible.

The jobs available were for unskilled laborers, and the pay was modest. Expenses were high and living conditions only passable. Unemployment rose, and cities found a whole new population mix within their boundaries. Not only had they lost sizeable tax revenues because of the defection of the middle class to suburbia, but the new arrivals were requiring more and more public services, which over the years increased in cost.

One other aspect of federal housing policy that had a negative effect on cities was the discrimination practiced by many private lending institutions. The FHA did not lend money directly to anybody; it merely insured the loan once a prospective home buyer had satisfied a private lending institution of his or her credit worthiness.

Dennis Judd asserts, "Financial considerations encouraged the FHA to promote social class and racial segregation. Segregation was synonomous with a safe investment. Additionally, FHA administrators shared the real estate industry's view that segregation was preferable to integration."[21]

In other words, a community was a sound investment if it was basically homogeneous—meaning, almost without exception, white. Selling a home to a family whose background or skin color differed from those in the neighborhood jeopardized the property values in that community. The National Association of Real Estate Boards endorsed this philosophy in its code of ethics. But what is more difficult to accept is the fact that the FHA subscribed to a similar set of principles in the belief that they were safeguarding home mortgages they had insured.

This policy effectively closed off the new suburban home market even to qualified black applicants, forcing them to find less desirable housing in the cities. The policy of segregated neighborhoods was often enforced through the use of racially restrictive covenants prohibiting a buyer from reselling a house to someone of a different race. The U.S. Supreme Court finally struck down these covenants in *Shelly* v. *Kraemer,* 334 U.S. 1 (1948). In 1968 Congress passed a Civil Rights Act, which included Title VIII, a Fair Housing Section (Public Law 90-284). This section barred discrimination in the sale or rental of housing, the financing of housing, and the provision of brokerage services. Nevertheless, racial discrimination in housing persists.[22]

For many homeowners and real estate brokers the prevailing sentiment is that homogeneous neighborhoods are better financial investments. In some metropolitan areas these views are reinforced by lending institutions that employ a technique known as redlining. Redlining is a device for delineating areas of a city or county that are considered less-desirable financial risks. The red line denotes an area within which the institution makes few if any loans, thereby taking away the potential for rehabilitation or growth in an economically depressed section of the city.[23]

Bankers and financial institutions are now prohibited by federal law from "writing off," or redlining, whole sections of a city. Instead they make loans for condominium conversions or for upper-income cooperative apartments in these areas but provide little financing for low-income housing tenants or apartment building owners or tenants who want to rehabilitate their apartments.

Biases in FHA lending practices continue today. Morris discusses FHA's current sunbelt-city orientation by pointing out that in 1975, the fifteen sunbelt states received 49 percent of FHA's mortgage insurance. Three of the fastest growing states—Florida, California, and Arizona—attracted almost 30 percent of the FHA mortgages. Just as the FHA helped the migration from central city to suburb with its mortgage policy, so today it is fueling the migration to the sunbelt. The FHA could be using its loan guarantees to shore up lending institution confidence in declining cities instead of following the market into the South and Southwest.[24]

## Federal Highway Programs

The federal government became involved in highways through the Highway Act of 1944, which allocated 25 percent of federal highway grants-in-aid for the construction of roads in cities. Traffic congestion in and around large urban centers had been increasing to the consternation of residents and commuters alike. The Bureau of Public Roads began advocating a nation-wide system of highways that would link all of the major population centers. In addition, it was felt that such a highway network would aid in the nation's defense by improving our capability to move military personnel and material quickly and efficiently around the country.

The major change in the development of the highway system occurred with the passage of the 1956 National Defense Highway Act. Congress changed the funding formula, increasing the federal share of highway con-struction projects from 50 percent to 90 percent. Coming just twelve years after the federal commitment to build a nationwide highway system, this change in funding not only accelerated the construction process, but it directly affected central cities.

In the 1944 to 1956 period, Americans used much of their newfound wealth to purchase automobiles, but a major drawback to auto ownership was the lack of an adequate system of roads and highways to permit safe and comfortable driving. As the burgeoning highway system began to develop in the late 40s and early 50s, the automobile became an increasingly important mode of transportation for millions of Americans.

The funding formula change of 1956 was a dramatic event in itself. When coupled with the FHA and VA policies of encouraging the develop-ment of single family homes in suburbia, a new trend was affirmed that had a profound effect on urban areas for at least the next generation. Where once the highway development system sought to assist commuters and aided com-mercial enterprises by linking large metropolitan areas, now a new pattern began to develop. More and more middle-income residents found living in suburbia less objectionable if they could get into their cars and commute to work on fast, new freeways. Furthermore, they could still enjoy the benefits of the central city's social, cultural, and night life now that transportation between home and central city had been made so much easier.

As more and more middle-class residents began to take advantage of the benefits of suburban home buying and easy access to the attractions of the central city, businesses began to appreciate the market and workforce potential of suburbia. In the 1950s huge shopping malls were opening in the highly developed suburban communities. Many of these malls contained branches of the best-known department and specialty stores in the central business districts. While this decentralization movement made sense for re-tailers and cut shopping time for suburban residents, it also deprived the central city of many tax dollars now paid to suburban governments.

The retail store movement was soon followed by the office building and factory boom. Land was plentiful and relatively cheap, and by the mid-1960s there were enough people living in suburbia to insure a good popula-tion mix from which to employ a workforce.[25]

As the highway system developed along with the expansion of subur-ban housing, the cycle of expansion and central city exodus was repeated. One commentator summed it up, "Like every transportation innovation preceding it, the new highway system drew the affluent farther away from the city. And with the expansion of credit fostered by the FHA and the VA, the middle and working classes were encouraged to trail along. The urban highway system made the land beyond the boundaries of the cities geographically accessible, while the FHA and the VA made it financially accessible to the growing urban population."[26]

Another issue emanating from the growth of the federal highway system was the negative impact this program had on inner-city neighborhoods and housing. As more and more highways that cut through the cities were planned, power struggles developed over the rights of way for the highways. Neighborhood groups fought to keep their homes from being demolished to make way for the new roads. In some cases the highways divided neighborhoods in half.

In Washington, D.C., legal action was successful in preventing an interstate highway from cutting through the city and destroying a number of homes and upsetting traditional neighborhood boundaries.

## THE FUTURE OF THE METROPOLITAN AREAS

Predictions about the future of metropolitan areas are often confusing. In the first place, some of the evidence is contradictory. It is often possible to cite opposing trends. And much of what passes for evidence has been carefully sifted by chambers of commerce or reform groups to lead to a particular conclusion.

But there is a second, and probably more profound, reason for the difficulty. It comes from the failure to distinguish sharply between two models of the metropolis. As a result, the analysis is often less focused than it could be.

The *historic model* stresses the linkages between the city and its suburbs. The impression is given that most suburbanites are directly dependent upon the city for their economic survival. The social and cultural dependence of the suburbs on the city is also emphasized.

The basic objection to the historic model is that it is outmoded in the 1980s. While it is still applicable to certain of the small and medium-sized metropolitan areas, it is rapidly becoming obsolete in regard to the largest of such areas, especially in the East and in the Midwest.

The *emerging model* emphasizes the autonomy of the suburbs. It suggests that the suburbs of New York City, Boston, Philadelphia, and Saint Louis, to cite a few prominent examples, will in all probability survive no matter how desperate the condition of the central cities becomes. The emerging model, which exists in many of the largest metropolitan areas, acknowledges that the suburbs have become increasingly independent of the cities economically and socially as well as politically. More and more jobs are found in these suburbs, as is shown by almost daily announcements that firms are abandoning downtown for suburban locations. Fewer and fewer suburbanites have any reason to come into the city at all, as life in the suburb becomes increasingly self-sufficient.

At the heart of the situation is the question of function. What does the city today do better than some other place? To confirmed urbanites, the answer may well be discouraging, for the big cities have been losing many of their historic functions. They are becoming less important, for example, as manufacturing and commercial centers. And ever since the advent of the automobile—about 1910—they have been losing out to the residential suburbs as attractive places in which to live.

The entire picture is complicated by the racial splits that seem firmly entrenched in the largest metropolitan areas. Yet it is vital to realize that the emerging or actual model of the metropolis was not created primarily by the heavy migration of blacks to the cities and the migration of whites to the suburbs. The movement of whites from the central cities began many decades ago, though black migration may have speeded it up in recent years. The basic reasons for departure were and remain mostly economic.[27] At least until the recession and inflation of the mid-1970s, one got more for one's money in the suburbs than in the cities. This was true both for home owners and for owners of industrial plants.

The belief by some that central cities and suburban communities appear to be coming closer together in political and socioeconomic characteristics is not borne out by the evidence. In fact, the emerging model appears to be an accurate picture of urban-suburban relations in the 1980s.

Sternlieb and Hughes, in testimony before Congress in 1979, pointed out that, by almost every important measure available, the central core of our largest cities was becoming a worse place in which to live and that suburbs were increasingly better off.[28] Citing demographic figures from 1977, Sternlieb and Hughes presented data on migration patterns, incomes, buying power, family structure, racial composition, and housing and commercial property abandonment to support their thesis that central cities were deteriorating badly.

The Advisory Commission on Intergovernmental Relations, in a 1980 report, demonstrated that taxable wealth and personal income were both growing faster in suburban areas than in central cities, thus widening the fiscal disparity between the two. Additionally, the Commission found that even though state and federal funding had become more responsive to central city needs, the central cities were under increasing pressure to increase both educational and non-educational services.[29]

Similar evidence has been prepared by the Department of Housing and Urban Development. In 1978, the Office of Community Planning and Development at HUD released a working paper that responded to an article stating that the urban crisis was over. The paper focused on income, employment, displacement, migration, and revenue sources and concluded that many of the nation's largest cities were still in serious trouble. The paper asserted that

many central cities still face severe economic, social, and environmental difficulties. Fiscal strain has not vanished and restricts the ability of many distressed cities to provide even conventional services and maintain or repair valued public investments in streets, sewers, and the like.[30]

In speculating on economic, social, and political trends in the suburbs, it is useful to realize to which of the two metropolitan models the particular area under examination more nearly corresponds. The chances are that more and more metropolitan areas will approximate the conditions postulated by the emerging model.

The fragmentation of power and authority, combined with autonomous units of government and racial and economic imbalances in metropolitan areas, has led to many proposals for reform and reorganization. Some of these will be discussed in the next chapter.

## NOTES

1. Office of Statistical Standards, Executive Office of the President, Bureau of the Budget, *Standard Metropolitan Statistical Areas* (Washington: U.S. Government Printing Office, 1967), p. vii. While this remains the basic document on the subject, occasional revisions are made to it.
2. Ibid., p. vii.
3. Ibid., p. 1.
4. Henry S. Reuss, *Revenue-Sharing* (New York: Praeger, 1970), p. 41.
5. Leo F. Schnore, "Forms of Government and Socioeconomic Characteristics of Suburbs," in *The Urban Scene,* ed. Schnore (New York: Free Press, 1965). Also see Thomas R. Dye, *Politics in States and Communities,* 4th ed. (Englewood Cliffs, N.J.: Prentice-Hall, 1981), pp. 326–27.
6. *Standard Metropolitan Statistical Areas and Standard Consolidated Statistical Areas: 1980,* U.S. Department of Commerce, Bureau of the Census (October 1981). Also see John Herbers, *New York Times,* May 31, 1981, pp. 1, 48.
7. *Standard Metropolitan Statistical Areas* and Herbers, p. 48. Also see Lowell W. Culver, "Changing Settlement Patterns of Black Americans, 1970–1980," *Journal of Urban Affairs* 4 (Fall 1982): 36–42; and Phillip L. Clay, "The Process of Black Suburbanization," *Urban Affairs Quarterly* 14 (June 1979): 405–24.
8. Bureau of the Census, *Current Population Reports, Technical Studies,* Series p. 23, No. 12 (July 31, 1964). For more recent data and analysis, see Mark Schneider, *Suburban Growth: Policy and Process* (Brunswick, Ohio: King's Court Communications, 1980), chap. 2.
9. See John C. Bollens, ed., *Exploring the Metropolitan Community* (Berkeley: University of California Press, 1961), pp. 17–18. A more recent study examining suburban patterns of residential segregation and fiscal inequality can be found in Mark Schneider and John R. Logan, "Fiscal Implications of Class Segregation: Inequalities in the Distribution of Public Goods and Services in Suburban Municipalities," *Urban Affairs Quarterly* 17 (September 1981): 23–36.
10. Leo F. Schnore, "The Socio-Economic Status of Cities and Suburbs," *American Sociological Review* 28 (February 1963): 76–85. Also see Leo F. Schnore, *Class and Race in Cities and Suburbs* (Chicago: Markham Publishing Company, 1972).
11. Frederick M. Wirt, "The Political Sociology of American Suburbia: A Reinterpretation," *The Journal of Politics* 27 (August 1965): 647–666. Also see Schneider, *Suburban Growth,* chap. 2.

12. For a discussion of suburbs and how they have changed over the years, see Frederick Wirt et al., *On the City's Rim: Politics and Policy in Suburbia* (Lexington, Mass.: D. C. Heath, 1972); and Anthony Downs, *Opening Up the Suburbs: An Urban Strategy for America* (New Haven: Yale University Press, 1973).

13. For an examination of different approaches to fiscal cutbacks, see Jeffrey McCaffrey, ed., "The Impact of Resource Scarcity on Urban Public Finance," *Public Administration Review* 41 (January 1981), whole issue.

14. Michael N. Danielson, *The Politics of Exclusion* (New York: Columbia University Press, 1976), p. 53.

15. *U.S.* v. *City of Black Jack, Missouri,* 508 F.2d 1179 (1974).

16. *Arlington Heights* v. *Metropolitan Housing Development Corporation,* 429 U.S. 252 (1977).

17. *Golden* v. *Planning Board of Town of Ramapo,* 39 N.Y.2d 359, 334 N.Y.S.2d 138, 285 N.E.2d 359 (1972).

18. *City of Petaluma* v. *Construction Industry Association of Sonoma County,* 522 F.2d 897 (1975).

19. Joseph P. Fried, *Housing Crisis U.S.A.* (Baltimore: Penguin Books, 1971), pp. 65–71.

20. Mark Schneider, *Suburban Growth: Policy and Process* (Brunswick, Ohio: Kings Court Communications, 1980), chap. 2. Also see Anthony Downs, *Opening Up the Suburbs: An Urban Strategy for America* (New Haven: Yale University Press, 1973), chaps. 1–3.

21. Dennis R. Judd, *The Politics of American Cities: Private Power and Public Policy* (Boston: Little, Brown, 1984), p. 283.

22. See Ronald E. Wienk et al., *Measuring Racial Discrimination in American Housing Markets: The Housing Market Practices Survey* (Washington: Department of Housing and Urban Development, 1979).

23. David Listokin and Stephen Casey, *Mortgage Lending and Race: Conceptual and Analytical Perspectives of the Urban Financing Problem* (Piscataway, N.J.: Center for Urban Policy Research, 1979). See the 1977 Community Reinvestment Act, which promotes reinvestment by lending institutions in their own communities.

24. Richard S. Morris, *Bum Rap on America's Cities* (Englewood Cliffs, N.J.: Prentice-Hall, 1980), p. 71.

25. For a discussion of the impact of federal transportation policy on urban areas, see Schneider, *Suburban Growth: Policy and Process,* pp. 13–34, 233–45.

26. Dennis R. Judd, *The Politics of American Cities,* pp. 294–95.

27. On these and related developments, see the Advisory Commission on Intergovernmental Relations, *Trends in Metropolitan America* (Washington, D.C.: ACIR, 1977).

28. George Sternlieb and James W. Hughes, "New Dimensions of the Urban Crisis," paper prepared for the Subcommittee on Fiscal and Intergovernmental Policy, Joint Economic Committee, Congress of the United States, March 20, 1979.

29. *Central City-Suburban Fiscal Disparity and City Distress 1977* (Washington, D.C.: Advisory Commission on Intergovernmental Relations, December, 1980).

30. "Whither or Whether Urban Distress," a response to the article "The Urban Crisis Leaves Town," by T. D. Allman, *Harper's Magazine* (December 1978), Office of Community Planning and Development, U.S. Department of Housing and Urban Development, 1979, p. 2. See also Robert P. Boynton, ed., *Occasional Papers in Housing and Community Affairs,* vol. 4 (Washington: U.S. Department of Housing and Urban Development, July 1979), whole issue.

# 9. THE POLITICS OF METROPOLITAN REORGANIZATION

One of the characteristics of government in the non-central-city areas of the metropolis is fragmentation. Suburban governmental services are provided by a large and diverse number of governmental units: municipalities, counties, towns, and overlapping special districts. There are usually several layers of government. As a result, residents are likely to receive public services from several different local governments.

Despite the differentiation among suburbs and the evident fragmentation of suburban political systems, one theme pervades the politics of suburbia: a politics of accommodation. There is general opposition in the suburbs to conflict for its own sake. The objective, on the contrary, is to achieve goals through cooperation. To what end? The general objective of the politics of accommodation has been to retain suburban autonomy in the face of steadily rising pressures for more goods and services.

The desire to retain autonomy is related to the very high value placed on self-government. The solution to the general problem of reconciling autonomy and efficiency has been found in the creation of a system of accommodations based on the use of specific devices such as special districts to supply such services as water supply and sewage disposal for contiguous suburban municipalities.

Intermunicipal cooperation is also a very common method for providing goods and services. This ranges from informal agreements to specific contractual arrangements. Sometimes counties are able to help suburbs adjust to new situations brought about by urban growth and social change. The greatest development along this line has taken place in California, where the urban county has played an important role in helping the suburbs to provide for increased public services. In addition, making use of their increased political clout, the suburbs are receiving more and more support from both state and federal governments.

The politics of accommodation has preserved local autonomy and is, therefore, viewed by most suburbanites as a decided success. But a price is paid for the maintenance of this autonomy. The increasing use of special districts and other devices—a form of functional autonomy—has shifted broad areas of public policy from locally elected officials to relatively autonomous and distant functional agencies that are insulated from the local political process.

In addition, most of the relationships are voluntary, and a suburb can withdraw from them if it can afford to pay the price of proceeding on its own. A community can also accommodate by refusing to act at all on particular problems. This may adversely affect the residents of the nonacting suburb (for example, a refusal to build sidewalks), but it is still an instance of the politics of accommodation.

## PROBLEMS CONFRONTING METROPOLITAN AMERICA

Migration patterns, economic inequities, federal policies, and inflation all have contributed to the political, economic, and social problems of central cities. Some of these problems can be understood better through an examination of the political and administrative implications of the development of metropolitan America.

One factor that causes problems for local governments seeking to cope with metropolitan problems is overlapping boundaries. Many metropolitan areas are not within the limits of a single political unit. Approximately 53 percent—174 out of 330—Metropolitan Statistical Areas have more than one county within their boundary. This makes it extremely difficult to develop a plan of action to encompass the whole MSA, which is made up of more than one political jurisdiction. These jurisdictions might not be in agreement on a number of issues central to formulating a coherent plan. These multi-county MSAs comprise 85 percent of the U.S. population.[1]

Another problem is that most local government units do not exercise complete political and administrative control within their boundaries. Special and school districts are the most obvious examples where service units overlap municipal or county government boundaries.

A similar set of problems arises from the disparities between tax and service boundaries. In some areas there is a direct relationship between the area covered and the source of revenues generated to pay for the service. However, in certain functional areas, such as water supply, sewage disposal, and mass transportation, facilities usually require a huge capital investment. This entails multijurisdictional planning, financing, and cooperation. These service areas are determined as much by population density and natural barriers as they are by political jurisdictional boundaries. In areas such as education, health, and law enforcement, problems of equitable financing arise, and these are compounded by cumbersome administrative procedures because of the involvement of numerous local governments.

In the Washington, D.C., Metropolitan Area, conflict developed over a number of issues during the planning and construction phases of the Metro subway system. These debates centered primarily around the financial contribution required of each local participating jurisdiction. The local governments raised questions about the number and the location of stations, the miles of track, and the number of passengers, all of which helped to impede the decision-making process at different times. In San Francisco the problems surrounding the Bay Area Rapid Transit (BART) system became so acerbic that some local political jurisdictions pulled out of the system during the planning stage and, as a result, BART does not service their jurisdictions.

The failure of local governments to respond effectively to metropolitan problems stems partly from the restrictions imposed upon these municipalities by the constitutions of the various states. State constitutions are the ultimate source of legal authority needed to attack metropolitan problems. However, since there are no formally established metropolitan area-wide governments in the United States, the subject does not come up in the constitutions themselves. As a result, one must turn to the interpretations of state constitutional provisions concerning the powers of local jurisdictions in order to see how metropolitan problems may be approached.

In this respect, Dillon's Rule, previously discussed, asserts the general principle that local governments are derivative; their powers come only by an express action of the state. Even though this view has been somewhat modified in recent years by the passage of home-rule charters in various municipalities, many state governments remain reluctant to grant wide latitude to local governments in questions of structure and powers.

This is especially true of the county. Even though a county may include the entire MSA within its boundaries, it normally does not possess the structural and functional flexibility to cope adequately with growing metropolitan problems. Alterations of county structure (such as city-county consolidation) are prohibited by many state constitutions unless a cumbersome referendum process is followed. Though state constitutions have often been amended, it has proved difficult to alter the structure of county governments through such a method. The county unit of government is generally protected by state constitutions.

This is not true, however, of many of the other local jurisdictions, which are not mentioned in some of the constitutions at all. The major responsibility for the multiplicity of local governmental units must be borne, therefore, not by the constitutions, but by the legislatures themselves. If they wished to do so, state legislatures could do a good deal more than they have done to encourage governmental reorganization in metropolitan areas.

The state legislatures also have an impact upon the autonomy of local governments by passing legislation that limits the taxing and borrowing powers of cities. Recent events in New York, Cleveland, and Wayne County, Michigan, might prompt some critics to applaud these restrictive measures and to argue even further that more stringent financial controls are required. However, local governments that cannot set their own tax rates and borrowing limits are hampered in their efforts at long-range planning, since they can never be sure in advance what financial decisions the state legislature will make in any legislative session.

Proposition 13 in California and proposition 2½ in Massachusetts placed severe limitations on the property tax rates local governments could set. This hampered local governments, forcing them to lay off workers, cut services, impose user charges, and increase other non-property taxes.[2] In Newark, New Jersey, the mayor was forced to lay off police officers and close drug rehabilitation programs as a result of federal aid cutbacks. New Jersey state law prohibited the city from increasing its own taxes to compensate for the reduced revenues.

Another consideration is that many metropolitan areas cross state lines. Over 20 percent of the nation's population is located in metropolitan areas that are interstate. Several thousand political jurisdictions are involved in the interstate problem. This issue is compounded by conflicting legislation, tax rate discrepancies, constitutional differences, and "turf" politics. All of this adds up to a history of only modest achievement in interstate agreements. At the present time, disputes are intensifying between Texas and New Mexico over water resources, between California and Nevada over boundary lines, and among New England states over fishing rights.

Another problem confronting local governments in metropolitan area problem-solving is the lack of metropolitan leadership. Each county, city, town, village, hamlet, and burg has someone either elected or appointed to a position of leadership who will represent and speak for the community. In addition, most of these political jurisdictions exercise some administrative and legislative authority within their boundaries. Trying to get all of these leaders together to agree on an areawide plan for the construction of a physical plant or the provision of a specific service is difficult. If the agenda for such a meeting includes the possibility of reorganizing the governmental structure in the metropolitan area, with all the possible implications for representation, leadership, bureaucrats, minorities, and services, then the prospects for success are diminished substantially.[3]

One last complicating issue needs to be mentioned. Much of the talk about metropolitan organization and reorganization focuses on how the multiple governmental units can be brought closer together to achieve the goals of coordination and economics of scale. What is often overlooked is that rather than seeking cooperative approaches, many local governments view the metropolitan area in terms of a market concept. In their view, local governments compete with one another for desirable residents, industry, and facilities. This factor tends to compound many of the other problems discussed above.

In Fairfax County, just outside of Washington, D.C., the Board of Supervisors established a commercial park at Tysons Corner that offers tax breaks to "desirable" corporations seeking to locate in the area. This policy helps to further unbalance tax and service relationships in the metropolitan area.

## CRITICAL ISSUES IN METROPOLITAN REORGANIZATION

Efforts to change governmental structure in metropolitan areas rarely succeed because they are logical, persuasive, or supported by large numbers of the affected residents. Rather, attempts at governmental reform usually become embroiled in a series of political and administrative conflicts, which, if unresolved, often mean defeat for the proposed change. The conflicts that have proven the most difficult to resolve concern taxes, representation, special interest groups, minority groups, bureaucracy, and service delivery.

## Taxes

Whenever local governmental reform is proposed, people are fearful that their taxes will go up. Usually they are right, because most governmental change does result in higher costs. Some observers have argued that reorganization along metropolitan lines will eliminate most of the duplication and overlapping of functions and services. Moreover, by expanding the base of the service area, the new government would be able to take advantage of economies of scale.

Taxes were reduced in both the Jacksonville and Indianapolis reorganizations, but this was attributed more to having a larger property tax base than to savings derived from efficiency or economies of scale. Other metropolitan reorganizations in Miami–Dade County and Nashville–Davidson County did not produce the lower taxes and cost savings that had been predicted by proponents of the new government.[4]

Much research remains to be done on post-reorganization tax rates and costs, with specific attention paid to the impact of external factors, such as increased federal funding to large, coordinated metropolitan areas. Jacksonville, Indianapolis, Miami, and Nashville all benefited financially from grants-in-aid immediately after their reorganizations.

One thing we have learned from a review of local government efforts to consolidate is that opponents of consolidation invariably raise the issue of increased taxes. If the proponents of governmental reform are unable to mount strong and convincing arguments to allay the fears of voters, defeat at the polls is likely.

## Representation

Representation becomes an issue in metropolitan consolidation because smaller, autonomous units of government provide citizens with a more personal and more responsive government. The residents know many of their elected officials personally and are used to smaller legislative bodies that represent fewer citizens.

Shifting to a metropolitan, or even a two-tier representative arrangement, often makes government seem larger and more remote than the existing local government. Representatives to local councils, once elected from small, homogeneous districts, often find that they have to campaign for election in larger districts composed of a more diverse population and represent a larger number of people. Therefore, the citizens feel uneasy about the new arrangement, and so do many of the less-politically-ambitious local representatives.

## Special Interest Groups

Special interest groups, like all of the other actors in the metropolitan political system, develop established patterns and channels of access and communication. These patterns and channels will be affected when a metropolitan reorganization proposal suggests changing or eliminating established agencies or eliminating elected council seats.

Each interest group reviews its own issues and strategies to ascertain how the new governmental arrangement will affect its potential for access to the system. Based upon this type of analysis they will decide whether to support or to oppose the reorganization. Minority groups, public service unions, and real estate interests historically have been very active participants in reorganization efforts.

## Minority Groups

The overwhelming percentage of the research conducted on the impact of metropolitan reorganization on minorities has been focused on blacks. It is fair to generalize that, in most cases, blacks have been very suspicious of plans for metropolitan reorganization.

The apprehension displayed by blacks towards metropolitan consolidation is usually couched in numerical and political terms. As black populations began to increase substantially in central cities, control of many of these governments passed into the hands of black elected and appointed local officials. Many of these officials mobilized their supporters into effective political organizations that, as they grew and matured, were able to recruit, nominate, and elect capable black officials to represent the interests of their communities.

Proposals for metropolitan reorganization threaten to undermine this developing black political power by diluting its voting strength over a broader geographical and population base. Attempts at consolidated governments in metropolitan areas almost always reduce the percentage of black population to total population in the area. In Jacksonville, this percentage change was from 44 to 25 percent, in Indianapolis from 27 to 17 percent, and in Nashville from 38 to 20 percent.[5]

Starting in the 1950s, it is easy to trace black opposition to proposals for metropolitan consolidation. Repeated efforts to reorganize both Cleveland and St. Louis met with opposition from black leaders and then black voters. In the 1960s both Nashville and Tampa, the former successful and the latter unsuccessful, were confronted with strong opposition from blacks. Over 55 percent of the black voters in Nashville and over 90 percent in Tampa voted against the reorganization.

The only two consolidation efforts in this country in which there was strong black support occurred in Jacksonville–Duval County, Florida, in 1967 and in Lexington–Fayette County, Kentucky, in 1972. In the former, 59 percent of the blacks voted for consolidation; in the latter, it was 70 percent.[6]

In both instances, there were some unique circumstances that helped to mobilize black support in favor of the consolidation. In Jacksonville, excessive corruption had resulted in waste, fraud, inefficiency, and numerous criminal indictments of local political officials. Residents were fed up and ready for a change. In addition, black leaders were involved in the consolidation movement from its inception. This heavy and early involvement allowed them to establish a bargaining position in the drawing of district lines that virtually guaranteed blacks three seats on the new consolidated government council. In exchange for participation in the process and an agreeable districting procedure, black leaders threw their support behind the consolidation effort.

In Lexington, a survey indicated that blacks were very concerned about being fairly represented on the new governing council. While blacks were not going to lose a great deal numerically under the new system, they realized they could solidify some existing political realities by insuring black domination in several of the new districts. In exchange for their electoral support, black leaders were able to draw favorable district lines insuring themselves of two or three seats on the new council.[7]

Despite the dilution of black voting strength that metropolitan reorganization might bring, some advocates of metropolitan government have argued that metropolitan reform would aid blacks. They point out that blacks, today, are gaining control of fiscally weakened central cities that have both a population with many needs and a severely limited tax base. These advocates of reform argue that minorities and the poor will be better off if new metropolitan-wide governments are created that can draw upon regional wealth to combat inner-city problems. Advocates of black power, however, question whether blacks could win control over these resources in a predominantly white metropolitan government area.

## Bureaucracy

Historically, bureaucrats have viewed political change from a conservative point of view. All things considered, they would prefer to see governmental structure and functions remain as they are. In many instances they have a vested interest in a continuation of the status quo or incremental change as opposed to the more dramatic upheavals caused by governmental consolidation or metropolitan government.

When reformers organize committees to begin planning structural change in the metropolis, it is often the bureaucrats who initially voice their apprehensions over recruitment, pay, promotion, and fringe benefits such as medical care, life insurance, holidays, vacations, and retirement provisions.

While at first glance these personnel issues might appear to have little to do with metropolitan reform, they often provide the engineers of consolidation with enormous political headaches. It is rare to find a metropolitan area where there is parity, or even the semblance of parity, on all of these issues. Until there is some agreement by the planning committee on these key personnel issues, there is unlikely to be bureaucratic support for the reorganization proposal. Since those public employees with the highest salaries or best fringe benefits are not likely to accept reductions, the political compromises necessary to gain bureaucratic support often require higher salaries and better fringe benefits for the bureaucrats on the lower end of the scale, resulting in higher costs for the new government. This often means that in order to win the support of the affected bureaucrats, proponents of government reorganization must often support reorganization plans that increase the costs of government, thus alienating the constituents.

## Service Delivery

Many of the most heated debates over metropolitan reform center on the question of which level of government under the new structure will deliver which services. Some of the pioneering work on this subject was published by the Advisory Commission on Intergovernmental Relations in the 1963 study *Performance of Urban Functions: Local and Areawide* and supplemented in other studies published in 1974.[8] The ACIR states that there are three important components in a service-level policy. These are "formulating criteria by which urban functions can be assigned, assessing the capabilities of the various institutional and procedural means of delivering assigned services, and determining what aspects of a function should be assigned to different types and levels of substate government."[9]

The ACIR established a set of criteria against which the assignment of services could be made. No effort was made to weigh or establish the relative importance of each criterion. The four criteria are economic efficiency, equity, political accountability, and administrative effectiveness.

The basic assumption underlying the allocation of services is that different levels of government will deliver the services. Some services are to be delivered from the metropolitan level, others at the local level, and the remainder are to be shared functions. The ACIR criteria are designed to permit each governmental function to be evaluated against the criteria and then assigned to the most appropriate level for delivery to citizens.

## Counties

Before turning our attention to the different types of reorganizations, we will first discuss counties. The discussion of the complex world of metropolitan America has omitted mention of the role of counties. Counties are an important component of the political system that affects the lives of residents of the metropolitan area.

Counties perform many services for citizens in metropolitan America. Some of the services spill over into other political jurisdictions. It would be much more convenient and politically expedient if each metropolitan area were contained in one county, but we have already noted that many metropolitan areas have multiple counties within their borders. Therefore, shifting responsibility for service delivery to counties is unlikely to be the entire answer to the metropolitan fragmentation problem.

Counties are the largest local governmental units in the country, several being larger than states. Counties also encompass many other forms of local government within their boundaries, including school districts, special districts, towns, and villages. They perform a wide range of services for their residents, including everything from housekeeping services to law enforcement and education. Counties are performing some local governmental functions in over three-fourths of the nation's largest cities.

Just as the types of services counties perform vary, so does the role of counties in different parts of the country. The one area of the country where counties do not play an important role is New England. The town has always been the primary unit of government in New England, and, since it was a successful governing system, it was not replaced by counties. Most New England states still retain their counties but delegate very few governmental functions to them.

In other regions of the country, counties play a paramount role in government. ACIR, in a profile of county government, reported that in the 150 urban county governments the functions performed most were the following:[10]

| Function | % of Total | Number |
|---|---|---|
| 1. Jails and detention | 97 | 145 |
| 2. Coroner's office | 87 | 130 |
| 3. Courts | 87 | 130 |
| 4. Tax assessment | 83 | 125 |
| 5. Public health | 80 | 120 |
| 6. Prosecution | 80 | 120 |
| 7. Probation and parole | 79 | 119 |
| 8. Police protection | 78 | 117 |
| 9. Roads and highways | 78 | 117 |
| 10. General assistance public welfare | 76 | 114 |

During the 1960s and 70s counties began to expand their role in providing services. This coincided, to some extent, with the growth and increased visibility of the National Association of Counties (NACO), headquartered in Washington, D.C. As NACO increased its membership, resources, and, consequently, its political influence in Washington, more people began looking to counties to help provide services.[11] (County revenues to pay for these services come from real estate and sales taxes, user fees, and grants from state and federal agencies.) Counties began to fill an important role between distressed cities and non-urban-oriented state legislatures. One researcher noted that counties were now spending almost 70 percent of their budgets on four key services: welfare, hospitals, education, and highways.[12]

Counties get mixed reviews from suburbanites who live in them. William Colman, who has observed the growth and development of counties over two decades, writes:

> For many years, there has been widespread adverse opinions about county government. This view is especially common in large cities. However, the suburbanites' view of county government varies according to the state or section of the country with which they are familiar. In Illinois, as well as a number of other midwestern industrial states, and Pennsylvania, for instance, many residents of suburban municipalities would share that adverse view. On the other hand, suburban residents in California, North Carolina, New York, Maryland, and Virginia would take a completely opposite view.[13]

Counties are often not thought of when the problems of large urban centers are being discussed; however, there is a historical relationship between the two worth noting. Caraley[14] singles out the major cities where there are no separate county governments. He divides these cities into three groups.

In group one are the cities that are part of areas designated as counties. These include New York, Philadelphia, Boston, New Orleans, Jacksonville, Indianapolis, and Nashville. The first four are products of consolidation movements effected before the turn of the century. The last three are products of consolidation since 1962.

The second group of cities are areas where the city and county are the same political jurisdiction—the city and county are one. Denver, Honolulu, and San Francisco comprise this group.

Group three has cities in which the city and county are separate but adjacent to one another. In this category are Baltimore and St. Louis, which were separated in the nineteenth century. Because of these variations it is difficult to generalize about county government, how it is organized, and what types of functions it performs.

Counties are usually organized politically under one of three types of government forms: commission, council-administrator, or council-executive. The form most often used is the commission, with over 75 percent of all counties using this system. About 20 percent of all counties now use a council-administrator form, first adopted by Iredell County, North Carolina, in 1927. The council-executive form is used in about 5 percent of the counties. Most of these are the large urban counties in metropolitan areas. However, in 1977, seventy-five counties in Arkansas changed from the commission form to the council-executive form because of a state mandate. This tended to swell the number of counties using the elected-executive plan.

The three forms of county government closely resemble their city counterparts. The commission form of government is comprised of elected commissioners who serve as the legislative body. At the same time, the commissioners exercise executive responsibility by heading different departments of government. The council-administrator form has an elected council that hires an administrator who is responsible to the council for implementing its policies. This form is similar to the council-manager government of cities. Under the council-executive form there are two distinct branches of government—executive and legislative. The independently elected executive is the political, administrative, and symbolic leader of the county, while the council exercises the legislative duties, including checking executive power when necessary. This form is closest to the strong-mayor form of government found in most large cities.

A 1982 survey survey by the International City Management Association (ICMA) counted over 3,000 counties.[15] About 21 percent of these are classified as metropolitan counties, since they are located in MSAs. Over 1,300 counties are located in the South and another 1,000 in North Central states. This means that the northeastern and western states have only about 20 percent of the nation's counties.

## Polycentrism vs. Metropolitanism

The dissatisfaction of residents with local governments in their metropolitan area has occasionally taken the form of movements to restructure government completely. This section examines the conceptual arguments as well as the alternative models of governance and the key political issues confronting policymakers who seek to reorganize political jurisdictions.

The conceptual debate focuses on the arguments between polycentrists and metropolitanists. The former favor the status quo, whereby each metropolitan area has a multitude of autonomous governments, each providing the level and type of service deemed necessary to satisfy its constituents. The latter approach suggests a consolidation of some or all of the local governments in the area, thereby providing similar services over a wider range of communities.

The polycentric model of governance is often referred to as the public choice approach, named by a group of scholars who have developed this model and whose adherents have published numerous articles and books explaining and applying the economic or market theories of the model.[16] The polycentrists believe that individuals are different and, as a result, desire different things, whether it be in governance structure or service quality or quantity. In the private sector, individuals satisfy their needs by purchasing goods and services according to what they want and what they can afford.

Some goods and services are not available through the private sector, which leads many individuals to express their preferences in different ways in the public sector. Environmental protection, disease control, and access to park lands are some of these publicly regulated and administered services. In the public sector, citizens can share in the benefits of these services equally. As Bish and Ostrom note, "Individuals *cannot be excluded* from enjoying a public good once it is provided for someone else; and one individual's enjoyment will not subtract from its consumption or enjoyment by others."[17]

TABLE 9.1
Cumulative Distribution of U.S. Counties

| Classification | All counties | Counties 2,500 & over | Counties 5,000 & over | Counties 10,000 & over | Counties 25,000 & over | Counties 50,000 & over | Counties 100,000 & over | Counties 250,000 & over | Counties 500,000 & over | Counties over 1,000,000 |
|---|---|---|---|---|---|---|---|---|---|---|
| **Total, all counties** | 3,041 | 2,940 | 2,764 | 2,316 | 1,359 | 748 | 374 | 156 | 68 | 20 |
| **Population group** | | | | | | | | | | |
| Over 1,000,000 | 20 | 20 | 20 | 20 | 20 | 20 | 20 | 20 | 20 | 20 |
| 500,000–1,000,000 | 48 | 48 | 48 | 48 | 48 | 48 | 48 | 48 | 48 | |
| 250,000–499,999 | 88 | 88 | 88 | 88 | 88 | 88 | 88 | 88 | | |
| 100,000–249,999 | 218 | 218 | 218 | 218 | 218 | 218 | 218 | | | |
| 50,000–99,999 | 374 | 374 | 374 | 374 | 374 | 374 | | | | |
| 25,000–49,999 | 611 | 611 | 611 | 611 | 611 | | | | | |
| 10,000–24,999 | 957 | 957 | 957 | 957 | | | | | | |
| 5,000–9,999 | 448 | 448 | 448 | | | | | | | |
| 2,500–4,999 | 176 | 176 | | | | | | | | |
| Under 2,500 | 101 | | | | | | | | | |
| **Geographic region** | | | | | | | | | | |
| Northeast | 196 | 196 | 195 | 189 | 178 | 132 | 84 | 42 | 18 | 5 |
| North Central | 1,051 | 1,016 | 932 | 753 | 410 | 204 | 107 | 37 | 15 | 4 |
| South | 1,376 | 1,348 | 1,300 | 1,108 | 610 | 298 | 119 | 45 | 18 | 4 |
| West | 418 | 380 | 337 | 266 | 161 | 114 | 64 | 32 | 17 | 7 |
| **Metro status** | | | | | | | | | | |
| Metro | 673 | 672 | 669 | 661 | 609 | 496 | 349 | 155 | 68 | 20 |
| Nonmetro | 2,368 | 2,268 | 2,095 | 1,655 | 750 | 252 | 25 | 1 | | |
| **Form of government** | | | | | | | | | | |
| Without administrator | 2,402 | 2,305 | 2,132 | 1,718 | 904 | 412 | 166 | 50 | 16 | 4 |
| With administrator | 639 | 635 | 632 | 598 | 455 | 336 | 208 | 106 | 52 | 16 |

Source: International City Management Association (Washington, D.C.: *The Municipal Year Book 1982*), p. XVII.

In the public sector, citizens express their preferences by voting, lobbying, testifying, picketing, or moving to another jurisdiction. The polycentrists view smaller units of government as being more capable of responding to diverse citizen preferences. As a consequence, they support multiple political jurisdictions in an area, each offering the type and quality of service most consistent with its resources and the demands of its citizens. The multiple governments in the area provide a market mechanism similar to that in which consumers shop for products and compare brands in a competitive system.

> Polycentric models are primarily concerned with maximizing the options of citizens to satisfy their preferences for public goods by making residential choices from a selection of governments with different combinations of services and taxes.[18]

Imagine yourself about to move to a large metropolitan area halfway across the country. You have no friends or relatives in the area, but you have made a list of the priority needs you want to satisfy before selecting one of the political jurisdictions as your new home. These needs might include quality of schools, access to public transportation, cost of housing, access to recreation or religious activities, tax rates, and proximity to work or cultural centers. Different people will assess these priorities differently and will try to select a new place to live based as much as possible on how close an area comes to meeting their needs.

The political jurisdictions, in a market sense, act as the providers of goods or services. Many of them go out of their way to publicize their assets, such as proximity to a recreational area or to a larger employer or the local train station. When there is a reasonable match between the priorities of the new arrival and the assets of the jurisdiction, then a new family moves into the community and the public choice model has worked.

When the priorities of individuals or families change, they reassess the assets of their political jurisdiction and then decide what action to take. Sometimes citizen groups lobby or testify to change government priorities. Occasionally, they try to elect a candidate who reflects their preferences for services. In some instances, families "vote with their feet" by moving to another community that appears to satisfy more of their needs than the community they are presently living in. In such a case, the private sector model of competition is working.

Since the numerous governments in the metropolitan area are not similar in size or service delivery, there is an opportunity for larger units to take advantage of some economies of scale that characterize large capital expenditures. The smaller units of government, on the other hand, are capable of providing the more personal social services, such as recreation, law enforcement, and health services.

The major arguments advanced for the polycentric approach include the following. First, more diverse preferences of constituents are satisfied, since there are numerous political jurisdictions to choose from. More jurisdictions mean greater choice. Second, varying service levels are provided by the local governments, permitting area residents to change locations as their priorities change. Third, smaller political jurisdictions provide greater access to governmental officials and, as a result, possibly better representation of constituent wishes. Fourth, smaller political jurisdictions are better suited to provide services requiring interpersonal relationships. Quality control and evaluation are easier to monitor. Fifth, competition among jurisdictions produces innovation and a need to improve efficiency and monitor costs.

Critics of polycentrism have countered with the following points. First, the public choice or market economy model is predicated upon a degree of freedom that is no longer a reality in the private sector. Government regulation, rate setting, oligopolistic practices, and quasi-public organizations have all interfered with the free market system. Second, the public choice model provision of voting with your feet is predicated upon the premise of a degree of mobility that simply doesn't exist in metropolitan areas. Neither poor people nor many minorities can satisfy their preferences under the polycentric system for reasons of economic want and racism. In other words, this model works primarily for middle-, upper-middle-, and upper-income whites. Third, the only real test of the polycentric model is to assess current metropolitan areas that reflect this approach. Yet, by all reasonable measures, these metropolitan areas are experiencing a variety of problems that some observers attribute to their fragmentation and duplication. Fourth, polycentrism tends to intensify parochial interests and exacerbate racial, ethnic, and economic cleavages within the metropolitan area rather than reducing them. Fifth, polycentrism does not maximize the use of scarce resources because there is no central allocation authority to redistribute these resources to where they might have the greatest impact in the area. Sixth, polycentrism cannot control "spillovers" when political units in the metropolitan area exercise autonomy within their boundaries. (Spillovers refer to positive or negative factors that result from the action of a local government. A high-quality educational system will benefit other jurisdictions in the area where its graduates settle and find jobs. A factory that pollutes the air or water produces negative spillovers to other political jurisdictions.) The inability to develop metropolitan-wide plans or control negative spillovers is a serious deficiency in an area plagued with rising costs and limited resources.

For many, the polycentric approach exemplified by the current governmental pattern in metropolitan America is insufficient to meet today's problems. Critics have argued there is too much fragmentation, duplication, and overlapping in multiple political units clustered together. Furthermore, within these metropolitan areas, there are fiscal disparities between the central city and many of the surrounding political jurisdictions. For all of these reasons, critics have begun to argue for new approaches that emphasize a more centralized and coordinated approach to problems, administered from a metropolitan level. The two most common responses to this perceived need have been city-county consolidation and federation.[19]

## City-County Consolidation

In city-county consolidation, a county and the cities within it merge into a single governmental unit. The achievement of consolidation usually includes the necessary state legislative approval. This is followed by popular approval at the polls in the central city and the other communities in the county.

New York, Philadelphia, Boston, and New Orleans achieved city-county consolidation in the nineteenth century. But our attention here will be focused on more recent efforts toward consolidation. In the 1950s, city-county consolidation plans were proposed for Nashville, Tennessee; Albuquerque, New Mexico; Macon, Georgia; Durham, North Carolina; and Richmond, Virginia. All were rejected by the voters in those areas.

But in the 1960s, several city-county consolidations did occur, the most notable being that in Nashville–Davidson County, Tennessee. In 1958, such a consolidation proposal received only 48 percent support from the electorate. Between 1958 and 1962, Nashville annexed a substantial portion (some fifty square miles) of Davidson County, which bordered the city. As a result, by 1962 a number of voters in the county believed they would fare better in a consolidated city-county government than by being annexed by the city of Nashville. Other voters wanted to strike back at Nashville's mayor, who was the leader of the annexation drive but an opponent of consolidation. He feared that his political power might be eroded under the proposed new government. In 1962, consolidation was approved by 57 percent of the total electorate in Nashville and the county.

One of the major features of the Nashville-Davidson County plan was the creation of two zones. One is the urban service district, composed at the beginning only of Nashville. The other zone is a general service district, including Nashville. Functions performed and financed on an area-wide basis through the general service district include schools, police, courts, welfare, transit, housing, urban renewal, health, refuse disposal, and the enforcement of building codes. Functions performed only in the urban service district, and also financed by it, include water supply, fire protection, intensified police protection, and street lighting and cleaning.[20]

What is the general evaluation of the Nashville–Davidson County consolidation thus far? Throughout the metropolitan area, improvement in the quality of public education, increased racial integration in the schools, additional water and sewer facilities, and coordinated tax assessment have been noted. A number of financial inequities have been eliminated by shifting various services and placing them on a county-wide rather than a city-wide tax base. On the other hand, it has been said that rural residents have had to pay higher taxes without gaining compensating benefits.

Students of government are mostly in agreement that some form of metropolitan reorganization is necessary. But is city-county consolidation politically feasible? In an important study of city-county consolidation from 1949 through 1974, Vincent L. Marando concludes that it is politically difficult to achieve this goal.[21] A summary of his findings is shown in Table 9.2. He makes the following principal points:

1. As the table shows, in the forty-nine reorganization referenda from 1945 through 1974, all adoptions occurred in single-county metropolitan areas.

2. Reorganization referenda generally fail. For every acceptance, there are three rejections.

3. The twelve voter-approved reorganizations have occurred in the seven states, mostly in the South, where the most attempts have taken place. Five of the successes occurred in Virginia, where state law grants all first-class cities a status independent of counties. This is a cause and effect relationship.

4. Reorganization was not successful in metropolitan areas of more than one million population. The voters in Cleveland and St. Louis turned down reorganization plans by rather hefty majorities.

5. The community problems that stimulated most governmental reform efforts were of a noncrisis nature. The only exception appears to be Jacksonville–Duval County, Florida. Here, the severity of urban problems stimulated considerable interest in reform. The reform movement was triggered by public concern over criminal indictments of certain government officials and the discreditation of the public schools. Reorganization was perceived as a means of getting rid of corrupt and incompetent officials and bringing good government to the area.

6. Voter response to reorganization proposals is complex. Interest normally begins with the civic associations, not the politicians. But eventually an opposition surfaces, and it has generally triumphed.

7. Movements to establish city-county consolidation tend to rest upon mass media campaigns. This has proved to be insufficient. "Political organization is necessary to gaining support for consolidation."[22]

## Analyzing Consolidations

An extensive review of city-county consolidation efforts, dating back to 1921, was conducted by Glendening and Atkins.[23] Their research revealed some interesting facts about this alternative to polycentric government. While city-council consolidation activity has been fairly constant over the years, there was increased activity during the 1970s. The successful consolidations in recent years occurred more often in the West than in the South, where many previous successes have been recorded. The primary reason for this appears to be an increasingly active interest on the part of the states, which have come to realize that fragmentation is impeding their ability to

TABLE 9.2
City-County Consolidation: Voter Support for Local Government Reorganization
1945–1974.

| Year | Reorganization referendum | Reorganization support (%) | |
|------|---------------------------|---------|--------|
| | | Success | Defeat |
| 1949 | Baton Rouge–East Baton Rouge Parish, La. | 51.1 | |
| 1952 | Hampton–Elizabeth County, Va. | 88.7 | |
| 1953 | Miami–Dade County, Fla. | | 49.2 |
| 1957 | Miami–Dade County, Fla. | 51.0 | |
| | Newport News–Warwick, Va. | 66.9 | |
| 1958 | Nashville–Davidson County, Tenn. | | 47.3 |
| 1959 | Albuquerque–Bernalillo County, N.M. | | 30.0 |
| | Knoxville–Knox County, Tenn. | | 16.7 |
| | Cleveland–Cuyahoga County, Ohio | | 44.8 |
| | St. Louis–St. Louis County, Mo. | | 27.5 |
| 1960 | Macon–Bibb County, Ga. | | 35.8 |
| 1961 | Durham–Durham County, N.C. | | 22.3 |
| | Richmond–Henrico County, Va. | | 54.0 |
| 1962 | Columbus–Muscogee County, Ga. | | 42.1 |
| | Memphis–Shelby County, Tenn. | | 36.8 |
| | Nashville–Davidson County, Tenn. | 56.8 | |
| | South Norfolk–Norfolk County, Va. | 66.0 | |
| | Virginia Beach–Princess Anne County, Va. | 81.9 | |
| | St. Louis–St. Louis County, Mo. | | 40.1 |
| 1964 | Chattanooga–Hamilton County, Tenn. | | 19.2 |
| 1967 | Jacksonville–Duval County, Fla. | 64.7 | |
| | Tampa–Hillsborough County, Fla. | | 28.4 |
| 1969 | Athens–Clarke County, Ga. | | 48.0 |
| | Brunswick–Glynn County, Ga. | | 29.6 |
| | Carson City–Ormsby County, Nvw. | 65.1 | |
| | Roanoke–Roanoke County, Va. | | 66.4 |
| | Winchester City–Frederick County, Va. | | 31.9 |
| 1970 | Charlottesville–Albermarle County, Va. | | 28.1 |
| | Columbus–Muscogee County, Ga. | 80.7 | |
| | Chattanooga–Hamilton County, Tenn. | | 48.0 |
| | Tampa–Hillsborough County, Fla. | | 42.0 |
| | Pensacola–Escambia County, Fla. | | 42.0 |
| 1971 | Augusta–Richmond County, Ga. | | 41.5 |
| | Charlotte–Mecklenburg County, N.C. | | 30.5 |
| | Tallahassee–Leon County, Fla. | | 41.0 |
| 1972 | Athens–Clarke County, Ga. | | 48.3 |
| | Macon–Bibb County, Ga. | | 39.6 |
| | Suffolk–Nansemond County, Va. | 75.7 | |
| | Fort Pierce–St. Lucie, Fla. | | 36.5 |
| | Lexington–Fayette County, Ky. | 69.4 | |
| | Tampa–Hillsborough County, Fla. | | 42.0 |
| 1973 | Columbia–Richland County, S.C. | | 45.9 |
| | Savannah–Chatham County, Ga. | | 58.3 |
| | Tallahassee–Leon County, Fla. | | 45.9 |
| 1974 | Augusta–Richmond County, Ga. | | 51.5 |
| | Portland–Multnomah County, Ore. | | 27.5 |
| | Durham–Durham County, N.C. | | 32.1 |
| | Charleston–Charleston County, S.C. | | 40.4 |
| | Sacramento–Sacramento County, Calif. | | 24.9 |
| | Total Outcome (#) | 12 | 37 |
| | Local Reorganizations Attempted | 49 | |

Source: Vincent L. Marando (New York: *National Civic Review*, February 1975), p. 77.

govern effectively. This has been very evident in Florida, Montana, Utah, Nevada, and Oregon.

The major obstacles confronting consolidation efforts have usually been the absence of state enabling legislation or state constitutional amendments authorizing proposed consolidations.[24]

Referenda attempts in small cities, with populations under 25,000, have been successful in two of every three attempts. However, referenda attempts in cities over 250,000 have all failed. Since 1921 there have been eighty-five referenda on consolidations, but they have occurred in only fifty-seven different communities.[25]

Glendening and Atkins point out that beginning in the late 1960s and continuing through the 1970s, there appeared to be a much more positive state attitude toward governmental consolidations. Besides the states mentioned above, facilitating legislation has also been passed in Arkansas, Kentucky, Washington, and Alaska.[26]

Consolidations have historically been linked with the southern states. An analysis of successful consolidation referenda indicates some refinement of this proposition. More than half the consolidation referenda were in southern states. However, these referenda were confined to four states. Virginia led the nation with thirteen cities holding referenda on consolidation, followed by Georgia with seven. Florida and Tennessee each had six cities. These thirty-two cities conducted forty-nine of the eighty-five referenda.

## Federation, or Two-Tier Plan

The federation, or two-tier government, reorganization plan has been the subject of much discussion as a possible technique for solving problems of the metropolis. What is involved is a two-level division of local government functions within a metropolitan area. Area-wide functions are assigned to an area-wide, or metropolitan government, with boundaries that take in all of the individual units. The local functions are left to the existing municipalities. In London, England, and Toronto and Winnipeg, Canada, the local units are called boroughs. There has been no specific adoption of this plan by any MSA in the United States.

It is claimed that the chief advantage of this plan lies in its ability to provide one metropolitan government to deal with regional problems while allowing the diverse municipalities to cope with their own local problems. Ideally, there is a blend of the requirements of metropolitan efficiency and local political identity and participation.

Despite these theoretical advantages, it is easy to see that barriers exist that work against the adoption of the plan in the MSAs in the United States. At the outset, there is the question of which functions will be assigned to which level of government. The decision will affect the relative strength of each of the two tiers. Second, the constitutions of the states that desired to permit federated government would have to be amended, as we observed earlier. Finally, the support of local officials and of their constituents would

TABLE 9.3
Number of City-County Consolidations Known To Have Been Held, 1921–1979

| Years | Annual Referenda Held | Total No. Passed | Northeast Referenda Held | No. Passed | North Central Referenda | No. Passed | South Referenda Held | No. Passed | West Referenda Held | No. Passed |
|---|---|---|---|---|---|---|---|---|---|---|
| 1921–1950 | 12 | 1 | 1 | 0 | 1 | 0 | 6 | 1 | 4 | 0 |
| 1951–1970 | 34 | 9 | 0 | 0 | 1 | 0 | 28 | 7 | 5 | 2 |
| 1971–1979 | 39 | 7 | 0 | 0 | 2 | 0 | 25 | 3 | 12 | 4 |

Source: International City Management Association (Washington, D.C.: *The Municipal Year Book 1980*), p. 69.

be indispensable for the plan to win approval within any particular MSA. If either the political leadership or the electorate in these areas felt threatened by the concept of a "big" metropolitan government, the chances of adoption of the plan would be slim. In this connection, it should be noted that two-tier governments were established both in Toronto and Winnipeg by *provincial* legislation, not by local referenda.

As a case study of the federal plan in action, it is useful to examine the scheme as it was developed and implemented in Toronto. This metropolitan region, with more than two million inhabitants, had experienced a very rapid population growth (about 75 percent in fifteen years), much of which had occurred in the suburban areas around the central city. Corresponding to this rapid population increase was a rise in problems confronting local jurisdictions, including poor planning, limited sewer and water facilities, poor transportation systems, rising pollution, and inadequate resources.

Studies of the situation led to a recommendation for a federation of the thirteen municipalities that make up metropolitan Toronto. Such a measure was introduced in the Ontario provincial legislature, and it became law on January 1, 1954. A Metropolitan Toronto Corporation was established to provide for the delivery of services that could be maintained on a local basis. In many problem areas, a sharing of functions between the metropolitan and the local governments was initiated, for example, in planning, local libraries, grants to cultural societies, snow removal, street cleaning, and traffic regulations.[27]

During the early years of the corporation, one of the vexing problems was that of representation. Each suburban municipality had one representative in the metropolitan government, although the municipalities varied in size from 10,000 to 360,000 people. Moreover, by the 1960s the total population of the suburban areas substantially exceeded that of the city of Toronto itself. Yet the city had representation equal to all of the suburban units. Change finally came in 1967, when the thirteen municipalities were consolidated into five boroughs and one city, and representation was made more equitable, with the boroughs receiving twenty representatives and the city twelve.

After three decades of effort, have there been any really major accomplishments of metropolitan Toronto? The answer is yes. The achievements include impressive strides in the public works area, with a new subway and new expressways, new water and sewage facilities, and plans for a regional park system. Efficiency of the police has been upgraded by centralization of the force. Perhaps the most significant accomplishment has been to increase the financial strength of metropolitan Toronto by broadening the tax base. This greater financial stability enabled Toronto to save an estimated $50 million through lower bond interest rates between 1954 and 1967.

Some critics have charged that metropolitan Toronto has overemphasized the construction of public works projects at the expense of certain social problems. In defense, the government has argued that it had to demonstrate a high level of visibility in order to generate and maintain support for the federation idea. In any event, there is almost universal agreement that life in Toronto today is vastly more comfortable, gracious, and safe than in Buffalo, Cleveland, or Chicago. It is therefore no accident that United States experts on urban problems have given, and will continue to give, very close attention to developments in both Toronto and Winnipeg.

On the other hand, Americans are beginning to make some attempts at government that ties together a whole region. In the Twin Cities area of Minneapolis and Saint Paul, government leaders decided a decade ago that some of their problems could be dealt with through a common effort.

At the heart of the Minnesota effort is the Metropolitan Council, a coordinating agency representing 139 municipalities and 50 townships. It has the final say on sewer and water systems, highway routes, mass transit, airports, solid waste, parks, land use, federal aid, and subsidized housing in 7 counties.

In the United States there are approximately 600 advisory councils that give advice on planning. But the Metropolitan Council is different. It has the power to approve the capital budgets of the metropolitan commissions in charge of parks, waste control, and mass transit. It has taxing authority and raised about 44 percent of its 1977 budget of $5.8 million through property taxes. In addition, it receives federal and state grants and revenue from fees charged local governments for various services. The regional council plan put into effect in Minnesota has drawn widespread attention from officials of other metropolitan areas.[28]

An interesting shift now appears to be taking place. While both southern and western states have increased the number of consolidation referenda, there appears to be a marked shift from the South to the West in terms of success. In both of these regions the metropolitan areas tend to have far fewer governmental units than metropolitan areas in the East. The smaller number of political jurisdictions to deal with may explain the higher success rate in these areas.

> What distinguishes the two groups is that until 1969 no Western state had achieved consolidation and since 1972 there have been no consolidations in the South. Three out of nine attempts have succeeded in the West since 1972, while the South has failed on eleven attempts. This is a striking reversal.[29]

## Procedural and Structural Reform in Metropolitan Areas

City-county consolidation is but one of several techniques used by local governments to cope with metropolitan-wide problems. Over the years, scholars have analyzed and compared a variety of approaches. Some of the best research on this subject appeared in the 1960s and early 1970s.[30] Much of that research is worth reviewing, since metropolitan areas have not undergone major structural changes in the past twenty years, and most of the proposals for change have been adopted in some form in some metropolitan areas.

It is important to keep in mind that it is virtually impossible to create a metropolitan government in large metropolitan areas today. For this reason, it is important to understand some of the procedural or incremental approaches used by metropolitan areas to lessen intergovernmental tensions and to increase metropolitan cooperation.

Martin and others have formulated a list of sixteen methods local governments can use to adapt to changing needs and circumstances. They range in complexity from informal meetings and cooperation to establishing a metropolitan-wide government or a regional agency. Items 1–8 represent *procedural* changes which can be accomplished with little or no impact on the structure of local government. The remaining approaches are *structural* modifications, since implementing these will require a structural change in government and a concomitant adjustment in political and administrative authority.

### Methods of Local Adaptation [31]

1. Informal cooperation
2. The service contract
3. Parallel action
4. The conference approach
5. The compact
6. Transfer of functions
7. Extraterritorial jurisdiction
8. Incorporation
9. Annexation
10. City-county separation
11. Geographical consolidation
12. Functional consolidation
13. The special district
14. The authority
15. Metropolitan government
16. The regional agency

*Procedural Adaptations*

Some of the procedural adaptations are further described below.

*Informal cooperation* is the desire on the part of two or more local government officials to cooperate in an effort to improve service. It might require nothing more than the sharing or exchanging of information or possibly the use by one government of equipment owned by another government.

The *service contract* is an agreement entered into by two or more governments in which one government agrees to provide a service and another agrees to pay for the service upon receiving it. The two governments enter into a legally binding agreement.

Service contracts have become popular for a number of reasons. Smaller political jurisdictions are able to obtain a service, such as water or sewage disposal, that they could never hope to provide for themselves except at a very high cost.

Service contracting is also appealing for a political reason. It allows a political jurisdiction to enter into an agreement to obtain a necessary local service without altering the structure of local government or ceding any of its political or administrative authority. The jurisdiction remains intact, but is able to provide the quantity and quality of service it deems necessary.

ACIR conducted a study on service contracting that involved over 2,300 municipalities, with just under 1,500 (63 percent) indicating they had participated in either formal or informal arrangements for services to be provided to their residents by either private companies or other governmental units. The results showed that cities with larger populations tended to enter into service agreements more frequently than smaller cities. There was no difference in the amount of service contracting entered into by central cities and suburbs.

Some other results of the study were:

- Service contracting is much more prevalent in the West than in the South.
- The council-manager form of government is most closely associated with the practice of service contracting, though over 50 percent of all other forms of local government also engage in the practice.
- Local governments are more likely to establish service agreements with counties than with other municipalities.[32]

Service contracting is now in use in all parts of the country. Some of the services most commonly contracted out are: jails and detention homes, police training, street lighting, refuse collection, and libraries. Most service contracts involve a single service, but, as the ACIR study pointed out, many central cities and suburban municipalities reported numerous instances where they receive service packages from another unit of government.[33]

The Lakewood Plan, named after the suburban Los Angeles community of Lakewood, carried the concept of contracting to the extreme. The plan was based upon the separation of the provision of services from the production of services in an effort to help the municipality take advantage of some economies of scale.

Lakewood, in the early 1950s, grew at a very rapid rate. Rather than trying to develop a service capability for delivering all of the necessary services, Lakewood opted to purchase the great majority of its services from other units of government. The plan became so popular and aroused so much interest that Los Angeles County began signing service contract agreements with political jurisdictions in the county for over fifty different services.

The success of the Lakewood Plan was based upon the ability of the local government to retain its political and administrative autonomy while meeting the service needs of the local constituents and businesses. Furthermore, it typified the market model in the public sector provision of services. Local governments could produce a service themselves, join with another local government in the coproduction of the service, purchase the service from a private contractor, or purchase the service from another unit of government under a service contract.

Two of the major criticisms voiced about the Lakewood Plan concern the bargaining position of the service recipient and the local government incorporation spawned by the inception of the plan. Some have argued that the county, as the dominant service provider, exercises too much influence in determining the quantity, quality, and price of services. Local governments might not have as many of the apparent options available to them for obtaining services as the market model might suggest.

The Lakewood Plan did not directly generate local government incorporations. However, the plan encouraged a number of local governments to incorporate because tax incentives were offered to them and the threat of annexation by the city of Los Angeles appeared real if they remained unincorporated. Since 1954, thirty-seven cities have incorporated and have begun receiving services from Los Angeles County under the Contract Cities Program. Hence, while contracting under the Lakewood Plan allowed municipalities to provide services more economically to their constituents, the plan also helped to foster increased metropolitan fragmentation.

*Parallel action* involves two or more governments that agree to pursue a common course of action. The governments pursue their agreed-upon commitments separately, even though the result is designed to benefit both parties. Parallel action is sometimes referred to as a joint power agreement. According to an ACIR survey of over 2,000 municipalities, this approach to metropolitan problem solving is growing in acceptance, particularly in the West.[34]

*The conference approach* consists of bringing together the top elected officials of governments in a metropolitan area. These officials meet on a regular basis to discuss problems of mutual interest and share information and ideas. Once these officials get to know one another, the discussions often progress to policymaking and implementation questions of actions affecting the whole metropolitan area. This approach is best typified by the development of the Council of Governments movement, which is discussed below.

*Transfer of functions* involves finding the most suitable unit of government to deliver a specific service and transferring the service to the most financially or administratively capable jurisdiction. This could involve a transfer from city to county, city to state, village to city, or county to state. Very often the jurisdiction seeking to effect the transfer recognizes the loss of administrative authority involved. However, this is weighed against both the rising costs involved in continuing to provide the service as well as the demands by local residents for a quality of service that can no longer be provided by the local government. Such a transfer of functions occurred in the 1970s when Madison, Wisconsin, turned over to the county responsibility for the airport that served the entire metropolitan area.

*Incorporation* is one method of adaptation that has an enormous impact upon the governmental structure of the metropolitan area. Incorporated areas are usually autonomous political jurisdictions having their own charters as a result of state legislative or constitutional action.

While incorporation sounds like a positive and progessive step for a growing and vigorous community to take, which often is the case, there are some disadvantages to this method of adaptation. First, incorporation often is taken as a defensive posture to ward off annexation by a larger political jurisdiction. Such a move is usually not a sound or clearly thought-out justification for incorporating. Second, many cities contend that lack of tighter controls on incorporation has led to much of the fragmentation and duplication of effort and expense in metropolitan America, thus making it increasingly difficult to develop and implement necessary metropolitan planning and coordination.

During the 1970s, about 600 communities incorporated in the United States. Only a handful of those incorporating in 1978 had populations exceeding 2,500. Texas recorded the highest number of incorporations in 1978 —twelve—followed by Missouri with five.[35]

*Structural Adaptations*

The major changes in metropolitan area governments occur because of structural adaptations. Some of the more common structural changes are discussed in this section.

*Annexation* is the acquisition of additional territory to enlarge the existing governmental jurisdiction. The annexed territory is almost always unincorporated, since many states tend to protect the sovereignty of incorporated areas by requiring a majority vote in both jurisdictions involved in the annexation. This has had the effect of increasing the political costs involved in mounting an annexation campaign.

Historically, annexation has been a very popular device for increasing the size of political jurisdictions. Most of America's largest cities achieved their present size as a result of annexations carried out towards the end of the nineteenth century. This was possible because the areas around these cities were sparsely populated and few, if any, incorporated areas existed to defend themselves against central city annexations.

The nature of municipal annexation has changed in the twentieth century. There are very few of the large nineteenth century-type annexations occurring because of local government incorporations. In addition, annexations are less likely to occur around the largest urban centers. The pattern appears to be that small to medium-sized cities are much more active in municipal annexations. We also know that annexations occur throughout the country, with the possible exception of the New England states. They are most likely to occur in areas where the populations in both the central city and the surrounding suburban areas are of similar socio-economic backgrounds, thus reducing many of the anxieties and apprehensions associated with peoples of diverse backgrounds and aspirations attempting to live together under one political system.

Older central cities are less likely to engage in annexation for a number of reasons. There is probably less unincorporated land available to annex, and the socio-economic differences between the central city and suburban residents are great, partially because of the age of housing, schools, and other capital stock.

Annexation is also more likely to occur when there is a council-manager form of government in the central city. This form of government appears to generate among citizens less animosity and fear of corruption and inefficiency than does a mayor-council form of government.

There are several ways annexation can be accomplished:

1. Legislative determination—boundary changes are the result of special legislative action in the state, usually initiated by the areas to be affected.
2. Popular determination—citizens use political power to support or defeat proposals that will alter their political and administrative power.
3. Municipal determination—local governments are given authority to expand their boundaries by their own elected officials, without the consent of the area to be annexed.
4. Judicial determination—courts become the final arbiter in deciding whether or not a proposed annexation can be implemented. In some cases they modify or amend the proposal.
5. Quasi-legislative determination—administrative agencies are entrusted with the responsibility of determining the validity of requests for annexations and other boundary adjustment proposals.[36]

What are the major strengths of annexation? First, annexation, unlike the creation of special districts, enhances the status and viability of local general-purpose government. Second, it permits the provision of services in a larger geographic area than would be possible before the city annexed the unincorporated territory. Third, it increases the tax base of the annexing jurisdiction.

But there are three principal reasons why annexation, popular in the nineteenth century, has lost much of its earlier appeal. In the first place, the absence of unincorporated territory around our cities precludes the widespread use of the device in the last decades of the twentieth century. Second, local officials of the area proposed for annexation are almost certain to campaign against it, due to their understandable fear that their jobs may be on the line. Third, unincorporated areas may engage in the process of becoming incorporated as a way to counter the threat of annexation by their neighboring city. Though such an action undoubtedly reflects the wishes of the residents of the territory, it very much compounds the problem of a multiplicity of fragmented local units within our MSAs.

During the 1970s, annexations continued at roughly the same pace as in the 1950s and 1960s. About 65 percent of the cities over 2,500 population experienced some boundary changes, most occurring because of annexations.

In looking at the number of people annexed by states during the 1970s, we find that Texas and Tennessee led the nation. They were followed in descending order by California, Kentucky, Florida, Indiana, Louisiana, Alabama, and Colorado. At the other end of the spectrum, Connecticut, New Jersey, and Vermont showed hardly any changes at all. The use of a liberal annexation policy in Texas helps to explain Houston's recent phenomenal growth. Houston's boundaries have continued to expand outward.

TABLE 9.4
Twenty Largest Annexations of 1978, by Estimated Population[1]

| City | Population annexed |
| --- | --- |
| Houston, Tex. | 51,700 |
| Savannah, Ga. | 35,300 |
| Colorado Springs, Colo. | 20,200 |
| Goose Creek, S.C. | 8,500 |
| Baton Rouge, La. | 8,500 |
| Albuquerque, N.M. | 7,700 |
| Brandon, Miss. | 6,200 |
| North Charleston, S.C. | 5,500 |
| Biloxi, Miss. | 4,700 |
| Pearl, Miss. | 4,400 |
| Starkville, Miss. | 3,500 |
| La Mirada, Calif. | 3,200 |
| Jackson, Tenn. | 3,100 |
| Glendora, Calif. | 2,800 |
| Cheyenne, Wyo. | 2,800 |
| Southside, Ala. | 2,600 |
| Birmingham, Ala. | 2,600 |
| Philadelphia, Miss. | 2,500 |
| Rapid City, S.D. | 2,500 |
| Longview, Tex. | 2,300 |

[1]Net of detachments. Data are estimates based on responses of local governments to the bureau's Boundary and Annexation Survey and do not constitute official Bureau of the Census estimates.
    Source: International City Management Association (Washington, D.C.: *The Munic Year Book* 1980), p. 65.

States in which the greatest number of square miles were added to cities because of annexation were Texas, Oklahoma, California, Alaska, Alabama, Tennessee, Illinois, and Florida. The ten cities with the largest number of people annexed during the 1970s were Houston (77,500); San Antonio (54,500); Chattanooga (47,900); Charlotte, N.C. (46,000); Baton Rouge (36,700); North Charleston, S.C. (34,900); Memphis (33,400); Jackson, Miss. (28,800); Savannah (26,400); and Colorado Springs (24,800).[37]

*Geographical consolidation* includes the city-county consolidations that were discussed above in reviewing the polycentric and metropolitan approaches. Consolidation movements are beginning to occur in different parts of the country, and as pressures mount for quality services at reason-

TABLE 9.5
Municipal Annexations of More Than 12,000 Population,[1]
2 January 1970 to 1 January 1979, in Rank Order

| Rank | City | 1970 population[2] |
|------|------|--------------------|
| 1. | Houston, Tex. | 77,494 |
| 2. | San Antonio, Tex. | 54,429 |
| 3. | Chattanooga, Tenn. | 47,915 |
| 4. | Charlotte, N.C. | 46,049 |
| 5. | Baton Rouge, La. | 36,741 |
| 6. | North Charleston, S.C. | 34,870 |
| 7. | Memphis, Tenn. | 33,412 |
| 8. | Jackson, Miss. | 26,846 |
| 9. | Savannah, Ga. | 26,388 |
| 10. | Colorado Springs, Colo. | 24,800 |
| 11. | Muncie, Ind. | 15,692 |
| 12. | Hendersonville, Tenn. | 15,224 |
| 13. | Redding, Calif. | 14,866 |
| 14. | Mount Prospect, Ill. | 13,931 |
| 15. | Roanoke, Va. | 13,503 |
| 16. | Gary, Ind. | 12,983 |
| 17. | Clarksville, Tenn. | 12,661 |
| 18. | Fairbanks, Alaska | 12,507 |
| 19. | La Mirada, Calif. | 12,152 |
| 20. | Clarksville, Tenn. | 12,010 |

[1]Based on the 1970 census of population.
[2]Data are net of detachments.

Source: International City Management Association (Washington, D.C.:
The Municipal Year Book 1980), p. 65.

able costs, local governments are going to be placed under increased pressure to initiate innovative techniques for delivering these services. City-county consolidation offers one possible approach to the problem. One area where this has been occurring has been in the consolidation of school districts, which has increased over the past ten years.

The special district is a unit of government created to provide one or more service functions. The overwhelming number of special districts are unifunctional. Special districts are autonomous units of local government that are administratively and fiscally independent. Their budgets are not approved by the local government, nor are they dependent upon local government appropriation processes. School districts, which are a form of special district, use taxing authority for their revenues. Non-school special districts rely more on user or service charges.

Special districts have been growing rapidly in recent years, although school districts are decreasing in number. The latter is due primarily to administrative and financial considerations leading to consolidations. The growth in other special districts appears to reflect the inability of local government to perform required services at a satisfactory level and at a reasonable cost.

There are over 28,000 special districts in the United States, an increase from 23,885 in 1972. The largest number of these are school districts. Special districts now outnumber both municipalities and townships. One of the primary reasons for their rapid growth is that special districts help local governments circumvent legal restrictions imposed by the state constitutions or state legislation. Special districts help to disperse the increasingly high cost of some needed local services and also permit local governments to evade taxing and debt limits imposed by the state.

Special districts are found in all areas of the country, and patterns are hard to define. Some urban states, such as Illinois, New York, California, Pennsylvania, and Washington, contain over 30 percent of the non-school special districts. At the same time, the urban states of Connecticut, Ohio, Massachusetts, and Michigan contain very few special districts.

TABLE 9.6
Scope of the Subnational System: Number of Governments in the U.S.

| Type of Government | 1962 | 1967 | 1972 | 1977 | 1982 |
|---|---|---|---|---|---|
| Total | 91,237 | 81,299 | 79,269 | 80,171 | 82,688 |
| U.S. Government | 1 | 1 | 1 | 1 | 1 |
| State Governments | 50 | 50 | 50 | 50 | 50 |
| Local Governments | 91,186 | 81,248 | 78,218 | 80,120 | 82,637 |
| Counties | 3,043 | 3,049 | 3,044 | 3,042 | 3,041 |
| Municipalities | 18,000 | 18,048 | 18,517 | 18,856 | 19,083 |
| Townships | 17,142 | 17,105 | 18,991 | 16,822 | 16,748 |
| School Districts | 34,678 | 21,782 | 15,781 | 15,260 | 15,032 |
| Special Districts | 18,323 | 21,264 | 23,885 | 26,140 | 28,733 |

Source: U.S. Bureau of the Census.

Special district boundaries vary according to the location, the service provided, and the needs defined. Sometimes the boundaries are coterminous with the existing political jurisdictions; in other cases they overlap into other cities, suburbs, counties, and even states. While this helps to disperse the cost of the service, it also raises many questions about the relationship of tax and service boundaries and the appropriate governance mechanism to administer the service. The governmental services most frequently delivered by special districts are fire protection, soil conservation, water supply, housing, and drainage control.

While special districts appear to solve some very basic problems confronting urban America, they have stimulated a great deal of debate and controversy. The major arguments advanced for creating a special district are: (1) It provides urban services where and when they are needed and limits costs and financial burdens to those directly affected. (2) Special districts eliminate much of the local government red tape and politics associated with service delivery. (3) Other types of governmental units cannot or will not provide these services. (4) Creation of a special district often thwarts more drastic actions, such as municipal annexation or city-county consolidation. A special district can be the lesser of two evils. (5) The purchasing of equipment or construction of facilities can be spread over a large taxpaying area and might also be achieved at a reduced rate due to economies of scale. (6) Removal of the service from the governmental unit appears to citizens to increase objectivity in decision-making, reduce politics in the allocation of services, and allow the service provider to maintain low visibility.

Critics of special districts feel there are many negative aspects: (1) Special districts provide some short-range solutions and reduce urgency associated with a service problem, but they do not solve long-range problems. (2) Administrative appointments to the special district are often a product of a patronage system. This diminishes the professional quality of the people responsible for delivering the service. (3) Costs are sometimes higher because the special district is competing with other nearby governmental jurisdiction, and duplication of services occurs. (4) There is not enough coordination among the agencies that provide services, and the creation of a special district only exacerbates this situation. (5) There is little popular control and accountability to the electorate, since many officers are appointed. Furthermore, their terms are often staggered, preventing a new administration from altering the makeup of the governing board, which might increase efficiency or improve service quality.

Special districts increase intergovernmental cooperation and allow for the more economical delivery of urban services. However, special districts achieve these goals at the cost of increasing metropolitan fragmentation and establishing relatively "invisible" governments, which are not easily held accountable to the public or its elected representatives.[38]

*The public authority* technique resembles the special district, but there are some important differences. Special districts are usually given the power to tax but are prohibited from issuing revenue bonds. The authority usually has the power to issue revenue bonds but not the power to tax. In some cases, both organizations possess both powers.

Since authorities raise much of their money in the bond market, they like to present a businesslike facade so as to receive the most favorable interest rates possible. To do this, authorities try to keep out of local political conflicts, which usually end up tarnishing their image. Authorities also try to avoid becoming embroiled in controversial issues of great concern to the public. In the early 1970s, the New York Port Authority allowed itself to become caught up in the debate over the public mass transit system in New York City. The Port Authority, with huge sums of money at its disposal, was virtually helpless to defend its image against critics who wanted the Authority to invest some of its money in the mass transit system. In the end, the debate subsided, but the Port Authority's image was badly tarnished.

The Port Authority, with a business and highway orientation, did not want to make a large investment in a losing proposition like mass transit. Pressure from mayors and public officials was not enough to sway the Authority's investment policy. The Port Authority then proceeded to build the World Trade Center in lower Manhattan with much of its surplus funds. For a while, vacancy rates were extremely high, and the State of New York became the single largest tenant. The actions of the Port Authority raise serious questions about accountability and responsibility of authorities that have enormous independent revenue raising capability.[39]

Other services provided by authorities include sewage disposal, parks, water supply, housing, and airports. Authorities, or metropolitan service districts, as they are sometimes called, are found in most large metropolitan areas. Some of the better-known ones are the Southern California Metropolitan Water District, Chicago Metropolitan Sanitary District, Seattle Port District, and the Massachusetts Bay Transit Authority.

*Metropolitan government,* as an approach to dealing with metropolitan problems, has been discussed above. The metropolitan government approach represents a major alteration in the political and administrative exercise in power. Since it threatens so many existing relationships, efforts to create metropolitan governments fail much more often than they succeed. Two-tier governments, federation, and city-county consolidations are all efforts that have had limited acceptance in the United States.

The only two metropolitan governance mechanisms operating in the United States today are found in the Portland, Oregon, Metropolitan Services District and the Metropolitan Council of the Twin Cities Area (Minneapolis-St. Paul). The two systems are very much alike except that in Portland the voters elect the councillors and the chief executive officer, while in the Twin Cities the councillors and the chairperson are appointed by the governor. The other major difference between the two governments is that the Twin Cities uses a tax-base sharing plan. The local governments in the area benefit directly from the economic growth that occurs each year in the regions.[40]

*The regional agency,* occasionally situations arise which cannot be resolved by any of the other approaches discussed above. Issues such as water supply, air and water pollution, mass transit, and economic development often exceed the capabilities of a few governments in a metropolitan area. In these circumstances the federal and state governments encourage the formation of regional agencies that overarch the metropolitan area and engage in planning, funding, or monitoring activities. Some of these agencies are the Federal Aviation Administration in airport planning and air traffic control; the Urban Mass Transportation Administration in transit planning in the Washington metropolitan area; and the Economic Development Administration in rural development areas.

## COUNCIL OF GOVERNMENTS

Earlier in this chapter we discussed a procedural mechanism—the conference aproach—for local governments to use in adapting to metropolitan problems. The conference approach is typified by the Council of Governments (COG) now found in hundreds of metropolitan areas. The purpose of this section is to define COGs, examine their growth and development in contemporary urban America, and assess their strengths and weaknesses in trying to cope with metropolitan problems.

A COG is a voluntary regional association composed of locally elected officials from the cities and counties in the metropolitan area. The members meet regularly to exchange ideas and opinions and to develop policies of value to the region. One of the primary concerns of COGs has been the preparation and implementation of a comprehensive plan for regional growth and development.

COGs have also been defined in several other ways. They are sometimes labeled "defensive coalitions." Several COGs were initially created by local officials as the least-consequential step in warding off more drastic action proposed by a state government or other political factions in the metropolitan area.

In the early days, many observers saw COGs as nothing more than regional planning commissions composed of elected officials rather than officials appointed by local governments or local planning authorities.

Another stereotype of COGs sees them as federal grant brokerage councils. This stereotype developed in the late 1960s, when COGs, as a result of the explosion in the grant-in-aid system and federal regulations granting them increased powers, began to play a much larger role in the processing of some grant applications and the administration, review, and monitoring of many others.

Finally, some critics have seen COGs as the first step in the process towards regional or metropolitan governmental autonomy. As such, they were to be watched carefully and constantly. Despite the fact that metropolitanism has not become a popular movement in this century and COGs have rather limited powers, critics have repeatedly warned us of the dangers inherent in the Council of Governments movement.[41]

The Council of Governments movement is a relatively recent phenomenon. The first COG is thought to have been formed in 1954 in Detroit. It was called the Detroit Area Supervisors Inter-County Committee and held meetings to discuss problems common to the metropolitan area governments.

In 1956, New York City Mayor Robert F. Wagner helped to establish the New York Metropolitan Regional Council, which was the beginning of the New York COG. These first two efforts were quickly followed by organizations established in 1957 in Washington, D.C. (the Washington Metropolitan Conference) and Seattle (The Puget Sound Government Conference). In 1958, Salem, Oregon, helped to initiate the Mid-Willamette Valley Intergovernmental Cooperation Committee, and in 1961, San Francisco established the Association of Bay Area Governments (ABAG).[42]

COGs have been initiated in a variety of ways. Some were started by local officials who sensed a need for better and more frequent communication among elected officials in a metropolitan area. This often led to a feeling that a more permanent organizational arrangement was required. Some COGs have been created because existing local organizations saw a need and encouraged local officials to begin meeting. In Southern California, the California League of Cities was very involved in encouraging the establishment of the Southern California Association of Governments (SCAG). As mentioned above, some COGs were created as defensive responses to an outside stimulus. This usually was based upon a desire to retain local autonomy while still meeting the mandates imposed by the state. In this case, a COG was seen as less threatening than alternative organizational arrangements.[43]

The COG movement developed at a fairly modest pace. There were several serious problems confronting COGs and not too many solutions. First, the COGs relied on member governments for dues with which to finance their activities. Given the adverse publicity some COGs generated because of their potential threat to local autonomy, it was easy to see that membership dues were a vehicle for limiting rather than encouraging growth and new program areas. Few COGs in the early 1960s had budgets over $100,000.

Limited financing also made it difficult to recruit high quality professional staff. City, county, state, and federal government agencies were also competing for these employees, and they offered decent salaries, good fringe benefits, and the prospects for promotion and professional growth.

A third problem concerned the relationship between the central city and the surrounding political jurisdictions. Both approached COGs with a great deal of apprehension. The central cities were wary because they couldn't understand what benefits could accrue to them from joining an organization that included a number of upper-middle-class suburbs. Moreover, the central city felt threatened under a one unit–one vote arrangement.[44] The suburban political jurisdictions also felt threatened, since they were fearful of having the COG become dominated by the central city. Under such an arrangement they could not see any benefits resulting from their participation.

A lot of hard work, negotiating, and compromising was employed in creating a number of COGs and keeping them afloat during their early years. The turning point in the development of the COG movement occurred in 1965, with the passage of Section 701(g) as an amendment to the 1954 Housing Act. This Act made organizations of locally elected officials in metropolitan areas directly eligible to receive funding under the planning assistance program.[45]

The amendment sought to foster greater metropolitan cooperation by assisting organizations composed of locally elected officials. Planning grants were made available to COGs and COG-like organizations for professional staffing; administrative expenses; organizational, fiscal, and planning studies; data collection; and regional planning for land use, transportation, housing, economic development, resource development, community facilities, and general improvement of the environment Approved activities were eligible for funding of two-thirds of their cost.

Almost overnight, COGs became important metropolitan organizations. The 701 funding was broad enough in scope to cover virtually every activity conducted or contemplated by existing COGs. The federal government was not only recognizing the existence of these organizations, but now was willing to encourage their growth and development.

The following year, Congress passed the Demonstration Cities and Metropolitan Development Act, sometimes referred to as the Model Cities Act. Section 204 gave further encouragement to COGs and for the first time appeared to vest some tangible power in them. This was done in an attempt to force independent local governments to begin thinking in metropolitan terms and begin comprehensive planning for the overall growth and development of their metropolitan areas.[46]

Section 204 stated that after June 30, 1967, applications for federal grants and loans in more than thirty different programs would have to be reviewed and commented upon by officials of either a state or regional agency. The review process was to be conducted by an agency composed of elected officials who assessed the program with respect to its consistency with the planned development for the area.

In 1968 Congress passed the Intergovernmental Cooperation Act designed to increase cooperation among the three levels of government in the political system. The following year the Office of Management and Budget issued Circular A-95, which required federal agencies to notify governors, legislators, or other designated officials of the purpose and amounts of grants being awarded to states or their political units.[47]

The A-95 program stimulated COG development by requiring that certain grant applications by local governments first go to regional clearinghouses for their comments on the program impact on metropolitan-wide issues. In some areas Regional Planning Councils continued to serve as the designated regional clearinghouse.

By 1971, over 100 programs were included in the A-95 review process. The metropolitan review function was often lodged with the Council of Governments, which had evolved into a brokerage style of operation, with staff capability to review grant proposals and negotiate modifications that conformed to the overall plan for metropolitan growth and development.

Table 9.7

| Year | Number of COGs |
|------|----------------|
| 1950 | 23 |
| 1963 | 126 |
| 1967 | 216 |
| 1970 | 253 |
| 1980 | 670 |

The growth of COGs paralleled the rapid expansion in the grant-in-aid system. The increase in numbers from 1963 to 1967 represents the added powers and money COGs received as a result of the passage of Section 701(g) in 1965 and Section 204 in 1966.

In 1983 the Reagan administration eliminated the regional review requirements of A-95, thereby eliminating one of its most important functions as far as local governments and COGs were concerned.

## Summary and Conclusions

COGs are a relatively new organizational arrangement in metropolitan America. They have both strengths and weaknesses. Their strengths appear to be the following:

- They serve as a metropolitan coordinating mechanism.
- Communications, data gathering, and information dissemination are often provided by COGs.
- They are easy to create.
- They are professionally staffed.
- They provide a public forum for the discussion of metropolitan issues and the brokering of interests.
- They engage in comprehensive metropolitan planning and development.

Their weaknesses are numerous. First, COGs lack substantial power and authority. They receive their directions from their member governments, and their political and administrative limits are determined by the rules and regulations of the federal agencies that fund them. Very few COGs have independent sources of power.

Second, COGs are voluntary organizations from which members can withdraw at any time. This potential threat hangs over each COG as it attempts to deal with metropolitan issues. In both Cleveland and Washington, D.C., member governments have withdrawn from the local COG for short periods of time.

Third, COGs have few independent sources of revenue; therefore, they are dependent for funding on a number of sources, which help to set their agenda.

Fourth, because they are agents of the local governments in the area, they tend to avoid the controversial social issues and concentrate on planning and development concerns. School bussing, gun control, and housing integration are not the types of issues many COGs debate. Furthermore, COGs require unanimity on an issue before moving forward. Since any government that perceives its interests to be negatively affected by an issue can withdraw from the COG, only safe or bland issues, which can gain unanimous support, are frequently debated.

Finally, the one government–one vote rule gives a veto on some issues to small political jurisdictions, thereby antagonizing the large political jurisdictions that have a majority of the area's population. In Cleveland, a long and bitter struggle in the Northeast Ohio Areawide Coordinating Agency (NOACA) erupted in the late 1960s, which led to HUD's decertifying NOACA in 1971 and cutting off about $5 million of funding. Cleveland felt it was being discriminated against since it had 25 percent of the population but only 6 percent of the votes in NOACA. Cleveland withdrew its support from NOACA and was suspended for non-payment of dues.[48]

COGs have come a long way since 1954 and have established themselves in all parts of the country. Their growth was rapid up to the mid

1970s, but it is likely to stabilize or possibly diminish in the 1980s.

COGs are heavily dependent upon federal spending, with only minimal financial support coming from state and local governments. Despite this, a relatively small percentage of the COGs (20 percent) have assumed a majority of the federal program responsibilities available to them.

The 1980s may prove to be the sternest test COGs have yet faced. The Reagan Administration is reducing federal support of numerous programs, forcing state and local governments to assume some of the financial and administrative responsibilities associated with these programs. It is still too early to determine what impact this changing federal policy will have on the traditional COG role of federal grant broker.

As already noted, federal funding was the chief catalyst in the creation and development of many COGs across the country. If regional planning and COG funding dry up under the Reagan Administration, few local governments, hard-pressed to finance their own services, will make up the cuts by increasing their own contributions. If this proves to be the case, COGs may suffer severe staff cutbacks, greatly diminishing their effectiveness; in some areas of the country COGs may disappear altogether. Still, if program responsibility is returned to states and local government, we may be ushering in a new era in metropolitan politics. The role local governments will want COGs to play will be one of the key issues in determining the future of COGs.

The problems confronting metropolitan America are enormous. For the past fifteen years the federal government has assumed less and less interest in the potential of metropolitan solutions to urban problems. The Reagan Administration has articulated a clear policy of New Federalism, which aims to return power and authority for numerous programs to the states.

Nowhere in America is there a serious movement for comprehensive metropolitan reform. The numerous, autonomous units of local government, which guard their resources carefully, make only incremental change a possibility. Incremental reforms do provide some benefits. They increase communication, problem solving, and cooperation among governments in the metropolitan area. However, the politics of accommodation, which preserves autonomy and fragmentation while providing for diversity, choice, and competition, also increases duplication of efforts, political and economic rivalries, and a lack of metropolitan planning.

The 1980s are proving to be a time of cutbacks and resource scarcity. The distribution of power in the metropolitan area is strongly inclined towards polycentrism. How much change we are willing to make in political and economic resource distribution may turn out to be the most important issue facing metropolitan America during the decade.

# NOTES

1. *Standard Metropolitan Statistical Areas and Standard Consolidated Statistical Areas: 1980* (Washington: U.S. Department of Commerce, Bureau of the Census, October 1981).

2.  For a discussion of these issues, see Jeffrey McCaffery, "The Impact of Re-
    source Scarcity on Urban Public Finance," *Public Administration Review* 41
    (January 1981), whole issue.
3.  These problems are all discussed in *Alternative Approaches to Governmental
    Reorganization in Metropolitan Areas* (Washington: Advisory Commission on
    Intergovernmental Relations, 1962); and Bernard J. Frieden, *Metropolitan
    America: Challenge to Federalism* (Washington: Advisory Commission on In-
    tergovernmental Relations, 1966), chap. I.
4.  For a discussion of this issue, see *The Challenge of Local Governmental Reor-
    ganization* (Washington: Advisory Commission on Intergovernmental Rela-
    tions, 1974), pp. 104–05; Stephen P. Eric, John J. Kirlin, and Francine Rabino-
    vitz, *Reform of Metropolitan Governments* (Washington: Resources for the
    Future, 1972); and William H. Wilken, "The Impact of Centralization on Ef-
    fectiveness, Economy and Efficiency," in *Organizing Public Services in Met-
    ropolitan America*, ed. Thomas P. Murphy and Charles R. Warren (Lexington,
    Mass.: D. C. Heath, 1974), pp. 107–26.
5.  *The Challenge of Local Governmental Reorganization*, p. 103.
6.  Ibid., p. 101–04.
7.  Ibid., pp. 101–04; and Dale Rogers Marshall, Bernard Frieden, and D. W.
    Fessler, *The Governance of Metropolitan Regions: Minority Perspectives*
    (Washington: Resources for the Future, 1972). Also see Tobe Johnson, *Met-
    ropolitan Government: A Black Analytical Perspective* (Washington: Joint Cen-
    ter for Political Studies, 1972).
8.  See *Government Functions and Processes: Local and Areawide* (Washington:
    Advisory Commission on Intergovernmental Relations, 1974). Also see How-
    ard W. Hallman, *Small and Large Together: Governing the Metropolis* (Bever-
    ly Hills; Sage Publications, 1977), chap. 13; and *Reshaping Government in
    Metropolitan Areas* (New York: Committee for Economic Development, 1970).
9.  *The Challenge of Local Governmental Reorganization*, p. 8.
10. *Profile of County Government* (Washington: Advisory Commission on Inter-
    governmental Relations, 1972), p. 23.
11. About two-thirds of the nation's counties are members of NACO.
12. Susan Walker Torrence, *Grass Roots Government: The County in American
    Politics* (Washington: Robert B. Luce, 1974), pp. 21–44.
13. William G. Colman, *Cities, Suburbs and States: Governing and Financing
    Urban America* (New York: Free Press, 1975), pp. 260–66.
14. Demetrios Caraley, *City Governments and Urban Problems* (Englewood Cliffs,
    N.J.: Prentice-Hall, 1977), pp. 115–16.
15. *The Municipal Year Book* (Washington: International City Management As-
    sociation, 1982), p. xvii.
16. The most important application of this model to urban political life is found in
    Vincent Ostrom, Charles Tiebout, and Robert Warren, "The Organization of
    Government in Metropolitan Areas," *The American Political Science Review*
    55 (December 1961): 831–42. Other useful works on this subject include
    Robert L. Bish, *The Public Economy of Metropolitan Areas* (Chicago: Mark-
    ham, 1971); Robert L. Bish and Vincent Ostrom, *Understanding Urban Gov-
    ernment: Metropolitan Reform Reconsidered* (Washington: American Enterprise
    Institute, 1973); and Vincent Ostrom and Elinor Ostrom, "Public Choice: A
    Different Approach to the Study of Public Administration," *Public Administra-
    tion Review* 31 (March/April 1971): 203–16.
17. Bish and Ostrom, *Understanding Urban Government*, p. 19.
18. Harlan Hahn and Charles Levine, eds., *Urban Politics: Past, Present and Fu-
    ture*, 2nd ed. (New York: Longman, 1984), p. 28.
19. For a discussion of these approaches, see *Reshaping Government in Metropoli-
    tan Areas;* and *Regional Governance: Promise and Performance* (Washington:

Advisory Commission on Intergovernmental Relations, 1973), chap. 1. The latter document presents several short case studies of the major governmental reorganizations in the U.S.

20. Brett W. Hawkins, *Nashville Metro* (Nashville: University of Vanderbilt Press, 1966); and Brett W. Hawkins, "Public Opinion and Metropolitan Reorganization in Nashville," *Journal of Politics* 28 (May 1966): 408–18.

21. Vincent L. Marando, "The Politics of City-County Consolidation," *National Civic Review* 64, no. 2 (February 1975): 76–81. Also see Vincent L. Marando, "City-County Consolidation: Reform, Regionalism, Referenda and Requiem," *Western Political Quarterly* 32, No. 4 (Dec. 1979): 409–21.

22. Marando, "The Politics of City-County Consolidation," p. 81.

23. Parris N. Glendening and Patricia S. Atkins, "City-County Consolidations: New Views From the Eighties," in *The Municipal Year Book* (Washington: International City Management Association, 1980), pp. 68–72.

24. Ibid., p. 68.

25. Ibid., p. 68.

26. Ibid., p. 68; and Marando, "The Politics of City-County Consolidations," pp. 76–81.

27. Two studies of the Toronto government are Frank Smallwood, *Metro Toronto a Decade Later* (Toronto: Bureau of Municipal Research, 1963); and Harold Kaplan, *Urban Political Systems: A Functional Analysis of Metro Toronto* (New York: Columbia University Press, 1967).

28. John J. Harrigan and William C. Johnson, *Governing the Twin Cities: The Metropolitan Council in Comparative Perspective* (Minneapolis: University of Minnesota Press, 1978).

29. Glendening and Atkins, "City-County Consolidations," p. 68.

30. Roscoe C. Martin, *Metropolis in Transition* (Washington: Housing and Home Financing Agency, 1963); and Bernard J. Frieden, *Metropolitan America: Challenge to Federalism* (Washington: Advisory Commission on Intergovernmental Relations, 1966). Also see *The Challenge to Local Government Reorganization* (Washington: Advisory Commission on Intergovernmental Relations, 1974); and *Alternative Approaches to Governmental Reorganization* (Washington: Advisory Commission on Intergovernmental Relations, 1962).

31. Martin, *Metropolis in Transition*, p. 3.

32. *The Challenge of Local Governmental Reorganization*, pp. 35–36. Also see Patricia S. Florestano and Stephen B. Gordon, "A Survey of City and County Use of Private Contracting," *The Urban Interest* 3 (Spring 1981): 22–29; and E. S. Savas, *Privatizing the Public Sector: How to Shrink Government* (Chatham, N.J.: Chatham House, 1982).

33. *The Challenge of Local Governmental Reorganization*, pp. 35–36. Also see Patricia S. Florestano and Stephen B. Gordon, "Public vs. Private: Small Government Contracting with the Private Sector," *Public Administration Review* 40 (January/February 1980): 29–34; and Richard M. Cion, "Accommodation Par Excellence: The Lakewood Plan," in *Metropolitan Politics: A Reader*, 2nd ed., ed. Michael N. Danielson (Boston: Little, Brown, 1971), pp. 224–26.

34. *The Challenge of Local Governmental Reorganization*, pp. 41–47.

35. *The Municipal Year Book* (Washington: International City Management Association, 1980), p. 64.

36. *The Challenge of Local Governmental Reorganization*, pp. 84–86.

37. *The Municipal Year Book*, 1980, pp. 65–67.

38. For a discussion of special districts and authorities, see *Regional Decision Making: New Strategies for Substate Districts* (Washington: Advisory Commission on Intergovernmental Relations, 1973), chap. II. Also see *Metropolitan Governance: A Handbook for Local Government Study Commissions* (Washington: National Academy of Public Administration, June 1980), chap. 7.

39. For a critical view of the New York–New Jersey Port Authority, see Robert A. Caro, *The Power Broker: Robert Moses and the Fall of New York* (New York: Vintage Books, 1975), chaps. 39–40.

40. For a discussion of the two plans, see *Metropolitan Governance: A Handbook for Local Government Study Commissions,* pp. 85–89. For an analysis of the Minneapolis Plan, see Harrigan and Johnson, *Governing the Twin Cities.* Miami, Nashville, and Indianapolis are more accurately classified as city-county consolidations.

41. For a discussion of the Council of Governments movement, see *Regional Decision Making: New Strategies for Substate Districts,* chap. III; and Bruce D. McDowell, "Substate Regionalism Matures Gradually;" *Intergovernmental Perspective* (Fall 1980): 20–26.

42. The early years of the Council of Governments movement are discussed in *Regional Decision Making: New Strategies for Substate Districts,* pp. 63–70.

43. See Royce Hanson, *Metropolitan Councils of Governments* (Washington: Advisory Commission on Intergovernmental Relations, 1966), pp. 3–5.

44. *Regional Decision Making: New Strategies for Substate Districts,* p. 80.

45. Ibid., pp. 56–58.

46. Ibid., pp. 140–42.

47. Ibid., pp. 143–64.

48. Ibid., pp. 83–86.

# 10. INTERGOVERNMENTAL RELATIONS

Intergovernmental relations (IGR) has become one of the most important aspects of U.S. politics in recent years. Local public officials exercise very few powers, implement very few programs, and provide very few services that are not in some way affected by decisions made in their state capitol or in Washington, D.C. With the extraordinary growth in domestic spending by the federal government over the past fifty years, there are hardly any local government functions that are not influenced by federal policymakers.

The dichotomy between federal policymaking and state or local policy implementation is a difficult one for students of urban politics to understand.

> In our system, broad policy goals and objectives are legislated by Congress. Administrative agencies then develop rules and regulations to guide the state, counties, and cities charged with the responsibility of implementing the programs.[1]

Just as local governments find it difficult to set policy goals and objectives without intrusions from the federal government, Washington officials find it equally burdensome to administer their programs without the cooperation of local officials. The relationship that has developed is one in which most domestic programs receive some funding from the federal government, but the management of these programs is left to state, county, and local officials.

The intergovernmental system of the United States is unique. It is a complex system comprised of intricate financial, administrative, and judicial relationships that do not fit easily into a pattern. But it is essential for students of urban politics to understand the governmental system since this system often indicates how power is distributed and exercised.

## IGR AND FEDERALISM

Several years ago a student in an undergraduate seminar asked a guest speaker why he kept using the terms *IGR* and *federalism* interchangeably.

The student found this confusing. The speaker stated that the two concepts meant basically the same thing and that everybody understood this. Obviously the student who asked the question did not, and neither do many other people, both students and practitioners. Reagan and Sanzone begin their book with this statement:

> Federalism—old style—is dead. Yet federalism—new style—is alive and well and living in the United States. Its name is intergovernmental relations.[2]

According to Reagan and Sanzone, old style federalism is a legal concept that focuses on the source of powers and how they are divided among the different levels of government. New style federalism is more pragmatic and action oriented and focuses less on division and separation of powers and more on sharing and interdependence.[3]

Morton Grodzins was one of the first to sense that assessing the powers of each level of government as it interacted with the others was not only cumbersome, but also unrealistic. Grodzins reoriented our thinking away from this structural approach and towards a view which stressed cooperation and sharing. He suggested we think of American federalism not as a "layer cake," with each level having separate and autonomous powers, but rather as a "marble cake" in which many different levels share in the decision-making and implementation of policies.[4]

There are several reasons for using the term *IGR* over *federalism*. Federalism implies a federal-state relationship, it implies a hierarchical set of relationships, and it has become too legalistic to accurately reflect contemporary relationships among the different levels of government.[5]

Finally, Glendening and Reeves define the difference by stating that IGR are much more inclusive and cover actions on all levels of government, while federalism is more narrowly focused on the relationship of the central government to the states.[6]

For purposes of this book we will use *IGR* to describe the political, administrative, and financial relationships among the many actors on the different levels of government. Wherever we discuss the theoretical or judicial relationships between the federal government and another level, we will use the term *federalism*.

## Evolution of the IGR system

Scholars differ markedly in their assessment of how the intergovernmental system has evolved in U.S. history. Deil Wright has divided the history of the country into six intergovernmental phases.[7]

| | |
|---|---|
| Conflict: | up to 1930 |
| Cooperative: | 1930s–1950s |
| Concentrated: | 1940s–1960s |
| Creative: | 1950s–1960s |
| Competitive: | 1960s–1970s |
| Calculative: | 1970s–1980s |

In each of these periods Wright examined three areas. What were the dominant policy issues? How did the participants view the system? And what mechanisms were used by the actors to process intergovernmental issues and achieve their objectives?

The conflict phase (up to 1930) was characterized by efforts to define appropriate spheres of action and jurisdiction among the different levels of government. Much of this was accomplished by the courts, particularly under Supreme Court Chief Justice Marshall in the early nineteenth century. However, the process whereby the various governments allocated functions and services and settled disputes was often bitter and conflictual.

The cooperation phase (1930–50) was highlighted by a common concern for stabilizing and improving the economic life of the nation and responding to the threats posed by the Depression and World War II. The twin evils of economic depression and international conflict increased the need for cooperation among the different levels of government. This supportive relationship was heightened by national efforts at planning, formula grants, and tax credits.

The 1940s–1960s are labeled the concentrated period. During this period a great deal of attention was paid to both increasing services and building new capital plants and equipment. As government expanded to meet these post-war needs there was a corresponding increase in the number of professionals required to manage the new programs. This new professional class was viewed by some observers as the beginning of a bureaucratic era labeled "the professional state."[8]

The creative phase of IGR (1950s–60s) derives its name from Lyndon Johnson's use of the term "creative federalism" to describe his approach to intergovernmental relations. This period was highlighted by increased attention to urban and metropolitan areas, with a specific focus on the poor and disadvantaged residents who inhabited those areas and who were clients of the agencies providing social services.

During this period, there was also a sizeable growth in the number of categorical grants. Many of these required involvement in planning and implementation of grant programs by the clients of the agencies delivering the services. All of this was consistent with the administration's goal of trying to end poverty.

The fifth phase in Wright's typology is the competitive period (1960s–1970s). By then, the number of grant-in-aid programs had grown to over 500. Coordination had become difficult, if not impossible, and program effectiveness was being assessed through a variety of mechanisms to help justify the large expenditures. Citizen involvement required time, attention, and patience, all of which were occasionally absent in interactions between bureaucrats and community groups. Tension and conflict escalated, and efforts to stabilize the system took the form of reorganization, regionalization, and revenue sharing.

The final phase in Wright's typology is called the calculative period (1970s–1980s). Wright suggested that this period begins in 1975 at the point when New York City was on the brink of bankruptcy. One major characteristic associated with this period was cutback management. Many state, county, and local governments perfected managerial techniques to assist them in making decisions to reduce or eliminate programs. These actions were taken in response to reductions in federal program funding, a weakened economy, and reduced revenues from taxes.[9]

A second characteristic of the calculative period Wright labels the "risk of noncompliance," which is directly related to the increase in the number of federal regulations applicable to state and local governments. Many local governments began asking themselves if they could afford to bear the costs associated with these rules and regulations. Another aspect of this problem dealt with the administrative capability to comply with all the applicable grant regulations. To some observers the intergovernmental system was becoming overloaded with excessive requirements, which were beginning to impede the effective operation of the system.

The phases of intergovernmental relations suggested by Wright are useful for our understanding of the historical changes that have occurred. Wright has interpreted numerous events in the intergovernmental area and has established different time frames to order these events. He provides us with a framework within which we can begin to analyze and understand the complexities of the intergovernmental system.

## Constitutional Questions

The theory of federalism, though not explicitly stated, was formulated at the Constitutional Convention. The Constitution provided for certain powers to be delegated to the federal government. Most of these powers are enumerated in Article I, Section 8. In the Tenth Amendment, the Congress sought to make clear where the powers they had not delegated should reside. The Tenth Amendment reads:

> The powers not delegated to the United States by the Constitution, nor prohibited by it to the States, are reserved to the States respectively, or to the people.

Some of the powers delegated to the national government include: taxing, regulation of interstate commerce, declaring war, entering into treaties, establishing post offices, and coining money. In Article I, Section 9, the Constitution lists certain powers that cannot be exercised by the national government. These include: suspending the writ of habeas corpus, passage of bills of attainder or ex post facto laws, and drawing money from the treasury unless it has been lawfully appropriated.

Article I, Section 10 lists several powers forbidden to the states. States are not allowed to enter into treaties, coin money, grant titles of nobility, impose duties, declare war, or pass bills of attainder or ex post facto laws.

This rather neat and orderly allocation of powers and constraints grew out of post-Revolutionary War political realities. Power resided with the thirteen former colonies. In order to form a union of the separate states it was agreed each state would have to give up some of its powers to a national government. The powers not delegated to the national government were to remain with the individual states.

However, the Tenth Amendment and the delegated powers clause must be viewed in the context of Article VI, which is sometimes called the supremacy clause. In this article the framers specified that the laws passed by Congress shall be the supreme law of the land and that judges throughout the country shall be bound by these laws. Article VI and the Tenth Amendment appear to be in conflict, but the Supreme Court has minimized this apparent conflict by broadly interpreting the "elastic clause" at the end of Article I, Section 8, to expand the power of the national government at the expense of the states.

One of the earliest tests of this conflict came in the famous Supreme Court case of *McCulloch* v. *Maryland* (1819).[10] In this case the Court upheld the right of the national government to establish a bank under the implied powers of the Constitution. The decision, written by Chief Justice Marshall, had a profound effect on the intergovernmental system thereafter. In the decision, Marshall said:

> This government is acknowledged by all to be one of enumerated powers. . . . That principle is now universally admitted. But the question respecting the extent of the powers actually granted is perpetually arising, and will probably continue to arise, so long as our system shall exist.

Marshall's view that the national government possessed all those powers that could reasonably be implied from the delegated powers was best expressed in his argument:

> Let the end be legitimate, let it be within the scope of the Constitution, and all means which are appropriate, which are plainly adapted to that end, which are not prohibited, but consist with the letter and spirit of the Constitution, are constitutional.

By broadly interpreting the "necessary and proper" clause of Article I, the Supreme Court had established that actions of the national government that appeared legitimate and were not strictly forbidden were within the purview of Congress.[11]

## Cities and States

One unique feature of the U.S. Constitution is that cities are not mentioned at all. In the 1980s it seems difficult to believe a nation with over 70 percent of the population living in metropolitan areas has no reference to cities or metropolitan areas in its legally binding constitution.

Cities have always been active centers of commerce, finance, and culture. This was true both before and after the Revolutionary War. Without any new powers or prohibitions emanating from the Constitution, cities and states continued to function as they had in colonial times. The cities sought to expand their powers and their independence, while the states sought to centralize control over the cities. Local government, which historically has been revered in our country, viewed itself as a countervailing force to the centralizing tendencies of state government.

Throughout the latter part of the eighteenth century and the first half of the nineteenth century, local governments staunchly resisted state pressures to centralize power. They continued to fight for power and authority that would allow them greater freedom to manage their own affairs. After numerous conflicts, the issue finally was resolved in Iowa in 1868, in the case of *City of Clinton* v. *Cedar Rapids and Missouri River Railroad,* presided over by Judge John F. Dillon (see Chapter 3).[12]

Throughout the nineteenth and early twentieth centuries, cities consistently sought to reverse or to modify the principles of Dillon's Rule. They were not very successful in altering the basic relationship between themselves and their states. In 1903, and again in 1923, the U.S. Supreme Court upheld the principle estabished by Judge Dillon, and it still stands today.[13]

However, the relationship between cities and states is not nearly as rigid as the strict interpretation of these court rulings implies. Over the years, states have legislated to grant their cities certain rights. The primary method for doing this has been through home rule, a technique whereby a state allocated power to its cities enabling them to have almost complete autonomy over local affairs. Home rule usually occurs through state law or provision in the state constitution. This grant of power can be either broad or narrow. In the broadest grant of power, the state has permitted the city to draft its own charter.

The power of home rule and the right to draft a charter do not fully explain how the city-state relationship has evolved. Cities have not remained passive, allowing the states to arbitrarily determine the scope of their powers. In New York, for instance, Mayor John V. Lindsay, sensing a strong anti-New York City bias in the state legislature, melded six of the largest cities in the state together into a coalition. They lobbied the state legislature for increased funding and more autonomy and created a miniature intergovernmental system within the state. By mobilizing the large cities to take action, Lindsay realized he was forcing the state to deal collectively with all large cities rather than with individual cities, where specific biases could manifest themselves.

Even though the states reign supreme within their borders, there has still developed a certain amount of local government autonomy. The state could legally modify the degree of local autonomy anytime it chose, but it would be extremely difficult to do so in practice. There are several reasons why this is so.

First, the largest concentration of people is still in the cities. This is where the voters are, and elected officials are not anxious to put themselves and their party in jeopardy by abridging local autonomy and upsetting urban voters.

Second, large numbers of public employees live and work in the major urban areas. Changes in state-city relationships will impact heaviest upon these people and possibly precipitate political and administrative unrest and anxiety.

Third, the cities are still the hub of most of the economic and commercial activity in the state. This activity translates into sales, income, and business taxes, all of which the state needs to finance its own programs. Therefore, the state is not anxious to alter existing political and administrative arrangements that might negatively affect the business or financial community.

Zimmerman has analyzed the varying degrees of local autonomy available to cities, counties, towns, and townships. In general, the states where local governments have a high degree of autonomy are Oregon, Maine, North Carolina, Connecticut, and Alaska. The least amount of local discretionary authority is found in Idaho, West Virginia, New Mexico, South Dakota, and Nevada. Zimmerman concluded his study by stating "that in most states general-purpose governments in fact do fall short of possessing broad structural, functional, and financing powers—particularly the last."[14]

## Cities and the Federal Government

Throughout most of the history of the United States, intergovernmental relations has meant a relationship between the federal government and the states. Over the past fifty years the system has included a third partner—the city. Several factors effected this changing role for the cities. First, cities began to grow in population; consequently, their voting strength increased. By 1920, a majority of the country's population lived in the cities, and national political officials began to pay greater attention to urban problems.

Second, there was the desire to fulfill the oft-stated goals of the "American dream." A capitalistic, free enterprise system functioning within a democratic political system encouraged us to practice more of what we were preaching. The overcrowded and often unsanitary conditions in our cities were a constant reminder of our past failures.

Third, the 1920s was a decade in which the nation's wealth increased substantially. This meant the federal government had sizeable resources available to initiate public programs in the cities when their problems increased.

Even though cities are not mentioned in the U.S. Constitution, they have become active partners in the intergovernmental system. In trying to define the role cities play in this system, scholars and politicians have developed a number of terms that help us to understand the complex world of intergovernmental relations.

*Cooperative federalism* implies a common sharing of responsibilities and goals by two or more levels of government. This can be federal-state, state-local, or federal-local. It is difficult to precisely pinpoint the beginning of cooperative federalism since there is some evidence of common sharing of ideas, objectives, and resources among the levels of government throughout our history. However, since the Roosevelt administration and the advent of the New Deal, cooperative federalism has become an accepted definition for the practice of IGR in our country.[15]

TABLE 10.1
States Ranked by Degree of Local Discretionary Authority, 1980

| A. Composite (all types of local units) | B. Cities Only | C. Counties Only | Degree of State Dominance of Fiscal Partnership* |
|---|---|---|---|
| 1 Oregon | Texas | Oregon | 2 |
| 2 Maine | Maine | Alaska | 2 |
| 3 North Carolina | Michigan | North Carolina | 1 |
| 4 Connecticut | Connecticut | Pennsylvania | 2 |
| 5 Alaska | North Carolina | Delaware | 1 |
| 6 Maryland | Oregon | Arkansas | 2 |
| 7 Pennsylvania | Maryland | South Carolina | 2 |
| 8 Virginia | Missouri | Louisiana | 2 |
| 9 Delaware | Virginia | Maryland | 1 |
| 10 Louisiana | Illinois | Utah | 1 |
| 11 Texas | Ohio | Kansas | 2 |
| 12 Illinois | Oklahoma | Minnesota | 2 |
| 13 Oklahoma | Alaska | Virginia | 1 |
| 14 Kansas | Arizona | Florida | 2 |
| 15 South Carolina | Kansas | Wisconsin | 1 |
| 16 Michigan | Louisiana | Kentucky | 2 |
| 17 Minnesota | California | California | 2 |
| 18 California | Georgia | Montana | 3 |
| 19 Missouri | Minnesota | Illinois | 2 |
| 20 Utah | Pennsylvania | Maine | 2 |
| 21 Arkansas | South Carolina | North Dakota | 1 |
| 22 New Hampshire | Wisconsin | Hawaii | 3 |
| 23 Wisconsin | Alabama | New Mexico | 2 |
| 24 North Dakota | Nebraska | Indiana | 2 |
| 25 Arizona | North Dakota | New York | 2 |
| 26 Florida | Delaware | Wyoming | 2 |
| 27 Ohio | New Hampshire | Oklahoma | 3 |
| 28 Alabama | Utah | Michigan | 1 |
| 29 Kentucky | Wyoming | Washington | 1 |
| 30 Georgia | Florida | Iowa | 2 |
| 31 Montana | Mississippi | New Jersey | 3 |
| 32 Washington | Tennessee | Georgia | 2 |
| 33 Wyoming | Washington | Nevada | 2 |
| 34 Tennessee | Arkansas | Tennessee | 2 |
| 35 New York | New Jersey | Mississippi | 3 |
| 36 New Jersey | Kentucky | New Hampshire | 3 |
| 37 Indiana | Colorado | Alabama | 2 |
| 38 Rhode Island | Montana | Arizona | 2 |
| 39 Vermont | Iowa | South Dakota | 2 |
| 40 Hawaii | Indiana | West Virginia | 1 |
| 41 Nebraska | Massachusetts | Nebraska | 3 |
| 42 Colorado | Rhode Island | Ohio | 2 |
| 43 Massachusetts | South Dakota | Texas | 3 |
| 44 Iowa | New York | Idaho | 2 |
| 45 Mississippi | Nevada | Colorado | 1 |
| 46 Nevada | West Virginia | Vermont | 2 |
| 47 South Dakota | Idaho | Missouri | 3 |
| 48 New Mexico | Vermont | Massachusetts | 1 |
| 49 West Virginia | New Mexico | – | 1 |
| 50 Idaho | – | – | 2 |

*Key:
  1–State dominant fiscal partner.
  2–State strong fiscal partner.
  3–State junior fiscal partner.
  Applies to states in column A.
Source: ACIR survey and staff calculation.

*Dual federalism* is the opposite of cooperative federalism and implies an intergovernmental system where the federal government and the state pursue separate goals and programs without a sharing of ideas, resources, or technical assistance.[16] While dual federalism is no longer representative of our intergovernmental system, some scholars believe the term did reflect earlier periods in American intergovernmental history. Walker, for instance, writes, "The period from 1789 to 1860, for the most part, reflected an adherence to these dual federal themes—constitutionally, politically and operationally."[17]

*Direct federalism* defines a relationship between federal and local governments which bypasses the states completely and gives cities and counties equal status with states. In 1937, the low-rent public housing program was the first federal program to make grants directly to the state. Since then, this facet of the intergovernmental system has continued to grow.

*Private federalism* describes a system that bypasses both state and local governments and gives grants directly to individuals or specialized institutions such as universities, research and consulting firms, and other non-governmental organizations. Most of these grants are project grants for specific purposes.

*Creative federalism* was a term first used by New York Governor Nelson Rockefeller and later adopted by President Lyndon B. Johnson. Johnson's concept of federalism was to broaden its scope to include within its boundaries as many of the potential actors as possible. This expanded concept of partnership included not only federal, state, and local governments, but also involved school districts, churches, businesses, and non-profit organizations. The concept of creative federalism was implemented through an increase in the number and dollar amounts of categorical grants. This changed the face of intergovernmental relations for the next generation by making the system much more complex and by establishing a whole new set of administrative and financial relationships, which, prior to 1964, had not existed.[18]

## Failure of the States

The city-federal government relationship grew for a number of historical reasons, as stated above. One other factor that helped to establish this relationship was the inability or unwillingness of the states to provide sufficient resources to the cities at a time when cities were in desperate need of aid. Several factors contributed to what has been sometimes referred to as the "failure of the states."

The most important obstacles to greater state assistance for the cities were the state constitutions, many of which were outmoded. Even though a number of constitutions were amended regularly, they still lacked timeliness and direction. Many constitutions exhibited a strong agrarian bias, even though the state had clearly become urbanized and industrialized.

In the late 1960s and early 1970s, many states undertook the long, arduous process of drafting new constitutions and submitting them to the voters for approval. In New York, opponents of the new constitution launched a carefully orchestrated advertising and publicity campaign, using radio, television, and billboards to arouse voter sympathy for their cause. In Maryland, opponents of the proposed new constitution singled out two or three minor points of disagreement and, based upon these few issues, launched a speaking and advertising campaign to defeat the whole constitution. In both New York and Maryland, the voters rejected the new constitutions, leaving political and administrative leaders to run their states within the existing constitutional frameworks. In Maryland, the governor used a combination of executive orders and legislation to achieve some of the same reforms which had been proposed in the rejected new constitution.

## The Role of the States in Urban Affairs

It is in the legislative, rather than in the executive, branch of state government that a continuing anti-urban bias is to be found. Historically, the major reason for this condition was the overrepresentation of small town and rural areas in the legislatures. Although the country was shown in the 1920 census to possess an urban majority, this fact was not reflected in the apportionment of state legislative seats. At that time, there was no way in which the state legislature could be forced to reapportion if it did not want to do so. As a result, the inequities in representation often reached startling proportions. Six votes cast in Cook County, Illinois, for example, had about the same electoral weight as one vote cast in certain downstate counties.

The U.S. Supreme Court finally untied this Gordian knot. The breakthrough came with the case of *Baker* v. *Carr* in 1962, a case involving apportionment in the Tennessee House of Representatives.[19] In the Tennessee legislature, the House had not been reapportioned since 1901. As a result, the areas of the state with the fastest growing populations were grossly underrepresented. In appeals to state courts, a group of city officials sought to force the state to reapportion. When these efforts failed, several Knoxville lawyers brought suit in a federal court in an effort to prevent state officials from enforcing the 1901 apportionment act. Among other things, the lawyers contended that citizens living in underrepresented areas were being deprived of the "equal protection of the law" guaranteed by the 14th Amendment of the United States Constitution. Acting on the basis of established precedent, the federal district court dismissed the suit on the grounds of lack of jurisdiction, and this decision was appealed to the Supreme Court.

In its opinion, the Court did not rule on the validity of the Tennessee act in question. It did, however, state that federal courts possessed jurisdiction to decide cases involving apportionment in state legislatures. It further held that this kind of action could be brought to the courts under the equal protection clause; that is, citizens who claimed their rights were deprived could challenge the state apportionment practices in federal court.

As a result of the Court's action, the doors of federal courts were now open to apportionment cases, and aggrieved citizens were quick to respond. On June 15, 1964, the Court rendered decisions in eight state apportionment cases. In one of them—*Reynolds* v. *Sims*—the Court gave recognition to the importance of the equality criterion by endorsing what came to be called the "one man–one vote" principle.[20] Under prodding from federal courts, the states, with considerable reluctance, embarked on a process of implementing this principle in their own legislatures. Consequently, most state legislatures are now reasonably fairly apportioned on a population basis.

## CHANGING NATURE OF STATE GOVERNMENT

Beginning in the late 1960s, a change of attitude and direction began to appear in the states. Sparked in part by the urban riots of the 1960s and in part by the election of a host of young, activist mayors—John Lindsay in New York, Kevin White in Boston, and Carl Stokes in Cleveland—the states began to focus more attention and more resources on the cities.

The changing image of state government was enhanced by four factors: (1) the move of the National Governors' Conference to Washington, D.C., (2) reapportionment, (3) the growth of metropolitan areas, and (4) the creation of departments of community affairs in state government.

In 1967 the National Governors' Conference (now the National Governors' Association, or NGA) moved its headquarters to Washington, D.C. This move gave the governors more visibility in the policymaking centers of government and created the appearance that the states were represented in Washington to take a more active role in issues that directly affected them. The new offices of the NGA established better communication links with influential members of Congress and government agencies and monitored key legislative and administrative actions on a daily basis. The NGA was not only able to impart the views of top state officials to government leaders, but it was now in a better position to notify appropriate state officials of what the federal government was doing and to mobilize these officials to take action when necessary.

Reapportionment has been discussed above, but it is worth mentioning that as a result of the reapportionment cases many states began to view their metropolitan areas in a different light. The growing power of suburbia became a political reality to many elected state officials.

The third factor also grew out of the reapportionment cases. Once the state legislatures were reconstituted, everyone could more accurately assess the real problem of metropolitan areas. Besides a lack of financial resources, it was clear that administrative and geographical problems also existed. The political fragmentation in most large metropolitan areas made it virtually impossible for any coordinated planning or program implementation to take place. Councils of Government, which many hoped would solve this problem, remained voluntary organizations with limited powers. The states began taking a closer look at their metropolitan areas.

One of the techniques employed by the states to monitor and assist their cities was the creation of a state office or department of community affairs. More than half the states have opened such offices, with most of them located in the executive branch, some with cabinet status. The community affairs offices organized resources and coordinated programs that dealt with city problems. As these offices developed they also began to serve as a vital link between funding agencies in Washington and local officials in city hall.

As the federal grant system continued to grow, the states began to play a pivotal role as the key financial intermediary in all but a few programs. Many large federal programs required states to pass through funds to local governments; other programs required state fiscal contributions or administrative oversight functions.

Each of these factors helped to increase the visibility of the states as actors in the intergovernmental system. However, forces were also at work within the states to help them to modernize their governmental structure to meet the political and administrative challenges of the last half of the twentieth century. A look at some of these changes will help us to understand how far the states have come in the past twenty years.[21]

The major change in constitutional reform emerged from the drafting and the adoption of new constitutions. No new state constitutions had been adopted between 1921 and 1945, but during the 1960s and 1970s eleven states adopted new constitutions, over forty states modernized their existing constitutions, and several others revised or rewrote important articles. In summarizing the constitutional changes, the ACIR concluded:

> Present day constitutions conform more closely to the principles of brevity and simplicity. In general, the substantially revised or rewritten documents included provisions to strengthen the executive powers of the governor, to unify the court system, to improve legislative capability and to extend home rule and tax authority for local governments. Further, they contain reasonable amendment or revision processes urged by reformers for many years.[22]

## Governor and Executive Office

One of the most serious weaknesses in state government was the failure to provide for strong executive leadership. The constraints placed upon executive power included two-year terms, non-reelectability, low salaries, lack of control over the budget, weak appointment and reorganization powers, and too many independently elected state officials.

The states have acted to correct many of these deficiencies. Only four states still have two-year terms for their governors. This is a sizeable decrease from 1960 when sixteen states had two-year terms. Similarly, only-five states now bar their governors from reelection, thereby reducing the lame duck liabilities of the elected chief executive. Half the states have reduced the number of elected state officials, thus giving the governor more control over the executive branch through the exercise of appointive powers.

In addition, governor's salaries have been raised from a median of $16,000 in 1960 to $50,000 in 1980. Governors have also been given greater powers to reorganize the executive branch of government. In half the states, departments and agencies have been overhauled, and clearer lines of authority and responsibility have been established. This, in turn, has helped to reduce overlapping and duplication.

Finally, almost all governors have been given greater budget authority. They are authorized to prepare and to present the annual budget as well as to monitor the expenditures being made. In this way the governor's authority for the budget closely resembles that of the President of the United States.[23]

## State Legislatures

The 1960s and 1970s also produced dramatic changes in the state legislatures. Perhaps the most dramatic reforms have occurred in how and when the legislature conducts its business. In the early 1960s only twenty state legislatures met each year. By 1980 three-fourths of the state legislatures met annually, and of the fourteen states that met biennially, several were called into special session by their governors on a regular basis. This change has allowed the states to keep current with the rapidly changing pace of events in American political, social, and economic life. A number of states, however, still limit the legislative session to sixty legislative days or less.

The state legislatures also took steps to professionalize their operations. In 1960 few states had year-round professional staffs for their key committees. By 1980 thirty-six states had implemented this reform in both houses, making it much easier for members to be briefed on changing aspects of the budget or legislation. New members assigned to committees could also be oriented quickly by the professional staff.

The legislatures have also opened many more of their committee meetings to the public and have begun recording roll call votes. At the same time, a number of states have passed conflict of interest laws, and others have greatly strengthened their lobbying laws by tightening up regulations on registration and disclosure of lobbying activities.

In another reform movement, brought on by the apparent increase in corruption on the state level, the legislatures began passing laws on campaign financing and ethics in government. These actions not only helped to identify illegal activities, but they went a long way toward improving the public image of state government and state legislatures in particular.

The state legislatures have also become much more involved in both the auditing and the oversight functions of government. Today over twenty legislatures have responsibility for auditing state programs. Over three-fourths of the state legislatures today are responsible for appropriating federal funds that come into the state. This almost doubles the number of states reporting they did so in 1975.[24]

## Judicial System

By the 1960s the state court systems had become the object of much criticism. Confusion, delay, and lack of accurate information impeded the smooth flow of justice. The reform movement was highlighted by revamped systems in the 1960s in California, Colorado, Illinois, Michigan, Nebraska, New Mexico, New York, Oklahoma, and Alabama. In the 1970s the reform movement continued. Most of the changes initiated were in the area of court administration and management. The state courts were integrated so that cases could be processed fairly and expeditiously, and accurate information was available to all concerned. Judicial selection procedures were standardized and, in many cases, depoliticized. Full-time professional staff were hired to administer the case load and oversee the record keeping and paperwork. Effective machinery was established in over 80 percent of the states to discipline and, if necessary, remove incompetent judges.

## Finance

One factor that contributed to the growth of federal-local relations was the need on the part of local government for increased financial assistance. The states, with their conservative legislatures and their negative attitudes towards cities, were not likely to provide these funds. In 1954 state aid, as a percent of local general revenue from own sources, amounted to 41.7 percent. Ten years later, in 1964, it had increased to only 42.9 percent. But as the states began to modernize and accept more responsibility for their troubled cities, the amount of state aid, as a percent of local general revenue from own sources, began to increase. In 1969, it moved up to 54 percent and in 1974 to 59.4 percent. It reached 60.8 in 1976, and in 1980 it was 63.6 percent before dropping back to 62.7 percent in 1981. This commitment to the cities was one additional factor in establishing the states as full and active partners in the intergovernmental system.[25]

The changing nature of the states and their increased dedication and involvement in the intergovernmental system prompted the ACIR to comment:

> Just 20 years ago states largely deserved many of the criticisms directed their way including descriptions such as "antiquated" and "weak sisters." Those who looked at the state in the 1930s or even in the early 1960s and decided that they lacked the capability to perform their roles in the federal system because they operated under outdated constitutions, fragmented executive structures, hamstrung governors, poorly equipped and unrepresentative legislatures, and numerous other handicaps should take another look at the states today. The transformation of the states, occurring in a relatively short period of time, has no parallel in American history.[26]

# THE EVOLUTION OF THE CITY IN THE INTERGOVERNMENTAL SYSTEM

From the Depression to the mid-1960s, the states, for a variety of reasons, were not very attentive to the growing problems confronting the cities. The intergovernmental system, which historically has been composed of two actors—the federal government and the states—expanded to include a third actor—the cities.

In addition to the failure of the states to respond to urban problems, there were several other factors that contributed to the rise of the city as a partner in the intergovernmental system. The most important factor in elevating the city to prominence was the cash grant-in-aid, which replaced the land grants initiated in the nineteenth century. The cash grant-in-aid system began to expand during the New Deal under President Franklin D. Roosevelt and had a profound effect on intergovernmental relations for the next fifty years.

A grant-in-aid can be defined as money transferred by the federal government to state or local governments to be used for specific purposes, but subject to rules and guidelines established in either the law or the administrative regulations. The urban grant-in-aid is a technique whereby a program of importance to both federal and local governments is implemented by the cities with technical assistance and financial support from the federal government.

Generally speaking, grants are either formula grants or project grants. A formula grant is distributed to all states and/or local governments in accordance with a formula written into the law. The distribution could be based upon population, per capita income, tax effort, or number of senior citizens or school-aged children. The recipient governments are entitled to the grants by virtue of the law, and they do not have to submit proposals and compete for the available funds, as is the case with other grants.

Project grants are designed to combat specific problems deemed important by Congress. These grants are not distributed to all political jurisdictions. Eligible jurisdictions are specified (e.g., urban counties, low income housing tenants), but the eligible jurisdictions must take the initiative in submitting a proposal to apply for the grant. Federal administrators, adhering to legislative guidelines and congressional appropriations, assess the proposals and make grant awards based upon evaluative criteria publicized in the request for proposal notice.

Project grants are either categorical grants or block grants. Categorical grants are designed for very narrow and specific objectives that Congress has determined to be in the national interest, e.g., vocational education, public libraries, forest land management. However, even within the categorical grants there are variations. Some categorical grants are formula-based in the legislation. Another variation is the open-end reimbursement grant—sometimes referred to as formula grants. In this grant the federal government agrees to compensate state and local governments for specific program costs. This approach eliminates the need for both competition among jurisdictions and a congressionally determined formula.

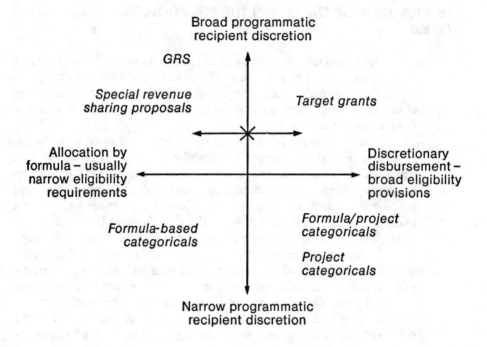

FIGURE 10.1
General Traits of Basic Forms of Intergovernmental Fiscal Transfers

Block grants are a relatively new phenomenon in IGR. Beginning in 1966 with the Partnership for Health Act and continuing through the 1970s, Congress began to enact block grants in community development, manpower training, criminal justice, and social services. These grants were much broader in scope than categorical grants and often have resulted from the consolidation of several existing categorical grants. There are far fewer strings attached to the grant; therefore, local officials have much greater discretion in administering this type of a grant. It was also felt by some officials that a few well-publicized block grants would have much greater visibility and impact than the several hundred smaller categorical grants.[27]

Beginning in 1972 the federal government initiated a new type of intergovernmental transfer. This was called revenue sharing, and it was different from either the formula grants or the project grants. Revenue sharing funds are distributed by formula with virtually no restrictions on how the money can be spent. Revenue sharing will be discussed in greater detail in the chapter on New Federalism.

A second factor for the emergence of the city as a key actor in the intergovernmental system was the Depression of the 1930s. The New Deal attempted to combat the economic woes of the nation by initiating large scale recovery programs. Most of these new programs were directed at the urban centers of the nation. Even though federal funding was used, local officials and local government agencies were charged with the responsibility for implementing these programs. By the time World War II ended, the cities had demonstrated for over a decade that they could be entrusted with responsibility for federal programs.

TABLE 10.2
Selected Characteristics of Major Types of Federal Grants

| Type of Grant | Recipient Discretion | Program Scope | Funding Criteria |
|---|---|---|---|
| Categorical a. Project | Lowest | Narrow-program | Federal Administrative Review |
| b. Formula | Low | Narrow-program | Legislative formula |
| Block | Medium | Broad-functional area | Legislative formula |
| General Revenue Sharing | High | Broadest-government operations | Legislative formula |

Source: George E. Hale and Marian Lief Palley, The Politics of Federal Grants (Washington, D.C.: Congressional Quarterly Press, 1981), p. 12. Reprinted with the permission of Congressional Quarterly Inc.

A third factor that increased the role of cities in the intergovernmental system was the growth of urban and metropolitan America in the post-World War II era. Not only did more people move into these areas, but as the population increased, so did the problems. The federal government became more conscious of the cities and their problems and passed legislation in the areas of highways (1956), slum clearance and urban renewal (1949), urban planning (1954), hospital construction (1946), waste treatment facilities (1956), and water pollution control (1956). Each of these programs helped to forge strong federal-city links and to increase the role of cities in the intergovernmental system.

The year 1932 serves as an important benchmark for cities and for the grant-in-aid system. In that year, about $10 million was transferred in grants from the federal government to the cities. During the next three decades that figure would increase dramatically. By 1960 federal aid to state and local governments had reached $7 billion. Prior to this time very few categorical grants were directed to cities or other substate jurisdictions. Only about 8 percent of the total went to cities.

## TABLE 10.3

### Federal Grants-in-Aid in Relation to State-Local Receipts from Own Sources, Total Federal Outlays and Gross National Product, 1955–1983

*(Dollar Amounts in Billions)*

| Fiscal Year[1] | Federal Grants-in-Aid (Current Dollars) | | As a Percentage of— | | | Federal Grants in Constant Dollars (1972 Dollars, GNP Deflator) | | Estimated Number of Federal Grant Programs | Grants for Payments to Individuals | |
|---|---|---|---|---|---|---|---|---|---|---|
| | Amount | Percent Increase or Decrease (-) | State-Local Receipts From Own Source[2] | Total Federal Outlays | Gross National Product | Amount | Percent Increase or Decrease (-) | | Amount | Percent of Total Grants |
| 1955 | $3.2 | 4.9 | 11.8 | 4.7 | 0.8 | $5.3 | n.a. | n.a. | $1.6 | 50.0 |
| 1956 | 3.7 | 15.6 | 12.3 | 5.3 | 0.9 | 5.9 | 11.3 | n.a. | 1.7 | 45.9 |
| 1957 | 4.0 | 8.1 | 12.1 | 5.3 | 0.9 | 6.2 | 5.1 | n.a. | 1.8 | 45.0 |
| 1958 | 4.9 | 22.5 | 14.0 | 6.0 | 1.1 | 7.4 | 19.4 | n.a. | 2.1 | 42.9 |
| 1959 | 6.5 | 32.7 | 17.2 | 7.0 | 1.4 | 9.6 | 29.7 | n.a. | 2.4 | 36.9 |
| 1960 | 7.0 | 7.7 | 16.8 | 7.6 | 1.4 | 10.2 | 6.3 | 132 | 2.5 | 35.7 |
| 1961 | 7.1 | 1.4 | 15.8 | 7.3 | 1.4 | 10.2 | -0- | n.a. | 2.9 | 40.8 |
| 1962 | 7.9 | 11.3 | 16.2 | 7.4 | 1.4 | 11.2 | 9.8 | n.a. | 3.2 | 40.5 |
| 1963 | 8.6 | 8.9 | 16.5 | 7.8 | 1.5 | 12.0 | 7.1 | n.a. | 3.5 | 40.7 |
| 1964 | 10.1 | 17.4 | 17.9 | 8.6 | 1.6 | 13.9 | 15.8 | n.a. | 3.8 | 37.6 |
| 1965 | 10.9 | 7.9 | 17.7 | 9.2 | 1.7 | 14.7 | 5.8 | n.a. | 3.9 | 35.8 |
| 1966 | 13.0 | 19.3 | 19.3 | 9.6 | 1.8 | 16.9 | 15.0 | n.a. | 4.5 | 34.6 |
| 1967 | 15.2 | 16.9 | 20.6 | 9.6 | 2.0 | 19.2 | 13.6 | 379 | 5.0 | 32.9 |
| 1968 | 18.6 | 22.4 | 22.4 | 10.4 | 2.2 | 22.5 | 17.2 | n.a. | 6.3 | 33.9 |
| 1969 | 20.3 | 9.1 | 21.6 | 11.0 | 2.2 | 23.4 | 4.0 | n.a. | 7.5 | 36.9 |
| 1970 | 24.0 | 18.2 | 22.9 | 12.2 | 2.5 | 26.2 | 12.0 | n.a. | 9.0 | 37.5 |
| 1971 | 28.1 | 17.1 | 24.1 | 13.3 | 2.7 | 29.3 | 11.8 | n.a. | 11.0 | 39.1 |
| 1972 | 34.4 | 22.4 | 26.1 | 14.8 | 3.1 | 34.4 | 17.4 | n.a. | 14.4 | 41.9 |
| 1973 | 41.8 | 21.5 | 28.5 | 16.9 | 3.3 | 39.5 | 14.8 | n.a. | 14.3 | 34.2 |
| 1974 | 43.4 | 3.8 | 27.3 | 16.1 | 3.1 | 37.7 | -4.6 | n.a. | 15.3 | 35.3 |

Exhibits:

| Year | | | | | | | | | | |
|---|---|---|---|---|---|---|---|---|---|---|
| 1975 | 49.8 | 14.7 | 29.1 | 15.3 | 3.4 | 39.6 | 5.0 | 448 | 17.4 | 34.9 |
| 1976 | 59.1 | 18.7 | 31.1 | 16.1 | 3.6 | 44.7 | 12.9 | n.a. | 21.0 | 35.5 |
| 1977 | 68.4 | 15.7 | 31.0 | 17.0 | 3.7 | 48.8 | 9.2 | n.a. | 23.9 | 34.9 |
| 1978 | 77.9 | 13.9 | 31.7 | 17.3 | 3.7 | 51.8 | 6.1 | 498 | 26.0 | 33.4 |
| 1979 | 82.9 | 6.4 | 31.3 | 16.8 | 3.5 | 50.7 | -2.1 | n.a. | 28.8 | 34.7 |
| 1980 | 91.5 | 10.4 | 31.7 | 15.8 | 3.6 | 51.2 | 1.0 | n.a. | 34.2 | 37.4 |
| 1981 | 94.8 | 3.6 | 29.4 | 14.4 | 3.2 | 48.5 | -5.3 | 539 | 40.1 | 42.3 |
| 1982 | 88.8 | -7.0 | 25.4 | 12.1 | 2.9 | 42.6 | -12.2 | 441[3] | 37.8 | 45.5 |
| *1983 est. | 93.5 | 6.0 | n.a. | 11.6 | 2.9 | 42.9 | 0.7 | 409[4] | n.a. | n.a. |
| *1984 est. | 95.9 | 12.6 | n.a. | 11.3 | 2.7 | 41.8 | -2.6 | n.a. | n.a. | n.a. |

Source: *Significant Features of Fiscal Federalism 1981–82 Edition*, Washington, D.C.: Advisory Commission on Intergovernmental Relations. 1983, p. 66.

*1983 and 1984 estimates based upon OMB assumptions published in the FY 1984 *Budget*. Grant-in-aid figures from *Special Analysis H*, Table H-7; federal outlays from *Budget*, Summary Table 23; GNP and GNP deflator figures from *Budget*, Secion 2, page 9. See *Special Analysis H* for explanation of differences between grant-in-aid figures published by the National Income and Product Accounts, Census and OMB.

n.a.—Not available.     est.—Estimated.

[1] For 1955–1976, years ending June 30; 1977–1982 years ending September 30.

[2] As defined in the national income and product accounts.

[3] Seventy-nine programs have been folded into nine block grants, and at least another twenty-six programs have not been funded as of November 1, 1981.

[4] Includes 398 categorical grants and 11 block grants.

Sources: ACIR staff computations based on U.S. Office of Management and Budget, *Budget of the United States Government*, (annual); Unpublished data from OMB Office of Financial Management; U.S. Department of Commerce, Bureau of Economic Analysis, *The National Income and Product Accounts of the United States, 1929–76, Statistical Tables*; *Survey of Current Business*, various issues: David B. Walker, *Toward a Functioning Federalism*, Cambridge, MA., Winthrop Publishers, Inc., 1981, p. 79.

## Expansion of the Grant-In-Aid System

During the 1960s and 1970s the grant-in-aid system expanded at a rapid rate. During the Johnson, Nixon, Ford, and Carter presidencies the number of categorical and block grants increased, and so did the dollars appropriated for these grants.

The 1980 figure was 539, including block grants, categorical grants, and revenue sharing. The number of grants began to diminish as the Reagan administration began consolidating categorical grants into block grants.

The expansion of the grant-in-aid system and the emergence of cities as partners in the intergovernmental system produced a number of changes in the system. First, there was a recognition of how large and how complex the problems of urban and metropolitan America were. Second, there was an understanding and a commitment to allocate public resources at the national level to solve public problems at the local level. Third, the federal government was able to exercise its influence to establish uniform standards for many programs and services across the nation. Basic standards have been set, and the administering agencies, in conjunction with state and local government, have developed a network of procedures, reports, regulations, and guidelines that all grant recipients must adhere to.

Fourth, as a result of the expanded grant-in-aid system, local government has been upgraded. Many urban areas have been encouraged to begin a number of new programs they otherwise might have ignored. In initiating these new programs, cities have conducted numerous needs assessments and have developed much more comprehensive inventories of their resources that could be applied to specific problem areas.

Fifth, several programs have made remarkable headway in achieving their stated goals. Among these are pre-school programs such as Headstart, Urban Mass Transportation Administration grants to numerous urban public transit systems, senior citizen programs, and water pollution and solid waste disposal programs.

Sixth, the concept of cooperative federalism has been broadened and strengthened. Today, big city mayors who have direct access to the agency officials as well as to the key senators and representatives who are responsible for policies affecting their cities are frequent visitors to Washington. When their chief elected executives are not in Washington, the big cities and the urban counties rely heavily on their national associations to speak for them and keep them informed about political and administrative decisions being made in Washington. Organizations such as the U.S. Conference of Mayors, the National League of Cities (NCL) and the National Association of Counties (NACO) have grown in importance in the 1960s and 1970s.[28]

In addition to personal contacts and representation through their associations, large cities and counties often establish their own offices in Washington to represent their interests. In some cases one person represents a number of cities and counties, and in other cases each local political jurisdiction opens its own office and pursues its own interests. By 1980 approximately 30 states and 100 cities had opened offices in Washington.[29]

TABLE 10.4
Types of Categorical Grants

| Formula-based | 1975 | | 1978 | |
|---|---|---|---|---|
| | Number | Percent | Number | Percent |
| Allotted formula | 96 | 21.7% | 106 | 21.5% |
| Project grants subject to formula distribution | 35 | 7.9 | 47 | 9.6 |
| Open-end reimbursement | 15 | 3.4 | 17 | 3.5 |
| Total formula-based | 146 | 33.0 | 170 | 34.6 |
| Project | 296 | 67.0 | 322 | 65.4 |
| Total | 442 | 100.0% | 492 | 100.0% |

Source: ACIR, *A Catalog of Federal Grant-In-Aid Programs to State and Local Governments: Grants Funded FY 1978* (Washington, D.C.: U.S. Government Printing Office, February 1979), p. 1.

The local government associations are often referred to as public interest groups (PIGs), and there are many who feel these organizations were largely responsible for the huge increases in both the number and the dollars allocated to grants that were passed in the 1960s and 1970s.[30] While the PIGs were instrumental in mobilizing their members to support a number of grant programs in health care, housing, transportation, education, and job training, they were also aided by other actors in the political arena. As more and more grant programs were proposed in Congress, specialized interest groups and associations developed to push their own causes and interests. They mobilized their resources and targeted their campaigns to key members of Congress and their staffs who would make the final decisions. Congress responded with equal vigor. Members of Congress, who in fact represent local interests in Washington, worked closely with both the public and the special interest groups to promote many new programs. Senators and representatives quickly became associated with specific issues, and many of them came to chair the subcommittees that were responsible for authorizing new programs. This often meant more power, more prestige, more staff, more visibility, and more office space. Since everybody involved had something to gain from the process, it was almost a certainty that the grant-in-aid program would continue to expand.

One interesting consequence to emerge from this expanded partnership was the concept of picket-fence federalism (PFF).[31] PFF depicted the linkage among the different levels of government by functional category. During the grant-in-aid expansion period, the federal government assumed responsibility for the major share of the funding, but the administration and implementation of the programs were delegated to state, county, and local officials. PFF illustrates the relationship of national to subnational decision-making and administrative units.

Since federal programs are funded and administered by functional agencies, the slats in the fence represent the major program areas as they span the three levels of government. The states and local governments were anxious to align their own departments with the functional departments at the federal level. This provided them with more knowledge, greater access, and clearer lines of administrative authority. Functional specialists and program managers on all levels of government were linked by the enabling federal legislation, funding limits, program rules and regulations, auditing and reporting requirements, and evaluation procedures. Program by program, federal bureaucrats worked on a continuous basis with their program counterparts in state and local governments. Once the bill was signed at the national level, elected officials on all levels found themselves excluded from policy decisions, since the authority and the funding for program implementation was conducted by the bureaucrats. State and local elected officials did not have the strength to counterbalance the powers federally funded programs invested in state, county, and local bureaucrats.

When state and local agencies failed to provide the quantity and quality of service citizens demanded, problems arose. Citizens found themselves at a disadvantage in trying to apply pressure on local elected officials to influence the administration of federally funded programs, whose guidelines and regulations had been written in Washington.

The bureaucratic agencies that accrued power through grant-in-aid programs were supported by a number of well-organized and influential special interest groups. These were the same groups that helped to pass the legislation and who then wanted to insure that the programs would be administered in a manner consistent with their interests.

In recent years local elected officials have begun to exercise greater oversight on federally financed grant programs. In addition, the federal government has modified some of its funding approaches. More money is now allocated to state and local governments, with fewer restrictions, thus giving elected officials greater discretion in how this money is spent. Still, the system is heavily dependent upon bureaucrats for administrative and policy decisions.[32]

The conflict between state and local elected officials and the bureaucrats from all three levels of government surfaced publicly in Pennsylvania in 1976. The Pennsylvania state legislature passed two bills, one of which required that all federal funds coming into the state be deposited in the general fund and be subjected to the state appropriation process. The second bill required that all federal funds be appropriated to state agencies through specific line items in the state budget. The first bill was passed over the governor's veto. Governor Milton Shapp was unwilling to see this power legislatively pass from the bureaucracy to the legislature, though it is doubtful that Shapp exercised much control over the administrative decisions made by the numerous program officers managing federal grants in the Pennsylvania bureaucracy. The state treasurer, acting under the law, refused to release federal funds for an operating program. The governor went into court to have the two laws declared unconstitutional. The lower court and the Pennsylvania Supreme Court both upheld the validity of the legislation, and the U.S.

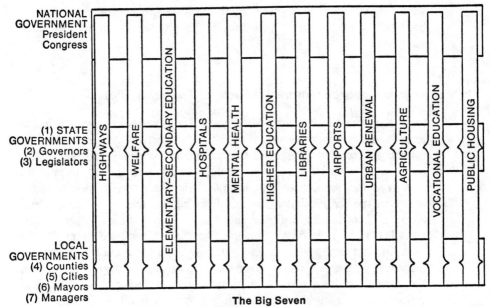

NATIONAL GOVERNMENT
President
Congress

(1) STATE GOVERNMENTS
(2) Governors
(3) Legislators

LOCAL GOVERNMENTS
(4) Counties
(5) Cities
(6) Mayors
(7) Managers

HIGHWAYS
WELFARE
ELEMENTARY-SECONDARY EDUCATION
HOSPITALS
MENTAL HEALTH
HIGHER EDUCATION
LIBRARIES
AIRPORTS
URBAN RENEWAL
AGRICULTURE
VOCATIONAL EDUCATION
PUBLIC HOUSING

**The Big Seven**

(1) Council of State Governments
(2) National Governors' Conference
(3) National Legislative Conference
(4) National Association of County Officials
(5) National League of Cities
(6) U.S. Conference of Mayors
(7) International City Management Association

FIGURE 10.2
Picket Fence Federalism: A Schematic Representation

Source: Reprinted from "Intergovernmental Relations: An Analytical Overview" by Deil S. Wright in November, 1974 of *The Annals* of the American Academy of Political and Social Science.

Supreme Court refused to hear the case, thus granting to the legislature the power to appropriate federal funds coming into the state.[33]

In 1975 ACIR conducted a survey that found few state legislatures carefully monitoring either the amount or the administration of federal dollars and programs coming into the state. In 1981, ACIR could report that almost 80 percent of the states appropriated federal funds coming into their state. The degree of oversight and assessment differs markedly from state to state, but as we enter a period of scarce resources and tightened federal budgets, the role of state legislatures in this process should become much more important.[34]

## Problems in the Intergovernmental System: The Local View

Not even the cities, which benefited greatly from the growth in the grant-in-aid system, were delighted with all aspects of this new source of money and technical assistance. As with almost every new program, issues surfaced that worried local government officials. One immediate problem concerned the question of centralization versus decentralization. As more and more power gravitated towards Washington, the role of the federal agency field office diminished in importance. An increasing number of decisions had to be made in Washington. President Nixon tried to modify the system by creating Federal Regional Councils (FRC) in ten regions around the country, but this new system had only a modest degree of success. Smaller units of local government historically have worked closely with field offices and have felt less confident in dealing with high-level bureaucrats in Washington who had little familiarity with local problems and programs.

A second problem local governments encountered was the relationship of local autonomy to federal control. Few local governments anticipated how much the federal government rules and regulations would mandate changes in their operations. Every time the local governments accepted money or were awarded a grant there were paperwork and legalistic requirements. Many local governments had to hire new staff just to comply with federal regulations, reporting, and auditing procedures. The larger the dollars and the higher the number of grants, the more control the federal government began to exercise over local government. As government programs were expanded, they began to overlap. A local government that administered a mass transit grant also had to comply with environmental quality regulations, civil rights laws, and equal employment opportunity guidelines. Small local political jurisdictions were overwhelmed by the rules and the paperwork.

As grants became more plentiful in the 1960s and 1970s, the competition for them intensified rapidly. Jurisdictions sought to maximize their opportunities by securing as many grants as possible. However, by the time the number of grants reached 400, some agencies were not able to distribute all of their allocated funds and some cities were not able to spend all of their grant funds. Questions began to arise about the efficacy of this whole competitive process. One of the most obvious things city officials noticed was that, despite all of the money they were receiving, the quality of life in their cities was not improving. Their problems, they concluded, were not really confined to the city, and federal programs should not be focused in that direction. Local officials sensed that the solution to many urban problems rested with a metropolitan approach. Yet Congress, with very few exceptions, seemed intent upon legislating programs for functional rather than geographical areas. Congress did mandate areawide planning requirements in more than 40 federal grant programs. In all fairness, some of the metropolitan approaches Congress embarked upon, (e.g., housing, planning, mass transit) were not received favorably by many central cities and their surrounding suburbs. The courts also tried to encourage a metropolitan approach in education and low income housing but only succeeded in exacerbating a lot of feelings.[35]

In a perfect world, the grant-in-aid system would provide a much needed rational approach to urban problem solving. However, in the highly pluralistic and politicized world of intergovernmental relations there are no incentives to be rational. The rational approach might consist of three separate steps:

1.  A local community establishes its priorities for the coming year based partially upon a needs assessment.
2.  The community then assesses its resources with respect to the priorities it has established.
3.  Grants are sought to provide funding for the differences between the priorities and the resources.

Since the federal grant-in-aid system has grown so large and so cumbersome, it has become extremely difficult for local governments to know about all of the available grants. Rather than risk the potential penalties for following a "rational plan," it becomes even more rational for local officials to seek the "sure grants" and skew their priorities. In fact, the grant-in-aid system provides a perverse set of incentives that rewards the irrational at the expense of the rational policymaker.

## Summary Comments on the Changing Federal System

As we have seen, the intergovernmental system of the 1980s is very different from the system of the 1960s. For the first time in a generation, we have witnessed (between 1981 and 1982) a decline in federal grants to state and local governments.

Some people have criticized the rapid expansion of federal involvement and authority in the 1960s as being both undesirable and a violation of the strict construction of the Constitution, specifically the Tenth Amendment. Others have welcomed the increased federal government activism in working jointly with state and local governments to help solve contemporary social and urban problems.

We have also seen the degree of federal intergovernmental activity explode dramatically in the 1960s to the point, according to Walker, where we no longer have a working cooperative system, but rather an overloaded, dysfunctional system.[36]

Overall, this expanded intergovernmental system with hundreds of grants has many advantages:

1. It stimulated states, counties, and cities to recognize, and then act on, some of the more pressing urban problems.
2. Federal programs assisted the truly needy with a number of programs, such as those for the blind, disabled, unemployed, disadvantaged, and homeless.
3. Many federal programs provided opportunities for states, counties, and cities to participate. This made the system more accessible to citizens than if it had been highly centralized in Washington.
4. Federal grant programs have stimulated local economies by providing funds for highways, housing, hospitals, mass transit, and job training.
5. Federal dollars have assisted local governments in dealing with problems that are national in scope—e.g., poverty, welfare, housing, pollution, and health care.[37]

On the other hand, this system has produced many disadvantages:

1. Federal programs and grants often exacerbated the cleavages between the central cities and their suburbs in such programs as highway systems and FHA housing.
2. Federal programs increased functional specialization and functional hierarchies as depicted in picket-fence federalism. This tended to diminish efforts at coordination and increase fragmentation and duplication.
3. As the grant-in-aid system grew, the problems of accountability and control become much more complex. Not only were there states, counties, and local governments, but federal legislation mandated the creation of semiautonomous and quasi-independent agencies, regional bodies, and authorities.
4. Federal programs set the tone for state and local governments. As mentioned above, local government budgets are skewed toward programs determined by federal officials. This inevitably distorts priorities and leaves many pressing problems unattended.
5. Categorical grants are targeted to narrow, specific issues usually publicized by special interest groups. These issues are not always the most pressing ones confronting local governments.
6. The number of federal programs today is so large that oversight has become extremely difficult and often remiss. To compensate for this, federal agencies often require excessive reporting systems that are costly and that antagonize the local governments that have to file them.[38]

These disadvantges have led to a movement to produce a "New Federalism," which limits the federal government's role and seeks to reduce the problems of an overloaded centralized system.

# NOTES

1. A. Lee Fritschler and Bernard H. Ross, *Business Regulation and Government Decision-Making* (Boston: Little, Brown, 1980), p. 123. Also see Arnold M. Howitt, *Managing Federalism: Studies in Intergovernmental Relations* (Washington: Congressional Quarterly, Inc., 1984).
2. Michael D. Reagan and John G. Sanzone, *The New Federalism*, 2nd ed. (New York: Oxford University Press, 1981), p. 3.
3. Reagan and Sanzone, *The New Federalism*, p. 3.
4. Morton Grodzins, "The Federal System" in *President's Commission on National Goals, Goals for Americans* (Englewood Cliffs, N.J.: Prentice-Hall, 1960). The marble cake analogy was first used by Joseph E. McLean, *Politics Is What You Make It*, Public Affairs Pamphlet, No. 181 (Washington, D.C.: Public Affairs Press, April, 1952), p. 5.
5. Deil S. Wright, *Understanding Intergovernmental Relations*, 2nd ed. (Monterey, Calif.: Brooks/Cole Publishing Company, 1982), pp. 16–18. The phases denote major characteristics of the period which explains why there is an overlap.
6. Parris N. Glendening and Mavis Mann Reeves, *Pragmatic Federalism: An Intergovernmental View of American Government*, 2nd ed. (Pacific Palisades, Calif.: Palisades Publishers, 1984), pp. 12–13.
7. Wright, *Understanding Intergovernmental Relations*, pp. 43–78.
8. See Frederick Mosher, *Democracy and the Public Service* (New York: Oxford University Press, 1968), chap. 4. Also see Herbert Kaufman, "Emerging Conflicts in the Doctrines of Public Administration," *American Political Science Review*, 50 (December, 1956): 1057–1073.
9. See Elizabeth K. Kellar, ed., *Managing With Less: A Book of Readings* (Washington, D.C.: International City Management Association, 1979).
10. *4 Wheat 316 (1819)*.
11. See Glendening and Reeves, *Pragmatic Federalism*, pp. 39–48; and Reagan and Sanzone, *The New Federalism*, pp. 7–12.
12. *24 Iowa 455 (1868)*.
13. *Atkins v. Kansas*, 191 U.S. 207 at 220–21 (1903) and *Trenton v. New Jersey*, 262 U.S. 182, 67L Ed 93, 43 SCT 534 (1923).
14. *Measuring Local Discretionary Authority* (Washington: Advisory Commission on Intergovernmental Relations, November 1980), p. 60.
15. Morton Grodzins, *The American System: A New View of Government in the United States*, ed. Daniel J. Elazar (Chicago: Rand McNally, 1966) and David B. Walker, *Toward a Functioning Federalism* (Boston: Little, Brown, 1981), p. 67.
16. For an elaborate definition of dual federalism see Edwin S. Corwin, "A Constitution of Powers and Modern Federalism," *Essays in Constitutional Law*, ed. Robert McCloskey (New York: Alfred A. Knopf, 1962), pp. 188–89.
17. Walker, *Toward a Functioning Federalism*, p. 47.
18. For a discussion of this new approach, see Walker, *Toward a Functioning Federalism*, pp. 101–04. Also see Paul E. Peterson, *City Limits* (Chicago: The University of Chicago Press, 1981).
19. *Baker v. Carr*, 369 U.S. 189 (1962).
20. *Reynolds v. Sims*, 377 U.S. 533 (1964).
21. For a discussion of these changes, see *State and Local Roles in the Federal System* (Washington: Advisory Commission on Intergovernmental Relations, 1981). Also see *The State of the States in 1974: Responsive Government for the Seventies* (Washington: The National Governors Conference, 1974).
22. *In Brief: State and Local Roles in the Federal System* (Washington: Advisory Commission on Intergovernmental Relations, 1981), p. 5.

23. For a discussion of the changes in the Office of Governor see Larry Sabato, *Goodbye to Good-Time Charlie: The American Governorship Transformed*, 2nd ed. (Washington: Congressional Quarterly Press, 1983).

24. *The Intergovernmental Grant System As Seen By Local, State and Federal Officials* (Washington: Advisory Commission on Intergovernmental Relations, 1977), p. 101. For a discussion of one of the more interesting court cases on this subject, see Fritschler and Ross, *Business Regulation and Government Decision-Making*, pp. 126–128.

25. *Significant Features of Fiscal Federalism 1980–81* (Washington: Advisory Commission on Intergovernmental Relations, 1981), p. 61. It should be noted that most state aid to local governments is given to counties and school districts rather than to general local government support.

26. *State and Local Roles in the Federal System*, p. 3.

27. For a discussion of the different types of grants, see Reagan and Sanzone, *The New Federalism*, pp. 57–60. Also see George E. Hale and Marian Lief Palley, *The Politics of Federal Grants* (Washington: Congressional Quarterly Press, 1981), pp. 100–111; and Walker, *Toward a Functioning Federalism*, p. 179. A valuable resource is *The Intergovernmental Grant System: An Assessment and Proposed Policies*, a series of fourteen studies published by the Advisory Commission on Intergovernmental Relations between 1976 and 1978.

28. For an analysis of the strategies and tactics of the public interest groups, see Suzanne Farkas, *Urban Lobbying: Mayors in the Federal Arena* (New York: New York University Press, 1971); and Donald H. Haider, *When Governments Come to Washington: Governors, Mayors and Intergovernmental Lobbying* (New York: Free Press, 1974). Also see B. J. Reed, "The Changing Role of Local Advocacy in National Politics," *Journal of Urban Affairs* 5 (Fall 1983): 287–298.

29. See Hale and Palley, *The Politics of Federal Grants*, pp. 56–58.

30. Aside from the three organizations mentioned, the other members of the public interest group coalition are the International City Management Association (ICMA), the National Governors' Association (NGA), the National Conference of State Legislatures (NCSL), and the Council of State Governments (CSG).

31. See Terry Stanford, *Storm Over the States* (New York: McGraw-Hill, 1967), pp. 80–81, and Wright, *Understanding Intergovernmental Relations*, pp. 63–65.

32. Wright, *Understanding Intergovernmental Relations*, pp. 63–65, and Fritschler and Ross, *Business Regulation and Government Decision-Making*, pp. 126–129.

33. For a discussion of *Shapp* v. *Sloan* (later changed to *Thornburgh* v. *Casey)*, see *Intergovernmental Perspective* 4 (Fall 1978): 5–6; and *Intergovernmental Perspective* 5 (Winter 1979): 28.

34. *The Intergovernmental Grant System as Seen by Local, State and Federal Officials* (Washington: Advisory Commission on Intergovernmental Relations, 1977), p. 101; and *State and Local Roles in the Federal System*, p. 8. Also see Advisory Commission Information Bulletin 82-1, p. 4.

35. Some of the more prominent cases are discussed in Chapter 8.

36. Walker, *Toward a Functioning Federalism*, pp. 3–16. Also see *Regulatory Federalism Policy, Process, Impact and Reform* (Washington: Advisory Commission on Intergovernmental Relations, 1984), chaps. 1, 3, 4.

37. See Reagan and Sanzone, *The New Federalism*, pp. 60–65; and John J. Harrigan, *Political Change in the Metropolis*, 2nd ed. (Boston: Little, Brown, 1981), pp. 357–58.

38. See *Summary and Concluding Observations, The Intergovernmental Grant System: An Assessment and Proposed Policies* (Washington: Advisory Commission on Intergovernmental Relations, 1978), pp. 4–6. Also see Harrigan, *Political Change in the Metropolis*, pp. 358–59.

# 11. THE NEW FEDERALISM

When Richard Nixon became president in 1969, he was committed to changing the existing balance of power in the intergovernmental system. He developed a program called the New Federalism. According to David Walker of the ACIR, the New Federalism "was ostensibly anticentralization, anticategorical, and anti-administrative confusion. In positive terms, it supported: greater decentralization within the federal departments to their field units; a devolution of more power and greater discretion to recipient units; a streamlining of the service delivery system generally; a definite preferring of general governments and their elected officials; and some sorting out of some servicing responsibilities by governmental levels."[1]

The New Federalism was based on the proposition that for forty years money and political power had been flowing from states and local governments to elected and administrative officials in Washington. The New Federalism sought to arrest this flow of power and to reverse it back to states and local governments. Implicit in the underlying theory of the New Federalism were several basic assumptions:

1. The federal government has too much power in the intergovernmental system.
2. The federal government should devolve some of this power to states and localities.
3. Cities and states want this power returned to them.
4. Cities and states have the political and administrative mechanisms necessary to receive this power.

The amount of power the federal government has in the intergovernmental system is difficult to assess, but it is doubtful that the federal government has all of the power with which it is credited. While federal officials pass laws and develop regulations and guidelines for state and local officials to follow, it is these state and local officials who have the responsibility for administering the programs and, hence, great discretionary power. With the large number of local units of governments receiving federal monies, federal agencies find it difficult to monitor and evaluate the administration of these programs. State and local officials who understand the limitations of the oversight functions of the federal government realize they have a good deal of administrative authority and discretion in program implementation.[2]

Another assumption was that cities and states wanted additional power and responsibility. While this might have been true for some of the larger cities and states, it was not true for all subnational units of government. With additional power there would be increased responsibility and accountability. Many local officials, however, found it convenient to blame the federal government whenever a program failed to meet its objectives. Under Nixon's New Federalism this could no longer be done. Moreover, local officials accustomed to receiving federal funds with guidelines might not want to confront the special interest groups and local bureaucrats if federal programs were to become less constraining.

Finally, there was the question of whether or not the states and cities were prepared to assume these proposed additional grants of power. Some critics felt that in 1969 the states were just beginning to emerge as partners in the intergovernmental system and were not yet ready to assume additional responsibilities. Cities that had been recipients of numerous grants and billions of dollars had very little to show for their efforts. Some policymakers were anxious to see more metropolitan planning and administration approaches, but fewer and fewer observers of city life felt enthusiastic about increasing the power of local officials as a means of solving urban problems.

The Nixon Administration's New Federalism was composed of three major programs: reorganization, regionalization, and revenue sharing.

President Nixon's reorganization proposal was introduced in January 1971.[3] It was based on the premise that before handing down power to state and local governments it was necessary to centralize policymaking in Washington. The technique for achieving this was to be the superdepartment concept already implemented in cities such as New York and Washington, D.C.

The reorganization proposal was not received enthusiastically by members of Congress, bureaucrats, and interest group members, who saw the plan as a way to restructure and, consequently, upset accepted channels of communication and influence. Others in government saw the reorganization proposal as an attempt by the Nixon administration to increase centralization in the intergovernmental system and to accrue more power in Washington. For these reasons the reorganization plan did not advance very far in the Congress, and eventually it died there.

A second component of the New Federalism, which *was* implemented, was regionalization. In 1969 Nixon established ten Federal Regional Councils (FRCs) in ten large cities to coordinate federal agency policymaking to assist program implementation at the state and local levels.[4]

During the Nixon and Ford administrations the FRCs met with varying degrees of success. Some FRCs were staffed with professionals of proven ability; others were not. Coordination among federal agencies in the field was difficult in some regions, while quite successful in others. Communication with local governments and community groups has been uneven and sporadic. Rotating leadership on the council and lack of continuity of agency representatives have also caused problems.

The FRCs in general were not very successful for two reasons. First, during the 1960s, when cities were faced with riots, mayors found a much

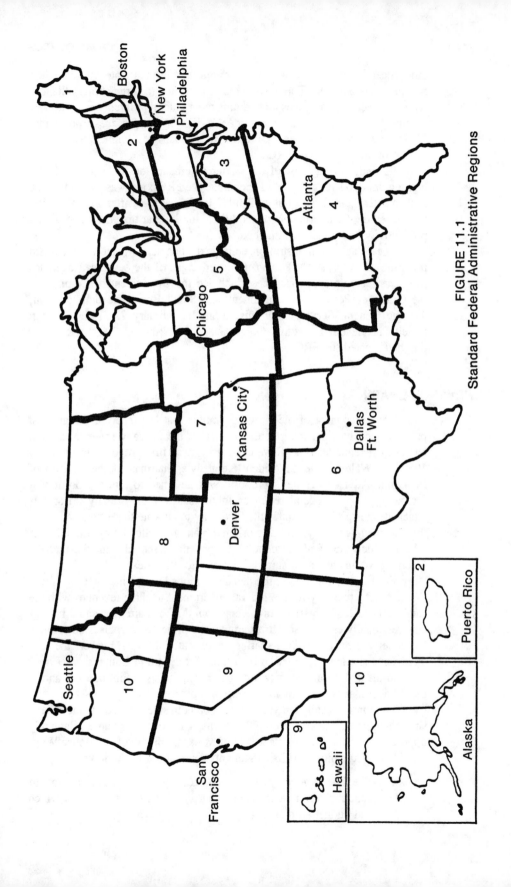

FIGURE 11.1
Standard Federal Administrative Regions

more receptive environment in Washington than in their state capitols when seeking financial help. The mayors quickly learned to forge strong alliances with bureaucrats in agencies that administered federal programs and with key members of Congress and committee staff who funded these programs. These alliances were not easily broken by promises of administrative decentralization in the form of FRCs.

Second, during most of the Carter administration there was virtually nothing done to strengthen or to encourage the FRCs; nor was anything done to dismantle them. It was not until July, 1979, that the Carter administration reaffirmed the basic principle of the FRCs, but by that time their appeal and productivity had greatly diminished.[5]

The Reagan administration embarked upon its own New Federalism program. In July, 1981, Reagan removed eight of the seventeen agencies from the regional councils. These included the Department of Commerce, the Office of Personnel Management, the Small Business Administration, and the General Services Administration. In February 22, 1983, Reagan issued Presidential Executive Order 12407, revoking the Executive Order that had created the FRCs.

## REVENUE SHARING

The component of the New Federalism that has received the greatest publicity and has had the greatest impact on the intergovernmental system has been revenue sharing. Revenue sharing was first proposed in the early 1960s by Walter Heller, President Kennedy's chairman of the Council of Economic Advisers. Heller's proposal was designed to return a portion of forecasted surplus federal revenues to the states with virtually no strings attached, thus giving the states the flexibility to allocate these funds any way they deemed necessary. Heller's original plan was followed by a number of others, which modified the details but kept the essential principle that the federal government return surplus revenues to the states.

For most of the 1960s, the debate continued over which approach was the most effective way for the federal government to share revenues with the states. Because of American involvement in the Vietnam War and a host of congressionally enacted social programs, the projected surpluses envisioned by Heller to finance revenue sharing never materialized. However, the idea of revenue sharing continued to be a topic for debate in Congress year after year. In the 89th Congress fifty revenue sharing bills were introduced, and in the 90th Congress the number increased to ninety bills.

For approximately ten years, forces on both sides argued the merits and shortcomings of the different bills. Perhaps no one was more adamantly opposed to revenue sharing than Wilbur Mills, Chairman of the House Ways and Means Committee. Mills' arguments centered on the following:

1. The federal government had no excess revenues, but it had lots of debts, which it would gladly share with the states, many of which had budget surpluses.

2. Revenue sharing was bad economic policy, since the level of government that collected the revenues was the level that should determine how the money is spent.

3. By returning money to the states and cities with no strings attached, the federal government would provide mayors, governors, council members, and state legislators with greater flexibility in program implementation. This, in turn, would allow these officers to achieve greater publicity and possibly encourage them to challenge the incumbent representative or senator.

The proponents of revenue sharing countered Mills' arguments by asserting that revenue sharing would provide the regional flexibility so obviously missing in the categorical grant-in-aid system, encourage greater innovation in programs, give greater discretion to local officials in administration and implementation, and greatly reduce the paperwork, auditing, and regulations that accompany most other federal programs.[6]

In October, 1972, Congress passed, and the President signed, the State and Local Fiscal Assistance Act, thus ending a decade of political conflict over the details of revenue sharing. The new law made available $30.2 billion to states and local governments over a five-year period. One of the last obstacles to overcome in passing the legislation dealt with the formula for distributing the money. The basic components of the formula were population, tax effort, and per capita income. Adjusting the weight of each factor in the formula almost proved to be too conflict-ridden and threatened, on several occasions, to kill the revenue sharing bill.[7]

The bill, as passed, allocated one-third of the money to the states and two-thirds to the local governments. Local governments had to spend their money on public safety, environmental protection, public transportation, health, recreation, libraries, social services, or financial administration. The states were not restricted to these categories; however, they were required to maintain the same level of aid to local governments (maintenance of effort) as they had the previous year. This was designed to prevent the states from using revenue sharing as an excuse to reduce funding levels to their cities. Neither states nor local governments were allowed to use revenue sharing funds to meet matching requirements of federal grant-in-aid programs.

The revenue sharing program was originally funded for five years and would have expired in 1977. However, a number of public interest groups sensed that revenue sharing could be a very important issue in a presidential campaign. By 1975 these groups, led by the National Association of Counties, began to urge Congress to renew revenue sharing in 1976. Both President Ford and candidate Jimmy Carter supported the early renewal effort, and Congress agreed with only token opposition.

The 1976 renewal of revenue sharing extended the program for 3¾ years, so it would expire once again during a presidential election year. This time $26 billion was appropriated, and most of the act remained unchanged except that revenue sharing funds could now be used as matching funds for other federal programs.

The 1980 battle to renew revenue sharing was a bitter political struggle. Because so many states had budget surpluses, a movement developed in Congress to eliminate the states from the program. Many members of Congress felt that the federal government needed the money more than the states did. Once again, public interest groups mobilized resources, developed information materials, and orchestrated the strategic assault on the key policymakers. After several months of political maneuvering, a series of compromises were reached that reauthorized revenue sharing for an additional three years. The states were excluded from the program in the first year but were included in the second and third years. However, money was never appropriated for the states. In 1983 Congress reauthorized the revenue sharing program for another three years.

While many members of Congress favored the idea of revenue sharing because it returned money to their political jurisdictions with very few strings attached, others were quite apprehensive. Since all units of local government were eligible for revenue sharing funds, the rich districts received money along with the poor. Gary, Detroit, Cleveland, New Orleans, and Newark received funds; but so did Scarsdale, New York; Grosse Point, Michigan; Palm Beach, Florida; and Shaker Heights, Ohio. Furthermore, the upper-middle and high-income communities have far fewer problems on which to spend their revenue sharing funds. Some of the communities added lights to their tennis courts and upgraded the quality of their golf courses. At a time when large urban areas were complaining of a shortage of resources, expenditures of this type rankled many in Congress.

Several studies were conducted to determine how state and local governments were spending their revenue sharing funds. In the Brookings Institution study of fifty-seven jurisdictions, it was reported that through fiscal year 1974 local governments were spending just over 50 percent of their revenue sharing funds on new or expanded operations, new capital expenditures, or increased pay and benefits, while only 37.3 percent of the states' expenditures were for these areas. However, in looking at areas such as program maintenance, tax reductions, and avoidance of borrowing, the results are quite different. The states spent 62.5 percent of their revenue sharing funds on these areas, while local governments only spent 47 percent.[8]

Unfortunately, not all of the studies of revenue sharing expenditures draw the same conclusions about how these funds were spent. In a study conducted by the General Accounting Office (GAO), it was reported that capital expenditures amounted to 33 percent of total revenue sharing direct-use expenditures.[9] These data were further complicated by the issuance of a report in 1976 by the National Science Foundation, which found that local governments greatly expanded their capital outlays, more revenue sharing funds were used to maintain or expand operating programs than to reduce or stabilize taxes, and most revenue sharing funds were used to support ongoing activities rather than to develop new approaches or programs.[10]

Another survey, conducted by David Caputo and Richard Cole, surveyed the chief administration officials of over 400 cities with more than

50,000 inhabitants. Caputo and Cole found that after an initial flurry of expenditures for capital expense projects, local governments began to expend more of their revenue sharing funds on ongoing programs that received the greatest attention in their local budgets—environmental protection, law enforcement, street and road repair, fire protection, and parks and recreation.[11]

One reason a program like revenue sharing is difficult to monitor concerns the concept of fungibility. "A grant is said to be *fungible* when the state or local government is able to use the grant for purposes other than those intended by Congress. When an agency receives a large grant, it may be able to use the federal funds to substitute for state or local monies."[12] Since almost all federal grant monies come into local government general revenues, it is difficult to trace specific funds within the city. Local officials have a great deal of discretion in the allocation of these funds; state and federal funding agencies, because of time and manpower constraints, are often forced to rely upon local government reporting mechanisms to assess how funds were spent. The reliability of these reports is often in doubt; consequently, government agencies, university researchers, or independent investigators collecting data from these governments and their reports can produce conclusions at variance with one another.

Revenue sharing as a source of revenue for state and local governments needs to be put in perspective. Thomas Muller of the Urban Institute, testifying before Congress in 1979, stated, "Let me briefly note that revenue sharing as a source of funds is much more important to cities than to states. In fiscal 1977, only 8/10 of 1 percent of all State revenue came from revenue sharing, or roughly $8 out of every $1,000. In comparison, almost 4 percent of all city revenues comes from revenue sharing. We thus have a ratio of almost 5 to 1 in relative importance of revenue sharing as a share of local in comparison to State budgets."[13]

President Nixon also proposed a Special Revenue Sharing program as a companion program to General Revenue Sharing. Special Revenue Sharing was to be funded at $11 billion, with $10 billion coming from existing categorical grant-in-aid programs and an additional $1 billion in new money. The $11 billion Special Revenue Sharing fund was to be used for grants in six major areas—education, transportation, law enforcement, job training, urban development, and rural development.

Congress reacted slowly to the Nixon proposals. Categorical grants are an important source of power and control for Congress. The Nixon plan would have consolidated many of the categorical grants into block grants, which were designed to reduce federal regulations and increase state and local authority. In Nixon's second term, Congress passed the Comprehensive Employment and Training Act (CETA) in 1973 and the Community Development Block Grant (CDBG) in 1974. The following year Congress approved Title XX of the Social Security Act.

While Nixon did not get the complete package of block grants he sought in his Special Revenue Sharing Program, he was able to persuade the Congress to add to the two block grants already on the books. These efforts at grant consolidation, decentralization of program authority, and greater state and local administrative discretion have been carried further by the Reagan administration.

The New Federalism of the Nixon administration received mixed reviews at best. The effort to reorganize the executive branch of government into superdepartments was a failure. The development of the FRCs was initiated for sound and logical reasons. However, for a number of reasons, some political and some administrative, the FRCs performed with mixed results. The major program of the New Federalism was, and still is, revenue sharing. Now more than a decade old, it continues to be fine tuned by Congress each time it is renewed. Nevertheless, it has become an important component in the tripartite federal funding mix of categorical grants, block grants, and revenue sharing by which funds are transferred annually to state and local governments.

## THE NEW PARTNERSHIP

President Carter's approach to the intergovernmental system consisted of a number of programs designed to accomplish a variety of goals. Some of these programs were old (welfare reform, increased housing for low and moderate income families, energy conservation), while others were new (hospital cost containment, Urban Development Action Grants, and the creation of new departments of Energy and Education). The Carter administration was in many ways symptomatic of the frustration that can befall a president who seeks to change the system either too quickly or without fully understanding its dynamic nature.

Candidate Carter had articulated his views and hopes for his New Partnership to a summer 1976 meeting of the United States Conference of Mayors.[14] In his address Carter talked of a number of themes he hoped to pursue as president. This speech indicated that Carter would attempt to blend aspects of Johnson's Creative Federalism with Nixon's New Federalism—two programs whose goals were quite contradictory. Carter spoke about expanding the federal-state-local-private partnership, focusing programs heavily on urban areas, bypassing state governments on some programs, targeting aid to cities in distress, and developing a wide range of new intergovernmental programs while expanding several existing ones. In this vein Carter was articulating the Creative Federalism philosophy of the Johnson administration. On the other hand, Carter spoke of fiscal restraints and caution, reducing the number of categorical grant programs, and reorganizing the federal executive branch of government. These were all programs characteristic of the Nixon administration's New Federalism. The inability to satisfactorily resolve these two conflicting approaches plagued the Carter administration throughout most of its four years in office.

The Carter administration's intergovernmental program emphasized three themes: (1) targeting of federal aid to troubled urban communities, (2) making greater use of public funds to promote private investment in cities, and (3) reducing the administrative red tape and paperwork associated with obtaining grants from the federal government.

David Walker, a critic of the Carter administration initiatives in the intergovernmental arena, wrote:

> The basic dilemma confronting any administration that now relies primarily on improved and uniform procedures and processes to strengthen intergovernmental management is that such efforts cannot be separated from the drastically expanded size, scope, and substantive concerns of today's intergovernmental programs and their recipients. Thanks to the legacies of Creative, New, and especially Congressional Federalism, no mere effort on the process and access fronts alone—no matter how persistent and massive—can bring uniformity, simplicity, and manageability to intergovernmental administration. Combined with consolidation, abolition, and devolution, proceduralism would have been a viable management strategy for the late seventies; alone it was ineffective.[15]

## NATIONAL URBAN POLICY

The focal point of President Carter's domestic policy program was the attempt to develop a national urban policy. This policy was intricately linked to the intergovernmental system and, had it been implemented, would have had a profound impact upon federal-state-local relations.

Since 1977 each president has been required to submit to Congress a biennial report on National Urban Policy. Shortly after taking office Jimmy Carter created an Urban and Regional Policy Group (URPG) with Patricia R. Harris, Secretary of Housing and Urban Development, as the chairwoman. The URPG was charged with the task of preparing the national urban policy report after consulting with the interested agencies and groups and developing programs consistent with the president's theme of a new partnership. The URPG was instructed to focus on:

- Economic revitalization of cities
- Targeting of federal aid to cities in need
- Immediate assistance to cities with critical needs
- Leveraging federal dollars by encouraging greater private investment
- Better program coordination[16]

The URPG encountered obstacles in preparing the report right from the start. Despite some general guidelines on the New Partnership, there was very little direction and virtually no participation from the White House in the preparation of the National Urban Policy. Yet all of the agencies participating in drafting the document knew the White House had some definite ideas on urban policy. Even within the Department of Housing and Urban Development, differences of opinion arose among those charged with the responsibility for reviewing and drafting proposals. These internal conflicts delayed the process and fostered an image of divisiveness and discord that was not helpful to the development of a rational policy.

Finally, HUD was given responsibility as the lead agency in developing the National Urban Policy. However, as one among equals, it was virtually impossible for HUD to exert any control over the other participating agencies. The Departments of Transportation, Commerce, Labor, Treasury, and HEW all participated in the development of the policy, but each department exercised a veto over proposals that appeared to have negative implications for them or their constituents. This meant that almost all innovative or controversial issues were subjected to lengthy consultation, and bargaining and negotiating became the key operating words in the URPG working sessions.[17]

The National Urban Policy submitted to Congress committed the federal government to the following:

- Encouraging and supporting efforts to improve local planning and management capacity and existing Federal programs
- Encouraging states to become partners in assisting urban areas (i.e., cities, counties, and other communities)
- Stimulating greater involvement by neighborhood and voluntary associations
- Providing fiscal relief to the most hard-pressed communities
- Providing strong incentives to attract private investment to distressed communities
- Providing employment opportunities, primarily in the private sector, to the long-term unemployed and disadvantaged in urban areas
- Increasing access to opportunity for those disadvantaged by a history of discrimination
- Expanding and improving social and health services to disadvantaged people in cities, counties, and other communities
- Improving the urban physical environment and the cultural and aesthetic aspects of urban life and reducing urban sprawl[18]

To achieve the goals established in the National Urban Policy Report, Carter introduced several new initiatives requiring $4.4 billion in budget authority, $1.7 billion in new taxes, and $2.2 billion in guaranteed loan authority in fiscal year 1979. For fiscal year 1980 the necessary budget authority was to be $6.1 billion, new taxes $1.7 billion, and $3.8 billion in guaranteed loan authority.[19] The new initiatives were divided into five categories: (1) improving the operation of federal, state, and local governments, (2) employment and economic development, (3) fiscal assistance, (4) community and human development, and (5) neighborhood and voluntary associations.

The first initiative consisted mostly of a series of executive orders issued by the president to tighten up the grant-in-aid process (discussed above) and to improve coordination among federal agencies, as well as among federal, state, and local governments. One of these executive orders initiated a process known as Urban and Community Impact Analysis (UCIA), which was designed to insure that proposed federal actions did not have a negative impact on urban areas. In fact, UCIA proved to be of limited value, since it did not have the force of law nor the active involvement of citizens and local governments. This prevented the clients on the receiving end of the policy from critiquing the agency views of a policy's impact. The agencies, on the other hand, could not be held accountable by the citizens, nor were they likely to present analyses suggesting that negative consequences might ensue from their proposed policies.[20]

Another executive order established the Interagency Coordinating Council (IACC) under Cabinet Secretary Jack Watson. This Council was composed of the assistant secretaries in the departments with major urban responsibilities. The IACC was charged with two responsibilities: first, to improve interagency coordination in standardizing paperwork—applications, reporting, and auditing by states and local governments; second, to resolve conflicts and cooperate on projects that were too large for a single agency to handle. Watson was generally applauded for his efforts in this area, but with entrenched functional hierarchies running from federal to state and local agency and a congressional subcommittee system that supported this functional specialization, there were very few successes to report.

The focus of the National Urban Policy was a series of new and expanded programs designed to achieve the basic principles of the New Partnership. The major pieces of proposed legislation were:[21]

### Employment and Economic Development

> *Labor Intensive Public Works*—targeted to high unemployment communities—about 60,000 jobs to help cities repair streets, buildings, parks. Cost: $1 billion.
>
> *Targeted Employment Tax Credit*—encourage business to hire disadvantaged young people 18–24. Tax credits to employers would start at $2,000 per worker in the first year and drop to $1,500 during the second year. Cost: $1.5 billion.
>
> *National Development Bank*—encourage businesses to locate or to expand in economically depressed urban rural areas. Bank would guarantee investments through a combination of grants, loan guarantees, and industrial reserve boards.
>
> *Economic Development Grants*—increases in both Urban Development Action Grants and Title IX of the Economic Development Administration program, both of which leverage private sector investment in urban areas. Cost: $275 million.

### Fiscal Assistance

> *Supplemental Fiscal Assistance Program*—to help states and local communities withstand the fiscal impact of high unemployment. Cost: $2 billion (2 years).

Other components of the National Urban Policy, with lower dollar estimates, were programs in housing rehabilitation, urban transportation, social services, self-help development program, community development credit unions, crime prevention, and the urban volunteer corps.

It is difficult to assess the success or failure of a major legislative effort such as the National Urban Policy proposals. In a democratic system every politician, including the president, knows that he or she will not achieve a perfect record on getting legislation passed. Furthermore, some legislation that does pass has been amended and modified to the point where the president no longer recognizes it, nor for that matter wishes to retain a proprietary interest in it. It is also fair to say that the most important legislative proposals are not necessarily the ones with the largest dollar requests, making it even more difficult to determine success in a comprehensive legislative package such as the urban policy proposal.

The announcement of Carter's National Urban Policy was not greeted with great enthusiasm. There had been much publicity concerning the process of putting the program together and several leaks about specific aspects of the policy. Anything short of a major change in federal government direction was not likely to excite the political actors who awaited its announcement.

The critics saw it more as an extension of the past than as a new policy for America's urban centers. They characterized it as rather bland, with few new exciting programs and the consolidation of several older ones. Moreover, they had been hoping for a much larger financial commitment from a Democratic president.[22]

Supporters of the program pointed to two innovations that appealed to them. First was the concept of greater involvement for the private sector. Many felt this was a renewed commitment to involve this underutilized resource more heavily in trying to solve some of America's pressing urban problems. Second, the supporters liked the idea of targeting federal aid where it was needed most rather than spreading the funds across the country to satisfy political interests.

By the end of 1978 thirteen pieces of legislation had become law. At least four of these—Elementary and Secondary Education Act, New York City Loan Guarantee, the Consumer Co-op Bank, and the CETA authorization—were not part of the original National Urban Policy proposals, but the Carter administration included them in assessing its progress towards a National Urban Policy during the legislative year.

The Employment Tax Credit was a major success. More modest victories were achieved with housing rehabilitation, the Urban Parks program, intermodal transportation, and the Social Services package. The major defeats were in the Labor Intensive Public Works Program, State Incentive Grant Program, and the Supplemental Fiscal Assistance program. Each of these represented a considerable sum of money, and their defeats must be viewed as damaging to any concerted national effort to solve America's urban problems.[23]

Was the dissection of the Carter National Urban Policy a defeat for a less than perfect program, or was it a commentary on the nature of processing political issues in a democratic political system? We think it is probably some of both, but more of the latter.

It is no accident that the United States is a country devoid of national policies. Whether the issue be health, transportation, housing, employment, energy, or urban areas, we have been unable to develop and to successfully legislate a national policy. Several presidents have tried (Nixon—welfare, Ford—energy, and Carter—urban), but each has failed.

The answer lies partly in the fragmented and highly decentralized nature of our political system. For any issue to be successfully processed through the federal decision-making structure requires it to be broken down into small, discrete proposals that can be easily assigned to relevant congressional subcommittees. These subcommittees, in conjunction with bureaucrats who are experts on the subject, lobbyists who are interested in the subject, White House staff who represent the president's views, and state and local officials who represent subnational units that have to implement the policies, join together to evaluate, modify, or reject proposed legislation.

There are rarely more than fifty actors involved in any one of these subsystems. The actors communicate with each other, meet occasionally, and try to reach the necessary compromises to move a proposal through to an enacted law. This can only be done when the subsystem is given a narrowly defined issue to deal with. Issues such as national urban, health, or energy policy are far too complex and cumbersome for a subsystem to handle. These issues raise questions that encompass more than one subsystem, and often several. This means someone has to try to pull together many disparate interests. The U.S. policymaking process has rarely been successful in achieving this, since there are few places where power is centralized in our system.

The alternative is to take a national policy proposal and break it down into smaller legislative packages and allow the subsystems to process them. This means that each discrete component of the policy will be handled in a different way, at a different time, by different actors. The results will be mixed, since the original policy will no longer represent a "national theme" but, having been dismantled, will in the end represent the rather narrow and specific views of the members of the subsystems.[24] There is no place in our decision-making structure where one individual or a few individuals have the power to pull together all the legislative proposals pertaining to a policy and refashion them into a national policy, as once conceived by the president.

Knowledge of subsystem politics helps to explain what happened to Carter's National Urban Policy. What started out in the White House as a comprehensive set of proposals to solve America's urban ills were treated individually as separate ideas to be weighed against the political interests of the bureaucrats, members of Congress, lobbyists, and state and local officials. The end result was a scorecard with some victories and some defeats, but no National Urban Policy.[25]

## NEW FEDERALISM—AGAIN

As a candidate for president, Ronald Reagan left little doubt about his views on the intergovernmental system. He repeatedly told audiences that he felt the federal government was too large, both in dollars spent and personnel employed. He further stated that the federal government had become too involved in the lives of citizens through the promulgation of extensive rules and regulations, many of which resulted from the federal programs enacted in Washington.

Reagan campaigned hard on the theme of reducing federal government spending and government intrusion in our lives. His plan was to decentralize power and authority back to the states and allow them to make their own administrative decisions and establish their own guidelines for program implementation.[26]

The Reagan program had an impact on the intergovernmental system on three different levels. First were the 1982 fiscal year budget cuts. Second was the program of consolidating categorical grants into block grants. Third was the New Federalism program. (Reagan used the same term as Nixon, but the Reagan program focused on increasing state responsibility for administering programs, whereas Nixon looked to local governments.) This was announced in Reagan's 1982 State of the Union message, in which he proposed swapping funding sources and functions between the federal government and the states and local governments.

## Budget Cuts

President Reagan sought to achieve his budget goals by reducing many program costs—except for defense spending, which was slated to increase from $162 billion in 1981 to $255 billion in 1984. The basic income security programs—"social safety net"—would increase slightly over the 1981–84 period. Almost all other domestic programs were to be reduced in budget allocations and were to have their eligibility requirements tightened. Finally, the Reagan administration proposed consolidating numerous categorical programs into block grants and reducing their funding levels by approximately 25 percent.[27]

Sizeable cuts, amounting to over $20 billion, were made in the 1981 budget. An additional $48 billion was to be cut from existing programs in the 1982 budget, amounting to about a 14 percent cut in state and local grants from the federal government. However, Congress was unable to pass the needed appropriations bills, so continuing resolutions were used to keep agencies funded, employees paid, and intergovernmental programs operating. Since most state legislatures began meeting in January, 1982, to work on fiscal year 1983 budgets, many of them were unable to accurately assess what level of federal funding they would have in a number of programs.

New Jersey, like many other states, was facing severe cutbacks in a number of programs, estimated to reach $700 million. Having just elected a new governor, the state found itself mired not only in guessing what level of federal funding would be forthcoming in 1982, but how a new governor was supposed to organize his administration, prepare a budget, and negotiate with interest groups and the legislature without any sound revenue projections.

A number of other states reported similar experiences in trying to make their economic projections in preparation for the fiscal 1983 budgets. Unlike the federal government, the states are required to balance their budgets. One Oklahoma legislator commented, "We have no information for '83 and a shortage of information for '82."[28] Reports from Washington, California, Arizona, Maryland, and Missouri all showed states with projected deficits being asked to plan future budgets and spending patterns without sufficient information to make sound judgments.

## Block Grants

The Reagan administration began examining the grant-in-aid system early in its first year. Consistent with the president's announced position, his aides began drafting plans to consolidate a number of categorical grants into block grants. Only five block grants had ever been passed by Congress— Partnership for Health Act, Law Enforcement Assistance Act, Community Development Block Grant, Comprehensive Employment and Training Act, and Title XX of the Social Security Act.

Reagan's approach to block grants also differed markedly from the approach taken by his Republican predecessors, Nixon and Ford. Whereas Nixon and Ford created block grants that bypassed the states and went directly to local governments, Reagan has chosen to make block grant payments directly to the states. Nixon and Ford felt they needed the political clout of the mayors in order to pass their programs, while Reagan viewed the governors as more politically essential in the passage of his block grant program. Under the Reagan proposals, states will pass money on to local governments, leaving these local units in a very tenuous position until those pass-through decisions are made.

In Spring of 1981 the ACIR reviewed the fiscal year 1982 budget revisions and produced the following list of block grant proposals along with the potential number of categorical grants that could be consolidated into these block grants.[29]

Highways (14)

Airports (2)

Education, State (32)

Education, Local (12)

Social Services (12)

Energy and Emergency Assistance (2)

Health Services (15)

Preventive Health Services (10)

Community Development (7)

Indian Programs (11)

Employment and Training (3)

Environment

Nutrition

Housing

Aging Services (5–7)

The actual legislative package of the Reagan administration called for consolidating eighty-five categorical grants-in-aid into seven block grants. These categoricals amounted to over $16.1 billion in 1981. Congress only enacted nine new block grants consolidating seventy-seven categoricals at about $7.5 billion. This result would seem to indicate that the Reagan administration fell far short of what it hoped to achieve in grant consolidation.[30]

Some of the block grants that passed were very different from the concept of block grants established in the 1960s and 1970s. Some existing categorical grants were rechristened block grants. The president received much of what he wanted in education, employment and training, health and social services, and energy assistance. However, in some education, health, and social services programs, Congress failed to go along with the president. The programs where the major consolidations took place were state education (37), preventive health and health services (6), alcohol and drug abuse (10), maternal and child health (9), social services (1), community services (7), low income energy assistance (1), and state community development (1).

Another aspect of these recent block grants that is noted by John Gist:

> The transfer of discretion over spending and the reduction of federal regulations usually associated with block grants is absent from all these new block grants. Federal agencies will continue to administer these programs until states express a desire to take them over. If and when they do, they must submit reports detailing the intended use of the funds, activities to be supported, areas and individuals to be served, and methods and criteria of allocating funds and a process for public comment.[31]

Some critics have suggested that Reagan's plan for grant consolidation and the creation of numerous block grants was subverted by Congress. Their argument suggests that, historically, Congress has passed very few block grants, and most of those passed between 1973–75. This is not a record that indicates strong support for the block grant concept. Block grants reduce the control Congress exerts over funding and guidelines and lodge that control with states and local governments. The logical conclusion was to give the president some of the block grants he wanted, deny him several others, and insure that several other categorical grants remained intact regardless of what they were called.

From Reagan's standpoint, the 1981 legislation was a success. While not getting all of the grant consolidation he wanted, he did achieve several victories and reduced the number of grants and the amount of dollars involved. If the White House had a hidden agenda, namely to use grant consolidation as a budget-cutting tool rather than a technique for reallocating power in the intergovernmental system, then a reassessment of who won and who lost in the 1981 intergovernmental struggle is in order.[32]

## New Federalism—1982 Style

In his January 1982 State of the Union address to the nation, President Reagan announced the scope, but not many of the details, of his New Federalism proposal. In accordance with his previously stated views that the states should begin to assume more responsibility for programs funded and administered by the federal government, the president proposed the following:

1. Beginning in 1984 the *federal government* would assume all responsibility, including costs, for the Medicaid program.
2. Beginning in 1984, the *states* would assume all responsibility, including costs, for the food stamp program and for the Aid to Families with Dependent Children (AFDC) program.
3. In 1984 the federal government would devolve to the states responsibility for an additional 43 programs, currently funded from over 100 federal grants.[33]

In the few weeks following the announcement of the new program, some of the details were made public. From a financial standpoint, the Reagan proposal recommended the following pattern. The states would take over AFDC and the food stamp program at a projected 1984 cost of $16.5 billion. In addition, the forty-three grant programs being turned back to the states would add an additional $30.2 billion to state expenditures in 1984 for a total of $46.5 billion in new expenditures.

However, the states would be relieved of their Medicaid costs, which in 1984 were estimated to be $19.1 billion. To make the New Federalism politically feasible the Reagan administration had to devise a plan to cover the balance of the expenditures the states would be obligated to make in 1984. The plan consisted of a federalism trust fund financed from federal excise taxes on alcohol, tobacco, gasoline, and windfall profits from the oil companies. The trust fund would provide $28 billion annually between 1984 and 1987. Assuming that all financial projections are correct, by 1984 the states would be expending $46.7 billion while receiving $47.1 billion. Beginning in 1988 the trust fund would be cut by 25 percent each year through a reduction in the excise taxes. As the fund was reduced, the states would have the option of raising their own taxes to make up the difference between their costs and the reduced revenue coming from the trust fund.

The forty-three programs scheduled to be turned back to the states included:

social, health, and nutrition services (18)

transportation (11)

community development and facilities (6)

education and training (5)

revenue sharing and technical assistance (2)

income assistance (1)

**Federalism program** (Fiscal 1984 in billions of dollars)

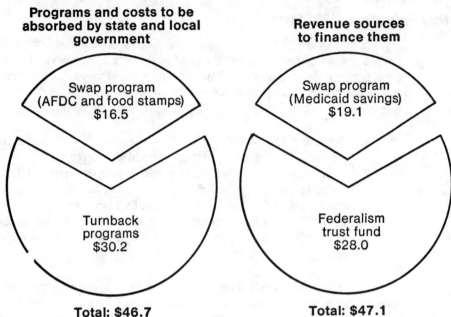

**Programs and costs to be absorbed by state and local government**

Swap program (AFDC and food stamps) $16.5

Turnback programs $30.2

Total: $46.7

**Revenue sources to finance them**

Swap program (Medicaid savings) $19.1

Federalism trust fund $28.0

Total: $47.1

**Turnback program** (Fiscal 1984 in billions of dollars)

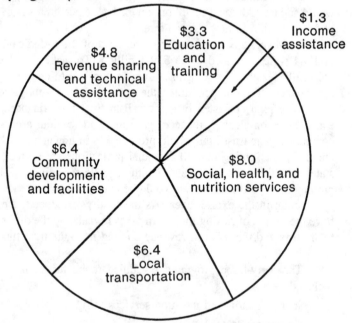

$3.3 Education and training

$1.3 Income assistance

$4.8 Revenue sharing and technical assistance

$6.4 Community development and facilities

$8.0 Social, health, and nutrition services

$6.4 Local transportation

Total: $30.2 billion

FIGURE 11.2

Source: Reprinted from *County News*, National Association of Counties.

The response from the cities, counties, and states was one of caution and concern. Cities and counties were very concerned about guaranteed pass-through features in the new proposals. The Reagan administration strongly supported this provision in areas such as mass transit, employment, and community development.

Also of great concern to states, cities, and counties was the issue of implementation strategy. Few details of the New Federalism program were announced by the president in his State of the Union message. State and local officials viewed this as an opportunity to influence the final implementation plans. At their annual meeting in Washington in 1982, the National Governors' Association (NGA) drafted a set of counter-proposals that they submitted to the Reagan Administration. The NGA seemed optimistic that they had established the groundwork for future negotiations with Reagan aides. The administration was pleased that NGA had developed some constructive ideas rather than rejecting the New Federalism program altogether.

In early March, after reviewing many of the comments and criticisms of the New Federalism, the administration offered a revised version of the plan, hoping to garner greater support for the program. The administration's revised proposal called for the states to assume responsibility for income maintenance programs for the nation's poor, while the federal government would agree to fund and administer the welfare assistance programs for the aged, blind, and severely disabled. It was hoped that by dividing the welfare burden between the national and subnational units of government, much of the opposition to the New Federalism program would disappear.

Local officials remained cool to the administration's proposals, pending final agreement on maintenance of their share of the federal funding. Black local officials urged the Reagan administration to incorporate antidiscrimination safeguards in the new legislation. State officials continued to believe that the poor were a national responsibility and welfare programs to aid them should be funded at the national level.[34]

The Congressional Budget Office (CBO) did its own analysis of the Reagan administration's New Federalism proposals and produced figures that varied greatly from those put forth by the administration.[35] CBO did not assume that the forty-three grant programs to be returned to the states would be cut, as proposed in the president's 1983 budget. Since there was mounting opposition to these cuts, the CBO projected that the states would inherit programs that were far more costly to run than the president suggested. These programs, the CBO suggested, would cost as much as $62 billion in 1984, not the $47 billion suggested by the administration.

Furthermore, the CBO predicted a higher rate of inflation than did the administration. This would not be offset by growth in the proposed federalism trust fund.

The failure of the Reagan administration to win the support of any of the major public interest groups was a severe setback for the New Federalism, the cornerstone of the president's domestic policy program. White House aides spent most of 1982 revamping and redrafting the New Federalism proposals with an eye towards developing a program that the governors would support.

In early 1983 the administration released the details of its revised New Federalism program. Gone were the federalization of Medicaid, the turnback program, the trust fund, and the state assumption of food stamps and welfare costs. In their place were proposals totaling $21 billion in the form of four new block grants in transportation, housing construction, social services, and community development. None of these block grants received serious consideration from Congress in 1983. The public interest groups seemed content to let them die, thus ending the Reagan administration's New Federalism effort.

## Enterprise Zones

In March, 1982, President Reagan unveiled his plan for revitalizing America's inner cities when he sent his proposal for enterprise zones to Congress. The Reagan proposal closely resembled a plan introduced in the House of Representatives in 1980 by Rep. Jack Kemp (R-N.Y.) and Robert Garcia (D-N.Y.).[36]

The Reagan plan is designed to attract businesses to the inner cities and increase employment in these areas. Modeled after the British plan announced in 1980, the new enterprise zone proposal would exempt participating businesses from the federal capital gains tax. In addition, businesses would be eligible for a number of special tax credits that could free them from as much as 75 percent of their corporate taxes. A further incentive is provided by the administration's effort at deregulation, which is aimed at easing restrictions on business corporations.

The president claimed that decades of massive federal spending programs had done little to improve the quality of life in America's cities. The proposed Enterprise Zone Act of 1982 calls upon the Department of Housing and Urban Development to create twenty-five zones a year for three years. State and local governments would nominate areas to be included, and HUD would make the final selection. Most areas chosen to become enterprise zones would probably be no more than one to two square miles in area. States and local governments could increase their chances of being selected by providing additional tax reductions and loosening up zoning, regulation, and licensing procedures. Enterprise zones were being established in three cities in Connecticut as a result of state legislation, and a similar bill had been enacted in the Maryland legislature.

Enterprise zone legislation raises many questions about who is likely to benefit from this program. On the one hand, the legislation would provide both tax and regulatory relief for moderate and large sized businesses. On the other hand, the failure of the administration's proposal to assist small businesses or provide job training funds or front-end capital leaves in doubt who will wind up with the projected benefits of the programs.[37]

## Summary and Conclusions

The intergovernmental system in the United States is complex, large, and often in a state of change. For the past decade and a half there have been periodic efforts to reform the system by reducing power and authority at the federal level and returning it to either the states or local governments. These efforts have been categorized under the heading of the New Federalism and have met with varying degrees of success.

We have seen that the federal government cannot solve all the problems in the states and local governments. There is a real need for a partnership arrangement among the different levels, and the essence of the debate centers on which levels should have which powers. This usually varies with the administration in power at the national level, and this debate is likely to continue with each succeeding administration.

Second, there is a need to involve the private sector in more activities performed by government. This involves much more than just turning functions of government over to corporations. Questions of accountability, citizen involvement, information sharing, equity, secrecy, and control have to be analyzed and resolved before large-scale privatization becomes a reality.

Third, we have learned that formulating and implementing a national urban policy is a very difficult process. The nature of the American political system is such that small, specific issues and programs are handled with greater ease than attempts to solve large, national problems in a comprehensive manner. President Carter formulated a national urban policy that was processed in a series of separate bills. Some passed, some died, and some were modified, but the results hardly represented a national urban policy. Even President Reagan, who enjoyed numerous political successes in Congress during his first two years in office, suffered defeat on his 1982 New Federalism proposal, which was rebuffed by the major interest groups and hardly discussed in Congress.

The issue of the New Federalism strikes at the heart of the intergovernmental system. The real issue is how power will be distributed and exercised in our political system. Republican administrations tend to take a decentralized view and seek to reduce federal power by returning authority for programs to state and local governments. Democratic administrations tend to see greater equity in the distribution of services if greater power resides in the federal arena.

Neither party has been powerful or persuasive enough to convince Congress to shift dramatically in one direction or the other since 1968. While almost everyone agrees that change is needed in the financial and administrative aspects of the intergovernmental system, there has yet to develop the necessary consensus to implement such change.

## NOTES

1. David Walker, *Toward a Functioning Federalism* (Boston: Little, Brown, 1981), pp. 104–05.

2. For a discussion of where power resides in the intergovernmental system, see A. Lee Fritschler and Bernard H. Ross, *Business Regulation and Government Decision-Making* (Boston: Little, Brown, 1980), pp. 133–38.

3. Nixon's reorganization proposal was contained in "The President's Message to the Congress Proposing the Establishment of a Department of Natural Resources, Department of Community Development, Department of Human Resources, and Department of Economic Affairs," March 25, 1971.

4. Executive Order 11647.

5. See *Fact Sheet, Federal Regional Councils* (Washington: The White House, July 20, 1979). Also see Fritschler and Ross, *Business Regulation and Government Decision-Making*, pp. 140, 143.

6. For a discussion of the arguments for and against revenue sharing, see Michael D. Reagan and John G. Sanzone, *The New Federalism*, 2nd ed. (New York: Oxford University Press, 1981), pp. 85–92.

7. For a discussion of the history and the politics of the Revenue Sharing Bill, see Paul R. Dommel, *The Politics of Revenue Sharing* (Bloomington: Indiana University Press, 1974); and Richard P. Nathan, Allen D. Manvel, and Susannah E. Calkins, *Monitoring Revenue Sharing* (Washington: Brookings Institution, 1975), pp. 344–372.

8. Richard P. Nathan and Charles F. Adams, Jr., *Revenue Sharing: The Second Round* (Washington: Brookings Institution, 1977), pp. 27–32.

9. *Revenue Sharing: Its Use By and Impact On Local Governments* (Washington: General Accounting Office, April 25, 1974), and *General Revenue Sharing— The First Actual Use Reports* (Washington: Office of Revenue Sharing, March 1974).

10. F. Thomas Juster, ed., *The Economic and Political Impact of General Revenue Sharing* (Washington: Government Printing Office, 1976), p. 5.

11. David A. Caputo and Richard L. Cole, "Revenue Sharing and Urban Services: A Survey," *Tax Review* 34 (October 1973). Also see Caputo and Cole, "General Revenue Sharing Expenditure Decisions in Cities Over 50,000," *Public Administration Review* 35 (March/April 1975): 136–42.

12. George E. Hale and Marian Lief Palley, *The Politics of Federal Grants* (Washington: Congressional Quarterly, 1981), p. 113; and Nathan and Adams, *Revenue Sharing*, pp. 77–80.

13. Thomas Muller, "The State Role in Revenue Sharing: A Fiscal Perspective," in *Revenue Sharing With the States*. Hearings before the Subcommittee on the City, Committee on Banking, Finance, and Urban Affairs, U.S. House of Representatives, 96th Congress, 1st Session, May 3, 1979, p. 2.

14. Jimmy Carter, "Address on Urban Policy to the United States Conference of Mayors," June 29, 1976.

15. Walker, *Toward a Functioning Federalism*, p. 118.

16. See Myron Levine, "The President and National Urban Policy," paper delivered at the annual meeting of the Northeastern Political Science Association Meeting, Newark, New Jersey, November 9, 1979, pp. 2–3.

17. For a discussion of the politics involved in developing the National Urban Policy, see Robert Reinhold, "How Urban Policy Gets Made—Very Carefully," *New York Times*, April 2, 1978, section 4, p. 1.

18. *The President's National Urban Policy Report*, August, 1978, p. 5.

19. "President's Message to Congress on the National Urban Policy," March 27, 1978.

20. See Levine, "The President and National Urban Policy," pp. 27–32 for an analysis of UCIAs. In March, 1982, President Reagan rescinded the 1978 Executive Order that created UCIAs, claiming they were burdensome and unnecessary. *Washington Post*, March 10, 1982, p. 21.

21. All of these legislative proposals are contained in "President's Message to Congress on the National Urban Policy," March 1978.

22.  "Carter Urban Policy: A Smorgasbord," *Congressional Quarterly Weekly Reports* (April 1, 1978), p. 782.
23.  For an analysis of the legislative struggle over the 1978 National Urban Policy, see Levine, "The President and National Urban Policy."
24.  For a discussion of subsystem politics, see Fritschler and Ross, *Business Regulation and Government Decision-Making,* chaps. 5–7.
25.  For a discussion of this issue with respect to Carter's National Urban Policy, see Levine, "The President and National Urban Policy," pp. 32–36.
26.  See President Reagan's inaugural address in *Weekly Compilation of Presidential Documents,* January 26, 1981.
27.  Office of Management and Budget, *Fiscal Year 1982 Budget Revisions,* and Congressional Budget Office, *An Analysis of President Reagan's Budget Revision for Fiscal Year 1982.*
28.  Jay Mathews, "States Unable or Unwilling to Shoulder 'Federalism' Burden," *Washington Post,* February 17, 1982, pp. 1, 4.
29.  *Intergovernmental Perspective* 7, no. 2 (Spring 1981): 9.
30.  For a breakdown of the block grants, see David B. Walker, Albert J. Richter, and Cynthia Cates Colella, "The First Ten Months: Grants-in-Aid, Regulatory and Other Changes," *Intergovernmental Perspective* 8, no. 1 (Winter 1982): 8–12. Also see Richard P. Nathan, "The Nationalization of Proposition 13," *P.S.* 14, no. 4 (Fall 1981): 752–56.
31.  John R. Gist, "The Reagan Budget: A Significant Departure From the Past," *P.S.* 14, no. 4 (Fall 1981): 742.
32.  For a discussion of the politics of block grant legislation in 1981 and its relationship to the Reagan budget, see Gist, "The Reagan Budget"; Nathan, "The Nationalization of Proposition 13," pp. 752–56; Walker, Richter, and Colella, "The First Ten Months," pp. 12–14; and Timothy J. Conlan, "Back in Vogue: The Politics of Block Grant Administration," *Intergovernmental Perspective* 7, no. 2 (Spring 1981): 8–15.
33.  *Washington Post,* January 28, 1982, pp. 1, 9.
34.  For a discussion of the major issues in the New Federalism program, see Herbert H. Denton, "White House Offers Federalism Deal," *Washington Post,* March 13, 1982, pp. 1, 6.
35.  Spencer Rich, " 'Federalism' No Even Swap, Hill Told," *Washington Post,* March 17, 1982, pp. 1, 6.
36.  For a discussion and an analysis of Enterprise zones, see Stuart M. Butler, *Enterprise Zones: Pioneering in the Inner City* (Washington: Heritage Foundation, 1980); and George Sternlieb and David Listokin, eds., *New Tools for Economic Development: The Enterprise Zone, Development Bank and RFC* (Piscataway, N.J.: Center for Urban Policy Research, 1981). The Reagan Administration proposal is discussed by Herbert H. Denton, "Reagan Proposes Enterprise Zones to Lure Business to Big-City Slums," *Washington Post,* March 24, 1982, p. 3.
37.  See Myron A. Levine, "The Reagan Urban Policy: Efficient National Economic Growth and Public Sector Minimization," *Journal of Urban Affairs* 5, no. 1 (Winter 1983): 20–24.

# 12. FINANCING URBAN AMERICA

In 1957, Baltimore, desperate for revenues to pay for salary increases won by city employees after a decade of spiraling municipal expenditures, enacted a 4 percent levy on all advertising outlays by newspapers, sign companies, television stations, and all others selling either advertising space or time. This tax was repealed—only one year after it was passed, when the Supreme Court of the United States declared that it was unconstitutional.

This is but one indication of the degree of desperation felt in city halls across the United States for additional revenue sources to pay for the increasingly expensive services that are expected in our cities today. Why is this sense of desperation so widespread, and why does it continue?

## REVENUES

### The Taxing Power

A tax is generally defined as a compulsory contribution for the support of government, exacted without regard for individual benefit. That is, people cannot refuse to pay a tax simply because they, as individuals, receive no particular benefit from it. The power of the states to tax is very broad and is subject only to limitations imposed by the federal and state constitutions. Local governments, on the other hand, possess only such taxing power as has been conferred on them by the states. State governments can and do pass statutes restricting the taxing powers of local governments. In short, a state legislature may levy any tax that it is not forbidden to enact, but local governments may only impose those taxes the states permit them to levy.

Because over the decades there has been a feeling that state legislatures could not altogether be trusted to levy taxes wisely, all state constitutions impose certain limitations upon the taxing powers of the states. Ordinarily these provisions take the form of exempting certain classes of property from taxation. It is common, for instance, to exempt from taxation all publicly owned property as well as property used for educational, religious, or charitable purposes. Most states provide exemptions of one sort or another for

## STATE AND LOCAL GOVERNMENT REVENUE
### $451.5 BILLION

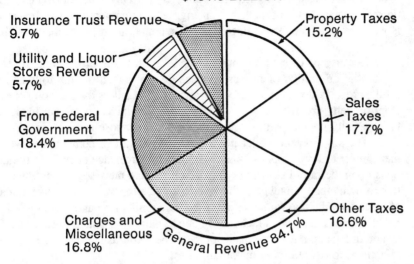

Insurance Trust Revenue
9.7%

Utility and Liquor
Stores Revenue
5.7%

From Federal
Government
18.4%

Charges and
Miscellaneous
16.8%

*General Revenue 84.7%*

Property Taxes
15.2%

Sales
Taxes
17.7%

Other Taxes
16.6%

U.S. Department of Commerce BUREAU OF THE CENSUS

## STATE AND LOCAL GOVERNMENT EXPENDITURE
### $434.1 BILLION

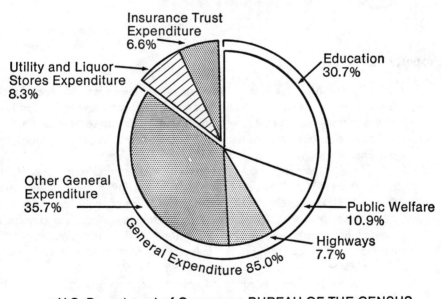

Insurance Trust
Expenditure
6.6%

Utility and Liquor
Stores Expenditure
8.3%

Other General
Expenditure
35.7%

*General Expenditure 85.0%*

Education
30.7%

Public Welfare
10.9%

Highways
7.7%

U.S. Department of Commerce BUREAU OF THE CENSUS

### FIGURE 12.1

Source: U.S. Bureau of the Census, *Government Finances in 1979–80* (Washington: U.S. Government Printing Office, 1981), pp. 2–3.

veterans. Other forms of exemption include "homestead" exemptions (under which owner-occupied homes are wholly or partially nontaxable), exemptions on certain kinds of industrial and agricultural properties, and, though it is not very common, some degree of tax exemption on the property of the elderly.

Because of these numerous exemptions, in many urban areas a very substantial proportion of real estate does not appear on the tax rolls. As a result, property-tax revenues are severely curtailed unless the rates on nonexempt property are increased. Obviously, such rate increases are not likely to be especially popular with those property owners whose taxes go up.

The tax problems of local governments are further compounded when their power to levy property taxes is subject to percentage or millage limitations upon the rates that may be imposed for stated purposes. As an illustration, a municipality may be authorized to levy up to five mills on each dollar of assessed valuation for street purposes, three mills for parks, two mills for health work, and so on. Practice, of course, varies from state to state, but it is not uncommon for the local voters to be allowed, through the use of referenda, to exceed these maximum rates.

Another limiting device, employed in several states, is an overall limitation on property taxes. Under this plan, the combined tax levies on a single piece of property may not exceed a maximum total rate. As we have noted earlier, the way local governments attempt to circumvent limitations of this type is to make increasing use of the special district.

## Property Taxes

The property tax is at the heart of urban finance and has been for the last 200 years. About 40 percent of municipal general revenue comes from property taxes. In the past few years, however, they have been declining in importance as local revenue sources. There are several reasons for this development.

Ideally, property taxes are both universal and uniform.[1] That is, the taxes are levied on all forms of property (universality) at the same rate (uniformity). Unfortunately, in the real world neither of these ideals has been maintained. As the different types of property multiplied, the concept of universality became unattainable. Real property—land improvement—is the easiest to reach through taxation. Real property is made up of visible, easily recognizable assets, and relatively immobile ones at that.

As we reached our advanced industrialized economic state, less and less personal wealth was in the form of real property. We now possess extensive personal property: home furnishings, appliances, and expensive automobiles at home, and inventories and equipment at work. All of these are harder to locate, since they have a lower degree of visibility, coupled with a higher degree of mobility. Any effort to locate items of this nature is bound to be quite expensive, time-consuming, and often unrewarding. Some

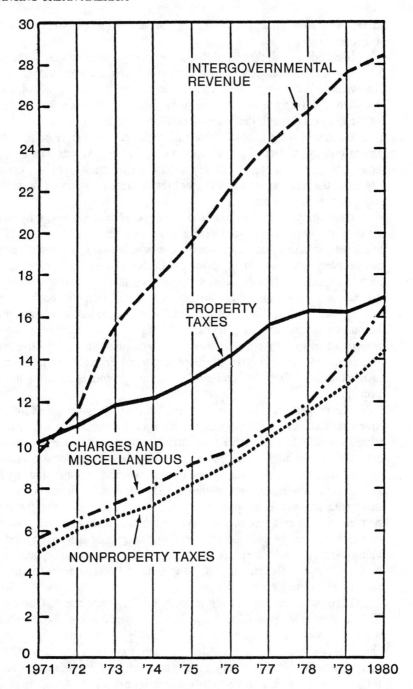

FIGURE 12.2
Trends in City General Revenue from Selected Major Sources:
1971 – 1980
(Billions of dollars)

Source: U.S. Bureau of the Census, *City Government Finances in 1979–80*
(Washington: U.S. Government Printing Office, 1981), p. 2.

governments find it possible to tax tangible personal property only by means of a formula.

In addition to all these problems, our society has developed to the point that even real and tangible personal property does not represent all of our true wealth. We now possess cash, stocks, and bonds, all of which are classified as intangible personal property. Many governments have tried to tax these assets through the property tax, but have failed. Most jurisdictions have abandoned the notion of universality and have concentrated their taxation efforts on real and tangible personal property. As one can see, this removes a significant portion of the wealth of the members of any community from the reach of any government that depends on property taxes as a major source of revenue.

Uniformity, too, has come into question. Most states began by requiring that all property be taxed at the same rate, but modifications of this position have taken place ever since those who legislate tax policy realized that property taxes would be more productive if they were based on the ability of the individual or business to pay and that industry and commerce can pay more than individual citizens can. Thus, different tax rates have been applied to the property of industrial and commercial development, on the one hand, and to purely residential property and the tangible personal property of its residents on the other. Although this is very productive, some states contend that equity is the more important criterion for taxation and have maintained their constitutional or statutory requirements for uniform property taxes.

The property tax, as studied by the Advisory Commission on Intergovernmental Relations, proves to be the item most in trouble in our domestic revenue system. In its report, ACIR called the property tax our "sick giant"[2] and traced its problems to several "tax overburdens," including overassessment of individuals with average and below-average incomes and the high costs of often inadequate administration. Also cited is the development of an inadequate tax base for property taxes; this has resulted from the division of the metropolitan area into residential, commercial, and industrial sectors, as well as from the concentration of large populations of the poverty-stricken within the city. All of these factors point up the problem facing many communities, namely, the inability of individuals and communities to raise any more money through property taxes.

Reforms in the tax, though needed, may not help much. One contention often brought up in discussions on local finance is that those who own no real property pay no property taxes. This is unfortunately false, as any tenant knows, since higher taxes are promptly passed on to them through higher rents, with the relatively minor exception of those under rent control in New York City. The gross injustice here seems not to be that these individuals do not pay property taxes, for in the long run they do, but rather that in some communities tenants may not vote on referenda dealing with proposed increases in the property tax.

The central problem in all cases of property taxation is one of assessment. A tax assessor is one who has the responsibility for determining the value of property for tax purposes. Under a well-administered tax system, this does not mean that the assessment determines the tax bill, though it often happens that way. The ideal system should work like this: the assessed valuation of all property in the taxing jurisdiction is divided by the amount of money to be raised through the tax, thus determining the tax rate; this is altered in accordance with limitations on taxes established by state laws and constitutions, and the actual tax rate is developed.

As one would suspect, it rarely works that way. First of all, different governments assess on different bases. Some assess at 100 percent of market value, others as low as 25 percent. Thus, under the same tax rate, taxes can and do differ tremendously. Most states now provide for an equalization procedure to adjust assessed valuations of each assessment jurisdiction so that they are more nearly equal. This, however, does not solve all of the problems. Within a single governmental unit, comparable parcels of land may be assessed at different ratios to their market values. This is sometimes due to the failure of the assessors to bring assessments up to date with changes in the market value of the real estate in the area. Newer property is assessed more recently and, therefore (given the inflation of the last two decades), bears a higher assessment than older property in the same area. This undermines the concept of uniformity in taxation. In other cases, undeveloped land is seriously underassessed through pressure applied by land developers and real estate interests, who wish to maintain tax assessments at levels of agricultural usage to maximize the profits gained when the land is later sold for residential, commercial, or industrial development.

To remedy this, some local governments have adopted the policy of assessing all land at its highest usage level. Thus, an old single-family dwelling in the central city area may easily be assessed at a much higher value when zoning and other land-use changes indicate that the site might be more profitably used for a high-rise apartment house or some other commercial development. Incredible as it may seem, citrus groves in Southern California suburbs are assessed as potential residential developments in recognition of the huge profits to be realized by such use. In such cases, with frequent reassessments to keep pace with the rapidly changing market, uniformity is near. There are, however, social costs involved. Land near suburban areas is virtually forced out of agricultural usage because the taxes make it uneconomical to maintain it as farm land. This does little to discourage the outward continuation of urban sprawl. Additionally, the assessment of deteriorating residential units at maximum tax rates results in a tax bill that owners cannot bear.

Property tax reform is indeed difficult, since most people will not support measures calling for higher taxes.[3] This problem is exacerbated by the inability of most municipal governments to control assessments and collections, functions usually performed on the county or township level. Reforms must come from the state legislatures, which to date have been unable to achieve a fully uniform property tax system. As some experts point out, local tax reform is just one facet of the dilemma facing American cities in the last quarter of the twentieth century.

## Sales Taxes

To supplement the revenue resources of local governments, forty-five states have authorized the imposition of sales taxes. Most of these are levied by municipalities, though counties may do so in some states, and this right has been extended to school districts in Louisiana. Over the past twenty years, the use of sales taxes has been on the upswing. Most states permit municipalities to levy a local sales tax in addition to state sales taxes, while retaining the collection and administration at the state level. This guarantees uniformity of collection and administration and reduces the costs for these services to the local governments. The end result is to produce a maximum revenue for local municipalities.

Sales taxes, though, have one major fault, and this is apparent at any governmental level on which the tax is imposed. Sales taxes are regressive, and severely so. This means that sales taxes create a greater burden for lower-income groups than for the wealthy, since the poor spend a greater proportion of their incomes on necessities. Sales taxes, when applied to groceries, medicine, and other necessities of life, are particularly distressing. For families with average incomes, such taxes are irritations; for those with incomes at or below the subsistence level, they may be unbearable.

## Income Taxes

As property taxes and sales taxes have failed to provide adequate revenues, many cities have begun to look for yet other ways to reach wealth within their borders. Since income taxes are so productive at the national level, they appear equally attractive on the state and local levels. Thus far, forty states have allowed some or all of their governments to levy income taxes. In some cities, such as Louisville, Kentucky; Columbus, Ohio; and Philadelphia, Pennsylvania, the income tax provides nearly half of local tax collections, increasing its attractiveness to other localities.

There are some serious problems with a tax of this nature. In areas where localities must collect and administer the tax, these costs run particularly high. Also, the question of payment of local income taxes by non-residents has raised controversies in every city that has adopted the income tax. Municipalities view the income tax paid by non-resident workers within their boundaries as a means of making suburbs contribute for the services of the central city. Suburban dwellers (who may be heavily taxed within their own communities) feel that such additional taxation for services they use only partially is unfair. The antagonism that inevitably results from such policies does little for the already strained relations between the neighboring communities. Though income taxes add appreciably to the funding of local governments, they do not appear to be long-run solutions to the revenue problems cities now face.

## Other Taxes and License Fees

Most cities are able to supplement their revenues through minor taxes and license fees. Many have adopted a wheel tax upon automobiles driven within the city by residents or commuters who work in the city. Other taxes of this type include those imposed on the sale of cigarettes, alcoholic beverages, and amusements. There also exist in many areas licensing requirements for the sale of alcoholic beverages, the operation of taxicabs, and other services. Licensing requirements serve a dual purpose: they regulate these activities while profiting from them. These taxes and fees, however, seldom provide a significant portion of local revenues.

## User Fees and Charges

Another popular form of taxation is the imposition of charges or fees for "services rendered." These are based on the amount of service used, so that only those who use the service pay for it. Most urban transit systems operate this way, as do public utilities providing water, power, and sewage disposal to the community. Other improvements (streets, sidewalks, and street lighting, for example) are often financed by special assessments against the property owners in the affected area. This seems to be an attractive idea, as it appeals to our basic sense of fairness. The problem lies, though, in the inability of many to pay the fees even though they do, in fact, need services. Public transportation is a good example of this; those who need it most—namely, those with no other form of transportation available to them—are the ones least able to pay for it. Thus, subsidies from general tax revenues are required for continuation of these services.[4]

As state and local governments struggled to balance budgets during the recession in the early 1980s, many turned toward an increased use of user fees. In some instances these fees are being imposed for the first time; in other jurisdictions existing user fees are being increased. According to a recent survey by the Joint Economic Committee of Congress, city revenue from user fees rose 21 percent between 1980 and 1982, making it the fastest growing source of city funds.

Recent surveys by the Advisory Commission on Intergovernmental Relations indicate that taxpayers prefer user fees to increases in other types of taxes by a wide margin. The Reagan administration is also partial to this technique because of its pay-as-you-go system.

## Intergovernmental Revenues

Currently, we see that more and more revenue for cities is being produced from sources outside the local governments. This money may take various forms. By sharing the tax revenues, states return to local governments a portion of some taxes collected within the local jurisdiction. An example of this is the popular motor fuel tax, of which a percentage of the revenue is returned to local jurisdictions to maintain and improve local streets and highways. These grants-in-aid have served as one response to the inability of the property tax and other taxes, charges, and fees to support local governmental activity.

Both state governments and the federal government have tended to emphasize categorical grant programs, which are directed as particular aspects of particular functions. The categories are determined by state and national authorities to be areas of national significance in which local inability or unwillingness to act is most serious. This external funding, and the often imposed requirement for matching funds from the local governments, have caused some to charge that the higher levels of government bureaucracy are taking over local functions, making crucial decisions with respect to policy considerations and local resource allocations. This can be true, but the grants-in-aid do not necessarily bring with them shifts in policy control.

This type of revenue is expected to continue and increase in importance, since federal and state governments possess superior revenue-producing capacities by virtue of their access to the progressive income tax. This means that the national and state governments can equalize the ability of local governments to meet the pressing demands of urban society by passing on funds to jurisdictions with tax bases that are inadequate to support these services. Some see room for improvement in this system, such as replacement of the categorical grant programs with block grant programs, enabling cities to decide for themselves which functions and services are most in need of help, and when.

The needs of America's urban areas continue to grow, yet cities are limited in their ability to respond by state constitutions and legislation. States impose tax limits and deny cities permission to impose other taxes. Taxes left for cities to impose are regressive and undesirable in the view of many of the local citizens.

## The New York City Fiscal Crisis

New York City's fiscal crisis cannot be traced to any one event or to the administration of any one mayor. The problems that plagued New York City in the late 1970s and early 1980s were the result of actions and policies implemented in the 1960s and early 1970s.

The riots that occurred in many American cities produced a public awareness of inner-city problems. City officials, responding to citizen demands, worked to initiate and increase many social service programs. Funding for some of these programs helped the poor to organize. Some of the newly organized groups sought to capitalize on their new powers by accelerating their demands for more social services. This cycle, when repeated several times, helped to swell local government budgets.

While this was occurring, local government unions were also pressing their demands for increased wages and fringe benefits. In addition, the number of public employees was also increasing. Mayor Wagner had developed a relatively harmonious relationship with the unions, sensing their political value in an election campaign. As a result, by the time John Lindsay became mayor in 1966, the unions were used to getting most of what they wanted from City Hall. Lindsay, however, was no friend of the local government unions. His administration was less than six hours old when it was faced with its first strike. Besides, Lindsay had campaigned and won by forming coalitions of blacks, Hispanics, and low income residents, many of whom were attacking the bureaucracy for being unresponsive.

Lindsay's first administration was constantly at war with the unions. The city suffered a number of strikes, and the unions successfully lobbied the state legislature when they found the Lindsay administration intransigent. Toward the end of his first administration, Lindsay found he needed the unions on his side if he was to govern the city effectively and be reelected in 1969.

> To win union support and to pay off his campaign debt, he gave the unions everything they demanded during the 1969–70 round of contract negotiations. In these ways, the civil service unions were able to secure substantial salary and benefit increases for city employees during his tenure, thereby compelling the mayor to increase expenditures for the agencies employing their members.[5]

Early in the 1970s, the economic situation in New York City worsened. Manufacturing jobs in the city decreased, inflation rates soared, and the Nixon administration began drastically cutting funding for poverty and community action programs. Revenues coming into the city could not keep up with expenditures. The Lindsay administration, in an effort to maintain social service program levels, tried to cover its projected revenue deficits by borrowing money on short-term notes. As these notes became due they were refinanced at higher and higher rates. Lindsay also used long-term borrowing for capital projects to finance the city's current operating expenses.

All of this came to a head as the Lindsay administration left office and Abraham Beame became mayor. The rising inflation rate, coupled with increasing interest rates and declining revenues brought on by a nationwide recession, exacerbated New York's financial plight.[6]

In May, 1975, Mayor Beame and New York Governor Hugh Carey descended, amid much publicity, on Washington to demand assistance. Without an immediate federal grant of $1.5 billion, they said, New York City would not be able to meet its payroll by the end of June, 1975.

Though President Ford talked to the New York dignitaries, the assignment to handle the matter was given to Treasury Secretary William E. Simon. When asked if he thought the president and Congress would bail out New York City as they had bailed out the Penn Central Railroad in 1970 and Lockheed Aircraft in 1971, Simon, a Wall Street broker, said with a note of sarcasm: "We're going to sell New York to the Shah of Iran. It's a hell of an investment." The responses of the mayor and the governor were, as it turned out, thoroughly predictable. New York City engaged in massive layoffs of civil servants and a lowering of standards of municipal services.[7]

As it turned out, the day before default day the state imposed a temporary solution on New York City in the form of the Municipal Assistance Corporation. Big Mac, as it was called, was set up to transform $3 billion in city short-term debt into state long-term debt. But strings were attached. Big

Mac was to receive stock transfer and sales tax revenues (more than $1 billion) that previously had gone to the city. In addition, Big Mac was instructed to impose its own auditing procedures on the city and to audit city agencies. Exasperated by what it considered a long train of city fiscal abuses, the state of New York felt it necessary to force financial controls on New York City as a condition for assistance.

Although both Governor Carey and Mayor Beame insisted that the bonds to be issued by Big Mac would prove irresistible to the financial community, doubt persisted as to whether New York City would be able to meet its long-range fiscal commitments. The setting up of the Municipal Assistance Corporation did spare the city the humiliation of defaulting on some of its debts. It did not, however, even remotely resolve the city's long-range fiscal crisis.

The crisis continued on a week-to-week basis. With considerable reluctance, the federal government set up a three-year program of loans to aid the city. In the meantime, the state of New York established an Emergency Financial Control Board, the chairman of which was the state's governor. The board virtually took control of the city's spending. In addition, approval of the board was required for adoption of the city's budget.

For the fiscal year 1978 New York City managed to develop a balanced budget. After complex negotiations, the proposed budget was approved by the Municipal Assistance Corporation and the Emergency Financial Control Board.

This action did not, however, end the long-term crisis. In fact, the 1978 budget was balanced by using over $1 billion in one-time revenues and by postponing the payment of obligations. Clearly, there was little reason for optimism in regard to long-term prospects.

Who are the actors in this involved game? They include, besides city and state officials and control boards, some important but relatively unknown performers. The banks are important, because they determine whether the city may borrow money through the sale of bonds. The municipal pension fund managers are important, because they are under pressure to buy city securities. If the city goes broke, so do the funds and their pensioners.

The actors also include the Securities and Exchange Commission, which from time to time issues judgments on the real value of New York City's securities. For example, in August, 1977, the commission charged that the mayor, six big banks, and Merrill Lynch (the country's largest brokerage house) had failed to inform investors of the city's dangerous financial condition.

Then there is the Banking Committee of the United States Senate. As an illustration of its interest, consider the action taken by Senators William Proxmire of Wisconsin, the committee chairman, and Edward A. Brooke of Massachusetts, its senior Republican. Over the 1977 Christmas holiday, the two senators sent a letter to President Carter. It said that New York City should not need, nor should it get, additional federal loans after the then-current "seasonal" loan program expired on June 30, 1978. The contention was that a strict financial plan, combined with increased state, pension-fund, and bank loans to the city, would enable it to meet its financial needs.

At this point Secretary of the Treasury W. Michael Blumenthal appeared on the scene. He indicated that he would recommend continuing the seasonal (that is, short-term) loans, but would gradually reduce them to zero.[8]

New York City will undoubtedly survive, but it surely has lost any pretense of fiscal autonomy. As for the principal actors (including thousands of anonymous investors), the morning's financial news makes for exciting, even invigorating, reading.

Ronald Reagan, as a presidential candidate, indicated during the campaign a considerable amount of distaste for the type of federal support the Carter administration had given New York City. After winning the election and assuming office, however, Reagan agreed that New York City could not be allowed to default on its obligations.

## The Urban Debt

As costs have increased and funds have become harder to find, urban governments are turning more and more frequently to borrowing in order to support their existing programs and encourage the growth of new ones. Most of the loans are of the long-term variety; they are used for capital expenditures such as equipment or municipal structures. The bonds that are sold to raise this money usually have a life as long as that of the goods purchased.

States have found many ways to regulate the urban debt. Many have found it desirable to limit severely the borrowing power of local jurisdictions. States may also have to place a ceiling on the amount of interest that localities pay on the bonds they issue, and many require local referenda to approve bond sales.

These general obligations, or full faith and credit bonds, are only one type of urban indebtedness and are often the only type restricted by the states. Other types include revenue bonds (which are usually employed for capital financing of urban services of the sort supported by user fees and charges) and lease-purchase agreements (which are often developed to enable the government to make capital expenditure for assets that seldom produce revenue).

The fact that local jurisdictions must develop these methods of adding to revenues, while avoiding debt limits within their states, should show sufficient reason as to why such debt limits are unrealistic. Many feel that the free operation of the bond market will control unwise borrowing by local jurisdictions. The bonds will never be sold if investors cannot be assured that the purchase is a reasonably safe one. To limit interest rates renders bond issues unsalable in a highly competitive money market. Investors favor municipal bonds now only because they feel that the federal income tax exemption for the interest on such bonds offsets the lower interest rates. If the exemption is ever eliminated, local governments will be forced to pay the going competitive rates of interest in order to borrow funds, which will, in turn remove state limitations.

The referendum requirement has impaired local borrowing power, since many citizens vote "No" because they feel that bonds will be coupled with tax increases. Many argue that it is unfair to burden future generations with this generation's debts. They fail to recognize that if a community needs a city hall and then saves for fifty years to build one, those whose taxes were spent will receive no benefit from its construction. On the other hand, if the money is borrowed now and taxes pay for it during the next fifty years, then those who use it will be paying for it.

## Expenditure Patterns

Cities spend more each year to provide the services demanded from them. When one looks at the increases in expenditure, making adjustments for population growth and inflation, one sees that the increases continue to grow each year. In some areas the increase in expenditures is more rapid than the growth in the Gross National Product, considered to be the best measure for the general growth of the economy. When the urban area is clearly defined, the function upon which the most money is spent is education. Also, counting both state and county expenditures in urban areas, far more money is spent on highway and street maintenance and construction than on police and fire protection.

Why are the expenditures growing so rapidly at the urban level of government? There are several answers. One is the desire for program expansion on the part of planners and administrators in urban governments. This type of upward pressure on expenditure levels is to be expected on all government levels, and serves only to mask the real reasons for rising expenditures.

Pressure for the expansion of public services (and therefore a cause for rising rates in these costs) is provided by the private sector in our cities' economy rather than the public one. Increases in the population of metropolitan areas have put increasing pressure on existing governmental services and facilities and have required an enormous expansion in expenditures just to stay even with demands. If per capita expenditures also increase, however, then population increases cannot account for all increases in costs. The forces of urbanization require additional new services and the continuation and maintenance of the old ones. Technological changes have brought with them massive demands for public services that are not directly related to the service needs of the citizenry. Industrial demands on public utilities have grown dramatically, requiring the construction of new facilities. Industrialization and technological developments have created demands for *new* public services, such as air and water pollution control, to keep the urban environment habitable. Physical scale expansion, made possible by new advances in transportation technology, has in turn made additional demands for streets and highways, as well as for more and better public transportation to carry larger and larger suburban populations between their residences and their places of work in other parts of the urban area.

Added to these burdens is the passage of time, the importance of which any automobile owner well knows. The older the existing equipment, the higher the costs for its maintenance in normal running condition. As the central cities deteriorate, more and more money must be spent just to keep them minimally habitable. To return them to ideal conditions would take massive sums of money—just as it would cost an enormous amount, probably greater than the original cost, to restore an old automobile to mint condition. Finally, citizens in urban society are no longer satisfied with the mere maintenance of old governmental service levels. Growth in national productivity and wealth has resulted in rising public expectations in all sectors, not the least important of which is the public one. We now see "the good life" as one of increasing opulence, with governmental service expectations changing accordingly. What we saw as "frills" yesterday we see as necessities today, and so our expenditures must continually grow.

## The Rising Cost of Government

In ordinary times, government receipts and government expenditures tend to balance out. In times of recession, when there is heavy borrowing, the key figure to examine is that of government indebtedness. Though the federal government can, and sometimes deliberately does, operate in the red, the Keynesian theory on which this practice is based does not apply to state and local governments. The maintenance of the national economy is a federal responsibility. The responsibility of the state and local governments is to raise adequate revenues to meet the expenditures incurred in providing the services and functions that their residents demand.

Direct general expenditure of state and local governments has steadily increased. For example, the combined totals rose from $51.9 billion in 1960, to $74.5 billion in 1965, $131.3 billion in 1970, $273 billion in 1977, and $430 billion in 1980. While this rise in part represents inflation, it mostly represents demands for new, improved, or extended services. As would be expected, the number of state and local government employees has also risen during the period, from 6.4 million in 1960 to over 12 million in 1983.

The best way to obtain an overview of the spending of state and local government is to examine Table 12.2 with care. The table illustrates the order of priorities in expenditures as established by state and local governments.

## THE BUDGETARY PROCESS

Deciding how much money a particular city needs to raise and how the available funds are to be spent lies at the heart of any urban political process.

TABLE 12.1
Governmental Expenditure, by Character and Object: 1979-80

| Item | Amount (millions of dollars) | | | | Percent | | | | Percent increases or decrease (−) from prior fiscal year | | |
|---|---|---|---|---|---|---|---|---|---|---|---|
| | All governments | Federal | State | Local | All governments | Federal | State | Local | All governments | Federal | State and local |
| Total expenditure .......... | 958,657 | 617,166 | 257,812 | 260,777 | 100.0 | 100.0 | 100.0 | 100.0 | 15.2 | 14.9 | 13.2 |
| Intergovernmental expenditure ... | (¹) | 90,836 | 84,504 | ¹1,757 | (¹) | 14.7 | 32.8 | 0.7 | (¹) | 6.6 | 11.2 |
| Direct expenditure .......... | 958,657 | 526,330 | 173,307 | 259,019 | 100.0 | 85.3 | 67.2 | 99.3 | 15.2 | 16.4 | 13.7 |
| Current operation .......... | 517,011 | 209,200 | 108,131 | 199,680 | 53.9 | 33.9 | 41.9 | 76.6 | 15.7 | 21.1 | 12.3 |
| Capital outlay ............. | 99,386 | 36,492 | 23,325 | 39,568 | 10.4 | 5.9 | 9.0 | 15.2 | 6.6 | -8.7 | 18.2 |
| Assistance and subsidies ... | 63,998 | 48,776 | 9,818 | 5,404 | 6.7 | 7.9 | 3.8 | 2.1 | 11.9 | 13.0 | 8.4 |
| Interest on debt .......... | 78,890 | 61,286 | 7,053 | 10,552 | 8.2 | 9.9 | 2.7 | 4.0 | 22.8 | 25.7 | 13.9 |
| Insurance benefits and repayments .......... | 199,373 | 170,576 | 24,981 | 3,815 | 20.8 | 27.6 | 9.7 | 1.5 | 16.7 | 15.8 | 22.5 |
| Exhibit: Expenditure for salaries and wages .......... | 250,886 | 86,990 | 48,793 | 115,103 | 26.2 | 14.1 | 18.9 | 44.1 | 10.3 | 10.9 | 9.9 |

Note: Because of rounding, detail may not add to totals.
− Represents zero or rounds to zero.
¹Net of duplicative intergovernmental transactions.
Source: U.S. Bureau of the Census, Government Finances in 1979–80 (Washington: U.S. Government Printing Office, 1981), p. 5.

No one can really be expected to enjoy paying taxes, and taxpayers' organizations and real estate interests use this antipathy to maintain anti-tax pressures on city councils, local governing boards, and other taxing agencies. Countervailing pressures are numerous. Citizen demands for municipal services continue to increase, in spite of having already reached unprecedented heights.[9] The bitter conflict engendered within the political process as a result may be relieved in part by the adoption of the municipal budget, or operating budget, which details the departmental programs and services for which money is expended on a day-to-day basis.

The responsibility for preparing the budget can vary among communities. In some, the executive (usually the mayor) is responsible; in others, the task falls on the city council, a legislative committee, or the executive in conjunction with a legislative committee. But in most cases, the mayor or city manager has the formal policy initiative for the budget. In larger cities, the chief executive has assistance in the form of a budget (or finance) director, whose job is to supervise the collection of data and formulate the budget within the guidelines set by the chief executive.

Even in the smallest of communities, the budget is an imposing document, beginning with the chief executive's budget message, an introduction designed to present the overall picture of policies and programs recommended for the community during the coming year. It seeks to explain and justify both the taxes and the expenditures in the budget. This message is followed by a summary of the general financial status of the community, indicating revenues and expenditures in major categories. The rest of the document is a detailed breakdown of all anticipated revenues and expenditures as compared with those of the previous fiscal year.

Before the budget can be drawn up, it must be decided where the money will go once it has been collected. This process of setting priorities is probably the most crucial point in the entire budgetary process.

It would not be unreasonable to expect that expenditure would vary from city to city because of the wide range of urban environments. Budget-makers, like other decision-makers, do not operate in a social vacuum; indeed, they cannot do so within the political context of their jobs. They respond to pressures and opportunities as they are perceived, and if forces are large enough, responses to them will tend to be alike. Most variations among expenditure levels in American cities have been found, not surprisingly, to be associated with variations in three population factors—socioeconomic status, age, and mobility.

Communities with many residents in the lower socioeconomic bracket spend more money per capita on police protection, fire protection, water systems, housing and urban renewal, parks and recreation, and employee retirement programs than do communities on a higher socioeconomic level. The older the population, the more it can be expected to spend on health care and hospitals, employee retirement, and parks and recreation. A more mobile population is usually indicated by greater municipal expenditures for interest on the urban debt, housing, and urban renewal.

## TABLE 12.2
### Governmental Expenditure by Function: 1979-80

| Item | Amount (millions of dollars) | Percent of total | Percent of general expenditure | Percent increase or decrease (−) from prior fiscal year | | |
|---|---|---|---|---|---|---|
| | | | | All governments | Federal | State and local[1] |
| Total expenditure ........... | 958,657 | 100.0 | (X) | 15.2 | 14.9 | 13.2 |
| Direct general expenditure ...... | 723,094 | 75.4 | 100.0 | 14.7 | 16.8 | 12.7 |
| National defense and international relations ........ | 149,459 | 15.6 | 20.7 | 16.3 | 16.3 | (X) |
| All other general expenditure .. | 573,636 | 59.8 | 79.3 | 14.2 | 17.1 | 12.7 |
| Education ............. | 143,830 | 15.0 | 19.9 | 11.1 | 6.4 | 11.5 |
| Public welfare ......... | 64,764 | 6.8 | 9.0 | 9.5 | 2.6 | 12.7 |
| Interest on general debt .... | 76,033 | 7.9 | 10.5 | 23.1 | 25.7 | 13.6 |
| Health and hospitals .... | 43,310 | 4.5 | 6.0 | 16.6 | 24.7 | 14.0 |
| Highways ............ | 33,745 | 3.5 | 4.7 | 16.4 | 3.8 | 17.1 |
| Natural resources ...... | 35,243 | 3.7 | 4.9 | 16.2 | 16.0 | 17.1 |
| Postal service ........ | 18,177 | 1.9 | 2.5 | 9.6 | 9.6 | (X) |
| Police protection ....... | 15,233 | 1.6 | 2.1 | 9.3 | 0.9 | 10.5 |
| Veterans' services, n.e.c. ..... | 12,504 | 1.3 | 1.7 | 7.7 | 7.7 | 15.1 |
| Sanitation .......... | 13,214 | 1.4 | 1.8 | 12.1 | (X) | 12.1 |
| Fire protection ........ | 5,718 | 0.6 | 0.8 | 11.1 | (X) | 11.1 |
| Other functions ....... | 111,865 | 11.7 | 15.5 | 16.2 | 23.3 | 12.5 |
| Utility expenditure ......... | 33,599 | 3.5 | (X) | 18.2 | (X) | 18.2 |
| Liquor stores expenditure ...... | 2,591 | 0.3 | (X) | 7.2 | (X) | 7.2 |
| Insurance trust expenditure ...... | 199,373 | 20.8 | (X) | 16.7 | 15.8 | 22.5 |

X Not applicable.
[1] Excludes intergovernmental expenditure.
Source: U.S. Bureau of the Census, *Government Finances in 1979–80* (Washington: U.S. Government Printing Office, 1981), p. 7.

Comparisons of this nature, however, are dangerous and can be misleading due to variations in the governmental structure in urban areas. Educational expenditures, for instance, were not mentioned in the above discussion because education in most communities is administered by an independent district with its own discretionary functions in taxation, expenditure, and budgetary process.

Also important is the location of the city within its metropolitan area. These factors are referred to as central city–suburban differences, differences that are usually studied as variations in levels of expenditure. This comparison breaks down with the addition of the dimension of governmental differences. Many are fond of quoting statistics showing how much more the suburbs spend on education than do the central cities. When the figures are studied in depth, however, we find that suburban educational expenditures are seldom included in municipal expenditures, since most suburban school districts are independent. This factor helps to contribute to a picture of higher governmental costs in central cities and lower ones in the suburbs—an unfortunate image that is an oversimplification.

Lately, we have seen the growth in popularity of another theory of local expenditure differences. Charles M. Tiebout bases his theory on an economic model that seeks to study municipalities as producers of goods and services in competition with other such producers for residents who fulfill the roles of consumers and voters.[10] These consumer-voters select as their place of residence a community whose service "package" comes closest to meeting their particular demands. This is seen as being especially true of suburban areas. Consumer-voters are seen as an important consideration in the selection of expenditure patterns that serve to maintain satisfaction among existing populations while attracting new residents and industries to the community.

The budget, therefore, becomes a policy instrument. In recent years, increasing effort has been put into its preparation. Since most city councils see their job as one of paring the budget, with an emphasis on reducing expenditures for some items and deleting others completely, the task of deciding what will be included in the budget and how much money will be allocated becomes crucial.

An appropriation act may be of the lump-sum type, or it may be itemized. Under the lump-sum plan, each spending agency is granted its funds in a single amount. While this approach encourages flexibility, which is desirable, its successful execution depends on the ability of department heads and their financial officers to plan carefully and competently.

In contrast, itemization of appropriations furthers administrative planning, but it may result in undue rigidity. Generally, highly segregated appropriations—how much may be spent for what—are looked on with disfavor by fiscal experts. One device they do favor in order to maintain administrative control while keeping a good deal of flexibility is the allotment system. Under this plan, each department head is required to divide the total appropriation into four or twelve parts, depending upon whether the allotments are quarterly or monthly. Expenditure controls are thereby established in that the accounting officer will not approve expenditures during a particular quarter or month in excess of the allotment. Of course, the expenditure pattern may be revised from time to time if the department head can make a good enough case to the chief executive.

The most commonly used budgeting process is the incremental approach. In the incremental approach, each municipal department assumes that it will receive at least as much funding in the upcoming fiscal year as it did in the current one. The only decision remaining is one of increase—how much more will this department need to run its desired programs next year?

Incremental budgeting also tends to minimize the amount of conflict inherent in the budgetary process, thereby lessening the opportunities for challenges to the budget as presented to the council. This encourages compromise among the various interest groups within the city as well as among the departments and agencies of the government itself.

## Capital Budgets

The capital budget complements the regular budgeting process as a financial planning tool. It details proposed capital expenditures and the means for financing them. A capital expenditure is used to construct or to purchase a facility that is expected to provide services over a considerable period of time.[11] Rather than raising tax rates each time a capital project is required, the local government sells bonds to finance the project. The process is similar to the way we purchase a home by taking out a mortgage and making monthly payments instead of paying for the home at the time of purchase.

A capital budget program is founded on economic base studies, land use reports, and population and migration studies. Data on existing industries, city economic history, and an analysis of economic development trends are contained in economic base studies. The land use reports reflect population densities and inventories of property developments. Population characteristics, income, and human resources are provided in population and migration studies.[12] These demographic studies help planners determine the future needs for schools, streets, parks, and highways.

Capital projects possess characteristics that incline them to be controlled through a capital budget. They are durable and have a long-term effect on communities; thus, they require long-range planning. Decisions about capital projects are irreversible for an extended period and, without adequate consideration, could result in long-lasting and costly mistakes. Another justification for the capital budget is that without special programming, important municipal expenditures would be postponed. Capital projects are also sporadic, and their tendency to be concentrated in short periods can be counteracted through the leveling effects of a planned schedule of bond offerings.[13]

In recent years it has become much more difficult to gain voter approval of bond referenda, particularly for schools. Business groups, parochial and private school parents, and childless couples have formed coalitions to keep taxes down by opposing many of these referenda.

The advantage of capital budgeting is that it makes possible some measure of long-range planning. Capital and operating budgets may be distinct parts of the same budget document or separate documents. This distinction has been made in the financial operations of large corporations for many decades, and governments have tended to imitate corporate practice in this and other fiscal areas.

Why do governments borrow? The most common purposes are: (1) in the anticipation of revenues, (2) for expenditures arising from emergencies, and (3) for construction of public improvements—most of which will last a long time. There is nothing immoral about a government's borrowing money; almost all governments find it necessary or desirable to do so at one time or another. It is when the debt ceiling, imposed by a constitution or statute, has been reached that the real problems begin. When, in the summer of 1975, the banks of New York City refused to buy a bond issue proposed by that city, everyone knew that New York City was on the brink of fiscal collapse. It survived, of course, but only at the sacrifice of numerous public services and the discharging of thousands of municipal employees.

## Financial Administration

We can directly ascribe some of the blame for our current urban economic crisis to the mismanagement of our urban finances on many different levels. The problem of assessments is a case in point. Many communities that still elect their assessment officials have burdened themselves (unnecessarily, at that) with unqualified and incapable assessors. The National Association of Assessing Officers now recommends that assessors be appointed and serve under a merit system. This would remove or lessen the pressures that are often applied by special interests. This point should be well taken by those communities that have had to indict their elected assessors (e.g., San Francisco, Oakland, San Diego, and Los Angeles) for felonies, including the taking of bribes.

Local pressures, however, are only one factor in the difficulties involving the whole assessment process. After the valuation of the property has been established, there are two methods by which it can be challenged. An individual may first appeal to the local office of tax appeals, which will review the assessment, perhaps adjusting it. After all administrative appeals are tried, the case may then be taken into the trial courts.

The second method is that of equalization. In every community, there is a local agency whose responsibility it is to make sure that all property is assessed properly. This agency has the power to raise or lower assessments in order to maintain fair market values at the established legal levels.

In addition, the assessor is faced with a growing number of properties that have been exempted from taxation. These properties include publicly owned real estate, as well as churches, charitable institutions, cultural organizations, veterans organizations, and others. The hopefully-apocryphal tale is one of the assessor who never assessed the property of one M. E. Church in the belief that it was tax exempt as a religious structure, when, actually, M. E. Church was simply the name of the property owner!

At any rate, these tax exemptions present a serious erosion of the urban tax base and are a concern for all governments. Any meaningful tax reform must bring with it a reduction of these tax exemptions to the barest possible minimum.

Attempts at tax reform present the same type of battle as initial taxation does. Reforms are always being suggested, but seldom are successful. If our cities are to keep their financial heads above water, however, they must begin to realize that some sort of tax reform is imperative. Since the tax that seems to be facing the greatest difficulties is the property tax, and since property taxes continue as the major important revenue source of most communities, it is the form of taxation most under fire by individuals and organizations that seek tax reform. Several major suggestions seem to be fairly universal.

Weaknesses in the system of taxation at all levels could be remedied by the initiation of an administration staffed and run by professionals. The elimination of such small assessing jurisdictions as townships and villages, while a politically unpopular suggestion, would acknowledge that such divisions are too small in area and population and too poor to finance an adequate assessment and collection program. Cities and school districts are more manageable in size and, therefore, form more reasonable divisions for efficient and successful financial administration.

When state governments limit tax ceilings for local jurisdictions, they often fail to take into consideration the varying fiscal capabilities of these localities. The elimination of these tax rate limits would facilitate the development of taxing policies that would be more suited to the individual communities they should be designed to serve. The opposition to a reform of this nature is enough, however, to render the removal of tax ceilings a politically unfeasible reform. Though we elect our local councils and feel that they are responsible and remain politically sensitive to the needs and desires of their constituents, we seem to fear that, given the power, they would go berserk and we could be faced with taxation amounting to confiscation. Why we allow taxing limitations to be set by other popularly elected officials who differ from their local counterparts only in their distance from their electorates is one question no expert seems to be able to answer.

Special levies, which many jurisdictions use to raise funds for anything from pensions for firemen to the support of art museums, are seen to be unnecessary as well as additional complications to any efficient fiscal system. The ideal would be to combine all these into one levy for the general fund.

States are beginning to answer the call of localities with inadequate property tax bases by allowing them to tax other forms of wealth. This developing emphasis on home rule in taxation policy is seen by many tax experts to be a good trend that should continue. The new emphasis on personal income taxes on the state and local level, while tapping a rich source, has brought with it many problems. For the most part, these tax gross income with no allowable exemptions. The tax is most often a flat rate tax, not the graduated type that forms the base for the federal income tax. Also, local income taxes rarely reach unearned incomes of interest, dividends, and capital gains. By taxing at a flat rate, these become regressive taxes, unfairly burdening those least able to pay them. Some labor leaders have gone so far as to term local income taxes "vicious" and "reactionary." The administration of these local income taxes is often inequitable, as both residents and non-residents are subject to income taxation on the local level. With the trend toward income taxation beginning in central cities and then being adopted in outlying suburbs, some individuals can have their gross income taxed twice—where they work and again where they live. Pennsylvania, one state that allows localities to tax income, has sought to eliminate this inequity by legislating that the place of residence should take precedence over the place of employment when both jurisdictions tax an individual's gross income. This regulation, however, does exempt Philadelphia, which was given exclusive powers to tax the gross income of the persons employed within its municipal boundaries.

## The Effect of Recession on State and Local Finance

The national recession of the early and mid-1970s, coupled with the unparalleled combination of inflation and massive unemployment, created severe financial problems for states and localities. But the impact was uneven. According to a survey by the Joint Economic Committee of Congress, an estimated $3.6 billion in new levies were added in the fiscal year that ended on June 30, 1975.[14] Of forty-eight states responding to the survey, twenty said they were raising existing taxes or imposing new ones—and some were doing both. These states added a total of $2.1 billion to their tax collections. Nearly 40 percent of the additional state taxes came from boosting levies on personal income.

Of 140 local governments surveyed by the committee, 52 raised taxes during the same fiscal year by a total of $850 million. Nationwide, local tax increases were reported to have gone up by a total of $1.5 billion, mostly on property and sales.

While they were increasing taxes, states and localities were also cutting back on services. The committee estimated that service cutbacks would save $3.3 billion. In addition, up to $1 billion in capital construction was delayed or cancelled.

Strapped for cash, the states engaged in vigorous warfare against tax dodgers. Particular targets were corporations that pay far less in taxes than the law demands, cigarette smugglers (who cheat Connecticut, for instance, out of an estimated $15 million annually), individuals who are supposed to pay sales taxes but refrain from doing so, and landlords who abandon properties in order to avoid property taxes. Especially in the Northeast, it was reported to be increasingly difficult to collect property taxes. In New York City, for example, the delinquency rate in 1975 stood at 7.6 percent, which meant adding $220 million to the $320 million in delinquencies already outstanding.

A survey was made in mid-1975 by the National League of Cities of sixty-seven cities.[15] The results underlined the findings of the congressional study. Forty-two cities planned to hike taxes or cut services, or both, and thirty-six had delayed capital improvement programs. What this amounts to is a reversal of a trend toward bigger budgets, new services, and expanding payrolls that had gone on for nearly thirty years in most cities.

Some examples illustrate the nationwide character of the crises. Detroit withdrew guards from public-housing projects. Cleveland cut its city payroll from 13,000 in 1970 to 10,800 in 1975. Baltimore cut its budget so drastically that the city payroll in 1975 was 25 percent less than it had been in 1972. Bridgeport, Connecticut, fired 15 percent of that city's entire payroll. Boston reduced the city subsidy to hospitals by 20 percent.

Chicago followed a different route. It made no cuts in services and fired no city employees. But it drastically raised taxes. Atlanta did the same thing. San Francisco cut its school budget and ruled out pay hikes for teachers. Dallas deferred purchasing equipment needed for its parks and recreational areas. Newark, New Jersey, simply fired large numbers of police and fire fighters. Hartford began to phase out its famous children's zoo. Berkeley, California, cut its library from twenty-six thousand to nineteen thousand volumes between 1972 and 1975 and reduced operating hours. The list could go on indefinitely.

Yet there was one big city that had lots of money to spend—Houston. In nearly every way, Houston was expanding. It undertook to spend $422 million in a two-year capital improvement program. Included in this expansion were 4,500 streetlights, a massive sewer-building and reclamation project, twelve new fire stations, three new branch libraries, and five neighborhood multiservice centers. It also planned to expand many departments, including the police. In addition, Houston purchased the local bus system in 1975 with federal help and ordered a hundred new buses. Not only were there no tax increases, but property taxes were *decreased* in 1975. In 1975, the city was running a small surplus. Needless to say, its bond rating was increased to AAA—the highest.

## Default and Bankruptcy

The financial difficulties of New York and scores of other cities in the mid-1970s naturally raised questions regarding the possibilities of default and bankruptcy by municipalities. A distinction must be made between the two items. Under default, the payment of bills is deferred (as happened in the case of New York State's Urban Development Corporation). Under bankruptcy, a court supervises the affairs of a debtor, deciding who should get paid for what.

In the Depression years before World War II, 140 cities defaulted on bond issues. But most recent cases of so-called municipal defaults deal with such things as toll-bridge authorities that can sell tax-exempt securities. These are known in the trade as *municipals*.

In 1946, Congress amended the bankruptcy laws by setting up a procedure for a court-supervised municipal bankruptcy. But most experts on the subject believe that federal bankruptcy laws simply would not have any practical application to New York or other large cities. For example, the law requires a city to file for court supervision, with the written consent to a payment plan of holders of 51 percent of the city's debt. But as one lawyer noted, "City debt is all over the place. Nobody knows who holds it." In addition, few politicians want their cities to be run by the courts.[16]

## Some Problems for the 1980s

The present trend toward limiting taxes is attributed to the passage of Proposition 13 in California in 1978. By constitutional amendment, ceilings were placed on local property taxes. Emboldened by their success in Proposition 13, Howard Jarvis and his associates placed Proposition 9 on the ballot during the summer of 1980. This would have cut state income taxes by 50 percent. Not wishing to go into statewide austerity, the California voters defeated Proposition 9 by a substantial majority.

Yet the move for mandated tax limitations continued. Several propositions relating to tax ceilings were on various state ballots for the elections of November 4, 1980. Of the proposals that were approved by the voters, Proposition 2½ in Massachusetts probably will have the most drastic effects. The amendment provided that the property tax level be reduced from 10 percent of its fair market value to 2½ percent.

As a result, Boston made immediate plans for 25 percent cuts in funds for the police and fire departments, 60 percent for the parks department, and 30 percent for the public works department.

Part of the frustration evidenced by Massachusetts voters in approving the amendment stemmed from the practice of the state legislature in adopting expensive programs and then mandating communities to pay for them through property taxes.[17] By the early 1980s, nineteen states had passed some form of tax limitation.

In 1981 and 1982 the states began raising taxes in an attempt to offset federal program cuts and declining revenues. Half of the states raised gas, motor, and fuel taxes, while sixteen states raised the tax on alcohol, eleven states raised cigarette taxes, thirteen increased sales taxes, and eight raised personal income taxes.

By 1983 the states were reacting to the economic recession in several different ways. Thirty-one states increased a variety of taxes in order to raise more than $8 billion. Forty-one states cut or limited their spending, and nineteen froze state employee salaries. Twenty-three states were forced to cut their workforce, while several states actually spent less money in 1983 than in 1982.[18]

The recession of the early 1980s has also had a devastating impact upon the cities. Faced with declining revenues and state restrictions on their taxing powers, cities were forced to look to their states and the federal government for financial assistance. However, the Reagan administration drastically reduced federal funding for domestic social programs. The states, many of which had been running budget surpluses in 1980, found themselves under severe financial pressure in 1981, 1982, and 1983. Several states ended the 1983 fiscal year with a deficit, making it extremely difficult for them to provide additional aid to their cities.

Responses to a survey administered by the Joint Economic Committee of Congress indicated that 43 percent of the responding cities had a 1982 budget deficit and 64 percent had a deficit in 1983. The biggest problems were in cities of 50–100,000 population.

Early in 1984 the National League of Cities (NLC) released the findings from its policy working paper on the fiscal outlook for cities in fiscal year 1984. The NLC paper concluded that about half the cities responding to their survey reported they were emerging from the recession in a strong position. However, these cities were not enthusiastic about a complete recovery in 1984.[19]

According to Roy Bahl of Syracuse University, it is virtually impossible to separate the performance of the national economy from the fiscal well-being of state and local governments.[20] In analyzing the factors that are likely to shape the outlook for cities in the 1980s, Bahl cited the U.S. economy as the most important.

The U.S. economy is growing more slowly in the 1980s than it did in the 1960s and 1970s. Over the past twenty years the Gross National Product (GNP) grew at an average rate of 4.5 percent per year. The most optimistic growth rate predictions for the 1980s are in the 3–4 percent per year range, and there are numerous economists who believe these figures may be too high.

A second factor relates to the uneven pattern of growth that is likely to occur. Not all regions of the country will grow at the same rate; consequently, some areas will be much harder hit during recessions than other areas. Over the years we have seen patterns develop in which some regions and their states go into a recession first and go in deeper than other regions. These hardest-hit regions also take longer to emerge and are usually worse off than their neighboring regions. The industrialized states in the Northeast and Midwest are typical of the pattern, and it is the large cities in those areas that feel the financial pressure the most.

A third issue in the 1980s is the regional shift in population. Almost all forecasters agree that the population migration of people from the North and East to the South and West will continue through the end of this century. The population shift away from the North and East has a negative impact on tax revenues, new businesses, and jobs. All of these effects fall hardest on the largest and most industrialized cities in the areas.

There is some speculation that a new economic equilibrium is beginning to emerge. Some areas in the South and Southwest have reached their saturation point and are no longer the appealing homelands they once were. With growth have come problems of crime, rising taxes, land use control, building codes, environmental concerns, educational quality, and inadequate public transportation.

Furthermore, the recession of the 1980s has hit the sunbelt pretty hard. California has serious unemployment, budget, and financial problems, while states like Texas and Louisiana for the first time have had to borrow funds from the federal government to meet their residents' claims for unemployment insurance. Lowering oil prices also reduced some of the attractiveness of living in the sunbelt. Sunbelt states produce oil, and lower prices mean less revenue.

The failure of Congress to pass a federal budget early enough in fiscal years 1982, 1983, or 1984, at the same time as the Reagan administration was cutting federal programs, upset state and local revenue projections. Under the best of circumstances, state and local governments are completing their annual budgets months before the federal budget is approved. Without a federal budget, even the best state and local revenue projects are suspect. Coupled with declining tax revenues, this creates a situation in which local governments are at the mercy of both national and international economic conditions and the uncertainty of federal budget and program decisions.

## Cutback Management

Perhaps the most serious problem facing local governments in the 1980s is going to be what Charles Levine calls organizational decline and cutback management. Cutback management refers to

> managing organizational change toward lower levels of resource consumption and organizational activity. Cutting back an organization involves making hard decisions about who will be let go, what programs will be scaled down or terminated, and what clients will be asked to make sacrifices.[21]

Limits on tax revenues, combined with large cuts in federal aid, have forced local officials to make better use of the available revenues. These officials are also learning to adjust to a shrinking revenue pie.

As more and more governments try to cope with a deteriorating economic environment, characterized by high interest rates, diminished tax revenues, high unemployment, and numerous bankruptcies, difficult political and administrative decisions will have to be made. Reducing the size and scope of local government raises several issues related to resource scarcity. First, unlike organizations that are growing, declining organizations have no incentives to offer their personnel. This reduces the likelihood that proposals for change will be received favorably. Second, public organizations have numerous built-in impediments to quick, effective management decision-making. These include civil service regulations, union contracts, and court orders on equal employment opportunity. Third, organizations undergoing budgeting, personnel, and program cuts develop low morale, which hampers the productivity necessary to overcome the cuts. Fourth, declining organizations become more conservative. Fewer risks are taken, and innovation and initiative wane.[22]

The hard choices to be made concern the tactics employed for reducing the size of the organization. The most frequently discussed issue is "equity vs. efficiency" approach. The equity approach is the one preferred by most managers, since it has an element of justice in it, it is easy to defend to client groups, and it requires little or no in-depth analysis to discriminate among programs. Each department is asked to take the same cut, thereby eliminating charges of favoritism or political influence.

The efficiency approach generates more problems because it requires targeting for cuts some programs that, after analysis, appear to be inefficient. Much staff time is required to assess each program's contribution to the overall mission of the department. Ranking programs and evaluating them economically, politically, and socially often leads to bitter debates. In some cases the methodology used in the assessment becomes more the issue than the program. Client groups also involve themselves in these deliberations, hoping to convince administrators that programs they favor are more worthy of continued departmental funding.

A third approach concerns the extent of the cuts to be made. Should organizations attempt to make small cuts each year, hoping that the economic situation will reverse itself and the agency will begin to grow again? Or should agencies resort to deep cuts early in the process and gamble that funding to rebuild the organization will be available in later years? Levine points out that the deep cut approach may make good management sense, but the decremental approach may be the only feasible political strategy available.[23]

Local governments have begun coping with cutback management in an effort to bring spending in line with revenues while continuing to provide services to citizens in need. Several studies have begun to analyze the administrative and political processes involved in cutback management.[24]

## Conclusions

We have tried to make the case that state and local finance is an integral part of the political process. The budget sets political, as well as economic, priorities. Revenue policy and expenditure policy both reflect the values of the society as perceived and understood by the political branches of government. From time to time, one or another emphasis may shift in response to changes in demands made upon the decision-making agencies.

Cities are faced with many problems, and a number of them are financial in nature. Severe revenue limits are placed upon cities by states, but city revenues are also severely limited by national economic policy, which has an impact upon inflation, unemployment, recession, and interest rates. This has been true in the growing cities as well as in the stagnating ones.

Given these difficult economic conditions, it is conceivable that cities will not be able to assume the responsibilities assigned to them under the various New Federalism proposals. To combat adverse economic factors that drive revenues down, cities often raise taxes. This can backfire by encouraging businesses to look elsewhere for more favorable tax situations, which lowers the home city's revenues again and perpetuates the cycle.

One alternative to raising taxes is for cities to begin a program of cutback management. Several techniques are available to city officials in determining how to reduce costs. Few of the choices are pleasant to make or easy to implement since they involve committing fewer resources to programs and employees. Each of these choices has political and administrative ramifications for the political actors in the city. Cutback management policies often help to redistribute power within the urban political system.[25]

# NOTES

1. Sumner Benson, "A History of the General Property Tax," in *The American Property Tax: Its History, Administration and Economic Impact,* ed. George C. S. Benson (Claremont, Calif., 1965), pp. 34–44, 52–59.

2. *State and Local Taxes: Significant Features, 1968* (Washington: Advisory Commission on Intergovernmental Affairs, 1968), p. 7. Also see *Significant Features of Fiscal Federalism, 1980–81* (Washington: Advisory Commission on Intergovernmental Relations, December, 1981), pp. 44–45.

3. In a survey conducted by the Advisory Commission, the property tax ranked just behind the federal income tax as the least fair tax paid by the public. See *Changing Public Attitudes on Governments and Taxes* (Washington: Advisory Commission on Intergovernmental Relations, 1981), p. 4.

4. For a discussion of different types of revenue sources, see Richard D. Bingham, Brett W. Hawkins, and F. Ted Hebert, *The Politics of Raising State and Local Revenue* (New York: Praeger, 1978), pp. 97–104.

5. Martin Shefter, "New York City's Fiscal Crisis: The Politics of Inflation and Retrenchment," *The Public Interest* 48 (Summer 1978): 108.

6. For a discussion of the New York City fiscal crisis, see Shefter, "New York City's Fiscal Crisis," pp. 98–127. Also see Charles H. Levine, Irene S. Rubin, and George G. Wolohojian, *The Politics of Retrenchment: How Local Governments Manage Fiscal Stress* (Beverly Hills: Sage Publications, 1981), pp. 21–35; Donald Haider, "Sayre and Kaufman Revisited: New York City Government Since 1965," *Urban Affairs Quarterly* 15 (December 1979): 123–45; and Robert W. Bailey, *The Crisis Regime: The M.A.C., the E.F.C.B., and the Political Impact of the New York City Financial Crisis* (Albany: SUNY Press, 1984).

7. Fred Ferretti, "Ford Rejects a Plea by Beame For Help," *New York Times,* May 15, 1975. A survey by the *New York Times* showed that New Yorkers were currently subjected to twenty-two different kinds of taxes. To meet the city's projected deficit, Mayor Beame was reported to be looking into additional types of taxes as well as increasing many of the existing ones. Peter Kihss, "New Yorkers Subjected to 22 Different Kinds of Taxes," *New York Times,* May 15, 1975.

8. Three other sources of information on New York's fiscal crisis are Fred Ferretti, *The Year The Big Apple Went Bust* (New York: Putnam, 1976); Raymond D.

Horton, *The City in Transition: Prospects and Policies for New York* (New York: City of New York, Temporary Commission on City Finances, 1977); and *Summary: The Long-Term Fiscal Outlook for New York City* (Washington, D.C.: Comptroller General of the United States, April 4, 1977).

9. For an overview of citizen feelings about taxes, see *Changing Attitudes on Governments and Taxes*, 1981.

10. Charles M. Tiebout, "A Pure Theory of Local Expenditures," *Journal of Political Economy* 64 (1956): 416–24.

11. J. Richard Aronson and Eli Schwartz, *Management Policies in Local Government Finance* (Washington: International City Management Association, 1975), p. 303.

12. Ibid., p. 310.

13. Ibid., pp. 304 and 306.

14. "Strapped for Cash, States Go After Tax Dodgers," *U.S. News and World Report*, June 23, 1975, pp. 66–68.

15. "How Slump Is Hurting Cities," *U.S. News and World Report*, June 30, 1975, p. 18. Also see *The States and Distressed Communities: The 1980 Annual Report* (Washington: Advisory Commission on Intergovernmental Relations, May, 1981).

16. Maurice Carroll, "Panel to Explore What Happens if City Defaults," *New York Times*, July 23, 1975.

17. See Marcia Whicker Taylor, "State Mandated Local Expenditures: Are They Panacea or Plague?", *National Civic Review*, vol. 69, no. 8 (September 1980): 435–441. She concludes: "Mandates need closer monitoring before the practice runs amok." Also see Peter J. May and Arnold J. Meltsner, "Limited Actions, Distressing Consequences: A Selected view of the California Experience," *Public Administration Review* 41 (January 1981): 172–79. One study that summarizes numerous urban cost cutting approaches is Robert W. Poole, Jr., *Cutting Back City Hall* (New York: Universe Books, 1980).

18. These data were compiled from reports of the Advisory Commission on Intergovernmental Relations and publications of several public interest groups such as the National Governors' Association.

19. See Francis Viscount, *City Fiscal Conditions and Outlook for Fiscal 1984: Resourcefulness vs. Resources* (Washington, D.C.: National League of Cities, December 1983).

20. Roy Bahl, "State and Local Government Finance in a Changing National Economy," paper delivered at the Annual Conference of the Urban Affairs Association, Flint, Michigan, March 24, 1982. An expanded version of this paper appears as Chapter 6 in *Financing State and Local Governments in the 1980s* (New York: Oxford University Press, 1984).

21. See Charles H. Levine, "More on Cutback Management: Hard Questions for Hard Times," *Public Administration Review* 39 (March/April 1979): 1; and Charles H. Levine, "Organizational Decline and Cutback Management," *Public Administration Review* 38 (July/August 1978): 316–25.

22. Levine, "More on Cutback Management," p. 180. Also see Mark Weinberg, "The Urban Fiscal Crisis Impact on Budgeting and Financial Planning Practices of Urban America," *Journal of Urban Affairs* 6 (Winter 1984): 39–52.

23. Levine, "Organizational Decline," p. 320; and Levine, "More on Cutback Management," pp. 181–82.

24. See Levine, Rubin, and Wolohojian, *The Politics of Retrenchment*, for a comparative analysis of how Oakland, Baltimore, Cincinnati, and Prince Georges County, Maryland, dealt with the issues of retrenchment. Also see Charles H. Levine, ed., "Organizational Decline and Cutback Management," *Public Administration Review* 38 (July/August 1978): 315–358; and Jeffrey McCaffery, "The Impact of Resource Scarcity on Urban Public Finance," *Public Administration Review* 41 (January 1981), whole issue. These two symposia contain

over fifteen articles on the subject of fiscal constraints in local governments and organizations in general.

25. For further references, see the following: L. Laszlo Ecker-Racz, *It's Your Business: Local and State Finance* (New York: National Municipal League, 1976); Charles H. Levine, *Managing Fiscal Stress: The Crisis in the Public Sector* (Chatham, N.J.: Chatham House, 1980); John E. Peterson and Catherine Lavigne Spain, *Essays in Public Finance and Financial Management* (Chatham, N.J.: Chatham House, 1980); Terry Nichols Clark and Lorna Crowley Ferguson, *City Money: Political Processes, Fiscal Strain and Retrenchment* (New York: Columbia University Press, 1983); and Robert W. Burchell and David Listokin, *Cities Under Stress: The Fiscal Crises of Urban America* (Piscataway, N.J.: Center for Urban Policy Research, Rutgers University, 1981).

# 13.   URBAN AMERICA IN THE 1980s

Our analysis has continued to point out that traditional brokerage politics has become outmoded in dealing with present-day realities of the urban political situation. In particular, we have noted how the group theory and community/state dichotomy of the pluralistic model are incapable of leading to the sound political decisions that are needed for our contemporary cities to survive.

Under the circumstances, it is natural to look for a more satisfactory explanation of urban politics than that offered by the now discredited official doctrine. A new model of urban politics—one that is in harmony with the present urban world—seems to be developing. An analysis of developments that are emerging from the real world of metropolitan and city politics may reveal at least some of the principal elements that will go into a new and more relevant model. To put the matter somewhat differently, if we could identify the leading elements in the developing New Style politics, we should be able to make considerable progress in building a new model to replace the pluralistic one, which we found to be no longer functional.

## NEW DEVELOPMENTS AND CHANGING RELATIONSHIPS

### Racial and Ethnic Realignments

Race and ethnicity, along with income and religion, have long provided fairly reliable indicators of how given sections of the electorate would vote. This has always been understood by brokerage politicians. During the last thirty years the relative impact of the different factors on voting behavior has been intensively studied by social scientists. There is nothing at all novel, then, in pointing to the existence of racial and ethnic voting patterns in urban areas.

What *is* different is the suggestion that large racial and ethnic groups should turn from the role of party-supporter to that of interest-group manipulator. It involves a shift from the idea, for example, that New York City blacks should automatically support the Democrats to the belief that blacks should back any party that offers the most to blacks. As Harry Bailey has said, "There does seem to be some indication that it—the black vote—is growing more sophisticated and is prepared to move to whichever parties and candidates offer the best policies and programs commensurate with Negro needs."[1] This might mean throwing the bulk of black strength to the Republicans one year, to the liberals or conservatives another year, and perhaps eventually back to the Democrats. This would be based on the conviction that the politics of interest groups offers a more substantial payoff than the politics of the traditional parties.

This is an extension of the bloc concept, which certain black leaders had in mind when they put together the necessary coalitions in Philadelphia and Chicago to elect black mayors. To the extent that this new politics of race is successful in large cities, it will involve the formation of new types of intrastate coalitions. This will be so because black-controlled urban parties will—for many reasons—have to come to understandings and arrangements with the white-dominated parties of the suburbs and of the states at large.

But blacks are not the only unassimilated racial group that seeks racial objectives through political action. A new militancy on the part of Mexican-Americans is emerging, and its urban manifestations are particularly evident in Los Angeles, San Antonio, Houston, and Denver. In Cesar Chavez, the organizer of agricultural workers, the Chicanos found their first leader of national stature. There are millions of Mexican-Americans in the United States, and many of them live in rural areas. Yet where they have heavy urban concentrations, they may be expected increasingly to play a more active political role—both inside the parties and as an interest group. Like "black power," "brown power" may take varying political forms. New alignments and new coalitions will undoubtedly be forged in many cities of California and the Southwest.[2]

Yet the newest rallying cry in urban politics relates not to black or brown groups but to white ethnic groups. As Paul Mundy, a Loyola University sociologist, put it: "The third generation remembers what the second generation would like to forget—its ethnic identity."[3]

"Ethnic power" comes from first- and second-generation "hyphenated" white Americans, most of whose members live in fifty-eight major industrial cities, and who are said to number over 40 million persons.[4] The roots of this large group lie in Central and Southern Europe. Its members are primarily in the working class. The "ethnic American" experienced a growing degree of frustration, dissatisfaction, and alienation throughout the 1960s.

In analyzing the reasons for this large-scale disaffection, Congresswoman Barbara Mikulski, a spokesman for the Polish community in Baltimore, singled out several factors.[5] These included unfavorable treatment of ethnic Americans in the mass media, neglect by all levels of government, inferior housing and educational facilities, and scorn from limousine-liberals. But the most important reason for complaint was economic. As members of the working class, ethnic Americans were too "rich" for their children to receive scholarship aid, too "poor" to afford private schooling, too "poor" to buy a house of their own, but too "rich" to qualify for Federal housing aid. Generally, they were losing ground economically, and they felt that no one noticed or cared. From their point of view, most government programs were tailored to help the blacks, or the suburban middle class, or the rich—never the 40 million ethnics.

Under these circumstances, city-dwelling ethnic Americans began to look more towards their own heritage.[6] In northern cities, communities of such citizens began to attach a new importance to a cultural identity that had earlier faded when confronted with the "American dream."

In striving to make themselves heard, ethnic groups deliberately adopted the same tactics that had been used by black civil rights activists. In Cleveland, for example, such groups demanded a voice on municipal boards and commissions. They also insisted on their right to examine school textbooks "to be sure an ethnic identity could be found in the history books our children study."[7] In Pittsburgh, the Pan Slavic Alliance, inactive for many years, was revived and began to agitate for government-sponsored research centers. Italian-Americans organized in order to expose misrepresentations of their group in the mass media.

It took some time for national religious leaders to take seriously the complaints arising from ethnic neighborhoods. In Chicago, many of these complaints were related to resistance to the efforts of the Rev. Martin Luther King, Jr., and other black leaders to desegregate all-white residential areas. The white ethnic communities were mostly Roman Catholic or Jewish. In looking for assistance, they turned to their national religious leaders, but the response, from the point of view of the ethnic groups, was inadequate and unhelpful.[8]

Eventually, when the national leadership began to understand the seriousness of the problem, in Chicago and elsewhere steps were taken to cope with the overall situation. The American Jewish Committee organized the first national "Consultation on Ethnic Americans" at Fordham University in June, 1968. A short while afterward the National Conference of Catholic Bishops established a Task Force on Urban Problems.[9]

Whether anyone can unite the Poles, Italians, Germans, Hungarians, Greeks, and others who constitute ethnic America into a cohesive electoral bloc would seem to be most unlikely. Yet, in particular cities at particular times, local electoral alliances of the ethnics could prove to be pivotal.

## Cities and Suburbs

The 1980 census confirmed what had been developing for the past fifteen years—the population of the suburbs continued to grow larger than that of the central cities. Looking into the political future, does this mean that the politics of metropolitan areas will increasingly be dominated by the politics of the suburbs? Will the political systems of the suburbs become the dominant systems in urban politics?

There are reasons for believing that the response to these questions is no. In the first place, America's suburbs vary economically, ethnically, and racially, and their political interests are not identical. Even though the suburban political systems are becoming increasingly autonomous in relation to the systems of the central cities, the suburban systems are not as alike as peas in a pod. They compete with each other as well as with the central cities. It is also a mistake to separate too sharply the governmental concerns of the suburbs from those of the central cities. Education, policing, and public housing may be locally managed, but transportation, air and water pollution, sewage disposal and water supply, welfare, and many aspects of land use and planning are usually considered to require regional management.

To put the matter in this way is not to deny that there are, more often than not, substantial political differences between the central cities and the suburbs. As was noted previously, the central city in the northern half of the country is now generally Democratic and is surrounded by Republican suburbs. There is the possibility that conflict over race in the central cities may drive a wedge in the Democratic party coalition between blacks and low-income white ethnics. Or substantial groups of working class ethnics might, given increasing affluence, move to the suburbs in response to what they regard as black aggression. In commenting on this situation, Thomas R. Dye has asserted that these party differences suggest that for many years to come it will be difficult, if not impossible, to achieve the consolidation of metropolitan governments.[10]

Though he did not stress the political aspects of consolidating governments in metropolitan regions, Charles E. Gilbert arrived at the same conclusion as Dye. Gilbert was dubious that regionalism, metropolitan government, or structural changes could bring about a rational public policy for large urban areas.[11] He came to this conclusion after studying the counties that surround Philadelphia. He favored a revitalization of county government as the most hopeful means of dealing with the needs of the metropolitan area. Admitting that some might find this position "seemingly conservative," Gilbert nonetheless added, "On the other hand, neither administrative, political, nor social analysis leads on to thoroughgoing regional consolidation."[12]

Known under various titles, but most frequently that of "metropolitan government," is a proposal that calls for the consolidation of the various units of government within the metropolitan region. The objectives have usually been stated in economic terms—for example, greater operating efficiency, enlarged financial resources, and more adequate public services. Taxpayers' organizations and economy leagues—self-appointed watchdogs over the public treasuries—were at one time the front ranks of organizations advocating metropolitan government.

In the last two decades the initial glow of enthusiasm for this plan has faded. One reason, suggested in Robert C. Wood's excellent study of the New York metropolitan region, is that only the planners like the scheme.[13] Wood and his associates engaged in an intensive examination of the "political economy" of the twenty-two-county region, which includes parts of three states. They found that the obstacles to regional government were formidable. Few political figures were desirous of any form of government consolidation.[14] When it came to business leaders, little favorable interest was forthcoming. Nor was there any evidence that the electorates in the

1,400 governments that constituted the metropolitan region were anxious for regional government. Quite to the contrary, according to Wood: "If the Region's leadership shows little inclination to take giant strides, it is not likely to be pushed by the electorate."[15] By and large, it could be inferred that the people were sufficiently satisfied with the existing situation so as not to demand drastic changes.[16]

Aside from public indifference to regional government, there also developed in some areas a mood of positive public hostility. An example comes from the Hartford region in central Connecticut. In the early 1960s metropolitan government was widely acclaimed as the device that would bring about a more equitable and efficient administration of services common to all units of the region. This belief was based in part on the success of the metropolitan water district. If consolidation worked in this area, why, it was asked, would it not operate equally well in others?

To the city planners in Hartford, metropolitan government at first looked like an easy solution to some of the city's problems. The well-to-do suburbs could share their financial and intellectual resources with the central city, presumably for the common benefit of all. As the financial implications of such brotherliness became apparent, hostility toward consolidation became vocal in West Hartford, Simsbury, Farmington, East Hartford, Glastonbury, Wethersfield, and Rocky Hill.

Another type of hostility developed that no one had foreseen. The supposed beneficiaries of metropolitan government, especially the blacks and Puerto Ricans in the North End of Hartford, began to reassess the demographic realities of metropolitan government. Under the existing system, they had a growing voice in the politics and government of the city, particularly in the public school system. Under the consolidation plan, the city population of 160,000 would have been swamped in the total regional population of half a million. By the end of the 1960–70 decade, leaders of substantial minority groups in Hartford were understandably chilly toward metropolitan government. Their reservations on this subject were widely shared throughout the city.

Similar reservations were expressed increasingly by central city minority communities across the country. During the 1970s these anti-regional attitudes did not change much. The growth of Councils of Government provided a mechanism for regional discussion, information exchange, and planned growth and development, but no serious movement emerged for full-scale regional government in any part of the country.

## Urban Areas and the State

One of the basic principles of the traditional American system of government is that cities and other urban areas possess only those powers delegated to them by the states. There is no inherent right to home rule, and even where the term is used, it tends to imply more self-determination than really exists. This is because the states have ordinarily regarded the cities as potential if not actual rivals and have hedged delegations of power with numerous and often irritating restrictions. Nonetheless, the states do bear a primary responsibility for the welfare of their urban citizens.

How well has this responsibility been met? In the opinion of experts in the field of state government, not very well. Daniel J. Elazar, for instance, a staunch supporter of federalism and of the power of state governments in general, has conceded that the states have fallen short of the mark in this area. He wrote, "there remains one major unsolved problem, whose importance cannot be overemphasized: that of the metropolitan areas. By and large, the states have been unwilling or unable to do enough to meet metropolitan problems."[17] The future role of the states, he added, will be determined by what they do or fail to do in dealing with this problem.[18]

As a result of this situation, the cities found themselves in a dilemma. On the one hand, they could wait for the solution to their problems until the states enjoyed a newfound prosperity. Or, refusing to sit tight until the Day of Awakening finally arrived, the cities could, and did, take their case directly to the federal government. Blocked by the states in their efforts to make progress in an over-the-center power play, the cities bypassed the states by an around-end maneuver. This strategy has suggested itself to many mayors, and they have employed it before federal agencies and Congressional committees.

Understandably, politicians and scholars who view the states as the keystone of the American governmental structure have been alarmed by this development. They see the tendency to create direct federal-city relationships as a challenge to state integrity, and cite the Office of Economic Opportunity grants to communities as frightening examples of what they have in mind.[19] There is, however, little evidence that the mayors of the largest cities, increasingly more desperate for funds, have been impressed by this line of reasoning.

## The New Federalism

During the 1970s many of the states made a commitment to work more closely with their troubled cities. This commitment involved the allocation of funds and personnel to urban issues and problems. Governors became more involved in their cities' problems, and state offices specifically designed to work on urban policy were created in numerous states. Much of this activity was initiated by the election in 1976, and again in 1980, of former governors to the presidency of the United States. Both Jimmy Carter and Ronald Reagan encouraged the states to become more active partners in the intergovernmental system. These initiatives, along with cutbacks in federal funding for domestic programs, have placed greater emphasis on the state rule in urban problems.

Perhaps the event of the 1970s that had the most dramatic impact upon state and local relations was the advent of the New Federalism, marked by the passage of the Revenue Sharing Bill in 1972 and its reenactment in 1976,

1980, and 1983. The New Federalism, initiated by the Nixon administration and embellished by the Reagan administration, sought to strengthen the role of the states in the intergovernmental system. To this end, the New Federalism sought to restore balance in the system by giving states more program responsibility and discretion. The 1980s are likely to become a decade of testing and adjusting to determine new intergovernmental relationships. Few of the actors in the system are pleased with the current arrangement, but the movement for change appears to be unstoppable. No one can predict how these intergovernmental relationships will change, but there is strong evidence that cities, counties, and states will need a long period of planning and working together before the changes are fully implemented and assessed.

## Other Factors Affecting Urban Areas

Two other factors are likely to have an important impact on the future of urban politics. These are the concerns with budget constraints and fiscal scarcity and the growing use of computers by local governments as a means of improving management capabilities by providing more timely and more accurate information to decision-makers.

From the late 1970s on, it has become apparent that funding for public sector programs, on all levels of government, has become difficult to sustain. Federal cutbacks, coupled with taxpayers' revolts in California, Massachusetts, and other states, have made it difficult to generate the same level of revenues needed to finance traditional urban service programs.[20] How far the funding cuts will go and what impact they will have on the nature of urban politics is hard to assess. It seems clear, however, that neither Congress nor the taxpayers are willing to provide the same amount of money they once did to aid urban areas. The evidence indicates that large amounts of federal, state, and local dollars thrown at a myriad of urban problems have not produced a marked change in the quality of urban life.

The second factor is of equal significance and is related to the first. As more and more local governments begin to introduce data processing into their day-to-day operations, they will have to justify the cost of leasing or purchasing this equipment by demonstrating either sustained cost savings in the long run or greater productivity by local employees, or both. Several problems related to computer technology have already begun to emerge. First, local governments lease or purchase their equipment independently. Thus, once their equipment is operational, they may no longer be compatible, in an information sense, with other local governments in the metropolitan area, region, or state. This will decrease the possibility of sharing information about mutual problems. Public Technology Incorporated and the International City Management Association are both working with local governments around the country to solve this problem.

Second, there is a problem of how to establish effective communications and working relationships among the elected, administrative, and technical personnel involved in the data processing needs and requirements of local government. Historically, communication among the three groups has been difficult. The technical people can provide information if they are given the right questions stated in precise terms. The administrative officials try to interpret what the elected officials want and then request this from the technical personnel. The elected officials have to make decisions quickly, while usually working part-time. They require information in a brief and timely manner, so it can be read, analyzed, and acted upon quickly. This puts pressure on both the administrators and the technical personnel to speed up their process by devising shortcuts. None of the three parties gets what it wants, and a valuable system installed for many good reasons often performs at less than full capacity. Elected, administrative, and technical personnel have begun working together to define information needs, state the needs in terms understandable to all parties, establish reasonable lead times, provide data and analysis that can be interpreted quickly and accurately and that can be translated into political and administrative policy.

Finally, there is the problem of managing the high technology revolution. Elected officials rarely have extensive background and experience in the technological aspects of communications and information processing. They rely heavily on administrative heads of departments and their own staff. But elected officials, most of whom are part-time, cannot effectively oversee the use and abuse of much of the information produced by the data processing revolution. The strides being made in improving the technological capabilities of data processing equipment far exceed the ability of elected and appointed officials to keep pace with the technicians or their equipment. One of the major problems facing urban managers in the 1980s will be how they manage the information explosion while minimizing the risks of leaks, misinterpretation of data, and excess capacity leading to lower productivity.[21]

Historically, control of information has been an important resource in local government decision-making. Failure on the part of local government officials to manage the technological revolution could have important implications for how power is distributed and exercised in urban areas.

## ELEMENTS OF THE NEW STYLE POLITICS

What can be said regarding the New Style, which is in the process of replacing Old Style politics? We are now in a position to identify those principal elements that we may expect to be included within the new and developing system.

The new system will have to be able to set up and enforce priorities to get things done. It is not yet clear how this may be achieved, but it is certain that some kinds of persuasion or coercion not currently employed under the present system will have to be utilized. There will have to be recognition of the idea that not every group and interest can advance at a rate determined by itself. Public authority will have to be just that—authority. Also, some new forms will have to evolve under the New Style politics.

To begin with, let us consider several forms that do not seem to have any particular future. Participatory democracy, often praised in the past, does not appear very promising as an element in the evolving New Style of politics. If it means anything, participatory democracy means that a person will have a direct voice in decisions affecting his own life. This sounds simple, but it is not. From a political point of view, participatory democracy, if taken literally, spells the end of representative government.

Recent experience with participatory democracy, notably involving community action agency boards, has not been encouraging. Voter turnout to elect representatives of "the poor" has almost universally been ludicrously low, perhaps because the real control over the War on Poverty funds remained in Washington and this condition undercut local interest. Nonetheless, the lack of participation by eligible residents in the election process creates doubt as to the value of this procedure.[22]

A second form—the so-called "students' movement"—also seems unlikely to become a harbinger of political developments in the new system. The movement probably hit its highest peak during the presidential primary campaign of Senator Eugene J. McCarthy in Wisconsin—at least, this is Theodore White's considered judgment.[23] During the 1970 congressional elections, student participation for the most part followed traditional patterns. There was not much of a movement in sight anywhere. On the other hand, there is reason to believe that student participation through the existing political forms is on the increase. And the lowering of the voting age to eighteen under the Twenty-Sixth Amendment guarantees further student involvement in urban politics. What seems unlikely in the immediate future is the development of an independent student movement.

This view is reinforced by the relative absence of "student issues" in the 1976 and 1980 presidential elections. Students, of course, participated in the campaigns of both major parties. But Watergate, and its attendant scandals, brought about an increase both in student apathy toward politics and widespread cynicism about the entire political process. This further undermined the possibility of creating an effective student movement.

It is sometimes said that a politics of confrontation may be expected to develop as an important form in the urban political process now unfolding. While such a political tactic may on occasion obtain satisfaction for immediate demands, this approach may well be negative and counterproductive in the long run, because confrontation politics inevitably isolates the group that espouses it from the rest of the body politic. A politics of confrontation, in the long run, is a politics of isolation. Since sustained movement toward political goals depends on the ability of groups to form and maintain coalitions, confrontation politics appears to be of limited utility.

In contrast to these approaches stands that of Common Cause. This group, which thinks of itself as a citizens' lobby, has called for "a renaissance of politics in this country."[24] It proposes to "repair the outworn machinery of government and renew the system."[25] It conceives of itself as a "third force," not a third party, in American politics.

In explaining the long-range goals of Common Cause, its founder,

John W. Gardner, and his associates speak in Olympian platitudes with which it would be hard for any reasonable person to disagree. When it comes to specifics, the group simply lists the great problems of our time and declares that solutions are in order. But one need not admire Gardner's high-minded and extremely vague prose in order to appreciate the truth of his pronouncements: the country is in trouble. The difficulty is that the cures that have so far been proposed by Common Cause are small steps toward reforming long-standing national institutions and practices.

The so-called lobby—it is really simply a citizens' interest group—operates in the best tradition of the upper-class reformers of sixty years ago. It may be considered to represent the reform element within the establishment. As such, it possesses a potential for stirring up political interest and action, but how much is impossible to say.

Much more likely to make an impact on the evolving New Style politics is the mass movement now being created in the ranks of America's black citizenry. Though in its infancy, this movement already shows signs of developing considerable political clout as well as savoir-faire. At the same time, parallel movements are slowly emerging from the Hispanic population. Such movements will surely play important roles in the new system of urban politics.

Indeed, it is possible that one of the great propelling forces of New Style politics will be the social movement that turns to politics for solutions to great issues. In addition to the black and the Hispanic movements, two more movements must be considered to possess a political potential. These are a consumers' movement and a women's movement. Given sufficient organization and financing, they might develop into permanent and important factors in the urban political process.

The consumer movement has accelerated its pressure on all levels of government to expand regulatory and promotional activity in this field. Generally, state and city governments have been highly responsive to consumer activism. A number of cities and states have established consumer affairs bureaus within the mayor's or governor's office or under the supervision of the district attorney or attorney general. As the issue becomes even more politicized, such administrative activity will be broadened.[26]

The women's movement, after several years of internal organizational problems, is beginning to have significant impact on local politics. The National Organization for Women, one of the many feminist groups, has thousands of local chapters throughout the country. In many cities, women who previously worked behind the scenes in party politics are now seeking and winning elective office. Feminists have become active lobbyists in favor of local legislation abolishing discrimination against women, establishing public day-care facilities, and safeguarding the rights of lesbians and homosexuals.[27]

The demise of the Equal Rights Amendment on June 30, 1982, is not likely to diminish the force of the women's movement. Aside from the fact that the amendment has been reintroduced, there is every reason to believe that many of the women's organizations operating at the local level will continue to be forceful advocates for issues of concern to them, and therefore important political actors in urban areas.

Another area where change is occurring and power relationships will be altered is the cooperation between the public and private sectors. As financial constraints increase, more and more local governments are going to look to the private sector for assistance. In some cases, this will involve contracting with corporations for the provision of services. In other situations, local governments will seek to turn over to private companies, on a competitive basis, responsibility for providing a service. Recently we have seen the growth of joint ventures where public and private sector organizations plan, invest, and develop projects together. These emerging alternatives to traditional public-private relationships are advantageous for both partners. Cities need additional resources in time of recession, and corporations see an opportunity to increase profits and make a contribution to the quality of life in the city where they do business. In each of these relationships, the distribution of power is altered, and the political actors must reassess their gains and losses.

Recently, Detroit and General Motors worked out a deal to build a new automotive assembly plant in a section of Detroit needing rehabilitation. The city supported the proposal because it meant keeping jobs in Detroit and retaining a big corporate taxpayer. However, there were costs associated with the plan. Hundreds of families had to be relocated so their homes could be destroyed to make way for the new plant. The social costs of such an upheaval are rarely calculated into public-private decisions of this type.

In the 1980s, it is likely that more urban areas are going to be faced with these difficult decisions. How the city officials weigh the costs of such proposals in terms of human resources and power relationships will help to determine the outcome of many urban policies in the late 1980s.

Finally—but perhaps the most important of all the new forms—is the almost spontaneous drive in the great cities for community control over certain community activities. Some, but by no means all, of the elements of this drive have their origin in local groups sponsored by the antipoverty program. Other sources include the desire for self-determination, now evident in many neighborhoods, and the generally current favorable attitude toward governmental decentralization at all levels.

Some words of caution are in order regarding community control. It should be understood that the constitutional rights of all citizens must continue to take precedence over decisions by neighborhood groups. In the event that there is a clash between a constitutional right and a decision by a community organization, the latter must yield. Furthermore, it must be recognized that community control may on occasion exacerbate political controversy, and that this may in turn make it difficult to obtain adequate government financing for projects the community would like to develop. It is also argued by some critics that the comparison of city neighborhoods with the suburbs is unreal and misleading.

Yet, in spite of all reservations, the concept of community control over certain activities that take place within the community possesses a very strong psychological attraction. This is especially observable in the rapidly growing black and Hispanic areas of the largest cities. The movement for community control has a very profound basis, and its roots go very deep. Beyond much doubt, the drive for community control will continue to gain momentum. More and more community and neighborhood groups will become involved in service delivery as a means of providing required services in a timely and effective manner and as a way of reducing costs for local governments.

Besides stressing new techniques for political activity and new forms for such activity, the new politics will also manifest some new features that distinguish it from the old politics. These characteristics may be summarized as follows:

1. There will be a rise of a new type of ethnic voting based on race. Class and racial voting will be highly correlated. Black solidarity will result in many black-dominated city halls.

2. There will be an increasing demand for welfare-state programs inside the cities. The disaffected do not have much use for the niceties and benefits of the free enterprise system.

3. Inside the cities, mini-federal systems based on the local communities may develop. Politics set in city hall would be administered by neighborhood organizations.

4. The cities will continue to forge a city-federal government axis, bypassing the states as much as possible.

5. The New Style politics will be marked by an increasing scope (or arena) of political activity and an increase in the intensity of that activity. Areas of life formerly not politicized will, in the process, become so.

6. Decreasing revenues brought on by national economic policy and declining federal aid will increase conflict in the cities and between cities and states. As a result, cutback management will continue to play an important role in local political decision-making.

7. Despite changes in the intergovernmental system resulting from New Federalism policies, the importance of federal aid to the health of cities will continue.

Whatever develops specifically, it is quite certain as a general proposition that the New Style politics will be played under a different set of rules. Not only will the rules change, but there will also be new actors and new goals. In the process of developing the New Style politics, there will be important attitudinal changes on the part of the citizens. For example, the traditional attitude toward winning and losing elections is very likely to be altered. Winning and losing elections will become less important as resources diminish and conflict increases. The ability to organize, agitate, and influence whoever is in office will be a critical factor in determining resource allocation.

It is from these materials—means, forms, and characteristics—that the New Style politics is being fashioned. As this style continues its rapid development, some of its attributes will be seen with more clarity. It will then be possible to gauge the relative importance of the particular attributes in relation to the total system. It will also be feasible to begin serious efforts to construct a new model of urban politics that will be useful in explaining and interpreting the New Style politics.

The militancy of the 1960s and 1970s has changed. The cries of black power and community control have been moderated and made more relevant to the political realities of the 1980s. Efforts to win political battles through riots and demonstrations have diminished. The new style of urban politics is manifest more in political organizing, campaigning, and voting than in violent outbursts.

The resources available to local governments in the 1960s and early 1970s have been drastically reduced. Conflict over the allocation of those resources will continue, but minority groups with the greatest needs will begin to use the ballot box more than they have in the past.

Black mayors have been elected in Los Angeles, Detroit, Newark, Washington, D.C., Gary, and Cleveland during the period of growing federal aid and urban unrest. In 1983, Chicago and Philadelphia both elected their first black mayors and Denver elected a Hispanic mayor. All three of these election victories were achieved through careful campaign planning and organizing and hard grass roots work by many interested inner-city residents determined to use the ballot box to achieve their ends.

Regardless of the style of politics or the issues being debated, it is still essential for students of urban politics to understand how power is distributed and exercised in the urban arena. While power relationships change rather quickly, knowledge of these changes remains one of the key ingredients to understanding who gets what from the political system.

## NOTES

1. Harry A. Bailey, Jr., "Negro Interest Group Strategies," *Urban Affairs Quarterly* 4, 1 (September 1968): 27–38, citation at p. 35.
2. See the article "Tio Taco is Dead," *Newsweek*, June 29, 1970, pp. 22–28. Also see *Puerto Ricans in the Continental United States: An Uncertain Future* (Washington: U.S. Commission on Civil Rights, October 1976).
3. See Bill Kovach, "Struggle for Identity: White Minorities Review Heritage," *New York Times*, November 27, 1970, p. 37. Also see Richard Krickus, *Pursuing the American Dream: White Ethnics and the New Populism* (Garden City, N.Y.: Anchor Books, 1976).
4. Barbara Mikulski, "He Came in Search of Freedom and a Job But What Did He Find?", *New York Times*, September 29, 1970, p. 43. Also see Michael Novak, *The Rise of the Unmeltable Ethnics* (New York: Macmillan, 1972), and Andrew M. Greeley, *Why Can't They Be Like Us?* (New York: E. P. Dutton, 1971).
5. Mikulski, p. 43.
6. Kovach, "Struggle for Identity," p. 37, and Greeley, *Why Can't They Be Like Us?*
7. Kovach, "Struggle for Identity," p. 37.
8. Ibid., p. 37.

9. See the article, "A Rising Cry: 'Ethnic Power,' " *Newsweek*, December 21, 1970, pp. 32–36.

10. Thomas R. Dye, *Politics in States and Communities*, 4th ed. (Englewood Cliffs, N.J.: Prentice-Hall, 1981), pp. 332–33.

11. See Charles E. Gilbert, *Governing the Suburbs* (Bloomington, Ind.: Indiana University Press, 1967).

12. Ibid., p. 315.

13. Robert C. Wood, *1400 Governments, The Political Economy of the New York Metropolitan Region* (Garden City, N.Y.: Doubleday Anchor Book edition, 1964).

14. Ibid., p. 210.

15. Ibid., p. 214.

16. Ibid., p. 216.

17. Daniel J. Elazar, ed., *American Federalism: A View from the States*, 2nd ed. (New York: Crowell, 1972), p. 208.

18. Ibid., p. 208.

19. On these points, see Elazar, *American Federalism*, p. 210.

20. See Charles H. Levine, ed., *Managing Fiscal Stress: The Crisis in the Public Sector* (Chatham, N.J.: Chatham House, 1980); and Charles H. Levine, Irene S. Rubin, and George G. Wolohojian, *The Politics of Retrenchment: How Local Governments Manage Fiscal Stress* (Beverly Hills: Sage Publications, 1981).

21. The problems and prospects of computer use in local government are discussed and analyzed in the following: Kenneth L. Kraemer and John Leslie King, *Computers and Local Government* (New York: Praeger, 1977); John Leslie King, "Local Government Use of Information Technology: The Next Decade," *Public Administration Review* 42, no. 1 (January/February 1982): 25–36; and Alana Northrup, William H. Dutton, and Kenneth L. Kramer, "The Management of Computer Applications in Local Government," *Public Administration Review* 42, no. 3 (May/June 1982): 234–243.

22. For a criticism of the whole program, including the role of the poor in choosing their local agency boards, see Daniel P. Moynihan, *Maximum Feasible Misunderstanding: Community Action in the War on Poverty* (New York: Free Press, 1969).

23. Theodore H. White, *The Making of the President 1968* (New York: Pocket Books, 1970), p. 149.

24. John W. Gardner, "Sign In," *Signature*, December, 1970, p. 10.

25. Ibid., p. 10.

26. For an excellent discussion of the political tactics of consumer groups, see Mark V. Nadel, *The Politics of Consumer Protection* (New York: Bobbs-Merrill, 1971).

27. *New York Times*, June 1, 1974.

# Appendixes A & B

# APPENDIX A

1980 Census Population for cities of 100,000 and Over by Rank Order
(Final counts as published in 1980 census advance reports by State,
Series PHC80–V. Includes revisions of 1970 census counts)

| Rank 1980 | City and State | 1980 census | 1970 census | Percent change, 1970–80 | Rank 1970 |
|---|---|---|---|---|---|
| 1 | New York, NY | 7,071,030 | 7,895,563 | −10.4 | 1 |
| 2 | Chicago, IL | 3,005,072 | 3,369,357 | −10.8 | 2 |
| 3 | Los Angeles, CA | 2,966,763 | 2,811,801 | 5.5 | 3 |
| 4 | Philadelphia, PA | 1,688,210 | 1,949,996 | −13.4 | 4 |
| 5 | Houston, TX | 1,594,086 | 1,233,535 | 29.2 | 6 |
| 6 | Detroit, MI | 1,203,339 | 1,514,063 | −20.5 | 5 |
| 7 | Dallas, TX | 904,078 | 844,401 | 7.1 | 8 |
| 8 | San Diego, CA | 875,504 | 697,471 | 25.5 | 14 |
| 9 | Phoenix, AZ[1] | 789,704 | 584,303 | 35.2 | 20 |
| 10 | Baltimore, MD | 786,775 | 905,787 | −13.1 | 7 |
| 11 | San Antonio, TX | 785,410 | 654,153 | 20.1 | 15 |
| 12 | Indianapolis, IN | 700,807 | 736,856 | −4.9 | 11 |
| 13 | San Francisco, CA | 678,974 | 715,674 | −5.1 | 13 |
| 14 | Memphis, TN | 646,356 | 623,988 | 3.6 | 17 |
| 15 | Washington, DC | 637,651 | 756,668 | −15.7 | 9 |
| 16 | San Jose, CA | 636,550 | 459,913 | 38.4 | 29 |
| 17 | Milwaukee, WI | 636,212 | 717,372 | −11.3 | 12 |
| 18 | Cleveland, OH | 573,822 | 750,879 | −23.6 | 10 |
| 19 | Columbus, OH | 564,871 | 540,025 | 4.6 | 21 |
| 20 | Boston, MA | 562,994 | 641,071 | −12.2 | 16 |
| 21 | New Orleans, LA | 557,482 | 593,471 | −6.1 | 19 |
| 22 | Jacksonville, FL | 540,898 | 504,265 | 7.3 | 26 |
| 23 | Seattle, WA | 493,846 | 530,831 | −7.0 | 22 |
| 24 | Denver, CO | 491,396 | 514,678 | −4.5 | 24 |
| 25 | Nashville–Davidson, TN | 455,651 | 426,029 | 7.0 | 32 |
| 26 | St. Louis, MO | 453,085 | 622,236 | −27.2 | 18 |
| 27 | Kansas City, MO | 448,159 | 507,330 | −11.7 | 25 |
| 28 | El Paso, TX | 425,259 | 322,261 | 32.0 | 45 |
| 29 | Atlanta, GA | 425,022 | 495,039 | −14.1 | 27 |
| 30 | Pittsburgh, PA | 423,938 | 520,089 | −18.5 | 23 |
| 31 | Oklahoma City, OK | 403,213 | 368,164 | 9.5 | 37 |
| 32 | Cincinnati, OH | 385,457 | 453,514 | −15.0 | 30 |
| 33 | Fort Worth, TX | 385,141 | 393,455 | −2.1 | 33 |
| 34 | Minneapolis, MN | 370,951 | 434,400 | −14.6 | 31 |

continued

## 1980 Census Population (continued)

| | | | | |
|---|---|---|---|---|
| 35 | Portland, OR | 366,383 | 379,967 | −3.6 | 36 |
| 36 | Honolulu, HI 2 | 365,048 | 324,871 | 12.4 | 44 |
| 37 | Long Beach, CA | 361,334 | 358,879 | 0.7 | 40 |
| 38 | Tulsa, OK | 360,919 | 330,350 | 9.3 | 43 |
| 39 | Buffalo, NY | 357,870 | 462,768 | −22.7 | 28 |
| 40 | Toledo, OH | 354,635 | 383,062 | −7.4 | 34 |
| 41 | Miami, FL | 346,931 | 334,859 | 3.6 | 42 |
| 42 | Austin, TX | 345,496 | 253,539 | 36.3 | 56 |
| 43 | Oakland, CA | 339,288 | 361,561 | −6.2 | 39 |
| 44 | Albuquerque, NM | 331,767 | 244,501 | 35.7 | 58 |
| 45 | Tucson, AZ | 330,537 | 262,933 | 25.7 | 53 |
| 46 | Newark, NJ | 329,248 | 381,930 | −13.8 | 35 |
| 47 | Charlotte, NC | 314,447 | 241,420 | 30.2 | 60 |
| 48 | Omaha, NE | 311,681 | 346,929 | −10.2 | 41 |
| 49 | Louisville, KY | 298,451 | 361,706 | −17.5 | 38 |
| 50 | Birmingham, AL | 284,413 | 300,910 | −5.5 | 48 |
| 51 | Wichita, KS | 279,272 | 276,554 | 1.0 | 51 |
| 52 | Sacramento, CA | 275,741 | 257,105 | 7.2 | 55 |
| 53 | Tampa, FL | 271,523 | 277,714 | −2.2 | 50 |
| 54 | St. Paul, MN | 270,230 | 309,866 | −12.8 | 46 |
| 55 | Norfolk, VA | 266,979 | 307,951 | −13.3 | 47 |
| 56 | Virginia Beach, VA | 262,199 | 172,106 | 52.3 | 77 |
| 57 | Rochester, NY | 241,741 | 295,011 | −18.1 | 49 |
| 58 | Akron, OH | 237,177 | 275,425 | −13.9 | 52 |
| 59 | St. Petersburg, FL | 236,893 | 216,159 | 9.6 | 61 |
| 60 | Corpus Christi, TX | 231,999 | 204,525 | 13.4 | 62 |
| 61 | Jersey City, NJ | 223,532 | 260,350 | −14.1 | 54 |
| 62 | Anaheim, CA | 221,847 | 166,408 | 33.3 | 81 |
| 63 | Baton Rouge, LA | 219,486 | 165,921 | 32.3 | 82 |
| 64 | Richmond, VA | 219,214 | 249,332 | −12.1 | 57 |
| 65 | Fresno, CA | 218,202 | 165,655 | 31.7 | 83 |
| 66 | Colorado Springs, CO | 215,150 | 135,517 | 58.8 | 103 |
| 67 | Shreveport, LA | 205,815 | 182,064 | 13.0 | 69 |
| 68 | Lexington–Fayette, KY | 204,165 | 108,137 | 88.8 | 139 |
| 69 | Santa Ana, CA | 203,713 | 155,710 | 30.8 | 87 |
| 70 | Dayton, OH | 203,588 | 243,023 | −16.2 | 59 |
| 71 | Jackson, MS | 202,895 | 153,968 | 31.8 | 90 |
| 72 | Mobile, AL | 200,452 | 190,026 | 5.5 | 68 |
| 73 | Yonkers, NY | 195,351 | 204,297 | −4.4 | 63 |
| 74 | Des Moines, IA | 191,003 | 201,404 | −5.2 | 64 |
| 75 | Knoxville, TN | 183,139 | 174,587 | 4.9 | 76 |
| 76 | Grand Rapids, MI | 181,843 | 197,649 | −8.0 | 65 |
| 77 | Montgomery, AL | 178,157 | 133,386 | 33.6 | 106 |
| 78 | Lubbock, TX | 173,979 | 149,101 | 16.7 | 92 |
| 79 | Anchorage, AK | 173,017 | 48,081 | 259.8 | – |
| 80 | Fort Wayne, IN | 172,196 | 178,269 | −3.4 | 72 |
| 81 | Lincoln, NE | 171,932 | 149,518 | 15.0 | 91 |
| 82 | Spokane, WA | 171,300 | 170,516 | 0.5 | 79 |
| 83 | Riverside, CA | 170,876 | 140,089 | 22.0 | 97 |
| 84 | Madison, WI | 170,616 | 171,809 | −0.7 | 78 |
| 85 | Huntington Beach, CA | 170,505 | 115,960 | 47.0 | 124 |
| 86 | Syracuse, NY | 170,105 | 197,297 | −13.8 | 66 |
| 87 | Chattanooga, TN | 169,565 | 119,923 | 41.4 | 121 |
| 88 | Columbus, GA | 169,441 | 155,028 | 9.3 | 88 |
| 89 | Las Vegas, NV | 164,674 | 125,787 | 30.9 | 113 |
| 90 | Salt Lake City, UT | 163,033 | 175,885 | −7.3 | 74 |
| 91 | Worcester, MA | 161,799 | 176,572 | −8.4 | 73 |
| 92 | Warren, MI | 161,134 | 179,260 | −10.1 | 70 |
| 93 | Kansas City, KS | 161,087 | 168,213 | −4.2 | 80 |

continued

1980 Census Population (continued)

| | | | | |
|---|---|---:|---:|---:|
| 94 | Arlington, TX | 160,123 | 90,229 | 77.5 | – |
| 95 | Flint, MI | 159,611 | 193,317 | −17.4 | 67 |
| 96 | Aurora, CO | 158,588 | 74,974 | 111.5 | – |
| 97 | Tacoma, WA | 158,501 | 154,407 | 2.7 | 89 |
| 98 | Little Rock, AR | 158,461 | 132,483 | 19.6 | 108 |
| 99 | Providence, RI | 156,804 | 179,116 | −12.5 | 71 |
| 100 | Greensboro, NC | 155,642 | 144,076 | 8.0 | 95 |
| 101 | Fort Lauderdale, FL | 153,256 | 139,590 | 9.8 | 98 |
| 102 | Mesa, AZ | 152,453 | 63,049 | 141.8 | – |
| 103 | Springfield, MA | 152,319 | 163,905 | −7.1 | 84 |
| 104 | Gary, IN | 151,953 | 175,415 | −13.4 | 75 |
| 105 | Stockton. CA | 149,779 | 109,963 | 36.2 | 136 |
| 106 | Raleigh, NC | 149,771 | 122,830 | 21.9 | 116 |
| 107 | Amarillo, TX | 149,230 | 127,010 | 17.5 | 111 |
| 108 | Hialeah, FL | 145,254 | 102,452 | 41.8 | 148 |
| 109 | Newport News, VA | 144,903 | 138,177 | 4.9 | 101 |
| 110 | Bridgeport, CT | 142,546 | 156,542 | −8.9 | 86 |
| 111 | Huntsville, AL | 142,513 | 139,282 | 2.3 | 99 |
| 112 | Savannah, GA | 141,634 | 118,349 | 19.7 | 122 |
| 113 | Rockford, IL | 139,712 | 147,370 | −5.2 | 93 |
| 114 | Glendale, CA | 139,060 | 132,664 | 4.8 | 107 |
| 115 | Garland, TX | 138,857 | 81,437 | 70.5 | – |
| 116 | Paterson, NJ | 137,970 | 144,824 | −4.7 | 94 |
| 117 | Hartford, CT | 136,392 | 158,017 | −13.7 | 85 |
| 118 | Springfield, MO | 133,116 | 120,096 | 10.8 | 120 |
| 119 | Fremont, CA | 131,945 | 100,869 | 30.8 | 150 |
| 120 | Winston–Salem, NC | 131.885 | 133,683 | −1.3 | 105 |
| 121 | Torrance, CA | 131,497 | 134,968 | −2.6 | 104 |
| 122 | Evansville, IN | 130,496 | 138,764 | −6.0 | 100 |
| 123 | Lansing, MI | 130,414 | 131,403 | −0.8 | 109 |
| 124 | Orlando, FL | 128,394 | 99,006 | 29.7 | – |
| 125 | New Haven, CT | 126,109 | 137,707 | −8.4 | 102 |
| 126 | Peoria, IL | 124,160 | 126,963 | −2.2 | 112 |
| 127 | Garden Grove, CA | 123,351 | 121,155 | 1.8 | 118 |
| 128 | Hampton, VA | 122,617 | 120,779 | 1.5 | 119 |
| 129 | Pasadena, CA | 119,374 | 112,951 | 5.7 | 128 |
| 130 | Erie, PA | 119,123 | 129,265 | −7.8 | 110 |
| 131 | Beaumont, TX | 118,102 | 117,548 | 0.5 | 123 |
| 132 | San Bernardino, CA | 118,057 | 106,869 | 10.5 | 143 |
| 133 | Hollywood, FL | 117,188 | 106,873 | 9.7 | 142 |
| 134 | Macon, GA | 116,860 | 122,423 | −4.5 | 117 |
| 135 | Youngstown, OH | 115,436 | 140,909 | −18.1 | 96 |
| 136 | Topeka, KS | 115,266 | 125,011 | −7.8 | 115 |
| 137 | Chesapeake, VA | 114,226 | 89,580 | 27.5 | – |
| 138 | Lakewood, CO | 112,848 | 92,743 | 21.7 | – |
| 139 | Pasadena, TX | 112,560 | 89,957 | 25.1 | – |
| 140 | Independence, MO | 111,806 | 111,630 | 0.2 | 130 |
| 141 | Cedar Rapids, IA | 110,243 | 110,642 | −0.4 | 133 |
| 142 | Irving, TX | 109,943 | 97,260 | 13.0 | – |
| 143 | South Bend, IN | 109,727 | 125,580 | −12.6 | 114 |
| 144 | Sterling Heights, MI | 108,999 | 61,365 | 77.6 | – |
| 145 | Oxnard, CA | 108,195 | 71,225 | 51.9 | – |
| 146 | Ann Arbor, MI | 107,316 | 100,035 | 7.3 | 154 |
| 147 | Tempe, AZ | 106,743 | 63,550 | 68.0 | – |
| 148 | Sunnyvale, CA | 106,618 | 95,976 | 11.1 | – |
| 149 | Elizabeth, NJ | 106,201 | 112,654 | −5.7 | 129 |
| 150 | Modesto, CA | 106,105 | 61,712 | 71.9 | – |
| 151 | Eugene, OR | 105,624 | 79,028 | 33.7 | – |
| 152 | Bakersfield, CA | 105,611 | 69,515 | 51.9 | – |

continued

## 1980 Census Population (continued)

| | | | | |
|---|---|---|---|---|
| 153 | Livonia, MI | 104,814 | 110,109 | −4.8 | 134 |
| 154 | Rortsmouth, VA | 104,577 | 110,963 | −5.8 | 131 |
| 155 | Allentown, PA | 103,758 | 109,871 | −5.6 | 137 |
| 156 | Berkeley, CA | 103,328 | 114,091 | −9.4 | 126 |
| 157 | Waterbury, CT | 103,266 | 108,033 | −4.4 | 140 |
| 158 | Davenport, IA | 103,264 | 98,469 | 4.9 | − |
| 159 | Concord, CA | 103,251 | 85,164 | 21.2 | − |
| 160 | Alexandria, VA | 103,217 | 110,927 | −7.0 | 132 |
| 161 | Stamford, CT | 102,453 | 108,798 | −5.8 | 138 |
| 162 | Boise City, ID | 102,451 | 74,990 | 36.6 | − |
| 163 | Fullerton, CA | 102,034 | 85,987 | 18.7 | − |
| 164 | Albany, NY | 101,727 | 115,781 | −12.1 | 125 |
| 165 | Pueblo, CO | 101,686 | 97,774 | 4.0 | − |
| 166 | Waco, TX | 101,261 | 95,326 | 6.2 | − |
| 167 | Durham, NC | 100,831 | 95,438 | 5.7 | − |
| 168 | Reno, NV | 100,756 | 72,863 | 38.3 | − |
| 169 | Roanoke, VA | 100,427 | 92,115 | 9.0 | − |

[1]Corrected count.

[2]The data listed here are for Honolulu census designated place, which essentially represents the Honolulu Judicial District. The city of Honolulu, coextensive with the county of Honolulu, is not recognized for census purposes.

# APPENDIX B

Standard Metropolitan Statistical Areas in the U.S. and
Their Constituent Counties

| | TOTAL | | TOTAL |
|---|---|---|---|
| *Abilene, TX* | 139,192 | *Anaheim-Santa Ana-* | |
| Callahan Co.* | 10,992 | *Garden Grove, CA* | 1,931,570 |
| Jones Co. | 17,268 | Orange Co. | 1,931,570 |
| Taylor Co. | 110,932 | | |
| | | *Anchorage, AK* * | 173,017 |
| *Akron, OH* | 660,328 | Anchorage Census | |
| Portage Co. | 135,856 | Division | 173,017 |
| Summit Co. | 524,472 | | |
| | | *Anderson, IN* | 139,336 |
| *Albany, GA* | 112,662 | Madison Co. | 139,336 |
| Dougherty Co. | 100,978 | | |
| Lee Co.* | 11,684 | *Anderson, SC* ** | 133,235 |
| | | Anderson Co. | 133,235 |
| *Albany-Schenectady-* | | | |
| *Troy, NY* | 795,019 | *Ann Arbor, MI* | 264,748 |
| Albany Co. | 285,909 | Washtenaw Co. | 264,748 |
| Montgomery Co.* | 53,439 | | |
| Rensselaer Co. | 151,966 | *Anniston, AL* * | 116,936 |
| Saratoga Co. | 153,759 | Calhoun Co. | 116,936 |
| Schenectady Co. | 149,946 | | |
| | | *Appleton-Oshkosh, WI* * | 291,325 |
| *Albuquerque, NM* | 454,499 | Calumet Co. | 30,867 |
| Bernalillo Co. | 419,700 | Outagamie Co. | 128,726 |
| Sandoval Co.* | 34,799 | Winnebago Co. | 131,732 |
| | | | |
| *Alexandria, LA* * | 151,985 | *Asheville, NC* | 177,761 |
| Grant Parish | 16,703 | Buncombe Co. | 160,934 |
| Rapides Parish | 135,282 | Madison Co.* | 16,827 |
| | | | |
| *Allentown-Bethlehem-* | | *Athens, GA* ** | 130,015 |
| *Easton, PA–NJ* | 636,714 | Clarke Co. | 74,498 |
| Carbon Co., PA* | 53,285 | Jackson Co. | 25,343 |
| Lehigh Co., PA | 273,582 | Madison Co. | 17,747 |
| Northampton Co., PA | 225,418 | Oconee Co. | 12,427 |
| Warren Co., NJ | 84,429 | | |
| | | *Atlanta, GA* | 2,029,618 |
| *Altoona, PA* | 136,621 | Butts Co.* | 13,665 |
| Blair Co. | 136,621 | Cherokee Co.* | 51,669 |
| | | Clayton Co. | 150,357 |
| | | Cobb Co. | 297,694 |
| *Amarillo, TX* | 173,699 | De Kalb Co. | 483,024 |
| Potter Co. | 98,637 | Douglas Co. | 54,573 |
| Randall Co. | 75,062 | | |

* indicates new area since 1970
** indicates new area as designated by the 1980 census

continued

## Standard Metropolitan Statistical Areas (continued)

| | | | |
|---|---:|---|---:|
| Fayette Co.* | 29,043 | Berrien Co. | 171,276 |
| Forsyth Co.* | 27,958 | | |
| Fulton Co. | 589,904 | *Billings, MT* | 108,035 |
| Gwinnett Co. | 166,903 | Yellowstone Co. | 108,035 |
| Henry Co.* | 36,309 | | |
| Newton Co.* | 34,489 | *Biloxi-Gulfport, MS* | 191,918 |
| Paulding Co.* | 26,042 | Hancock Co.* | 24,537 |
| Rockdale Co.* | 36,747 | Harrison Co. | 157,665 |
| Walton Co.* | 31,211 | Stone Co.* | 9,716 |
| | | | |
| *Atlantic City, NJ* | 194,119 | *Binghamton, NY-PA* | 301,336 |
| Atlantic Co. | 194,119 | Broome Co., NY | 213,648 |
| | | Susquehanna Co., PA | 49,812 |
| *Augusta, GA–SC* | 327,372 | Tioga Co., NY | 37,876 |
| Aiken Co., SC | 105,625 | | |
| Columbia Co., GA* | 40,118 | *Birmingham, AL* | 847,360 |
| Richmond Co., GA | 181,629 | Jefferson Co. | 671,197 |
| | | St. Clair Co.* | 41,205 |
| *Austin, TX* | 536,450 | Shelby Co. | 66,298 |
| Hays Co.* | 40,594 | Walker Co. | 68,660 |
| Travis Co. | 419,335 | | |
| Williamson Co.* | 76,521 | *Bismarck, ND* | 79,988 |
| | | Burleigh Co. | 54,811 |
| *Bakersfield, CA* | 403,089 | Morton Co. | 25,177 |
| Kern Co. | 403,089 | | |
| | | *Bloomington, IN* | 98,387 |
| *Baltimore, MD* | 2,174,023 | Monroe Co. | 98,387 |
| Anne Arundel Co. | 370,775 | | |
| Baltimore Co. | 655,615 | *Bloomington-Normal, IL* | 119,149 |
| Carroll Co. | 96,356 | McLean Co. | 119,149 |
| Harford Co. | 145,930 | | |
| Howard Co. | 118,572 | *Boise City, ID* | 173,036 |
| Baltimore city | 786,775 | Ada Co. | 173,036 |
| | | | |
| *Bangor, ME*** | 83,919 | *Boston, MA* | 2,763,357 |
| Penobscot Co. (pt) | 81,244 | Essex Co. (pt) | 329,844 |
| Waldo Co. (pt) | 2,675 | Middlesex Co. (pt) | 1,028,356 |
| | | Norfolk Co. (pt) | 595,704 |
| *Baton Rouge, LA* | 493,973 | Plymouth Co. (pt) | 159,311 |
| Ascension Parish* | 50,068 | Suffolk Co. (pt) | 650,142 |
| East Baton Rouge Par. | 366,164 | | |
| Livingston Parish* | 58,655 | *Bradenton, FL* | 148,442 |
| West Baton Rouge Par.* | 19,086 | Manatee Co. | 148,442 |
| | | | |
| *Battle Creek, MI* | 187,338 | *Bremerton, WA*** | 146,609 |
| Barry Co. | 45,781 | Kitsap Co. | 146,609 |
| Calhoun Co. | 141,557 | | |
| | | *Bridgeport, CT* | 395,455 |
| *Bay City, MI* | 119,881 | Fairfield Co. (pt) | 332,211 |
| Bay Co. | 119,881 | New Haven Co. (pt) | 63,244 |
| | | | |
| *Beaumont-Port Arthur-* | | *Bristol, CT* | 73,762 |
| *Orange, TX* | 375,497 | Hartford Co. (pt) | 63,030 |
| Hardin Co.* | 40,721 | Litchfield Co. (pt) | 10,732 |
| Jefferson Co. | 250,938 | | |
| Orange Co. | 83,838 | *Brockton, MA* | 169,374 |
| | | Bristol Co. (pt) | 16,623 |
| *Bellingham, WA* | 106,701 | Norfolk Co. (pt) | 5,026 |
| Whatcom Co. | 106,701 | Plymouth Co. (pt) | 147,725 |
| | | | |
| *Benton Harbor, MI*** | 171,276 | *Brownsville-Harlingen-* | |

continued

## Standard Metropolitan Statistical Areas (continued)

| | | | |
|---|---|---|---|
| San Benito, TX | 209,680 | Chicago, IL | 7,102,328 |
| Cameron Co. | 209,680 | Cook Co. | 5,253,190 |
| | | Du Page Co. | 658,177 |
| Bryan-College Station, TX* | 93,588 | Kane Co. | 278,405 |
| Brazos Co. | 93,588 | Lake Co. | 440,372 |
| | | McHenry Co. | 147,724 |
| Buffalo, NY | 1,242,573 | Will Co. | 324,460 |
| Erie Co. | 1,015,472 | | |
| Niagara Co. | 227,101 | Chico, CA** | 143,851 |
| | | Butte Co. | 143,851 |
| Burlington, NC* | 99,136 | | |
| Alamance Co. | 99,136 | Cincinnati, OH-KY-IN | 1,401,403 |
| | | Boone Co., KY | 45,842 |
| Burlington, VT** | 114,070 | Campbell Co., KY | 83,317 |
| Chittenden Co. (pt) | 110,064 | Clermont Co., OH | 128,483 |
| Franklin Co. (pt) | 2,818 | Dearborn Co., IN | 34,291 |
| Grand Isle Co. (pt) | 1,188 | Hamilton Co., OH | 873,136 |
| | | Kenton Co., KY | 137,058 |
| Canton, OH | 404,421 | Warren Co., OH | 99,276 |
| Carroll Co.* | 25,598 | | |
| Stark Co. | 378,823 | Clarksville-  | |
| | | Hopkinsville, TN-KY* | 150,220 |
| Casper, WY** | 71,856 | Christian Co., KY | 66,878 |
| Natrona Co. | 71,856 | Montgomery Co., TN | 83,342 |
| Cedar Rapids, IA | 169,775 | Cleveland, OH | 1,898,720 |
| Linn Co. | 169,775 | Cuyahoga Co. | 1,498,295 |
| | | Geauga Co. | 74,474 |
| Champaign-Urbana- | | Lake Co. | 212,801 |
| Rantoul, IL | 168,392 | Medina Co. | 113,150 |
| Champaign Co. | 168,392 | | |
| | | Colorado Springs, CO | 317,458 |
| Charleston-North | | El Paso Co. | 309,424 |
| Charleston, SC | 430,301 | Teller Co.* | 8,034 |
| Berkeley Co. | 94,727 | | |
| Charleston Co. | 277,308 | Columbia, MO* | 100,376 |
| Dorchester Co.* | 58,266 | Boone Co. | 100,376 |
| Charleston, WV | 269,595 | Columbia, SC | 408,176 |
| Kanawha Co. | 231,414 | Lexington Co. | 140,353 |
| Putnam Co.* | 38,181 | Richland Co. | 267,823 |
| Charlotte-Gastonia, NC | 637,218 | Columbus, GA-AL | 239,196 |
| Gaston Co.* | 162,568 | Chattahoochee Co., GA | 21,732 |
| Mecklenburg Co. | 404,270 | Muscogee Co., GA | 170,108 |
| Union Co. | 70,380 | Russell Co., AL | 47,356 |
| Charlottesville, VA** | 113,568 | Columbus, OH | 1,093,293 |
| Albermarlo Co. | 50,689 | Delaware Co. | 53,840 |
| Fluvonna Co. | 10,244 | Fairfield Co.* | 93,678 |
| Greene Co. | 7,625 | Franklin Co. | 869,109 |
| Charlottesville city | 45,010 | Madison Co.* | 33,004 |
| | | Pickaway Co. | 43,662 |
| Chattanooga, TN-GA | 426,540 | | |
| Catoosa Co., GA* | 36,991 | Corpus Christi, TX | 326,228 |
| Dade Co., GA* | 12,318 | Nueces Co. | 268,215 |
| Hamilton Co., TN | 287,740 | San Patricio Co. | 58,013 |
| Marion Co., TN* | 24,416 | | |
| Sequatchie Co., TN* | 8,605 | Cumberland, MD-WV** | 107,782 |
| Walker Co., GA | 56,470 | Allegany Co., MD | 80,548 |

continued

## Standard Metropolitan Statistical Areas (continued)

| | | | |
|---|---|---|---|
| Mineral Co., WV | 27,234 | Wayne Co. | 2,337,240 |
| | | | |
| *Dallas-Fort Worth, TX* | 2,974,878 | *Dubuque, IA* | 93,745 |
| Collin Co. | 144,490 | Dubuque Co. | 93,745 |
| Dallas Co. | 1,556,549 | | |
| Denton Co. | 143,126 | *Duluth-Superior, MN-WI* | 266,650 |
| Ellis Co. | 59,743 | Douglas Co., WI | 44,421 |
| Hood Co.* | 17,714 | St. Louis Co., MN | 222,229 |
| Johnson Co. | 67,649 | | |
| Kaufman Co. | 39,015 | *Eau Claire, WI** | 130,507 |
| Parker Co.* | 44,609 | Chippewa Co. | 51,702 |
| Rockwall Co. | 14,528 | Eau Claire Co. | 78,805 |
| Tarrant Co. | 860,880 | | |
| Wise Co.* | 26,575 | *El Paso, TX* | 479,899 |
| | | El Paso Co. | 479,899 |
| *Danbury, CT* | 146,405 | | |
| Fairfield Co. (pt) | 126,985 | *Elkhart, IN** | 137,330 |
| Litchfield Co. (pt) | 19,420 | Elkhart Co. | 137,330 |
| | | | |
| *Danville, VA*** | 111,789 | *Elmira, NY** | 97,656 |
| Pittsylvania Co. | 66,147 | Chemung Co. | 97,656 |
| Danville city | 45,642 | | |
| | | *Enid, OK** | 62,820 |
| *Davenport-Rock Island* | | Garfield Co. | 62,820 |
| *Moline, IA-IL* | 383,958 | | |
| Henry Co., IL | 57,968 | *Erie, PA* | 279,780 |
| Rock Island Co., IL | 165,968 | Erie Co. | 279,780 |
| Scott Co., IA | 160,022 | | |
| | | *Eugene-Springfield, OR* | 275,226 |
| *Dayton, OH* | 830,070 | Lane Co. | 275,226 |
| Greene Co. | 129,769 | | |
| Miami Co. | 90,381 | *Evansville, IN-KY* | 309,408 |
| Montgomery Co. | 571,697 | Gibson Co., IN* | 33,156 |
| Preble Co. | 38,223 | Henderson Co., KY | 40,849 |
| | | Posey Co., IN* | 26,414 |
| *Daytona Beach, FL** | 258,762 | Vanderburgh Co., IN | 167,515 |
| Volusia Co. | 258,762 | Warrick Co., IN | 41,474 |
| | | | |
| *Decatur, IL* | 131,375 | *Fall River, MA-RI* | 176,831 |
| Macon Co. | 131,375 | Bristol Co., MA (pt) | 145,963 |
| | | Newport Co., RI (pt) | 30,868 |
| *Denver-Boulder, CO* | 1,619,921 | | |
| Adams Co. | 245,944 | *Fargo-Moorhead, ND-MN* | 137,574 |
| Arapahoe Co. | 293,621 | Cass Co., ND | 88,247 |
| Boulder Co. | 189,625 | Clay Co., MN | 49,327 |
| Denver Co. | 491,396 | | |
| Douglas Co.* | 25,153 | *Fayetteville, NC* | 247,160 |
| Gilpin Co.* | 2,441 | Cumberland Co. | 247,160 |
| Jefferson Co. | 371,741 | | |
| | | *Fayetteville-* | |
| *Des Moines, IA* | 338,048 | *Springdale, AR** | 177,850 |
| Polk Co. | 303,170 | Benton Co. | 78,115 |
| Warren Co.* | 34,878 | Washington Co. | 99,735 |
| | | | |
| *Detroit, MI* | 4,352,762 | *Fitchburg-Leominster, MA* | 99,957 |
| Lapeer Co.* | 70,038 | Middlesex Co. (pt) | 12,325 |
| Livingston Co.* | 100,289 | Worcester Co. (pt) | 87,632 |
| Macomb Co. | 694,600 | | |
| Oakland Co. | 1,011,793 | *Flint, MI* | 521,589 |
| St. Clair Co.* | 138,802 | Genesee Co. | 450,449 |

continued

## Standard Metropolitan Statistical Areas (continued)

| | | | |
|---|---:|---|---:|
| Shiawassee Co.* | 71,140 | Polk Co., MN | 34,844 |
| *Florence, AL** | 135,023 | *Grand Rapids, MI* | 601,680 |
| Colbert Co. | 54,519 | Kent Co. | 444,506 |
| Lauderdale Co. | 80,504 | Ottawa Co. | 157,174 |
| *Florence, SC*** | 110,163 | *Great Falls, MT* | 80,696 |
| Florence Co. | 110,163 | Cascade Co. | 80,696 |
| *Fort Collins, CO** | 149,184 | *Greeley, CO** | 123,438 |
| Larimer Co. | 149,184 | Weld Co. | 123,438 |
| *Fort Lauderdale-* | 1,014,043 | *Green Bay, WI* | 175,280 |
| *Hollywood, FL* | 1,014,043 | Brown Co. | 175,280 |
| Broward Co. | | | |
| | | *Greensboro-Winston-* | |
| *Fort Myers-* | | *Salem-High Point, NC* | 827,385 |
| *Cape Coral, FL** | 205,266 | Davidson Co.* | 113,162 |
| Lee Co. | 205,266 | Forsyth Co. | 243,683 |
| | | Guilford Co. | 317,154 |
| *Fort Smith, AR-OK* | 203,269 | Randolph Co. | 91,861 |
| Crawford Co., AR | 36,892 | Stokes Co.* | 33,086 |
| Le Flore Co., OK | 40,698 | Yadkin Co. | 28,439 |
| Sebastian Co., AR | 94,930 | | |
| Sequoyah Co., OK | 30,749 | *Greenville-* | |
| | | *Spartanburg, SC* | 568,758 |
| *Fort Walton Bch, FL*** | 109,920 | Greenville Co. | 287,913 |
| Okaloosa Co. | 109,920 | Pickens Co. | 79,292 |
| | | Spartanburg Co.* | 201,553 |
| *Fort Wayne, IN* | 382,961 | | |
| Adams Co.* | 29,619 | *Hagerstown, MD*** | 113,086 |
| Allen Co. | 294,335 | Washington Co. | 113,086 |
| De Kalb Co.* | 33,606 | | |
| Wells Co.* | 25,401 | *Hamilton-* | |
| | | *Middletown, OH* | 258,787 |
| *Fresno, CA* | 515,013 | Butler Co. | 258,787 |
| Fresno Co. | 515,013 | | |
| | | *Harrisburg, PA* | 446,072 |
| *Gadsden, AL* | 103,057 | Cumberland Co. | 178,037 |
| Etowah Co. | 103,057 | Dauphin Co. | 232,317 |
| | | Perry Co. | 35,718 |
| *Gainesville, FL** | 151,348 | | |
| Alachua Co. | 151,348 | *Hartford, CT* | 726,114 |
| | | Hartford Co. (pt) | 601,079 |
| *Galveston-Texas* | | Litchfield Co. (pt) | 4,884 |
| *City, TX* | 195,940 | Middlesex Co. (pt) | 27,220 |
| Galveston Co. | 195,940 | New London Co. (pt) | 7,761 |
| | | Tolland Co. (pt) | 85,170 |
| *Gary-Hammond-East* | | | |
| *Chicago, IN* | 642,781 | *Hickory, NC*** | 130,207 |
| Lake Co. | 522,965 | Alexander Co. | 24,999 |
| Porter Co. | 119,816 | Catawba Co. | 105,208 |
| *Glen Falls, NY*** | 109,649 | *Honolulu, HI* | 762,874 |
| Warren Co. | 54,854 | Honolulu Co. | 762,874 |
| Washington Co. | 54,795 | | |
| | | *Houston, TX* | 2,905,350 |
| *Grand Forks, ND-MN** | 100,944 | Brazoria Co. | 169,587 |
| Grand Forks Co., ND | 66,100 | Fort Bend Co. | 130,846 |

continued

## Standard Metropolitan Statistical Areas (continued)

| | | | |
|---|---|---|---|
| Harris Co. | 2,409,544 | Sullivan Co., TN | 143,968 |
| Liberty Co. | 47,088 | Unicoi Co., TN | 16,362 |
| Montgomery Co. | 128,487 | Washington Co., TN | 88,755 |
| Waller Co.* | 19,798 | Washington Co., VA | 46,487 |
| | | Bristol city, VA | 19,042 |
| *Huntington-Ashland,* | | | |
| *WV-KY-OH* | 311,350 | *Johnstown, PA* | 264,506 |
| Boyd Co., KY | 55,513 | Cambria Co. | 183,263 |
| Cabell Co., W VA | 106,835 | Somerset Co. | 81,243 |
| Greenup Co., KY* | 39,132 | | |
| Lawrence Co., OH | 63,849 | *Joplin, MO** | 127,513 |
| Wayne Co., W VA | 46,021 | Jasper Co. | 86,958 |
| | | Newton Co. | 40,555 |
| *Huntsville, AL* | 308,593 | | |
| Limestone Co. | 46,005 | *Kalamazoo-Portage, MI* | 279,192 |
| Madison Co. | 196,966 | Kalamazoo Co. | 212,378 |
| Marshall Co.* | 65,622 | Van Buren Co.* | 66,814 |
| *Indianapolis, IN* | 1,166,929 | *Kankakee, IL** | 102,926 |
| Boone Co. | 36,446 | Kankakee Co. | 102,926 |
| Hamilton Co. | 82,381 | | |
| Hancock, Co. | 43,939 | *Kansas City, MO-KS* | 1,327,020 |
| Hendricks Co. | 69,804 | Cass Co., MO | 51,029 |
| Johnson Co. | 77,240 | Clay Co., MO | 136,488 |
| Marion Co. | 765,233 | Jackson Co., MO | 629,180 |
| Morgan Co. | 51,999 | Johnson Co., KS | 270,269 |
| Shelby Co. | 39,887 | Platte Co., MO | 46,341 |
| | | Ray Co., MO* | 21,378 |
| *Iowa City, IA** | 81,717 | Wyandotte Co., KS | 172,335 |
| Johnson Co. | 81,717 | | |
| | | *Kenosha, WI* | 123,137 |
| *Jackson, MI* | 151,495 | Kenosha Co. | 123,137 |
| Jackson Co. | 151,495 | | |
| | | *Killeen-Temple, TX** | 214,656 |
| *Jackson, MS* | 320,425 | Bell Co. | 157,889 |
| Hinds Co. | 250,998 | Coryell Co. | 56,767 |
| Rankin Co. | 69,427 | | |
| | | *Knoxville, TN* | 476,517 |
| *Jacksonville, FL* | 737,519 | Anderson Co. | 67,346 |
| Baker Co.* | 15,289 | Blount Co. | 77,770 |
| Clay Co.* | 67,052 | Knox Co. | 319,694 |
| Duval Co. | 570,981 | Union Co.* | 11,707 |
| Nassau Co.* | 32,894 | | |
| St. Johns Co.* | 51,303 | *Kokomo, IN** | 103,715 |
| | | Howard Co. | 86,896 |
| *Jacksonville, NC** | 112,784 | Tipton Co. | 16,819 |
| Onslow Co. | 112,784 | | |
| | | *La Crosse, WI** | 91,056 |
| *Janesville-Beloit, WI** | 139,420 | La Crosse Co. | 91,056 |
| Rock Co. | 139,420 | | |
| | | *Lafayette, LA* | 150,017 |
| *Jersey City, NJ* | 556,972 | Lafayette Parish | 150,017 |
| Hudson Co. | 556,972 | | |
| | | *Lafayette-West* | |
| ·*Johnson City-Kingsport-* | | *Lafayette, IN* | 121,702 |
| *Bristol, TN-VA** | 433,638 | Tippecanoe Co. | 121,702 |
| Carter Co., TN | 50,205 | | |
| Hawkins Co., TN | 43,751 | *Lake Charles, LA* | 167,048 |
| Scott Co., VA | 25,068 | Calcasieu Parish | 167,048 |

continued

## Standard Metropolitan Statistical Areas (continued)

| | | | |
|---|---:|---|---:|
| Lakeland-Winter | | Asbury Pk., NJ* | 503,173 |
| Haven, FL* | 321,652 | Monmouth Co. | 503,173 |
| Polk Co. | 321,652 | | |
| | | Longview-Marshall, TX* | 151,752 |
| Lancaster, PA | 362,346 | Gregg Co. | 99,487 |
| Lancaster Co. | 362,346 | Harrison Co. | 52,265 |
| | | | |
| Lansing-East | | Lorain-Elyria, OH | 274,909 |
| Lansing, MI | 468,482 | Lorain Co. | 274,909 |
| Clinton Co. | 55,893 | | |
| Eaton Co. | 88,337 | Los Angeles-Long | |
| Ingham Co. | 272,437 | Beach, CA | 7,477,657 |
| Ionia Co.* | 51,815 | Los Angeles Co. | 7,477,657 |
| | | | |
| Laredo, TX | 99,258 | Louisville, KY-IN | 906,240 |
| Webb Co. | 99,258 | Bullitt Co., KY* | 43,346 |
| | | Clark Co., IN | 88,838 |
| Las Cruces, NM* | 96,340 | Floyd Co., IN | 61,169 |
| Dona Ana Co. | 96,340 | Jefferson Co., KY | 684,793 |
| | | Oldham Co., KY* | 28,094 |
| Las Vegas, NV | 461,816 | | |
| Clark Co. | 461,816 | Lowell, MA-NH | 233,410 |
| | | Middlesex Co., MA (pt) | 225,320 |
| Lawrence, KS* | 67,640 | Hillsborough Co., NH (pt) | 8,090 |
| Douglas Co. | 67,640 | | |
| | | Lubbock, TX | 211,651 |
| Lawrence- | | Lubbock Co. | 211,651 |
| Haverhill, MA-NH | 281,981 | | |
| Essex Co., MA (pt) | 231,223 | Lynchburg, VA | 153,260 |
| Rockingham Co., NH (pt) | 50,758 | Amherst Co. | 29,122 |
| | | Appomattox Co.* | 11,971 |
| Lawton, OK | 112,456 | Campbell Co. | 45,424 |
| Comanche Co. | 112,456 | Lynchburg city | 66,743 |
| | | | |
| Lewiston-Auburn, ME | 72,378 | Macon, GA | 254,623 |
| Androscoggin Co. (pt) | 72,378 | Bibb Co. | 151,085 |
| | | Houston Co. | 77,605 |
| Lexington-Fayette, KY | 318,136 | Jones Co.* | 16,579 |
| Bourbon Co * | 19,405 | Twiggs Co.* | 9,354 |
| Clark Co.* | 28,322 | | |
| Fayette Co. | 204,165 | Madison, WI | 323,545 |
| Jessamine Co.* | 26,653 | Dane Co. | 323,545 |
| Scott Co.* | 21,813 | | |
| Woodford Co.* | 17,778 | Manchester, NH | 160,767 |
| | | Hillsborough Co. (pt) | 111,732 |
| Lima, OH | 218,244 | Merrimack Co. (pt) | 16,562 |
| Allen Co. | 112,241 | Rockingham Co. (pt) | 32,473 |
| Auglaize Co.* | 42,554 | | |
| Putnam Co. | 32,991 | Mansfield, OH | 131,205 |
| Van Wert Co. | 30,458 | Richland Co. | 131,205 |
| | | | |
| Lincoln, NE | 192,884 | McAllen-Pharr- | |
| Lancaster Co. | 192,884 | Edinburg, TX | 283,229 |
| | | Hidalgo Co. | 283,229 |
| Little Rock-North | | | |
| Little Rock, AR | 393,494 | Medford, OR** | 132,456 |
| Pulaski Co. | 340,613 | Jackson Co. | 132,456 |
| Saline Co. | 52,881 | | |
| | | Melbourne-Titusville | |
| Long Branch- | | Cocoa, FL* | 272,959 |

continued

## Standard Metropolitan Statistical Areas (continued)

| | | | |
|---|---|---|---|
| Brevard Co. | 272,959 | Hillsborough Co. (pt) | 114,221 |
| | | | |
| *Memphis, TN-AR-MS* | 912,887 | *Nashville-Davidson, TN* | 850,505 |
| Crittenden Co., AR | 49,097 | Cheatham Co.* | 21,616 |
| DeSoto Co., MS* | 53,930 | Davidson Co. | 477,811 |
| Shelby Co., TN | 777,113 | Dickson Co.* | 30,037 |
| Tipton Co., TN* | 32,747 | Robertson Co.* | 37,021 |
| | | Rutherford Co.* | 84,058 |
| *Meriden, CT* | 57,118 | Sumner Co. | 85,790 |
| New Haven Co. (pt) | 57,118 | Williamson Co.* | 58,108 |
| | | Wilson Co. | 56,064 |
| *Miami, FL* | 1,625,979 | | |
| Dade Co. | 1,625,979 | *Nassau-Suffolk, NY** | 2,605,813 |
| | | Nassau Co. | 1,321,582 |
| *Midland, TX* | 82,636 | Suffolk Co. | 1,284,231 |
| Midland Co. | 82,636 | | |
| | | *New Bedford, MA* | 169,425 |
| *Milwaukee, WI* | 1,397,143 | Bristol Co. (pt) | 153,965 |
| Milwaukee Co. | 964,988 | Plymouth Co. (pt) | 15,460 |
| Ozaukee Co. | 66,981 | | |
| Washington Co. | 84,848 | *New Britain, CT* | 142,241 |
| Waukesha Co. | 280,326 | Hartford Co. (pt) | 142,241 |
| | | | |
| *Minneapolis-St. Paul,* | | *New Brunswick-Perth-* | |
| *MN-WI* | 2,114,256 | *Amboy-Sayreville, NJ** | 595,893 |
| Anoka Co., MN | 195,998 | Middlesex Co. | 595,893 |
| Carver Co., MN* | 37,046 | | |
| Chisago Co., MN* | 25,717 | *New Haven-West* | |
| Dakota Co., MN | 194,111 | *Haven, CT* | 417,592 |
| Hennepin Co., MN | 941,411 | Middlesex Co. (pt) | 11,195 |
| Ramsey Co., MN | 459,784 | New Haven Co. (pt) | 406,397 |
| St. Croix Co., WI* | 43,872 | | |
| Scott Co., MN* | 43,784 | *New London-* | |
| Washington Co., MN | 113,571 | *Norwich, CT-RI* | 248,554 |
| Wright Co., MN* | 58,962 | Middlesex Co., CT (pt) | 9,287 |
| | | New London Co., CT (pt) | 214,281 |
| *Mobile, AL* | 442,819 | Washington Co., RI (pt) | 24,986 |
| Baldwin Co. | 78,440 | | |
| Mobile Co. | 364,379 | *New Orleans, LA* | 1,186,725 |
| | | Jefferson Parish | 454,592 |
| *Modesto, CA** | 265,902 | Orleans Parish | 557,482 |
| Stanislaus Co. | 265,902 | St. Bernard Parish | 64,097 |
| | | St. Tammany Parish | 110,554 |
| *Monroe, LA* | 139,241 | | |
| Ouachita Parish | 139,241 | *New York, NY-NJ* | 9,119,737 |
| | | Bronx Co., NY | 1,169,115 |
| *Montgomery, AL* | 272,687 | Bergen Co., NJ* | 845,385 |
| Autauga Co.* | 32,259 | Kings Co., NY | 2,230,936 |
| Elmore Co. | 43,390 | New York Co., NY | 1,427,533 |
| Montgomery Co. | 197,038 | Putnam Co., NY* | 77,193 |
| | | Queens Co., NY | 1,891,325 |
| *Muncie, IN* | 128,587 | Richmond Co., NY | 352,121 |
| Delaware Co. | 128,587 | Rockland Co., NY | 259,530 |
| | | Westchester Co., NY | 866,599 |
| *Muskegon-Norton Shores-* | | | |
| *Muskegon Hgts, MI* | 179,591 | *Newark, NJ* | 1,965,304 |
| Muskegon Co. | 157,589 | Essex Co. | 850,451 |
| Oceana Co.* | 22,002 | Morris Co. | 407,630 |
| | | Somerset Co.* | 203,129 |
| *Nashua, NH* | 114,221 | Union Co. | 504,094 |

continued

Standard Metropolitan Statistical Areas (continued)

| | | | |
|---|---|---|---|
| Newark, OH** | 120,981 | Owensboro, KY* | 85,949 |
| Licking Co. | 120,981 | Daviess Co. | 85,949 |
| | | | |
| Newburgh- | | Oxnard-Simi Valley- | |
| Middletown, NY** | 259,603 | Ventura, CA | 529,899 |
| Orange Co. | 259,603 | Ventura Co. | 529,899 |
| | | | |
| Newport News- | | Panama City, FL* | 97,740 |
| Hampton, VA | 364,449 | Bay Co. | 97,740 |
| Gloucester Co.* | 20,107 | | |
| James city Co.* | 22,763 | Parkersburg- | |
| York Co.* | 35,463 | Marietta, WV-OH* | 162,836 |
| Hampton city | 122,617 | Washington Co., OH | 64,266 |
| Newport News city | 144,903 | Wirt Co., WV* | 4,922 |
| Poquoson city* | 8,726 | Wood Co., WV* | 93,648 |
| Williamsburg city* | 9,870 | | |
| | | Pascagoula-Moss | |
| Norfolk-Virginia Beach- | | Point, MS* | 118,015 |
| Portsmouth, VA-NC | 806,691 | Jackson Co. | 118,015 |
| Currituck Co., NC* | 11,089 | | |
| Chesapeake city, VA | 114,226 | Paterson-Clifton- | |
| Norfolk city, VA | 266,979 | Passaic, NJ | 447,585 |
| Portsmouth city, VA | 104,577 | Passaic Co. | 447,585 |
| Suffolk city, VA* | 47,621 | | |
| Virginia Beach city, VA | 262,199 | Pensacola, FL | 289,782 |
| | | Escambia Co. | 233,794 |
| Northeast | | Santa Rosa Co. | 55,988 |
| Pennsylvania | 640,396 | | |
| Lackawanna Co. | 227,908 | Peoria, IL | 365,864 |
| Luzerne Co. | 343,079 | Peoria Co. | 200,466 |
| Monroe Co.* | 69,409 | Tazewell Co. | 132,078 |
| | | Woodford Co. | 33,320 |
| Norwalk, CT | 126,692 | | |
| Fairfield Co. (pt) | 126,692 | Petersburg-Colonial Hgts- | |
| | | Hopewell, VA* | 129,296 |
| Ocala, FL** | 122,488 | Dinwiddie Co. | 22,602 |
| Marion Co. | 122,488 | Prince George Co. | 25,733 |
| | | Colonial Hgts. city | 16,509 |
| Odessa, TX | 115,374 | Hopewell city | 23,397 |
| Ector Co. | 115,374 | Petersburg city | 41,055 |
| | | | |
| Oklahoma City, OK | 834,088 | Philadelphia, PA-NJ | 4,716,818 |
| Canadian Co. | 56,452 | Burlington Co., NJ | 362,542 |
| Cleveland Co. | 133,173 | Bucks Co., PA | 479,211 |
| McClain Co.* | 20,291 | Camden Co., NJ | 471,650 |
| Oklahoma Co. | 568,933 | Chester Co., PA | 316,660 |
| Pottawatomie Co.* | 55,239 | Delaware Co., PA | 555,007 |
| | | Gloucester Co., NJ | 199,917 |
| Olympia, WA** | 124,264 | Montgomery Co., PA | 643,621 |
| Thurston Co. | 124,264 | Philadelphia Co., PA | 1,688,210 |
| | | | |
| Omaha, NE-IA | 570,399 | Phoenix, AZ | 1,508,030 |
| Douglas Co., NE | 397,884 | Maricopa Co. | 1,508,030 |
| Pottawattamie Co., IA | 86,500 | | |
| Sarpy Co., NE | 86,015 | Pine Bluff, AR | 90,718 |
| | | Jefferson Co. | 90,718 |
| Orlando, FL | 700,699 | | |
| Orange Co. | 471,660 | Pittsburgh, PA | 2,263,894 |
| Osceola Co.* | 49,287 | Allegheny Co. | 1,450,085 |
| Seminole Co. | 179,752 | Beaver Co. | 204,441 |

continued

## Standard Metropolitan Statistical Areas (continued)

| | | | |
|---|---|---|---|
| Washington Co. | 217,074 | *Kennewick-Pasco, WA* | 144,469 |
| Westmoreland Co. | 392,294 | Benton Co. | 109,444 |
| | | Franklin Co. | 35,025 |
| *Pittsfield, MA* | 90,505 | | |
| Berkshire Co. (pt) | 90,505 | *Richmond, VA* | 632,015 |
| | | Charles City Co.* | 6,692 |
| *Portland, ME* | 183,625 | Chesterfield Co. | 141,372 |
| Cumberland Co. (pt) | 164,413 | Goochland Co.* | 11,761 |
| York Co. (pt) | 19,212 | Hanover Co. | 50,398 |
| | | Henrico Co. | 180,735 |
| *Portland, OR-WA* | 1,242,187 | New Kent Co.* | 8,781 |
| Clackamas Co., OR | 241,919 | Powhatan Co.* | 13,062 |
| Clark Co., WA | 192,227 | Richmond city | 219,214 |
| Multnomah Co., OR | 562,640 | | |
| Washington Co., OR | 245,401 | *Riverside-* | |
| | | *San Bernardino-* | |
| *Portsmouth-Dover-* | | *Ontario, CA* | 1,557,080 |
| *Rochester, NH-ME*** | 163,880 | Riverside Co. | 663,923 |
| Rockingham Co., NH (pt) | 53,568 | San Bernardino Co. | 893,157 |
| Strafford Co., NH (pt) | 79,390 | | |
| York Co., ME (pt) | 30,922 | *Roanoke, VA* | 224,548 |
| | | Botetourt Co.* | 23,270 |
| *Poughkeepsie, NY** | 245,055 | Craig Co.* | 3,948 |
| Dutchess Co. | 245,055 | Roanoke Co. | 72,945 |
| | | Roanoke city | 100,427 |
| *Providence-Warwick* | | Salem city | 23,958 |
| *Pawtucket, RI-MA* | 919,216 | | |
| Bristol Co., MA (pt) | 87,820 | *Rochester, MN** | 91,971 |
| Bristol Co., RI (pt) | 46,942 | Olmsted Co. | 91,971 |
| Kent Co., RI (pt) | 151,425 | | |
| Newport Co., RI (pt) | 4,040 | *Rochester, NY* | 971,879 |
| Norfolk Co., MA (pt) | 5,857 | Livingston Co. | 57,006 |
| Providence Co., RI (pt) | 560,429 | Monroe Co. | 702,238 |
| Washington Co., RI (pt) | 54,440 | Ontario Co.* | 88,909 |
| Worcester Co., MA (pt) | 8,263 | Orleans Co. | 38,496 |
| | | Wayne Co. | 85,230 |
| *Provo-Orem, UT* | 218,106 | | |
| Utah, Co. | 218,106 | *Rock Hill, SC*** | 106,720 |
| | | York Co. | 106,720 |
| *Pueblo, CO* | 125,972 | | |
| Pueblo Co. | 125,972 | *Rockford, IL* | 279,514 |
| | | Boone Co. | 28,630 |
| *Racine, WI* | 173,132 | Winnebago Co. | 250,884 |
| Racine Co. | 173,132 | | |
| | | *Sacramento, CA* | 1,014,002 |
| *Raleigh-Durham, NC* | 530,673 | Placer Co. | 117,247 |
| Durham Co. | 152,785 | Sacramento Co. | 783,381 |
| Orange Co. | 77,055 | Yolo Co. | 113,374 |
| Wake Co. | 300,833 | | |
| | | *Saginaw, MI* | 228,059 |
| *Reading, PA* | 312,509 | Saginaw | 228,059 |
| Berks Co. | 312,509 | | |
| | | *St. Cloud, MN** | 163,256 |
| *Redding, CA*** | 115,715 | Benton Co. | 25,187 |
| Shasta Co. | 115,715 | Sherburne Co. | 29,908 |
| | | Stearns Co. | 108,161 |
| *Reno, NV* | 193,623 | | |
| Washoe Co. | 193,623 | *St. Joseph, MO* | 101,868 |
| | | Andrew Co.* | 13,980 |
| *Richland-* | | Buchanan Co. | 87,888 |

continued

## Standard Metropolitan Statistical Areas (continued)

| | | | |
|---|---|---|---|
| St. Louis, MO-IL | 2,355,276 | Sarasota, FL* | 202,251 |
| Clinton Co., IL* | 32,617 | Sarasota Co. | 202,251 |
| Franklin Co., MO | 71,233 | | |
| Jefferson Co., MO | 146,814 | Savannah, GA | 230,728 |
| Madison Co., IL | 247,671 | Bryan Co.* | 10,175 |
| Monroe Co., IL* | 20,117 | Chatham Co. | 202,226 |
| St. Charles Co., MO | 143,455 | Effingham Co.* | 18,327 |
| St. Clair Co., IL | 265,469 | | |
| St. Louis Co., MO | 974,815 | Seattle-Everett, WA | 1,606,765 |
| St. Louis city, MO | 453,085 | King Co. | 1,269,749 |
| | | Snohomish Co. | 337,016 |
| Salem, OR | 249,895 | | |
| Marion Co. | 204,692 | Sharon, PA** | 128,299 |
| Polk Co. | 45,203 | Mercer Co. | 128,299 |
| | | | |
| Salinas-Seaside- | | Sheboygan, WI** | 100,935 |
| Monterey, CA | 290,444 | Sheboygan Co. | 100,935 |
| Monterey Co. | 290,444 | | |
| | | Sherman-Denison, TX | 89,796 |
| Salisbury-Concord, NC** | 185,081 | Grayson Co. | 89,796 |
| Cabarrus Co. | 85,895 | | |
| Rowan Co. | 99,186 | Shreveport, LA | 376,646 |
| | | Bossier Parish | 80,721 |
| Salt Lake City- | | Caddo Parish | 252,294 |
| Ogden, UT | 936,255 | Webster Parish* | 43,631 |
| Davis Co. | 146,540 | | |
| Salt Lake Co. | 619,066 | Sioux City, IA-NE | 117,457 |
| Tooele Co.* | 26,033 | Dakota Co., NE | 16,573 |
| Weber Co. | 144,616 | Woodbury Co., IA | 100,884 |
| | | | |
| San Angelo, TX | 84,784 | Sioux Falls, SD | 109,435 |
| Tom Green Co. | 84,784 | Minnehaha Co. | 109,435 |
| | | | |
| San Antonio, TX | 1,071,954 | South Bend, IN | 280,772 |
| Bexar Co. | 988,800 | Marshall Co. | 39,155 |
| Comal Co* | 36,446 | St. Joseph Co. | 241,617 |
| Guadalupe Co. | 46,708 | | |
| | | Spokane, WA | 341,835 |
| San Diego, CA | 1,861,846 | Spokane Co. | 341,835 |
| San Diego Co. | 1,861,846 | | |
| | | Springfield, IL | 187,789 |
| San Francisco- | | Menard Co.* | 11,700 |
| Oakland, CA | 3,252,721 | Sangamon Co. | 176,089 |
| Alameda Co. | 1,105,379 | | |
| Contra Costa Co. | 657,252 | Springfield, MO | 207,704 |
| Marin Co. | 222,952 | Christian Co.* | 22,402 |
| San Francisco Co. | 678,974 | Greene Co. | 185,302 |
| San Mateo Co. | 588,164 | | |
| | | Springfield, OH | 183,885 |
| San Jose, CA | 1,295,071 | Champaign Co.* | 33,649 |
| Santa Clara Co. | 1,295,071 | Clark Co. | 150,236 |
| | | | |
| Santa Barbara-Santa | | Springfield-Chicopee- | |
| Maria-Lompoc, CA | 298,660 | Holyoke, MA-CT | 530,668 |
| Santa Barbara Co. | 298,660 | Hampden Co., MA (pt) | 432,127 |
| | | Hampshire Co., MA (pt) | 86,291 |
| Santa Cruz, CA* | 188,141 | Tolland Co., CT (pt) | 8,473 |
| Santa Cruz Co. | 188,141 | Worcester Co., MA (pt) | 3,777 |
| | | | |
| Santa Rosa, CA | 299,827 | Stamford, CT | 198,854 |
| Sonoma Co. | 299,827 | Fairfield Co. (pt) | 198,854 |

continued

## Standard Metropolitan Statistical Areas (continued)

| | | | |
|---|---|---|---|
| *State College, PA*** | 112,760 | Creek Co. | 59,210 |
| Centre Co. | 112,760 | Mayes Co.* | 32,261 |
| | | Osage Co. | 39,327 |
| *Steubenville-* | | Rogers Co.* | 46,436 |
| *Weirton, OH-WV* | 163,099 | Tulsa Co. | 470,593 |
| Brooke Co., WV | 31,117 | Wagoner Co.* | 41,801 |
| Hancock Co., WV | 40,418 | | |
| Jefferson Co., OH | 91,564 | *Tuscaloosa, AL* | 137,473 |
| | | Tuscaloosa Co. | 137,473 |
| *Stockton, CA* | 347,342 | | |
| San Joaquin Co. | 347,342 | *Tyler, TX* | 128,366 |
| | | Smith Co. | 128,366 |
| *Syracuse, NY* | 642,375 | | |
| Madison Co. | 65,150 | *Utica-Rome, NY* | 320,180 |
| Onondaga Co. | 463,324 | Herkimer Co. | 66,714 |
| Oswego Co. | 113,901 | Oneida Co. | 253,466 |
| | | | |
| *Tacoma, WA* | 485,643 | *Vallejo-Fairfield-* | |
| Pierce Co. | 485,643 | *Napa, CA* | 334,402 |
| | | Napa Co. | 99,199 |
| *Tallahassee, FL* | 159,542 | Solano Co. | 235,203 |
| Leon Co. | 148,655 | | |
| Wakulla Co.* | 10,887 | *Vineland-Millville-* | |
| | | *Bridgeton, NJ* | 132,866 |
| *Tampa-* | | Cumberland Co. | 132,866 |
| *St. Petersburg, FL* | 1,569,492 | | |
| Hillsborough Co. | 646,960 | *Victoria, TX*** | 68,807 |
| Pasco Co.* | 194,123 | Victoria Co. | 68,807 |
| Pinellas Co. | 728,409 | | |
| | | *Visalia-Tulare-* | |
| *Terre Haute, IN* | 176,583 | *Porterville, CA*** | 245,751 |
| Clay Co. | 24,862 | Tulare Co. | 245,751 |
| Sullivan Co. | 21,107 | | |
| Vermillion Co. | 18,229 | *Waco, TX* | 170,755 |
| Vigo Co. | 112,385 | McLennan Co. | 170,755 |
| | | | |
| *Texarkana, TX-* | | *Washington, DC-MD-VA* | 3,060,240 |
| *Texarkana, AR* | 127,019 | Arlington Co., VA | 152,599 |
| Bowie Co., TX | 75,301 | Charles Co., MD* | 72,751 |
| Little River Co., AR* | 13,952 | District of Columbia | 637,651 |
| Miller Co., AR | 37,766 | Fairfax Co., VA | 596,901 |
| | | Loudoun Co., VA | 57,427 |
| *Toledo, OH-MI* | 791,599 | Montgomery Co., MD | 579,053 |
| Fulton Co., OH* | 37,751 | Prince Georges Co., MD | 665,071 |
| Lucas Co., OH | 471,741 | Prince William Co., VA | 144,703 |
| Monroe Co., MI | 134,659 | Alexandria city, VA | 103,217 |
| Ottawa Co., OH* | 40,076 | Fairfax city, VA | 19,390 |
| Wood Co., OH | 107,372 | Falls Church city, VA | 9,515 |
| | | Manassas city, VA* | 15,438 |
| *Topeka, KS* | 185,442 | Manassas Park city, VA* | 6,524 |
| Jefferson Co.* | 15,207 | | |
| Osage Co.* | 15,319 | *Waterbury, CT* | 228,178 |
| Shawnee Co. | 154,916 | Litchfield Co. (pt) | 32,707 |
| | | New Haven Co. (pt) | 195,471 |
| *Trenton, NJ* | 307,863 | | |
| Mercer Co. | 307,863 | *Waterloo-Cedar* | |
| | | *Falls, IA* | 137,961 |
| *Tucson, AZ* | 531,263 | Black Hawk Co. | 137,961 |
| Pima Co. | 531,263 | | |
| | | *Wausau, WI*** | 111,270 |
| *Tulsa, OK* | 689,628 | Marathon Co. | 111,270 |

continued

## Standard Metropolitan Statistical Areas (continued)

| | | | |
|---|---|---|---|
| West Palm Beach-<br>Boca Raton, FL | 573,125 | Salem Co., NJ | 64,676 |
| Palm Beach Co. | 573,125 | Wilmington, NC | 139,238 |
| | | Brunswick Co. | 35,767 |
| Wheeling, WV-OH | 185,566 | New Hanover Co. | 103,471 |
| Belmont Co., OH | 82,569 | | |
| Marshall Co., WV | 41,608 | Worcester, MA | 372,940 |
| Ohio Co., WV | 61,389 | Worcester Co. (pt) | 372,940 |
| Wichita, KS | 411,313 | Yakima, WA* | 172,508 |
| Butler Co. | 44,782 | Yakima Co. | 172,508 |
| Sedgwick Co. | 366,531 | | |
| | | York, PA | 381,255 |
| Wichita Falls, TX | 130,664 | Adams Co. | 68,292 |
| Clay Co. * | 9,582 | York Co. | 312,963 |
| Wichita Co. | 121,082 | | |
| | | Youngstown-Warren, OH | 531,350 |
| Williamsport, PA* | 118,416 | Mahoning Co. | 289,487 |
| Lycoming Co. | 118,416 | Trumbull Co. | 241,863 |
| Wilmington, DE-NJ-MD | 524,108 | Yuba City, CA** | 101,979 |
| Cecil Co., MD | 60,430 | Sutter Co. | 52,246 |
| New Castle Co., DE | 399,002 | Yuba Co. | 49,733 |

**Source:** PHC80-V (Advance Reports)
U.S. Bureau of the Census, August 1981.

# Name Index

Alioto, Joe, 99
Allman, T. D., 9, 10
Arnstein, Sherry, 99, 101, 103
Atkins, Patricia S., 189, 191

Bachrach, Peter, 27, 28, 29
Bahl, Roy, 288
Bailey, Harry, 294
Banfield, Edward C., 9, 16, 26, 59, 61, 79, 80
Baratz, Morton S., 27, 28, 29
Beame, Abraham, 41, 73, 273, 274
Bish, Robert L., 184
Blumenthal, W. Michael, 275
Bradley, Tom, 80
Brooke, Edward A., 274
Burr, Aaron, 61
Byrne, Jane, 72, 80

Cahn, Edgar, 99
Caputo, David A., 105, 246, 247
Caraley, Demetrios, 183
Carey, Hugh, 274
Carter, Jimmy, 16, 232, 244, 245, 248, 249, 250, 252, 253, 274, 299
Cavanaugh, Jerome, 99
Chavez, Cesar, 295
Childs, Richard, 49
Clark, Joseph S., Jr., 63
Cole, Richard I., 105, 117, 246, 247
Colman, William, 183
Cornwell, Elmer E., Jr., 67
Crenson, Matthew, 28
Cunningham, James V., 55
Curley, James M., 63

Dahl, Robert, 24, 25
Daley, Richard J., 26, 35, 56, 57, 61, 65, 68, 72, 73, 75, 80, 101
Daley, Richard M., 73
Dillon, John F., 36, 218
Domhoff, G. William, 20, 21, 27
Douglass, H. Paul, 160
Dye, Thomas R., 17, 90, 297

Eggers, Frank Hague, 62
Elazar, Daniel J., 299

Feinstein, Dianne, 44
Fish, Hamilton, 62
Ford, Gerald, 232, 242, 253, 255, 273
Fowler, Edmund P., 90

Garcia, John, 15, 260
Gardner, John W., 303
Gibson, Kenneth, 96, 99
Gilbert, Charles E., 297
Ginsburg, Sigmund G., 35
Gist, John, 256
Glendenning, Parris N., 189, 191, 214
Gosnell, Harold F., 66, 67
Green, Edith, 101
Grodzins, Morton, 214

Hague, Frank, 62, 64, 65
Hale, George E., 229
Hahn, Harlan, 129
Harrington, Michael, 98
Harris, Patricia R., 249
Hatcher, Richard, 56, 96, 99
Hatry, Harry, 144, 145
Heller, Walter, 244
Hofstadter, Richard, 69
Hughes, James W., 177
Hunter, Floyd, 22, 23
Hynes, John B., 63

Jacobs, Jane, 4
Jarvis, Howard, 287
Johnson, Lyndon, 98, 215, 221, 232
Jones, Bryan, 141, 142
Jones, Samuel N., 89
Judd, Dennis, 167

Kemp, Jack, 260
Kennedy, John F., 98, 244
Kenny, John V., 62
King, Martin Luther, 98, 296
Koch, Ed, 80

# Subject Index

## THE BOOK MANUFACTURE

**Urban Politics, Third Edition,** was typeset by Autographics, Monterey Park, CA. It was printed and bound at Kingsport Press, Kingsport, Tennessee. Cover design was by John Goetz. Internal design was by the F.E. Peacock Publishers' art department. The typeface is Times Roman with Helvetica display.